WOMEN AND THE
IRISH REVOLUTION

Women and the Irish Revolution

FEMINISM, ACTIVISM, VIOLENCE

Edited by
LINDA CONNOLLY

Irish Academic Press

First published in 2020 by
Irish Academic Press
10 George's Street
Newbridge
Co. Kildare
Ireland
www.iap.ie

© Linda Connolly and the contributors, 2020

978-1-78855-153-3 (Paper)
978-1-78855-154-0 (Kindle)
978-1-78855-155-7 (Epub)
978-1-78855-156-4 (PDF)

A CIP catalogue record for this book is
available from the British Library.

All rights reserved. No part of this publication may be reproduced, stored in a retrieval system, or transmitted, in any form or by any means (electronic, mechanical, photocopying, recording or otherwise) without the prior written permission of both the copyright owner and the publisher of this book.

Typeset in Minion Pro 11/14 pt

Front cover: Jack B. Yeats, *Communicating With Prisoners* (c.1924) © Estate of Jack B. Yeats, DACS London/IVARO Dublin, 2020

Back cover: The Commissiart of Cumann na mBan
(Courtesy of Cork Public Museum, Conlon Collection)

Cover design by RiverDesignBooks.com

Merrion Press is a member of Publishing Ireland.

CONTENTS

Acknowledgements   vii
Preface by Liz Gillis   ix
Notes on Contributors   xii
Acronyms   xvi

Introduction: Women in Ireland's Revolution, 1917–1923: Marginal or Constitutive?   1
Linda Connolly

PART I

1. Nationalism and Feminism: The Complex Relationship between the Suffragist and Independence Movements in Ireland   17
Louise Ryan

2. Comradeship: Feminists and Revolutionaries in Holloway Prison, 1918–1919   33
Lucy McDiarmid

3. Gendered Memories and Belfast Cumann na mBan, 1917–1922   47
Margaret Ward

4. Cumann na mBan, Martial Women and the Irish Civil War, 1922–1923   68
John Borgonovo

5. Women's Political Representation in Dáil Éireann in Revolutionary and Post-revolutionary Ireland   85
Claire McGing

PART II

6. Towards a Further Understanding of the Sexual and Gender-based Violence Women Experienced in the Irish Revolution   103
Linda Connolly

7. Compensation Claims and Women's Experience of Violence
   and Loss in Revolutionary Ireland, 1921–23   129
   Marie Coleman

8. Female Fatalities in County Cork during the Irish War of
   Independence and the Case of Mrs Lindsay   148
   Andy Bielenberg

9. The Homefront as Battlefront: Women, Violence and
   the Domestic Space during War in Ireland, 1919–1921   164
   Mary McAuliffe

PART III

10. 'When we've licked the wounds of history': Literary
    Representations of Women's Experiences of the War of
    Independence and Civil War   183
    Ailbhe McDaid

11. Commemorating the Irish Revolution: Disremembering
    and Remembering the Women and Children of the
    Tuam Mother and Baby Home   198
    Sarah-Anne Buckley and John Cunningham

12. Brightening   216
    Doireann Ní Ghríofa

    Endnotes   218
    Index   259

ACKNOWLEDGEMENTS

The genesis of this collection was a public conference held in the Royal Irish Academy, Dublin on 1st September 2017, and a project which was funded by an award from the Irish Research Council, New Foundations (Decade of Centenaries) scheme. The Irish Research Council is an essential resource for achieving research excellence in Ireland and I am grateful for this essential support. My colleagues in the Maynooth University Social Sciences Institute, especially Orla Dunne, Anne Hamilton-Black and Rhona Bradshaw, as always assisted me in hosting the conference and in completing the project. I am fortunate to work in a collegial and dynamic research environment at Maynooth University.

All of the contributors to the conference and to this collection are to be commended for undertaking and producing such detailed research on women's lives and experience of revolution. Sincere thanks are also due to Jennika Baines of Indiana University Press, Dr Oona Frawley and Professor Guy Beiner for their support in completing this book and to two anonymous reviewers for very useful and positive feedback on the manuscript. I am particularly grateful to Conor Graham of Irish Academic Press for publishing this book bang in the middle of the COVID-19 pandemic and to Patrick O'Donoghue for his outstanding editorial support.

I am indebted to Dr Andy Bielenberg, Dr John Borgonovo, Dr Marie Coleman, Dr Pádraig Yeates, Dr John Dorney, Aaron Ó Maonaoigh, Dr Seán William Gannon and Dr Pádraig Óg Ó Ruairc for suggesting archival sources and sharing information, at different stages. Liz Gillis contributed an insightful preface to the collection. In addition, Eleanor Hooker and Doireann Ní Ghríofa, at different stages, both provided encouragement and wrote powerful, evocative poetry. Thank you all for your support and solidarity.

The journey Edel Doherty, Frank Fagan and I undertook in securing an Irish Military Archives file documenting the shameful attack of Maggie Doherty on 27 May 1923 has been a huge inspiration. We hope she and other unspoken women will be remembered during the commemoration of the Irish Civil War in 2022 alongside other victims.

A number of speaking invitations afforded me opportunities between 2016 and 2020 to test out some of the key ideas underpinning my research on women, violence and the Irish revolution, in the best of places and always in excellent company. Sincere thanks to Dr John Borgonovo (UCC Decade of Centenaries Lecture Series), the West Cork History Festival (Simon and Victoria Kingston, and Bishop Paul Colton), the John Hewitt Summer School (Dr Myrtle Hill), the late Professor David Fitzpatrick, Dr Fionnuala Walsh and the TCD Long Room Hub on the occasion of David's retirement, Féile an Phobail (Professor Bill Rolston), Wexford Public Library, NUIG Irish Centre for the Histories of Labour and Class (Dr Sarah-Anne Buckley and Dr John Cunningham), the National Museum of Ireland (Collins Barracks, Helen Beaumont and Diarmaid Bolger), the National University of Ireland (Dr Emer Purcell and Dr Attracta Halpin), Glasnevin Museum (Georgina Laragy) and the National Library of Ireland (Bríd O'Sullivan).

As always, it is the help and support of my much-loved family – especially Andy, Benjamin, Rosa and Emily Mary Bielenberg – that has enabled me to publish a new book in the midst of our otherwise busy life together and during the unanticipated pressure caused by the COVID-19 lockdown period of 2020. Míle buíochas agus grá mór. *Ní Saoirse go Saoirse na mBan.*

Note: the contents of this book should not be used in any media outputs, documentaries, artistic or fictional work without the knowledge or consent of the authors who spent long periods researching, writing and editing their contribution to this book.

Professor Linda Connolly
Mount Leinster, August 2020

PREFACE

'What did the Women do anyway?' Lil Conlon felt so strongly about this statement that she decided to put on record exactly what the women of Ireland did during the Irish revolution. Conlon was a founding member of Cumann na mBan in Cork and was an active participant during the years 1914–23. She had expected a book to be written about the women's role in the revolution to coincide with the fiftieth anniversary of the Easter Rising. As she stated:

> The Executive [of Cumann na mBan] were in a position to undertake such a work, as all Branches throughout the country submitted monthly reports dealing with activities, etc., and their Organisers furnished them with complete surveys from the Provinces. They had the rein in their hands.[1]

Conlon took it upon herself to write the story and her book *Cumann na mBan and the Women of Ireland 1913–25* was published in 1969. This was a fitting time as it was the fiftieth anniversary of the beginning of the War of Independence, a fact that would not have been lost on Conlon.

And while books had been written about women and the Irish revolution as early as 1922, they were books focusing on individuals. No one had written the story of what it was like for those women who were active, what they did, how they felt and what effect the conflict had on them. More importantly no one had written of the experiences of those who were not involved, the women who witnessed the events, who experienced the revolution from a different perspective. Conlon changed that. As she claimed, 'This book does not purport to be a history – it is simply a pot-pourri of bitter-sweet memories culled in the garden of Yester-Year'.[2] But it was a start.

Others followed Conlon's lead. Historians such as Dr Margaret MacCurtain and Dr Margaret Ward blazed a trail in bringing forth the women's experience of the revolution. Since their pioneering work, more and more historians have followed in the footsteps of MacCurtain and Ward, bringing to life an aspect of the Irish revolution that had been cast to one side.

The task of discovering the stories of the women has been made so much easier in recent years thanks to the release of new material from archives across the country, most notably the Military Archives in Dublin. The Military Service Pension Collection is the gift that keeps on giving. These files, which were never intended for public release, are revealing so much about the activities of Cumann na mBan *and* more importantly the personal impact the revolution had on women.

Just one example of how rich this collection is. While researching the book *'We Were There': 77 Women of the Easter Rising*, co-authored with Dr Mary McAuliffe, members of the Inghinidhe na hÉireann Branch, Cumann na mBan noted in their applications that they had taken part in Lá na mBan in June 1918. Every other applicant just mentioned that they had been involved in anti-conscription activities. None, except for the Inghinidhe women mentioned specifically Lá na mBan. On digging a little deeper a whole story emerged of how the women played a crucial part in the anti-conscription campaign in 1918. Lá na mBan took place on 9 June 1918 in which the women of Ireland took a stand and signed a pledge refusing to take the place of any man in the workforce who was forcibly conscripted into the British Army. Two-thirds of the women of Ireland signed the pledge. Forty thousand women signed it in Dublin alone. What is so important about Lá na mBan was that it gave the women a voice. Although women over the age of thirty had won the right to vote, there was no representation for the younger women. Lá na mBan gave them that opportunity to be a part of something and was a pivotal moment for women in Ireland. That one event politicised so many, and unlike the Volunteers, whose numbers reduced after the threat of conscription had passed, the opposite happened with Cumann na mBan. Branches were set up all over the country. And thankfully in 2018 this event was commemorated in places such as City Hall and the Mansion House in Dublin.

The 1916 Easter Rising was the training ground for Cumann na mBan and the women of the Irish Citizen Army. When the men were imprisoned, it fell to the women to build up support. Although defeated, the Rising was just a battle in a war that was only beginning, and the women were determined to play their part. And that is exactly what they did. While carrying out their regular duties of fundraising, first aid etc., during the War of Independence and later Civil War, they went above and beyond what it was believed a woman could and *should* do. They were intelligence operatives, they were propagandists, they were gun runners, they were scouts, they were judges in the republican courts and much more. And all of this work was carried out without question and at great danger to their safety, both physically and mentally.

But that is only one side of the story. Although there were thousands of members of Cumann na mBan, there were a lot more women who were not. What of those women whose husbands or children were involved, or those who assisted the IRA but were not a member of any organisation, and of course those who were not involved at all, the civilians? Their stories are just as important as those who participated.

And this is exactly what this book has done. Like Conlon's work, this book is the start of something. A journey telling the story of the Irish revolution from the perspective of women; be they participants or civilians. It is a story that has been relegated to the sidelines for too long. We owe it to those who lived through those times, to ourselves and to future generations to have the women's narrative where it belongs, beside that of their male counterparts.

So to return to the statement that spurred Lil Conlon to write her book, *What did the Women do anyway?* Well as this book shows, they did an awful lot, more in fact than was previously known. They were revolutionaries, they were witnesses, they were victims, they were people and they *are* a central part of the story of the Irish revolution. The contributors and editors of this book are to be commended for their work. Lil Conlon would be proud.

Liz Gillis
July 2020

NOTES ON CONTRIBUTORS

Andy Bielenberg is a Senior Lecturer in the School of History at University College Cork. He has published a number of books, including *The Irish Diaspora* (editor), *Ireland and the Industrial Revolution* and *An Economic History of Ireland since 1920*. His articles have been published in several international journals, including *Past and Present, Economic History Review, Éire Ireland, Textile History, Explorations in Economic History,* and *Irish Economic and Social History*. He has recently published new research on war and revolution in County Cork in 1914–23, conflict migration and the Protestant exodus from the south of Ireland in 1919–23.

John Borgonovo is a Lecturer in the School of History at University College Cork. He is the author of a number of articles and books, including *The Battle for Cork: July–August 1922, Spies, Informers, and the Anti-Sinn Féin Society: The Intelligence War in Cork City, 1920–21* and *Florence and Josephine O'Donoghue's War of Independence: A Destiny that Shapes our Ends*. He is an editor of the *Atlas of the Irish Revolution*.

Sarah-Anne Buckley is a Lecturer in History at the National University of Ireland Galway and co-director of the Irish Centre for the Histories of Labour and Class. Her research interests include the history of child welfare in Ireland and Britain, the history of marginalised groups of women and children, the social history of Ireland in the twentieth century, and more recently the history of youth. Her first book was on the history of the Haematology Association of Ireland and a second book, *The Cruelty Man: Child Welfare, the NSPCC and the State in Ireland, 1889–1956*, was published in 2013 with Manchester University Press. She is current chair of the Irish Women's History Association.

Marie Coleman is a Reader in History at Queen's University Belfast. She is joint editor of the journal *Irish Historical Studies*, a committee member of the Economic and Social History Society of Ireland, secretary of the

Ulster Society for Irish Historical Studies, and a member of the Royal Irish Academy's National Committee for Historical Sciences and of the advisory committee to the Military Service Pensions Project. Her books include *County Longford and the Irish Revolution 1910–1923*, *The Irish Sweep: A History of the Irish Hospitals Sweepstake 1930–1987* and *The Irish Revolution 1916–1923*. She has also written a number of academic journal articles on revolutionary veterans, gender in the revolution and the experience of southern Protestants during the revolution.

Linda Connolly is Professor of Sociology and Director of the Maynooth University Social Sciences Institute. She is an author and editor of a number of books, including *The Irish Women's Movement: From Revolution to Devolution*, (co-editor) *Social Movements and Ireland*, (co-author) *Documenting Irish Feminisms* and (editor) *The 'Irish' Family*. She has published a number of chapters and articles and led research projects on the Irish women's movement, social movements, family, gender equality, Irish studies, and gender-based and sexual violence.

John Cunningham is a Lecturer in History at the National University of Ireland Galway and co-director of the Irish Centre for the Histories of Labour and Class. His research interests include Irish local history, the moral economy, and global syndicalism. He has served as an editor of *Saothar* and his publications include *Unlikely Radicals: Irish Secondary Teachers and the ASTI, 1909–2009*, *A Town Tormented by the Sea: Galway, 1790–1914* and *Labour in the West of Ireland: Working Life and Struggle*.

Mary McAuliffe is an Assistant Professor in Gender Studies at University College Dublin in the School of Social Policy/Social Justice. Her research interests include social history, Irish women and politics, memory and history, gender and Irish biography, war/military history and oral history. Her most recent books are *Margaret Skinnider*, (co-author) *Richmond Barracks 1916: We Were There – 77 Women of the Easter Rising* and (co-editor) *Kerry 1916; Histories and Legacies of the Easter Rising*. Other publications include *Fanny Taylors (1867) Irish Homes and Irish Hearts* and (co-editor) *Palgrave Advances in Irish History*.

Ailbhe McDaid is an Irish Research Council Postdoctoral Fellow in the School of English at University College Cork. Her current project is entitled 'Domestic Disruptions: Women, Literature and Conflict, 1914–1923'. She has held research and teaching positions at University of Liverpool, Maynooth

University and University of Otago, and her publications include articles in *Irish Studies Review, New Hibernia Review* and *Journal of War and Culture Studies*. Her book *The Poetics of Migration in Contemporary Irish Poetry* was published by Palgrave Macmillan in 2017.

Lucy McDiarmid is Marie Frazee-Baldassarre Professor of English at Montclair State University in New Jersey. Her books include *The Irish Art of Controversy* and *Poets and the Peacock Dinner: The Literary History of a Meal*, which appeared in paperback in October 2016. Her most recent book, *At Home in the Revolution: What Women Said and Did in 1916*, was published by the Royal Irish Academy in 2016. She is a former president of the American Conference for Irish Studies.

Claire McGing is a member of the senior management team at the Institute for Art, Design and Technology, Dun Laoghaire, leading on equality, diversity and inclusion. She has published research on gender politics and Irish politics, including chapters in the 2011, 2016 and 2020 editions of *How Ireland Voted* and reports, including on women's representation in Irish local government for the National Women's Council of Ireland.

Doireann Ní Ghríofa is a bilingual Irish writer. Among her awards are the Rooney Prize for Irish Literature, a Seamus Heaney Centre Fellowship, the Ireland Chair of Poetry bursary, the Michael Hartnett Award, and most recently, the Ostana Prize. Her fifth book, a bilingual selection of poetry *Lies*, was published in 2018. Her first prose title, *A Ghost in the Throat*, was published in 2020.

Louise Ryan is a Professor of Sociology at London Metropolitan University and a Fellow of the Academy of Social Sciences. She has published extensively in a range of international journals on migration, social networks, gender, religion and Irish women's history. Her recent books include (co-author) *An End to the Crisis of Empirical Sociology? Trends and Challenges in Social Research*, (co-author) *Migrant Capital: Networks, Identities, Strategies, Winning the Vote for Women: the Irish Citizen Newspaper and the Suffrage Movement in Ireland*; and (co-editor) *Irish Women and the Vote: Becoming Citizens*.

Margaret Ward is Honorary Senior Lecturer in History at Queen's University, Belfast and former director of the Women's Resource and Development Agency. Amongst her many publications are *Unmanageable Revolutionaries:*

Women and Irish Nationalism, Maud Gonne: A Life (1990), *Hanna Sheehy Skeffington: Suffragette and Sinn Féiner, Her Memoirs and Political Writings* and *Fearless Woman: Hanna Sheehy Skeffington, Feminism and the Irish Revolution.*

ACRONYMS

ASU	Active Service Unit
BMH	Bureau of Military History
GHQ	General Head Quarters
GPO	General Post Office
ICA	Irish Citizen Army
IRA	Irish Republican Army
IWFL	Irish Women's Franchise League
IWSF	Irish Women's Suffrage Federation
IWSS	Irish Women's Suffrage Society
MA	Military Archives
MP	Member of Parliament
MSP	Military Service Pension
MSPC	Military Services Pension Collection
NAI	National Archives of Ireland
NLI	National Library of Ireland
OC	Officer Commanding
OPW	Office of Public Works
PTSD	Post Traumatic Stress Disorder
RIC	Royal Irish Constabulary
TD	Teachta Dála
TNA	The National Archives
WS	Witness Statement
WSPU	Women's Social and Political Union

INTRODUCTION
Women in Ireland's Revolution, 1917–1923: Marginal or Constitutive?

LINDA CONNOLLY

Jack Goldstone has defined a revolution as 'an effort to transform the political institutions and the justifications for political authority in society, accompanied by formal or informal mass mobilisation and non-institutionalised actions that undermine authorities'.[1] Ireland experienced a distinctive and much debated revolution in the early decades of the twentieth century that sought to undermine British governance and incorporated episodes of civil unrest linked to loyalism, trade unionism, socialism, feminism and physical force republicanism. In the period after the Easter Rising of 1916, a period of protracted tension between constitutional nationalism and recourse to violence for political ends culminated in a destructive civil war that overshadowed the foundation of the State. The Anglo-Irish War of Independence (21 January 1919 to 11 July 1921) was followed by the Irish Civil War (28 June 1922 to 24 May 1923) between pro- and anti-Treaty republicans.

This phase of 'the Irish Revolution' is both a complex and thorny question in Irish women's studies. Women remained extremely active and important in Irish revolutionary movements and campaigns in the period after the 1916 Rising. At the same time, one of the major outcomes of the revolution was the introduction of a succession of restrictions on Irish women's social and political rights on the part of the new State. Although women continued to exercise agency in a variety of ways in society, the fusion of a deeply conservative Catholic and State ideology from 1922 on created a particularly regressive climate for women and feminist activists in Ireland that persisted for several decades.[2] Women were formally relegated to family duties, and repressive laws intended to encourage the birth of more children were subsequently passed.[3] The memory and impact of women's important political and military role in the revolution became largely *forgotten* and erased.

Valentine M. Moghadam has observed that internationally the study of revolutions 'has produced a prodigious body of scholarship that is nonetheless deficient in one area: attention to gender in the unfolding of revolutions and the building of new states.'[4] Moghadam broadened the scope of the study of diverse types of revolutions by taking into account emerging literature on women and revolutions. She drew particular attention to the continued absence of gender in theories of revolution and elaborated on the existence of two models of gender relations pursued by revolutionaries across time and place. A women-in-the-family-model was followed in the twentieth century by Mexico, Algeria, Iran and Eastern Europe, among others.[5] In all of these cases, Moghadam argues, the strong roles played by women in making revolutions were rolled back by new regimes stressing ideologies of gender difference – a model that clearly applies to Ireland's revolution and its aftermath. In Russia, China, Cuba, South Yemen, Vietnam, Nicaragua and elsewhere, by contrast, women gained more formal and actual rights, despite the recuperation of their autonomous organisations by the states that emerged. Moghadam concludes that the discernment of these patterns and the argument that revolutions necessarily possess a gender dimension opens up a space for further understanding the causes, course, and outcomes of revolutions.

Moghadam's contention that gender, unlike class or the State or the world-system, is not seen as a constitutive category applies to the Irish case.[6] Until recently, geography, ethnicity, religion and class have been widely considered core variables, constitutive of the revolution that occurred in Ireland, while gender was typically treated as marginal, separate or consignable to the sub-fields of women's history and women's studies.[7] The importance of doing more work on gender and incorporating gender was often noted but not fully attempted in influential work. Yet feminist scholars and women's historians had been working on these issues for some decades and had already provided a body of work available for consideration.[8] David Fitzpatrick, for instance, remarked that: 'Between 1912 and 1922, Ireland experienced revolution in several senses.'[9] But the edited volume *Terror in Ireland* did not include a chapter or sustained section of a chapter on women and violence (or indeed very many chapters written by women) – which seemed to suggest that women were not greatly impacted by the very serious forms of violence occurring during the Irish revolution.[10] Likewise Kissane provided very few references to 'women' or 'gender' in his detailed treatise of the Irish Civil War (women are, for instance, fleetingly mentioned on page 229)[11] and stated that 'Irish historians have done little to define the parameters of Irish democracy or authoritarianism as they existed in 1922 or afterwards.' However, quite substantial publications in women's history and feminist studies on 'the limits of democracy' imposed on women in Ireland (that is, half the population) before and after 1922 were not referred to.[12]

The experience of women and Irish women's revolutionary history have been better incorporated into more recent texts on the Irish revolution though this is by no means a universal or even trend.[13] It is timely, therefore, to explore these issues further in this volume. Women from different backgrounds and places in Ireland were revolutionary activists in not insignificant numbers in this period and indeed experienced Ireland's revolution 'in several senses' including by grappling with and embracing the liberating promises of feminism, nationalism and socialism, in diverse ways. Women were also profoundly impacted by the overall violence and tumult of this era as 'ordinary' civilians and loyalists.[14] Some of the most understudied aspects of women's lives during the Irish revolution includes the history of private life, wartime sexuality, motherhood, friendships and romantic relationships and experiences – all of which were heavily policed during and after the revolution, as this volume demonstrates.

Following Moghadam, this book explores the question 'what is a revolution, and in what way is it gendered?' in the context of the Irish revolution.[15] The question of 'what is a revolution,' and more specifically what was the fundamental essence and natue of the 'Irish' revolution, have been widely debated in terms of theories, scope and definition.[16] Gender is also critical to understanding the nature, scope and outcome of all revolutions, which is an issue that merits further consideration in Irish revolutionary studies and debates.[17] As Joan Scott has argued, gender is a 'useful category of historical analysis.'[18] In light of this, the chapters in this volume specifically explore the role and diverse experience of women as an important dimension of the revolution. The Irish revolution in the period after the Rising as a *process* was most certainly gendered. The roles men played as leaders, combatants, victims and parliamentarians have been extensively documented and connected to the course and outcome of the Irish revolution for some time. New work on men and masculinity in the revolution continues to emerge.[19] The aim of this book, however, is to advance new, additional scholarship and perspectives in Irish sociology, history, politics and literary studies on women's equally complex and varied role. Several questions arise. What did women do individually and in political and military organisations? What happened to women, in this period? And how can the experience of women in different situations, as civilians, activists and family members, be further documented and interpreted? In agreement with Thébaud 'looking at the history of women and developing gender-based approaches changes and complicates our understanding of war – both of particular wars and of the general phenomenon of war.'[20] Current convergence around a certain number of themes in the study of women, gender and wars, including the processes that accompany the exit from war, private life in wartime, and gendered and sexual violence require greater consideration in Irish revolutionary studies. A comprehensive gender-based approach has the potential to further complicate and expand the received understanding of the impact and outcome of Ireland's revolution.

Historiography and Commemoration

A significant number of academic articles, research monographs and edited collections, documenting different aspects of the political and violent dynamics of this dramatic and contested phase of 'revolution' exist.[21] Pioneering women's historians and feminist scholars have, for over four decades, worked relentlessly to locate women's role and experience alongside a male-dominated narrative of revolution and war in Ireland, and a prodigious body of scholarship is now evident.[22] Margaret Ward foregrounded the study of women in the Irish revolution in 1983 for a whole generation of scholars that followed in her groundbreaking text, *Unmanageable Revolutionaries*. Other important and sophisticated surveys of gender, nationalism, unionism, socialism and feminism, as well as biographies and studies of women's organisations, followed.[23] In addition, a solid body of work on various aspects of first wave feminism, the women's movement and the Irish revolution has developed since the 1980s.[24] Any claim that Irish women's role and experience in the revolution is not fully integrated into the established canon because the necessary scholarship does not exist is therefore inaccurate and unduly serves to airbrush the existing framework and empirical foundation established by key studies. More work undoubtedly needs to be done on gender and women, as this collection demonstrates, but a prodigious body of work on women and the Irish revolution has existed for a number of decades.

Women's history and women's challenge to masculinist historiography was treated as marginal during the nationalist/revisionist/post-colonial 'history wars' of the 1980s in Irish studies, and it continues to be ignored in very new interventions.[25] A recent article on the subject in Irish historiography completely omits women's history from a very comprehensive discussion and even suggests leading revisionists: 'All entered manhood and the academy at the outbreak of the Troubles.'[26]

Although dedicated scholarship on women and revolution continues to prosper, uneven access to 'the canon' also continues to translate into structural employment issues and citation practices (women and work on women receive significantly less citations in academic publications).[27] Nonetheless, important new studies and texts in women's history and feminist research, often strongly shaped or buttressed by earlier pioneering work, continue to emerge on the role of women in the revolution.[28] A broad spectrum of methodologies employed to study or incorporate women's role in the Irish revolution has in recent years ranged from entirely new, in-depth empirical research, typically conducted over a long period on newly released, previously unused sources, to summarising existing published work on women in general historical surveys. The Irish State's 'decade of centenaries' programme has also clearly influenced the production of women's public history in recent years. Several articles on women in the revolution have appeared on online platforms and public history fora.[29] The role of individual women in the 1916 Rising received attention during the 2016 State-led commemoration. At the same time, feminist scholars had to publicly challenge the prevalence of male dominated panels and conferences at the start of the year. The State's dedicated centennial commemoration of votes for women in 2018 also engendered renewed interdisciplinary interest in women's political history, feminist research and the history of feminism and the women's movement in Ireland and the United Kingdom, where a number of public and academic events were held.[30] A number of interdisciplinary conferences since 2018 on gender, class and political participation were also funded by the State, the National University of Ireland and the Irish Research Council.

The question of how the period of revolution after the Rising was significantly shaped by women and gender issues, as well as an understanding of the impact war and terror had on women in this period, requires even more focused attention now, however, not least in light of the more difficult, final stage of the State centennial commemorations – encompassing the ending of the War of Independence and onset of a divisive civil war. Any tendency to airbrush women out of the more violent and contentious episodes of the revolution must be avoided if an inclusive and full appraisal of this period is to be arrived at. Violence against women, including sexual violence, is a difficult aspect of the past but it is also an unavoidable truth. In agreement with the Irish President Michael D. Higgins: 'We must not be afraid to face the past, including all of the violence and cruelties released from pent-up exclusions, deprivations and humiliations. Let us not look with any trepidation towards the commemorations of the coming years, lest we be tempted to avert our gaze, take refuge in evasion, or seek to ignore the difficult questions they shall raise for us all.'[31] A key question addressed in this collection is, in a moment of national remembrance, if violence cuts to the heart of the State's foundation, how and in what ways is this gendered? And why was the violence women experienced marginalised, minimised or negated in the official histories of this period for such a long time? The role of women and the importance of considering gender in understanding the direction and outcome of other twentieth-century wars and civil wars (for instance, the Spanish Civil War and the Greek Civil War) is recognised internationally but this comparative dimension needs to be more systematically considered in Irish revolutionary studies.[32] The fact that the Irish revolution was clearly smaller in scale than other twentieth-century wars is not a reason to diminish or de-contextualise gender-based violence that did occur (such as forced hair cutting, physical violence, intimidation and sexual assault).

As the chapters by Ward and Borgonovo in this volume demonstrate, building on earlier work, the experience and the long-term fate of republican women, including in Cumann na mBan in the Civil War, is also being further revealed in valuable sources (such as the retrospective Bureau of Military History witness statements of men and some women gathered in the 1950s and in the Military Service Pensions Collection from the period). Indeed, the much-used patrilineal metaphor to describe the Civil War in Ireland as a conflict of 'brother against brother' is automatically disrupted when the divergent roles and positions women adopted during the Civil War, including within and between families, are examined in these sources. The family or the 'home front' (where women are often located if men are on the run or engaged in guerrilla warfare) likewise requires further consideration in the Irish context. Revolutions, it can be argued, are as much made and promulgated in the kitchen as in other locales, with women not just engaged in running the domestic space in the face of external, violent threats and attacks but also constructing it as a political space for ideas, strategies and military planning and establishing support systems for rebels and other women subjected to violence and intimidation. The elision of gender combined with the concomitant silence and solidarity of women in family structures is a recurrent theme in conflict situations internationally. Brett Schmoll, for instance, in the context of the pueblos in Spain, suggests:

Regrettably there has been little historical attention paid to gender in the pueblos during the Spanish Civil War. Due to the paucity of written records of the experience of motherhood during the war, the project makes use of oral sources. The men and women of these pueblos recall vivid images of their mothers during the war, memories of overwhelming fear and onerous labor; in so doing, they reveal the inherent value of their daily life during the war. The perception of mothers, as portrayed in the prescriptive literature of the 1930s in Spain, conflicts with the experience of motherhood during the Spanish Civil War. An examination of the impact of this war on mothers in this region of Spain reveals that they, whether through silence or solidarity, developed a culture of coping, a vigorous motherhood shaped by the specific social and historical circumstances in which these women found themselves. A close look at Castilian pueblos during the Spanish Civil War suggests that the war altered more than the economic and political life; instead it shook the very foundations of the Spanish family.[33]

In political and military terms, women widely participated in feminist, socialist and republican causes, as well as in unionist efforts to conserve the role of the United Kingdom in Ireland, during the broad period classified as the Irish revolution.[34] The revolution also clearly incorporated a first wave feminist social movement that fought for a range of causes, including votes for women which was in part achieved in 1918. But, like the women in the pueblos, women from various backgrounds in Ireland also maintained homes and families or engaged in onerous work in the face of adversity and danger. Commemorating the centenary of an internal civil war in 2022–23 in Ireland may well be difficult and risk reopening 'old' wounds and divisions. But, a commemoration that solely focuses on men's role in the war and in the foundation of the State will merely reassert the male narrative that prevailed, marginalised and silenced women's voice and experience of this phase of the revolution for decades.

This book aims to bring together new research in chapters that explore (in Part I) important aspects of women's participation in political and revolutionary activities in the 1917–23 period (in feminist politics, nationalist women's organisations, prisons and political institutions/parties, including during the Anglo-Irish Treaty debate) and (in Part II) the impact of terror and war on women throughout this period (including violence perpetrated against women). The representation of the trauma experienced by women in this period, including in literary sources, and the prioritisation of heroic remembrance over 'forgotten' and marginalised women are addressed in the final part of the book (Part III). The question of who we remember and how we remember in a moment of national commemoration arises in relation to the recovery work that has been necessary to rewrite women back into the received narrative of the Irish revolution. The narrative of the Irish revolution as essentially a chronology of great men and male militarism, with women presumed to have either played a subsidiary role or no role at all and/or to have escaped the worst brutalities of war compared to men, requires continued vigilance and correction, as the chapters in this volume demonstrate.

Margaret Ward has stated that:

> the significance of women has remained hidden within historical records, waiting for the understanding of someone who wants to know what women did, what they thought and how they were affected by the upheavals of the past century. To give serious consideration to their role involves a reappraisal for their subsequent exclusion from political and economic life.[35]

The experience of women in heretofore hidden records and in new sources made available in recent years needs to be further considered as a core dynamic both in new historical tomes of the period and in the programme of key events to be commemorated in Ireland. A 'women's section' of the decade of centenaries cannot be confined and left behind in the commemoration programme that marked female suffrage in 2018. More difficult questions require critical attention in the years ahead, such as the violence women experienced in the period covering the War of Independence and the Civil War and its aftermath (including State violence), as well as the marginalisation of women in the political process that established the Irish State. The role of women in the revolution in Northern Ireland also requires much more analysis and inclusion, as Margaret Ward demonstrates in her chapter. As extensive analysis of women's role and experience in civil wars and revolutionary conflicts internationally has shown, the gendered nature of war and conflict is not a separate or ancillary question that can be downplayed in any context. Nor are women simply mere victims or bystanders of conflicts that are steered by male political leaders or militants. Gender and women's studies scholars are not bystanders either – feeding our very detailed, often life-long research as token references or summary material into tomes and articles billed as the 'authoritative' or 'new' texts on the revolution. The story of women *is* the story of the revolution *in equal measure*. The granting of suffrage in 1918; the complex role of women as activists in the revolution, including their complex relationships with each other; the parliamentary role of women in the foundation of the new State; the wider impact of conflict, trauma and violence on women during the War of Independence and Civil War; and how we remember, write and represent these questions are core questions in Irish revolutionary studies. All these issues require further analysis, integration, recovery work and consideration, if this critical period of Irish history is to be adequately understood.

Book Outline

The chapters in Part I of the book explore women's activism in feminist and nationalist campaigns and movements, and in the debates concerning the establishment of the Irish Free State. The extension of suffrage to (some) women in 1918 was clearly a landmark development in Irish women's history and in the period of revolution. In Chapter 1, Louise Ryan introduces the complex and multifaceted relationship that developed between feminism and nationalism in this period – a central dynamic in the wider revolution. Historically, in many countries campaigning for independence (such as Ireland and India), feminism and nationalism were often regarded as competing priorities. In particular, the relationship between women's liberation and national liberation was complicated by the role of tradition. This chapter focuses on the tense relationship between feminism and nationalism in Ireland and demonstrates how, by challenging double moral standards, hypocrisy and conventional morality, Irish suffragists represented a feminist analysis of Irish society. However, like feminists in other countries engaged in anti-colonial struggles, Irish suffragists had to negotiate a tricky path between demanding women's rights and risking the antagonism of groups demanding the nation's right to self-determination. The challenge for feminism was in trying to reconcile traditional images of Irish womanhood with a modern women's movement demanding equality and rights. This frequently led to conflict with nationalists and to a contestation of 'tradition' whereby feminists attempted to redefine or reinvent traditional images of Irish womanhood. A tension between tradition and modernity, including in relation to gender roles and feminism, is a major feature and outcome of revolutions globally, and Ireland's revolution was no exception.

Moving beyond the method of individual biographies, the relationship *between* well-known female revolutionary leaders and comrades is explored and dissected in Chapter 2. Drawing on various published and unpublished first-person accounts of their stay in Holloway Prison by Kathleen Clarke, Maud Gonne MacBride, Constance Markievicz, and Hanna Sheehy Skeffington, Lucy McDiarmid considers the different forms of friendship and cross-class tensions among the women themselves. Sources examined include Clarke's published memoir and unpublished letters to her sister Madge Daly, Gonne's witness statement for the Bureau of Military History and her letters to W.B. Yeats, Markievicz's Prison Letters, and an unpublished memoir by Sheehy Skeffington. Benedict Anderson has stated that the nation is 'imagined as a community because, regardless of the actual inequality and exploitation that may prevail in each, the nation is always conceived as a deep, horizontal comradeship.'[36] Analysis of the women's narratives of their encounters in Holloway reveals the strains and stresses in that 'comradeship'.

Chapters 3 and 4 further advance the history of nationalist women in Cumann na mBan (the Irish republican women's organisation formed in Dublin in 1914), in the north and south of Ireland, and investigate the role of the organisation in the Civil War. In Chapter 3, Margaret Ward explores the life and work of Belfast-based activists, including Winifred Carney, who served in the GPO throughout the 1916 Rising and was the best known of the Cumann na mBan northern members. In the words of Elizabeth Corr, Carney had 'done her duty like a woman.' Corr and five of her colleagues had travelled to Dublin and throughout Ulster to warn of the confusion arising out of the countermanding orders on the eve of the Rising, but Belfast Cumann na mBan was to find the circumstances in which it operated to be very different in the aftermath of the events of Easter Week. Using unpublished journals and witness statements, this chapter will explore the challenges northern republicans faced as nationalist forces regrouped, Sinn Féin developed and the War of Independence began in earnest.

John Borgonovo, in Chapter 4, summarises how recent scholarship has expanded our understanding of Cumann na mBan as an active force during the Easter Rising and War of Independence period. Yet, relatively little attention has been paid to the republican women's organisation during the Irish Civil War. The military aspect of the Civil War has been presented in Irish historiography as an almost exclusively male story. However, this chapter examines Cumann na mBan from the perspective of Civil War participants. A survey of political and military activity and a comparison of the organisation during the Civil War with its War of Independence predecessor is provided. The findings suggest the organisation may have become more militarised and militant as it attempted to fill the vacuum left by the crumbling anti-Treaty IRA in late 1922 and early 1923. While the Civil War is often described as a war 'brother against brother', this chapter will argue that the conflict also had a 'sister against sister' dimension, with pro- and anti-Treaty Cumann na mBan forces coming into conflict with one another directly and indirectly.

In Chapter 5, Claire McGing summarises how the Dáil debates on the Anglo-Irish Treaty from December 1921 to January 1922 provided women TDs (elected members of Dáil Éireann) with the first occasion in which they voted on a major political issue. During the weeks of debate the six women deputies remained unwavering in their opposition to the document. What is particularly interesting is that these women claimed to substantively represent the views of ordinary women voters while numerous men on the pro-Treaty side sought to discredit these claims by painting the women TDs as nothing more than bitter widows, too emotional for politics and, in some cases, even mentally unstable. This chapter provides a gendered analysis of the Treaty debates. It explores how gendered assumptions and norms were produced and reproduced by the women and men who were TDs in the course of the Treaty debates, and suggests it formed a negative basis for women's access to politics in the later years of the Irish Free State and beyond.

Part II of the book focuses on the widespread and often traumatic impact violence, intimidation and protracted conflict had on women during the Irish revolution. My own extended chapter, Chapter 6, contextualises in detail the ways in which historians have conceptualised and framed violence against women, and thus violence more generally, in the period covering the War of Independence and the Civil War and its aftermath. The chapter specifically argues that historians of the Irish revolution need to take women's experience of violence further into account. The masculinist, militaristic frame work at the heart of Irish historiography should be transformed in order to arrive at a more complex and inclusive view of the dynamics of violence, throughout this period. Valuable new sources from this period recently made available contain detailed information, discussed in this chapter, on the widespread use of forced hair cutting, in particular, as a form of sexual policing and gender-specific punishment meted out by all sides in the conflict (crown forces and republicans). New cases of sexual violence that have recently come to light are also addressed. The question of whether sexual violence was rare in Ireland's revolution or more common than has been presumed to-date is explored.

In Chapter 7, Marie Coleman examines evidence of compensation claimed and awarded to women as a result of personal injury or damage to property after the revolution. It draws on the Irish Grants Committee's files for compensation given to Irish loyalists to examine the impact of political violence on loyalist women. Themes examined include the nature of violence experienced by these women (including physical attacks, intimidation and the economic effects of commercial boycotts), the impact which this had on their health and whether or not they remained in Ireland after independence. It also uses the recently released Military Service Pension Collection to examine the impact of involvement in revolutionary activity on combatant women, mostly members of Cumann na mBan. Pensions awarded for injuries and illness provide an insight into the physical and psychological effects that revolutionary activity had on them. The economic impact on families whose husbands, sons or brothers died as a result of the conflict will also be examined through pensions and gratuities that were awarded to dependents, which are also in this collection.

Andy Bielenberg, in Chapter 8, focuses on the scale of fatalities during the revolution. Irish historians have written extensively on the men killed during the War of Independence and Civil War as combatants. The historiography of the revolution in Cork, including episodes of violence in the Bandon Valley, has provoked particularly intense debate in Irish revolutionary studies. More civilian victims of the revolution were killed in Cork than in any other county in Ireland in this period. However, very little attention has been given to the stories behind the thirteen women who were killed in Cork during this period. This chapter examines the circumstances of the women killed in Cork county during the War of Independence, specifically. It explores their movements up to their death, their backgrounds and life stories, and the cause of their death, thereby addressing an invisible story in the history of 'lives lost' during the Irish revolution and in the otherwise much-debated history of the revolution in Cork.

Justin Dolan Stover has demonstrated how the nature of the conflict in Ireland meant that violence intruded on personal and intimate family spaces.[37] In Chapter 9, Mary McAuliffe further reviews the way in which 'women's spaces' – home, farm and community – were attacked in deliberate attempts to terrorise. The histories of these 'home invasions', including burnings, attacks and night raids, and the particular experiences of women in what was constructed as their safe and respectable space are rendered invisible in a male-centric narrative. In addition, how the work of women in these spaces – caring, feeding, grieving, working – is politicised and becomes in many ways dangerous during war arises.

In Chapter 10, Ailbhe McDaid considers the act of bearing witness and the complications of traumatic memory in women's experiences of conflict during the Irish revolution. How do women testify to the grief and trauma of witnessed and remembered violence in their own words? And how is women's witnessing presented in contemporaneous and retrospective literary works? Drawing on individual women's testimonies from the Bureau of Military History and the Military Service Pension Collections as well as literature written in and about the period, this chapter highlights how women's experiences of bearing witness raise key questions about the ethics of representation, the construction of cultural memory and the articulation of traumatic memory relating to the Irish revolution.

In the final chapter, Sarah-Anne Buckley and John Cunningham address the question of how the revolution has been selectively represented, commemorated and memorialised in a case study. In Tuam, County Galway, the now-notorious building that housed women who had children out of wedlock had a complex history as a place of incarceration, having been a workhouse and a military prison prior to becoming a mother and baby home. Even before the building was requisitioned by the British authorities in 1920, local officials of the proto-State had shown a disposition to police the sexual behaviour of workhouse inmates through republican courts. Later, when six anti-Treatyite prisoners were executed there during the Civil War, the site became iconic for republicans. After the new Free State shut down the workhouse system, the Archbishop of Tuam prevailed upon the public authorities to relocate a mother and baby home to the building under the auspices of the Bon Secours Sisters. For their part, the Sisters took care to preserve the scene of the 1923 executions, later facilitating the erection of a republican monument. In 2017, however, a public scandal broke when a Commission of Investigation confirmed that local historian Catherine Corless's earlier finding that the bodies of up to 800 dead infants were buried in a mass grave on the same site was *true*. The careful remembering of the republican martyrs (and indeed the respect paid to the remains of members of the Bon Secours order buried there) contrasts starkly with Irish society's systematic concealment of the predominantly working-class unmarried mothers who were confined there and in other institutions and the evident disregard for the bodies of the many hundreds of children who perished within its walls. The interplay of gender, stigma and revolutionary 'veneration' on the site of a controversial mother and baby home at Tuam is explored and leads to the question – who do we remember?

Each chapter in this volume explores specific and diverse aspects of women's experience in the revolution, in the period after the 1916 Rising. The complex role of women as activists, the detrimental impact of violence and social and political divisions during the War of Independence and Civil War on women, the role of women in the foundation of the new State and dynamics of political marginalisation, remembrance and forgetting are explored in detail. Fundamentally, it is hoped that the text as a whole will prompt new public conversations and questions about the complex experience of women and their legacy in this period. A poem by Doireann Ní Ghríofa, entitled *Brightening*, poignantly reflects on these themes and completes the collection.

PART I

Chapter 1

NATIONALISM AND FEMINISM:

The Complex Relationship between the Suffragist and Independence Movements in Ireland

LOUISE RYAN

The relationship between feminism and nationalism globally is complex and multifaceted.[1] In the early decades of the twentieth century, for countries embroiled in anti-colonial struggle, including Ireland, feminism and nationalism were often regarded as competing priorities.[2] However, that is not to suggest that these were oppositional movements. On the contrary, it has been suggested that feminism and nationalism emerged in the same discursive environment.[3] Feminism was a critical dynamic in the development of the Irish revolution, including the 1917 to 1923 period, encompassing the War of Independence and the Civil War.

The relationship between women's liberation and national liberation was complicated, in part, by gendered evocations of traditional culture, practices and identities.[4] Nationalist movements tended to use traditions not only as a source of national identity but also as a way of differentiating between the indigenous culture and heritage of the nation and the 'alien' influences of imperial culture. Within nationalism rhetoric, that 'alien' culture was frequently presented as immoral, evil and dangerous. In Ireland, as indeed in many other countries striving for independence, nationalist discourse tended to ascribe women a limited range of roles within a narrow repertoire of maternal iconography.[5] Hence, women were constructed as the keepers of traditional moral and social order.[6] However, a small but vocal group of activists took an opposing viewpoint.

In this chapter, drawing on the body of work I have developed over the last twenty years, the complex role of feminism and feminist activists during the Irish revolutionary period is contextualised and interrogated. Now, in the early twenty-first century, with nationalist movements again on the rise across Europe, it seems an appropriate time to revisit and reappraise the ways in which feminists in the past engaged with nationalism, especially in anti-colonial contexts. I argue that by challenging double moral standards, hypocrisy and conventional morality, Irish suffragists represented a feminist analysis of Irish society. However, like feminists in other countries engaged in anti-colonialism, such as Poland[7] or India,[8] for example, Irish suffragists had to negotiate a tricky path between demanding women's rights and risking the antagonism of groups demanding the nation's right to self-determination. The challenge for feminism was in trying to reconcile traditional images of Irish womanhood with a modern women's movement demanding equality and rights.[9] This frequently led to conflict with nationalists and to a contestation of 'tradition' whereby feminists attempted to redefine or reinvent traditional images of Irish womanhood. While focusing on the tense relationship between feminism and nationalism in Ireland, the chapter draws on some analytical frameworks from the wider international literature. In so doing, I aim to analyse some of the strategies feminists used to reposition feminism within narratives of national identity and nation-building.

Feminism and Nationalism

Over the last decade or so there has been renewed feminist interest in the issue of nationalism. Far from the assumed death of the nation-state in a rapidly globalising world, it has been increasingly realised that the nation-state and hence nationalism remain salient forces in twenty-first century societies.[10] In the early twenty-first century, the rise of ultra-nationalist groups in Europe has underlined the urgency of taking nationalism seriously. Without wishing to under-estimate the specificities of modern nationalist movements, I argue that much can be learned from an understanding of historical movements. In particular, how feminists had engaged critically with nationalist movements over one hundred years ago, at the start of the twentieth century.

In Ireland, in recent years, there has been growing interest in the active role played by women in the nationalist campaign for independence.[11] The centenary commemorations of the 1916 Rising included several celebrations of the role of women.[12] However, women's activism should not be analysed only through the lens of nationalism. There were other groups of women in the early twentieth century who had a more complex relationship with the nationalist movement.[13] Irish suffrage activists offered new insights into gender inequalities. In developing their critical analysis, these campaigners were part of a long history of feminist thinking in Ireland going back to pioneers like Anna Wheeler.[14] While many suffragists supported the aim of Irish self-determination, nonetheless, they refused to blame all social evils on colonialism or to assume that national independence would solve all social problems. Instead, they challenged the prevailing power relations and patriarchal order throughout all the social, economic and political institutions of societies.

Of course, Ireland was not alone in experiencing the thorny relationship between colonialism, nationalism and feminism. As discussed at length elsewhere,[15] in countries such as India, feminists not only had to engage with the oppressive force of colonial rule but also the constraining influence of gendered nationalist discourses, which constructed idealised masculinity and femininity in relation to tropes like 'Mother India'.[16] There is scope for more comparative research in the analysis of suffrage history. It would be interesting to see new comparative work on suffragism in Ireland and India, for example. But that is beyond the remit of this chapter.

As a sociologist, I am interested in drawing upon theoretical analyses of gendered nationalist discourses and counter-discourses. In so doing, it is necessary to consider how nationalism and feminism have been mutually constitutive of each other. According to Haque, feminism and nationalism emerged as part of the great reformism programme at the end of the nineteenth century, 'not only enriching one another in the process but also each bearing traces of the discourses and practices against which it self-fashioned itself (e.g. feudalism, monarchy, patriarchy, tradition and so on)'.[17] Feminist scholars have long debated the complex relationship between nationalism and feminism.[18] Indeed, as Liddle and Joshi have argued, while nationalists and feminists were united on issues where women's demands also furthered the nationalist cause, there were splits over issues that posed a direct challenge to male privilege.[19] Many nationalist men were 'forced to admit that whilst they were determined to resist national subordination they did not want to forgo their own domination of women'.[20] As Haque argues, 'Disillusioned and embittered, advocates of female interests' felt the need 'to re-examine the whole national/social question vis-à-vis the interests of women'. In so doing, 'a new course of action is adopted, re-aligning the priorities of nation and women. The process gets under way by delinking the two agendas: feminist and national. From then on, the fight for the rights of women becomes an agenda in its own merit.'[21]

These observations from international scholarship offer useful insights into the processes taking place in Ireland. Irish feminists, although in many cases supportive of Irish self-determination, argued that nationalist men were using women to further the national cause but were offering those women no guarantee of rights, citizenship or equality in an independent Ireland.[22]

Although the relationship between nationalism and feminism is multi-faceted and cannot be reduced to one single issue, I am particularly interested in how disputes about 'national tradition' often underpinned these tense relationships. 'Despite all its modern paraphernalia, the discourse of nation, for instance, is always torn between its adherence to a glorious past (revivalism) and its commitment to a (cosmopolitan) future brighter than the present.'[23] This echoes what Tom Nairn has described as the 'Janus quality' of nationalism – two faces – one looking backwards to history, the other looking forwards to the future.[24] Anne McClintock has gone further, arguing that the gendering of nationalism and, in particular, the trope of family makes this Janus quality possible.[25] While men are associated with the public world of business and decision-making, where they can build the nation's future, women represent tradition and links with the past that they should dutifully preserve in the family, in other words, passing on language, religion and culture to the children.[26] George L. Mosse, in his influential, classic text on gender and nationalism, notes that 'woman as a national symbol was the guardian of the continuity and immutability of the nation, the embodiment of its respectability'.[27] The portrayal of women as symbols of the nation renders invisible the everyday reality and challenges that women may endure within society.[28] National identity often glorifies masculinity while keeping women in narrow, family-oriented roles.[29]

Nationalist movements tend to use traditions not only as a source of national identity but also as a way of differentiating between the indigenous culture and heritage of the nation and the influence of the alien imperial culture. As I have demonstrated elsewhere, in my earlier work on Irish national and provincial newspapers, the alien culture is frequently presented as immoral, evil and dangerous.[30] Radhakrishnan examines the strategic use within nationalism of what he terms as the insider/outsider dichotomy.[31] He sees this dichotomy as a line of exclusion between the native 'insider' culture and the foreign 'outsider' culture. The latter is deemed negative and seen as a threat to the native culture. As Radhakrishnan puts it, women become the ground of allegorical transactions of national history. The inner self, the locus of identity, is associated with the home, the family, where the woman is keeper of the traditional way of life that must be protected from corrupting influences. Citing the work of Chatterjee, Radhakrishnan claims that once one has grasped the insider/outsider dichotomy one can see more clearly how gender roles develop into an ideology of nationalism.[32]

Katrak points out that such traditions may have been deeply oppressive of women: 'The arena of female sexuality – fertility/infertility motherhood; the sexual division of labour – is the site of certain "traditions" most oppressive for women.'[33] In the particular context of anti-colonial struggles, Katrak says that such traditions became a source of national identity against foreign domination, but as a result, women's idealised social positioning was reinscribed within such limiting traditional roles in the name of national liberation. The nationalist movement thus may appear contradictory; on the one hand inviting women into the public sphere to engage in active protest for the nationalist cause, while on the other hand, limiting women to purely traditional roles. Moreover, many male nationalist leaders have tended to assume that once the nation has been liberated from imperial domination, women would simply leave the public sphere and return to the private world of domesticity.[34] Of course, feminists in many contexts across the world have found this unacceptable and clashed on numerous occasions with the nationalist leaders.[35] Irish feminists too had some rather interesting views on tradition, as will be discussed in more detail later in this chapter.

As has been well documented, Irish feminists active in the campaign for enfranchisement were deeply affected by nationalism.[36] In the context of anti-colonial struggles, nationalist movements can pose serious questions for feminism. In the following section, focusing on the Irish suffrage movement, I analyse how feminists in early decades of the twentieth century engaged with national self-determination while simultaneously developing a sharp critique of a male-dominated society. Drawing on the theoretical framework outlined above, especially the concept of nationalism as a gendered Janus-faced discourse, I aim to offer deeper insights into the ways in which suffragists engaged with and sought to interrogate constructions of 'traditions' in the Irish context.

Suffragism and 'Masculine Political Ideals'

Although Irish suffrage societies were set up in the latter part of the nineteenth century, only in the early twentieth century did the movement grow and develop a higher public profile.[37] There are a number of reasons for this: the emergence of a group of highly educated women who had obtained university degrees but found most professions closed to them, the example of the wider international suffrage movement, including the British-based campaign, and also the cultural revival which was then taking place in Ireland. Cultural nationalism provided an important backdrop to Irish feminism. Many of the best known and most active suffragists of this period were highly involved in the arts, literature and theatre.[38] Within this milieu of creativity and radical critique, suffragism in Ireland underwent an important transformation from genteel drawing room 'get togethers' to militancy and activism.[39]

It is not the aim of this chapter to provide a history of the Irish suffrage movement. That has been presented elsewhere.[40] Nevertheless, some brief context is required to underpin the later analysis. Thus, as Rosemary Cullen Owens has written in her path-breaking book, *Smashing Times*, the period from 1912 to 1914 can be described as the heyday of Irish suffragism, the movement growing to a membership of over 3,000.[41] New societies were springing up around the country and by 1911 an umbrella group – the Irish Women's Suffrage Federation (IWSF) – was established to coordinate the many new, and geographically scattered, groups. Within a few years, the IWSF had over twenty member societies.[42] That there were so many diverse societies throughout the country, reflects the different political, religious and geographical divisions among suffragists and points to the complex political context in Ireland at that time.

From the very beginning of suffrage agitation in Ireland, the dual influences of the nationalist movement and the international women's movement are apparent. British and American feminists regularly visited Ireland. According to Clíona Murphy, the relationship with American suffragists, in particular, offered Irish campaigners the opportunity to reach out beyond the narrow confine of the British Isles.[43] Thus, being part of a wider international movement was important for Irish suffragists.[44] The significance of internationalism in early feminist movements needs to be highlighted. As Jo Vellacott has shown, many suffragists believed that they had an important contribution to make to all international questions and refused to be limited by national boundaries.[45]

Nonetheless, the complexities of national boundaries are well illustrated by the sometimes tense relationship between suffragists in Ireland and Britain. While Irish suffragists initially had a good deal of contact with British suffragists, it is important to recognise the differences between the two movements. While British suffragists were seeking votes for women from their own government in Westminster, Irish suffragists were demanding enfranchisement from what was, in effect, a foreign parliament based across the Irish Sea. Some Irish suffragists were frustrated that their British sisters did not recognise the specificities of the Irish context.[46] In addition, Irish suffragists were increasingly frustrated by the lack of support from Irish-elected representatives at Westminster.

Throughout this period various attempts were made to introduce suffrage bills at Westminster; however, several of these measures were voted down by the Irish Parliamentary Party (IPP). Why was this so? The attitudes of the IPP to women's suffrage were complex. Indeed, some Irish MPs such as Willie Redmond expressed support for female enfranchisement, while others such as his brother, the party leader John Redmond, were more hostile.[47] John Redmond believed that the primary objective of the IPP was to gain Home Rule for Ireland. In order to achieve this, the IPP relied on the support of the Liberal Prime Minister Asquith, who happened to be anti-female enfranchisement. Thus, John Redmond and many other Irish MPs not only saw the suffrage issue as a distraction from the Home Rule cause but also worried that if women were enfranchised, Asquith would carry out his threat to resign from power. The potential loss of a key ally in the campaign for Home Rule, may well have reinforced Redmond's and the IPP's hostility to the suffrage cause. The IPP decision to vote against suffrage measures in 1912–13 earned them the resentment of not only the British suffrage movement but also suffragists in Ireland.[48]

By campaigning for female enfranchisement, suffragists were adamant that women could not simply rely on the chivalry of men to represent their interests. Writing in April 1914, Louie Bennett of the Irish Women's Suffrage Federation made this point clearly: 'Probably no country has suffered more severely than Ireland as a victim of purely masculine political ideals'.[49] She criticised the political policy of sacrificing every other interest to Home Rule as 'short-sighted'. This was leading the country into financial ruin, she claimed. However, she added that in the last few decades new movements had emerged in which women had played a crucial role. Such movements included literary and cultural as well as educational and professional campaigns. The entry of women into local government, she argued, had done much to highlight poverty and poor housing conditions. Legislation was, she claimed, urgently needed to improve both the health, education and shelter of children as well as the pay and conditions of working women. Based on past performances, Bennett asserted, men simply could not be relied upon to represent the best interests of women: 'It is not possible for the women of Ireland any longer to accept things as they are, or to leave the welfare of their country, their people and their children to the care of men.'[50] Here Bennett was indicating the need for a new approach by women, a challenge to the conventional ways of doing things.

The response of the Irish suffragists to Home Rule was varied, reflecting wider political divisions. Firstly, there were different responses in terms of strategies and tactics. At a rather simplistic level, it is possible to divide the

Irish suffrage movement into two broad camps of constitutionalists, who campaigned within the law, and militants, who actively sought to break the law in an attempt to gain more publicity for their cause. Irish constitutional suffragists, while wary of antagonising the Home Rule lobby, nevertheless insisted that the government should enfranchise women and so give them a voice in deciding on Home Rule. The majority of Irish suffragists belonged to constitutional groups, such as the Irish Women's Suffrage Federation, Munster Women's Franchise League and Irish Women's Reform League.[51] The constitutionalist position was challenged by the militant Irish Women's Franchise League (IWFL) and Irish Women's Suffrage Society (IWSS), which refused to put women's campaign for the vote in second place to the Home Rule campaign. They argued for an 'anti-government' strategy which would mean bringing down the Liberal government if necessary. Such a policy, however, could seriously jeopardise Home Rule. Nevertheless, as I have argued at length elsewhere, this dichotomy between the militant and constitutional suffragists should not be exaggerated in the Irish case.[52] Militancy in Ireland never reached the extremes witnessed among the Women's Social and Political Union (WSPU) led by Emmeline Pankhurst and her daughters in Britain.[53]

Rather than dividing Irish suffragists into militants versus constitutionalists, it is probably more important to understand the deeper political differences that underpinned the movement. On the one hand, it is necessary to note that many Irish suffragists, across both the militant and constitutional camps, supported Irish self-determination. For example, despite their opposition to prioritising Home Rule above all other campaigns, a number of militant suffragists, such as Hanna Sheehy Skeffington, were sympathetic to nationalism.[54] On the other hand, to add a further layer of complexity in the Irish context, there were also unionist suffragists who opposed Home Rule and wanted Ireland to remain part of the union with Britain.[55] These divisions between nationalists and unionists and between constitutionalists and militants were potentially destabilising to a unified suffrage movement in Ireland.[56]

As discussed at the start of this chapter, women's relationship with nationalism is complex and multi-faceted. As Gerardine Meaney has also observed, it is important to contextualise nationalism against the wider backdrop of colonialism.[57] A critique of nationalism should not be interpreted as support for colonial rule. While being critical of nationalist politicians, feminist activists were not averse to employing nationalist iconography and drawing upon an idealised image of the past, to legitimate a contemporary role for women in public life.[58] Many Irish suffragists were influenced by the cultural revival movement, which provided an iconography of Gaelic warrior queens as symbols of female empowerment. Contributors to the suffrage newspaper, the *Irish Citizen* (1912–20), frequently drew upon romantic and idealised images of the Gaelic civilization of yore.[59] For example, in September 1912, Sidney Gifford (writing under her pen name *John Brennan*) argued that:

> In the Gaelic civilisation, which was never quite cast down and trampled out, and which the Gaelic League and Sinn Féin organisation are attempting to rebuild, the woman was the equal of the man in all things; she was never the woman of the harem, but the proud and independent comrade of her mate.[60]

She went on to argue that this 'fine old' Gaelic civilisation 'peeps out through the worn particles of English influence'.[61] This piece by Gifford is important and illuminating. It provides a clear example of a counter-narrative to the hegemonic colonial discourse. Gifford asserts that, far from civilizing Irish savages, as the English colonial discourse usually claimed, colonialism had instead attempted to suppress a sophisticated pre-existing Irish civilization.

Suffragists regularly invoked this counter-narrative of a great Gaelic civilization where women allegedly had equality with men. An editorial in the *Irish Citizen* newspaper of September 1916 says of Ireland: 'as of old her civilization was based on feminism'. These sentiments are again reflected in another *Irish Citizen* editorial in November 1917, when the principles of inequality are rejected as 'the teaching of an alien civilization', in other words, Britain.[62] This notion that sex inequality was not something endemic to Ireland but in fact imposed by British rule was repeated many times and can be analysed through the lens of the insider/outsider dichotomy, discussed earlier. The outsider or alien culture, of the coloniser, is presented as negative, while the native culture is seen as good and pure.[63] However, rather than simply interpreting this as a typical nationalist rhetoric, it is possible to offer a different explanation. These arguments may equally have been part of a feminist strategy. Suffragists were often accused, by their critics, of being all too eager 'to forsake the good old ways'. Why can't suffragists 'be content to go on as we were and not do all these unheard of things?'[64] In an article entitled 'Women in Ancient Ireland', Dora Mellone set out to challenge these criticisms. She argued that, far from being new and unheard of, powerful female characters, such as Queen Maeve and the warrior Scathach, were much in evidence in ancient Ireland. Thus, by tracing a direct lineage from these ancient female figures to modern day feminists, suffragists sought to underline their legitimacy and dispel their critics. Hence, suffragists argued that far from being a new and imported idea, which had no place in Irish society, feminism was as Irish as Queen Maeve. Moreover, suffragists used this apparent Gaelic, feminist heritage to criticise contemporary nationalists, as in April 1917 when the editor of the *Irish Citizen* demanded of Sinn Féin, 'Will it be true to the fine traditions of Ireland's past, when Ireland's men and women were equally honoured and equally free?'[65]

Nowhere was the complexity between feminism and nationalism more apparent than in the fraught relationship between suffragists and the nationalist women's organisation Cumann na mBan. As noted earlier in this chapter, nationalism can provide a platform for mobilising women in support for national independence.[66] Cumann na mBan was set up in 1914 as a women's auxiliary to the Irish Volunteers, the main function being to raise funds for the Volunteers.[67] Many suffragists were furious by what they saw as 'slave-like' behaviour on the part of these women. In May 1914 a heated correspondence took place in the pages of the *Irish Citizen* newspaper between Cumann na mBan and the paper's editor Francis Sheehy Skeffington.[68] The editor criticised Cumann na mBan as 'thoroughly reactionary' and as 'opposed to the best interests of the women's movement in Ireland'. The editor claimed that the nationalist women were tying themselves to the 'chariot wheel' of John Redmond and the Irish Parliamentary Party.[69] Helena Moloney and Mary MacSwiney, members of Cumann na mBan, quickly responded, saying that there could be no talk of women's freedom while the nation itself was still in bondage to Britain.[70] The editor pointed out that there was no guarantee that women would be enfranchised even when Ireland gained political independence and judging on the past performance of John Redmond and the IPP it seemed extremely unlikely.[71] This debate is similar in many ways to debates going on in other countries engaged in anti-colonial struggles.[72] The apparently competing priorities of national rights over women's rights have frequently sparked tensions and distrust.[73]

After the nationalist uprising of Easter 1916, the political landscape in Ireland changed dramatically.[74] Several supporters of the suffrage cause were amongst those killed during the uprising, including the socialist leader James Connolly, as well as Francis Sheehy Skeffington and the cartoonist Ernest Cavanagh. Although suffragists continued to demand immediate enfranchisement from Westminster, there was also a new relationship between Cumann na mBan and the suffrage movement. Historians such as Margaret Ward and Beth McKillen have suggested that part of this new relationship may be related to the transformation which occurred in Cumann na mBan itself after the Rising.[75] Certainly the memoirs of Cumann na mBan activist

Lil Conlon illustrate a marked change in the attitudes and behaviour of the nationalist women as their movement became larger, more vocal and more autonomous from the Irish Volunteers.[76] With Constance Markievicz as President, Cumann na mBan was more prepared to assert women's rights and engage in campaigns around women's issues. This was clearly illustrated by their cooperation with suffragists in the campaign against the reintroduction of the Contagious Diseases Acts.[77] However, despite this cooperation, the two groups of women continued to demand different things; suffragists refused to relinquish their demand for immediate female enfranchisement.

Despite their differences, suffragists in Ireland were united in the view that women needed to be empowered at every level of society, not just by gaining voting rights but by gaining admittance to all public institutions. So long as women depended on men, they were at risk of exploitation and abuse.[78] In making these demands, suffragists exposed many of the hidden realities of early twentieth-century Irish society. In so doing, they not only attacked politicians, nationalist as well as unionist, but also the judiciary, employers and the Church.

The Suffragist and the 'Man-Run System of Society'

Over many years, I have sought to show that Irish suffragists had a much broader agenda than simply the enfranchisement of women.[79] Thus, while it is clearly important to acknowledge the significance of the national question for feminism in Ireland, it would be wrong to discuss the suffragists only within that context. Their critique of nationalist politicians was part of a wider feminist analysis of Irish society. Leading suffragists were critical of conventional culture, both implicitly and explicitly – by word but also by deed.[80] They were prepared to discuss publicly subjects like child abuse, incest, rape and marital violence, hence challenging taboos around indecent and unsuitable topics for 'ladies'. Suffragists, both militant and constitutional, raised these issues at public meetings, in speaking tours around the country and in the *Irish Citizen* newspaper. Suffragists not only condemned the under-reporting of these offences in Irish society but also brought a feminist lens to analysing the power dynamics that underpinned these crimes. Suffragists pointed out that one reason why such things went on in secret was because the professions were male-dominated and unwilling to address the abuse of women and children. One solution, therefore, was to make more women aware of what was really going on and encourage women to enter the professions where they could exert some influence on policy and decision-making. As one writer to the *Irish Citizen* newspaper put it, 'It was the knowledge that women had no protection and need expect none under a man run system of society which provided all the driving force of the suffrage agitation.'[81]

Suffragists asserted that women had the right to participate at every level of the legal system, as judges, jurors and lawyers. Suffragists from across the political spectrum argued that women could never expect justice from a system which was so male-biased and which excluded women from its profession.

The pages of the *Irish Citizen* newspaper regularly reported court cases where crimes like rape and child abuse appeared not to be taken seriously by the all-male judiciary. The Watching the Courts Committee was set up by the Irish Women's Reform League to monitor court cases involving women and ensure that such cases were given publicity so that women were made aware of what was going on.[82] Cases involving the 'seduction of servant girls' were commonly reported in the *Irish Citizen*. For example, in 1913 under the headline, 'The Ruin of Young Girls in Ireland', the editorial reported a case recently heard by the Recorder of Dublin. The case involved a 15-year-old girl who became pregnant while employed as a servant. This was the second time the case had appeared in court, and on each occasion the all-male jury failed to reach a verdict: 'The jury's disagreement was, no doubt, in some measure due to the very able manner in which the defending counsel played upon their masculine prejudices, pointing out to them that any one of them might one day find himself in a similar position to the man in the dock.' For the editor, this was clear evidence of the need for women on juries: 'A woman on the jury might have reflected that any young girl might any day find herself in the pitiful plight of the ruined girl.'[83] Suffragists sought to highlight cases such as this in order to expose the cruelty that existed in Ireland but which was usually concealed from public view. As the *Irish Citizen* newspaper reported, 'Not one word of this case was allowed to appear in any Dublin newspaper. This is how the press created the legend that there is no sexual viciousness and no danger to young girls in Ireland.'[84]

In addition to increasing public awareness about sexual abuse, suffragists also wished to expose domestic violence. Elizabeth Priestley-McCracken argued that: 'Wife beating is of common occurrence and is suffered in most part in silence by the victim for the sake of her social or financial position or for the sake of her children.'[85] Suffragists were keenly aware that the privacy of the domestic sphere enabled men to abuse their wives in secret, especially since the legal system was so unsupportive of women. Women who were financially dependent on men were in no position to complain about this treatment. As noted earlier in the chapter, the domestic arena, much romanticised within national rhetoric, is a site where women are especially vulnerable to exploitation and abuse.[86] Suffragists sought to disconnect such romanticism from the reality of hardship, poverty and suffering within many Irish households.

The rights of working women were the particular concern of the Irish Women's Reform League. They were closely connected with the women's trade union movement, which was gaining some ground in Ireland at the time.[87] Many suffragists strongly supported trade unionism and encouraged women to join a union.[88] Nonetheless, some suffragists were aware that middle-class women knew little about the experiences of working women. In an attempt to overcome such ignorance, the Irish Women's Reform League set about publicising working conditions in sweat shops and factories in Dublin and Belfast. For example, Winifred Carney, secretary of the Irish Textile Workers Union, wrote to the *Irish Citizen* to highlight the plight of women in the Belfast linen industry.[89] She asserted that 'many Belfast mills are slaughter-houses for women and penitentiaries for children'. She went on to describe women working 'in a super-heated atmosphere, with clothes drenched … hands torn and lacerated as a consequence of the speeding up of the machinery'. Yet, despite this hard toil, the wages were low: 'a wage less than some of our pious mill owners would spend weekly upon a dog'. In a series of articles published in the *Irish Citizen* in 1913, Ethelred Browning of the Irish Women's Reform League described the working conditions of women in several Dublin factories and workshops. She ended with an impassioned plea: 'women factory inspectors, women law makers, women police, women on the jury, women lawyers, women everywhere, that is the need of our country'.[90]

In this way, suffragists sought not only to expose the abuse of women but also to show that men could not be trusted to protect women's interests. Thus, only by empowering women to protect themselves could these societal ills be addressed. With this argument, suffragists challenged the long-held conventional wisdom that men in public life protected women. Instead, suffragists accused male leaders, including nationalists, of hypocrisy and double moral standards.

Suffragists and the 'Ventilation of Evils'

In addition to the suppression of the true extent of physical abuse of women in Ireland (in the home as well as in the workplace) some suffragists were equally concerned about the social construction of female morality. This led them to explore the double moral standard. In two articles that appeared in the *Irish Citizen* of 1917, this topic was skilfully explored by Margaret Connery.

She began by boldly asserting, 'In all ages men have been great sticklers for the observance of a code of conventional morality – on the part of women.' The standard bearers of this modesty cult in Ireland, she continued, were the clergy.

> A Revd clergyman preached in Co. Sligo recently in a whirlwind attack on the 'glad neck' and the 'pneumonia' blouse, and declared '*it is appalling to see Irish girls parading their nakedness in this way*' and he was inclined to think they should be refused Communion when they came to the altar dressed in this way.[91]

Connery humorously retorted that 'hitherto the cure of souls and the cure of pneumonia have been recognised as belonging to two distinct and well defined professions'. It was a pity, she added, that this clergyman did not have a sense of humour and could have avoided this 'futile storm in a tea cup'. But Connery did not limit her critique to humble priests. She was not afraid to criticise the leader of the Catholic Church in Ireland, Cardinal Logue. He had recently 'expressed himself in a somewhat similar strain to an audience composed entirely of men'. His subject matter was 'the shortness of women's skirts and the density of their stockings'. Connery expresses her outrage: 'one would think that the length of the European War would present itself as a more urgent human problem to set before Irish Catholics than the length of women's skirts'. As noted earlier, 'woman' as a national symbol represents the respectability of the nation.[92] Within this national discourse women are the keepers of national traditions and values.[93] Hence, any women judged to be immoral in any way are blamed for undermining national honour. As argued elsewhere, the Catholic Church were especially vocal in their condemnation of any hint of 'immorality' among Irish women as a threat to national culture, identity and sovereignty.[94]

Connery has been described as one of the most active suffragists in Ireland.[95] A member of the militant, Irish Women's Franchise League, she was forthright in her views and clearly not afraid to attack the double moral standards propounded by the Church and other male-dominated institutions in Ireland. While clergymen and lawyers criticised any hint of immorality among women, they were prepared to ignore the appalling conditions in factories and the inhuman living conditions of many Irish families in overcrowded slum dwelling. Connery called for the 'ventilation of evils' in our society. She argued that the Church should put its collective efforts into tackling these problems. Once again suffragists were prepared to raise issues rarely discussed in polite society:

In Ireland, as elsewhere, public morals must continue in an unhealthy state while we tolerate the shameful double moral standard, while we have the crying evil of sweated wages paid to our women workers and while the thousands of our Catholic citizens life means the indecent herding of number of persons of both sexes and all ages into one room where every function of humanity has to be performed.[96]

The suffragists' critiques of cultural convention and double moral standards brought them on to topics rarely discussed publicly by 'ladies'. One such topic was the 'girl mother'. In September 1915 Marion Duggan, who had a Bachelor of Law Degree and was, a member of the Irish Women's Reform League and the Irish Women's Workers' Union, wrote an article in the *Irish Citizen* describing how young single mothers faced a life of poverty and degradation while the fathers of their children were rarely affected in any way. Duggan suggested that children born outside of marriage should be made wards of court and the fathers tracked down for maintenance.[97]

Of course, it would be naïve to suggest that all suffragists in Ireland were cultural rebels or espoused radical views on social morality. In seeking to protect women from physical, economic and sexual abuse, some suffragists sought to eradicate the double moral standard by advocating a new moral standard by which both men and women should abide. An article in the *Irish Citizen* in July 1919 reminded the reader that for certain types of men sex had become an obsession, a disease. Men had restricted women's sphere of activities to the mere exercise of the sex function: 'which in practice results in denying her a human status and reducing her to a condition of pure animalism'. Economic freedom for women was the key according to the writer: 'any considerable improvement in our moral standards must inevitably keep pace with the growth of women's power and influence in the public life of the community'.[98]

Conclusion

Irish suffragists constituted far more than a vote for women campaign group. As discussed in this chapter, the suffragists' agenda extended to a wide range of feminist concerns. As visibly illustrated through the pages of the *Irish Citizen*, as well as the many public events organised across the country, suffragists were not afraid to tackle some of the most serious, and indeed secretive, problems facing Irish society in the early twentieth century. In so doing, they challenged the traditional gender ideology underpinning patriarchal authority.

However, nationalism made the suffragists' demands more complex and perhaps also more intriguing. The specific situation in Ireland provided an important backdrop to the suffrage movement. Thus, the Irish suffrage movement faced particular challenges that set them apart from suffrage campaigns in most western countries. Irish suffragism was inextricably linked to nationalism. Although suffragists were, on occasion, very critical of the nationalist movement, they were always keenly aware of the impact of nationalism on suffragism. The specific political and geographical location of Ireland influenced both suffragist analyses and practices. Irish suffragists, like suffragists in other sites of anti-colonial struggle, such as India[99] for example, found themselves in the difficult position of demanding votes from the British Parliament at Westminster amid growing calls for national self-determination and independence from British control.

Drawing on the work of scholars such as Mosse, Nairn, Radhakrishnan and McClintock, I have suggested how issues around tradition, colonialism, history and identity posed very serious questions for suffragists. As I have shown in this chapter, many Irish suffragists actively engaged with these constructions of past glories and traditions by offering feminist critiques, reinterpretations and counter-narratives. Hence, while established scholarship has argued that nationalism had a Janus-quality, I would suggest that feminism has also adopted a sort of Janus-quality. As demonstrated by the examples of writers such as Sidney Gifford (John Brennan) and Dora Mellone, there was a strategy to position feminism back into a pre-colonial past of gender equality, where strong women like Queen Maeve exerted authority in Irish society. In this way suffragists sought not only to challenge the representation of feminism as an alien, 'outsider', colonial import but furthermore to claim feminism as part of ancient Irish heritage. In so doing, they constructed a Janus-quality for feminism by simultaneously looking back to a 'glorious' Gaelic past and forward to a bright future of women's rights and equality.

Irish women did win partial enfranchisement from Westminster under the terms of the Representation of the People Act in 1918. Newly enfranchised Irish women were instrumental in electing the first woman to the British Parliament, when Constance Markievicz topped the poll in Dublin St Patrick's Ward, though she did not take her seat at Westminster. However, they had little time to savour such success since, within one year, Ireland was plunged into a war with Britain during which some of the most extreme outrages were inflicted upon Irish women.[100] Once again, it was clear that Irish women could not separate themselves from the wider political issues of Ireland's independence.

Chapter 2

COMRADESHIP:
Feminists and Revolutionaries in Holloway Prison, 1918–1919

LUCY McDIARMID[1]

> Then they began to quarrel in a ladylike way then for relief turned to me and I became a buffer state.
>
> *Kathleen Clarke, Notebook, NLI*

The 'they' in the quotation from Kathleen Clarke's notebook are Maud Gonne and Constance Markievicz, and the sentence describes the three women's conversations in Holloway Prison in 1918. Like many well-known Irish male activists, the women were charged with participation in the alleged 'German Plot', a fabrication of the British government created to justify arresting all the major militant Irish nationalists and thereby to prevent them from speaking out against conscription. Hanna Sheehy Skeffington (imprisoned under 'our old friend DORA', the Defence of the Realm Act, though not for the 'German Plot') joined the women in Holloway for two days in August but was released after she went on hunger strike.[2] Gonne, Markievicz, and Clarke were in Holloway for different but overlapping periods of time between May 1917 and March 1918.[3]

Clarke's 'buffer state' metaphor associates the small group of women with the macropolitical realm: each one is a 'state', two of them enemies, and one of them neutral in the conflict between the two more important states. By implicitly politicising the relations among the women, Clarke interprets the way they act in prison in terms of each one's power relative to that of the others. The adjective 'ladylike' adds an interesting dimension to the metaphor of the states and their international relations, because it introduces the social distinction between Clarke and the other two women, a distinction all three were aware of.

All the women in Holloway during this period – the three 'states' and Sheehy Skeffington as well – wrote accounts of the time spent in prison, and the complexity of the relations among them becomes clear in their own words. One model through which to consider the political and social implications of their narratives is Benedict Anderson's well-known statement that the 'imagined community' which is the nation 'is always conceived as a deep horizontal comradeship.' And that comradeship enables an absolute loyalty, the kind that these women felt:

> it is this fraternity that makes it possible, over the past two centuries, for so many millions of people, not so much to kill, as willingly to die for such limited imaginings.[4]

This is the national feeling that Clarke expressed when, early in her imprisonment, she wrote to her sister Madge Daly in Limerick, 'We are all satisfied if our arrest will in any way help the cause dearer than life to us.'[5]

The basic facts of the women's political lives make their sorority clear: they were all activists, all republicans and later anti-Treaty, and all connected to the 1916 Rising either as widows or participants. But the horizontality of their sisterhood is not always present in their prison narratives. The documents they left on the subject of their imprisonment in Holloway show the importance of the vertical as well as the horizontal. Their writings reveal that within a pre-existing sisterhood there was a struggle to establish a hierarchy. The horizontality of the women's sisterhood was – in Holloway, at least – complicated by the vertical, hierarchical issues of *status* and *dominance*. Hence, for instance, the word 'ladylike' in Clarke's sentence: the two tall, wealthy, former debutantes, formerly Protestant women, did everything in a 'ladylike' way. For 'relief', as Clarke puts it, they turned to a short, middle-class, Catholic Irish woman; she was the buffer.[6]

I

In men's accounts of prison life – written by men also jailed for the 'German plot' or for other reasons around the same time – the horizontality, the 'comradeship', is more visible. The gendered distinction in Irish prison memoirs of this period may not be typical of all such accounts, but the men's narratives emphasise more explicitly the fellowship and collaboration of prison life. Edward Moane, in Usk Prison for the 'German Plot', refers to the other prisoners as 'my comrades', as does his fellow Usk prisoner, Frank Drohan.[7] Both of them list all the names of the other prisoners there. Their accounts emphasise the way the men established a collective sense of identity as they claimed agency even while imprisoned: 'After we were a while there, the place was little like a prison at all as we made our own of the place.'[8] The greater the negligence of the prison authorities, the stronger grew the bond among the men. When the governor of Usk failed to place the men suffering from the flu in a separate location, the healthy men took care of the sick: 'We arranged … that two of us would stay up each night to attend the sick.'[9] After the death of Dick Coleman, they 'demanded that a doctor should be sent to the prison.'[10]

On some occasions, as a form of protest, the men joined in collective action against the prison authorities to destroy all prison property within reach. In Belfast Prison in the spring of 1918, as Eamon Ó Duibhir tells the story, the men fought the locking up of an Irishman with ordinary criminals by carefully orchestrated violence:

> we broke the cell windows and tore holes in the side walls between the cells. Our crowd had got hold of big nails and pieces of iron. The centre walls between the cells were made of one brick only, and when you got one brick loose it was easy to pull down the remainder. We wedged the doors, and then the Governor's trouble was to get us out of the cells before the wing of the prison was wrecked. In two hundred cells this rumpus was going on and the noise was terrific.[11]

The man in question was returned to the political prisoners' cells only after a series of punishments for those involved in the protest.

The men's collaboration often resulted in tricks played on the warders. In Gloucester Jail, where Robert Brennan was biding his time in 1918–19, his fellow prisoner J.K. Reilly 'insisted that the doctor had ordered him a glass of whiskey' instead of the medicinal tonic the prisoners were compelled to take every night against flu. He kept demanding, 'Where's my whiskey?' and so, in solidarity, 'we all backed him up.' Before long the governor of the prison came up with an entire bottle of whiskey that Seán McEntee – encouraged by Brennan – claimed as his own, one wrongfully withheld from him. When the governor surrendered the bottle to McEntee, he took over the situation. '[G]o and get your mugs', McEntee said, and the prisoners who were not teetotallers 'made a grand night of it.'[12]

In the men's prisons in 1918, there was usually a 'vertical' dimension to the comradeship, but it was a hierarchy for self-government carefully established by the men. In Usk, order was kept by Arthur Griffith. As Brennan writes, 'A.G., as we called him, was the prisoners' spokesman and he was easily the most cheerful man among the dozen internees.' On one occasion, when an argument between Pierce McCann and Ginger O'Connell 'nearly came to blows', Griffith prevented the blows by asking Brennan 'how I had found Fred Murphy the last time I was in Wexford.' Brennan told a shaggy dog story that went on for so long and in such bizarre detail that the two men forgot their fight.[13]

In Belfast Prison (a month before the 'German Plot' arrests), the men were more organised, as Eamon O'Duibhir explains in his witness statement:

> The prison control run by us consisted of the Commandant and Vice Commandant. [Austin] Stack, naturally, was the Commandant ... and Joe McDonagh was the Vice Commandant. With them there was a Captain for each floor. There were three floors and these were comprised of double rows of cells separated by a thin strip of wire netting. I happened to be one of those floor Captains. Frank McGrath was another, and E. de Blaghd the third. ... Our business was to see that everything was done properly in the prison, that floors and cells were kept spotlessly clean, that everybody kept themselves spic and span as far as they could, and that there was regular attendance at the baths and at the outdoor games so that the prisoners kept in good health. The outdoor games were mostly rounders, as there wasn't room for any other game in the part of the grounds we occupied. We insisted that all rules should be carried out fully and completely, for the good of the prisoners and for the keeping of discipline so necessary in a body of men like ours. I remember one time Hugo McNeill, who has since been a General in the army, and Seán Downey from Golden in this county, had a bit of an argument, ending in a battle with the fists. We had them brought before the council to decide what we would do with them. When he had looked around the council and saw that Co. Tipperary had a majority on it, Downey stated very firmly that he was defending the honour of Tipperary owing to some derogatory remark that Hugo MacNeill passed upon it, and he hoped, of course, that he would get off fairly soft. Instead, both of them got a job to go on their knees every morning for a week to scrub the basement floor of the prison, and that was some job with the crowd coming in and out and having a laugh at them, but they did it all right and they certainly had no more rows about Tipperary and Dublin.[14]

This military hierarchy, with its strict discipline, was easily organised among men who had served together in brigades and battalions, and it was accepted by all of them.

II

For the women held in Holloway, such collective assertions of power would have been difficult to achieve; most of the time there were only three of them, and from November 1918 until the middle of February 1919 there were only two. Markievicz, Gonne, and Clarke, who were together in Holloway for a significant amount of time, did not constitute a sufficiently large group to create a system of self-government, and the need for one seems never to have occurred to them. Moreover, they were not badly treated. The only time they joined in action against the prison authorities was the time Markievicz stole the wardress's report book, and she and Clarke

> had great fun reading it. Every move we made was recorded, from the time our cells were opened in the morning until we were locked up at night. According to her report, I ate nothing, Madame ate everything, and ate all day.[15]

In addition, the women held in Holloway had no common military experience. Markievicz had been second in command at the College of Surgeons during the Rising, but in the more loosely structured Citizen Army. Maud Gonne had organised Inghinidhe na hÉireann, and Kathleen Clarke had been a member of Cumann na mBan, but neither of those organisations had functioned in terms of military ranks and discipline.[16] For the two days Hanna Sheehy Skeffington was held in Holloway, she followed the practices of women in the suffrage movement and refused food, but the other women did not participate in the hunger strike.[17]

Although they had not been members of a single battalion or brigade, the four women in Holloway constituted a sisterhood of long standing. They were members of a network of activist Irish women who worked together for many national causes and admired one another. Gonne and Sheehy Skeffington had gone with other women 'as a deputation to the Corporation' to seek support in supplying meals to Irish schoolchildren when the English School Meals Act of 1910 neglected to include Ireland. Markievicz was a member of Inghinidhe na hÉireann, which Gonne had founded in 1900; as Gonne wrote to John Quinn after the Rising, 'Constance Markievicz was like a sister to me.' In her witness statement for the Bureau of Military History,

Gonne writes of Markievicz, 'She was a great woman and I always think she does not get the credit she should.' Kathleen Clarke, explaining her support of Markievicz's attack on MacNeill at the 1917 Sinn Féin Ard Fheis, says of her, '[H]ere was a woman who had come out and risked her life, had been sentenced to death and imprisoned for her participation in the Rising, and Irishmen were ready to do violence to her for attacking a man whose action had caused the failure of the Rising, and who had not participated in it.'[18] Commenting on Sheehy Skeffington's arrival in Holloway in August 1918, Clarke notes, 'She was a very highly-gifted woman, and one of the straightest I ever met, and I had a great admiration for her.'[19]

The women's sisters were also part of the extended sisterhood. Maud Gonne's only sister Kathleen died while she was in Holloway, but the other three women had sisters who provided an important support system to the rebel women in prison. Markievicz's account of her time in Holloway is recorded in a book of letters to her sister Eva Gore-Booth, and Clarke wrote dozens of letters (unpublished) to her sister Madge.[20] After Clarke's release from Holloway in February 1919, but before her sister Madge could arrive to escort her back to Ireland, 'Miss Eva Gore-Booth invited me to stay with her … She was the essence of kindness to me, though I was a perfect stranger to her, but as a friend of her sister that she loved she thought she could never do enough for me.'[21] And Markievicz was grateful for the corollary kindness. When one of Clarke's sisters stayed with Eva Gore-Booth, Markievicz wrote Eva, 'I was so glad that you were able to repay them a little for all their goodness to me. Their house was a home to me, when I was 'running' round that part of Ireland. They fed me up and looked after me, and I just came and went as I liked.'[22]

Sheehy Skeffington writes in her unpublished account of this period that her sister Mary Kettle helped her evade re-arrest under the Cat and Mouse Act when she was released. She says that British authorities made a '… final effort at face-saving by writing to Mrs Kettle to say that I was to reside with her, asking that she saw to it that I met no Sinn Féiners there! This she naturally declined so it was dropped.'[23] Clarke wrote to her sister Madge: 'If you are in Dublin, see Mrs Skeffington (–) she will tell you all about us' and added that 'Madame … sends her love.'[24] During their time in prison, Markievicz was sketching Clarke, who sent the pictures to her sons, and Markievicz wanted to know if any of the Clarke boys had an interest in becoming artists. The three women were always sharing food, and late in their stay, when they were given kitchen equipment, they cooked together.

It was, then, within the context of an abiding sisterhood that the conflicts about status and dominance among the three women prisoners took place.

When there were three women in Holloway, the two who were more alike – older, wealthier, born Protestant – competed with one another in social status, at least as Clarke tells the story:

> In the early days of our imprisonment, when we were out for exercise, Madame Markievicz and Madame MacBride walked up and down the exercise yard together, discussing their mutual friends and acquaintances, and disputing as to which of them had the highest social status. Madame Markievicz claimed that she was far above Madame MacBride; she belonged to the inner circle of the Vice-Regal Lodge set, while Madame MacBride was only on the fringe of it. I sometimes listened to them, quite amused; I was outside their social circle, and had nothing in common with them socially. Madame Markievicz took pains to make me aware of the social gulf between us; it didn't worry me. I walked up and down alone, reading the Irish newspaper, eager for news from Ireland.[25]

As Clarke says in the notes for her memoir, she acted as a 'buffer state'; she is the peaceful, non-combative one:

> Both ladies would come in to my cell and unload their grievances on me separately. They were not on such good terms with each other as at first; Maeve was this and that, Connie was that and this. When one came in, the other went out. I had to listen and sympathise with each of them; it became quite a strain.[26]

The Markievicz–Gonne argument implicitly creates a hierarchy that has a third term, Clarke, at the bottom. Her own metaphors deconstruct the hierarchy: she changes her marginal position to a type of independence and the 'gulf' between us to a national distinction. Clarke is 'outside their social circle' and walks 'up and down alone … eager for news from Ireland'. Pacing back and forth in the prison yard, the other two are closed in an Anglo-Irish past, while she looks outward to the Irish-Ireland present. Their discussions omit Clarke; she is not in contention for the status each of them claims.

When Gonne was released in October, the direct conflict between Clarke and Markievicz began. The two of them were alone together from the end of October 1918 until 18 February 1919, and both comment on the strain, but in different tones. In the unpublished notes for her memoir, Clarke writes, 'She urged me to call her Connie but I could not forget her first attitude to me so easily and Madame she remained to me.' Markievicz's remark in a letter to

Clarke immediately after Clarke's release has a bit of an edge: 'I miss you very much ... I wonder whose head you are snapping off now!'[27] And when, just after her release, Clarke was staying with Eva Gore-Booth, Markievicz wrote to her sister, 'I've no one to bully now, and she needs it.'[28] The bullying seems to have bothered Clarke more than the head-snapping-off bothered Markievicz. As Clarke wrote later of Markievicz, 'In spite of all the things I said to her when she annoyed me from time to time, we still were very good friends, she said she loved me, but I fear I would not go as far as that.'[29] The effusive affection of Markievicz – 'urged me to call her Connie', 'she said she loved me' – was not entirely accepted, or not entirely believed, by the more restrained Clarke. The effusions felt like bullying to her; she found Gonne easier to get along with because, as she wrote, 'she always accorded you the right to think and act for yourself and she was very gentle and courteous'.[30]

The major site of conflict for all the women was the body. The most obvious and most visible bodily issue was height. The women in Holloway were not the only people at this time to associate height with caste superiority. In Elsie Mahaffy's diary of the Rising, the social value attributed to height appears frequently. She was the daughter of the Trinity Provost John Mahaffy, and the people she admired, such as Captain Bowen-Colthurst, were handsome and tall; she was bewildered that such a 'tall, lovely creature' as Constance Gore-Booth had 'lost her shame and dignity and married a Pole' and 'left our class for that of Larkin and Connolly.' Mahaffy also noticed that the man striding in front of the surrendering rebels from Boland's Mills was 'a tall fine looking lad – hatless and very pale – obviously of gentle blood [de Valera, of course]. The rest were a low, motley crew'.[31]

Clarke notes the same dichotomy in the three women in Holloway Prison. She writes, 'The Governor and Matron usually walked through the yard on their morning rounds while we were there, and they had a few words with us in passing. The Governor always asked how was little Mrs Clarke; I suppose I did look small beside the other two ladies, who were both very tall.' The next sentence makes clear the connection between height and dominance:

> When Madame Markievicz did talk to me in those early days, I sensed a certain amount of patronage in her tone and manner, that I was not prepared to take from anybody. It appeared to worry her that such an insignificant little person as myself was put in prison with her. Again and again she said to me, 'Why on earth did they arrest such a quiet, insignificant person as you are?'[32]

The language of size forms part of a discourse of power, and it is clear that Clarke is fighting for her place in an implicit hierarchy: she 'was not prepared to take from anybody' the tone of 'patronage' that she heard in the governor's tone either. And Gonne was clearly proud of her height, which was of course always increased by almost another foot when she wore one of her grand feathered hats. She includes in her witness statement a remark about her own height and that of the Gore-Booth sisters: 'I had previously seen, but not spoken to her [CM], at a ball in London at which she and her two sisters, who were as tall as myself, were pointed out to me. I was asked on that occasion whether all Irish girls were as tall as we.'[33]

The idea of dominance is also pervasive in issues relating to food and eating. For prisoners, as for Persephone in the underworld, for humans abducted by fairies, for Catholics given soup by Protestants, and for the 1913 strikers' children fed by English socialists, the intimacy of feeding is associated with the control of identity.[34] To some extent, the struggle to control eating took place between the women and the prison authorities. Hanna Sheehy Skeffington went on hunger strike and maintained control of her body in other ways. As she wrote, 'I wanted to be as weak as possible to make forcible feeding harder and walked about to tire myself out.'[35]

Maud Gonne took control of her body in a different way. Instead of going on hunger strike, as she had initially wanted to, she 'started auto-suggestioning' herself 'to get thin'. She writes, 'I had to eat normally, yet in three months I lost three stone and became a living skeleton.'[36] At any rate, she told the prison doctor that she had TB, which she had in fact suffered from thirty years earlier. Her release in October was to a nursing home, and from there she escaped in disguise to Ireland.[37]

Clarke's prison eating habits took shape in opposition not to the Holloway authorities but to Markievicz. When she arrived, she was asked if she wanted to pay for her meals to be 'sent in', as Markievicz did. By her own account she responded 'that of course was Madame's business, but ... I certainly was not going to pay for my meals.'[38] In a series of arguments with the prison doctor over various somatic issues, Clarke's battles occurred on two fronts. She fought over regular prison food, which was inedible, as opposed to the 'hospital diet', which was much better – and over the amount of time allowed for exercise – one hour fresh air daily as opposed to the freedom to go outside anytime. The same pattern obtained in both arguments. The doctor said no; Clarke persisted. The doctor acceded to her request; Clarke then insisted that the same privileges be given to the other women, 'my friends', and the doctor acceded again.

the prison diet was so repulsive I could not eat it ... I was eating so little the wardress noticed it ... The doctor came and put me on what he called hospital diet. Instead of cocoa, I got tea and a rice pudding with a glass of milk for dinner, and then he very kindly put Madame MacBride on the same diet. Madame Markievicz was still getting her meals in.[39]

The fight to get more exercise time is described as a minor revolution:

At first we were only allowed out of our cells for one hour out of the twenty-four. I told my fellow-prisoners that I would fight for better conditions. I put down for the doctor, and told him that if I did not get more fresh air than I was getting, my health would suffer. As a result, we got two hours' exercise. This did not satisfy me, and I ... asked for more ... I kept on, and eventually my persistence was rewarded, and we were allowed out for most of the day. This made a great change in Madame Markievicz's health.[40]

These arguments were not simply Irish victories over English officials: they were Clarke's victories on behalf of the Irish women prisoners. They show that the 'quiet, insignificant' little person was the one most qualified to lead the rebellion. Her victories – as she describes them – not only improved the health of one of the taller 'ladies' but, more importantly, challenged the hierarchy of the three women as the other two had constructed it.

As these narratives make clear, Clarke's complaints were as much about Ascendancy domination as about British authority. The general issue of bodily health also functioned as a site of conflict among the women. It is clear from their accounts that the prison officials wanted to keep them alive, but they argued with one another about who controlled information about their health. Gonne, who wanted to be released immediately (hence her 'auto-suggestioning'), wrote to the *Irish Independent* about her health and Clarke's, and Clarke wrote, 'I was angry and I asked Mrs McBride how dare she write out such a thing, had she any realisation of the trouble she would cause my mother and family, and it was all the more wicked when it was not true. She was not ill, in body anyhow, Madame M was not ill and I was not as ill as she stated. I just danced at her, I was in such a fury.'[41]

Clarke made the same complaint about Markievicz: she and no one else had the authority to spread information about her health. At a later date, Markievicz wrote to Madge Daly about Clarke's health, and Clarke wrote to Madge herself to reframe the information:

> Don't let the report about my health worry you, there's nothing very much the matter with me except rheumatism. I have been pretty bad with that, but I'm nearly better, I was in bed with it when Madame wrote, & I did not know she was writing, but be quite easy in your mind about me.[42]

As Clarke records in the notes for her memoir:

> Madame Markievicz became a nuisance. I told her one day she would make an occupation of me and advised her to cease, get another occupation and mind her own business. But what will Madge say to me if I see you dying before my eyes and do nothing. I have no intention of dying before or behind your eyes or anywhere else, I said. You annoy me badly with your fussing, looking for a thrill you are, well get another one.
> We had lots of tiffs.[43]

Clarke could have had no idea that Markievicz in letters to her sister Eva was describing Clarke as 'frail', 'feeble', and 'not so well'.

Gonne's 'auto-suggestioning' and insistence on her TB, which led to her release, helped Clarke also, because serving as the 'buffer state' had been exhausting: 'I had to listen to each of their grievances separately, sympathise and keep my mouth shut. It became quite a strain in the end and I was glad for that reason if no other when Madame was released.'[44] Clarke was indeed in bad health, and after her release in February, she collapsed and had to spend six weeks in a nursing home. On the other hand, it is worth noting that she – the 'frail', 'feeble', 'little' woman – lived to be 94, and Markievicz, she who (as Clarke wrote) 'had the biggest appetite I ever saw in man or woman', only lived to be 59.[45]

Besides their own bodies, the Irish women in Holloway competed to control space. Clarke fiercely defended her authority over her cell. Markievicz, she writes:

> sat on the end of my bed, painting and smoking and chatting and after some time I noticed she had her cigarette ash all over my bed. She was flicking the water from her paint brush all over my floor and generally causing a mess which annoyed me as I hated any disorder in my cell. I got up and said, clear out. Why, what's wrong Kathleen? Poor Madame looked the picture of alarm. Why, I said, look at the mess you've made. I'll clear it up Kathleen. … no you won't, I said, get out, stay out, so out.

> She went out quite humbly and sat outside in the passage painting and every now and then I'd hear a big sigh coming from her. Next morning she came to my cell gate and said through the bars, may I come in, Kathleen?[46]
>
> No, you may not ... Why? ... You are too disorderly ... But Kathleen, I won't be, I'll bring a plate for my cigarette ash, and a jar to flick my paint brushes into, and I won't throw any stubs on the floor ... I said, 'No, I don't want you, I'm fed up with you.' She went away, and after some time she came back and said, 'But Kathleen, I'm lonely.' I could not resist that plea, so I yielded, saying, 'Come in so, but remember the conditions, out you go if you don't keep them.[47]

Clarke controlled the borders of her cell absolutely, as a kind of miniature Ireland. She defined and enforced the 'conditions'. Her territoriality replicated the territorial autonomy the Irish rebels were struggling for. There she could set the terms by which people were allowed to enter and leave her room. In Clarke's account of the conversation, she appeared to take pleasure in her power to kick the tall 'big house' woman out of her cell and in her own *noblesse oblige* in allowing the lonely, dependent prisoner back in.

Clarke and Gonne both took credit for upgrades in the larger territory, the wing of Holloway in which the Irish women prisoners lived. Clarke did not read Gonne's witness statement, because the Bureau of Military History did not make the statements public until 2003, and Clarke died in 1972. Nor did Gonne, who died in 1953, read Clarke's *Revolutionary Woman*, which was first published in 1991. As Gonne tells it, her family connection with one of the justices inspecting the prison deserves credit for persuading the prison authorities to change the women's living quarters. Markievicz and Gonne were originally housed in 'the syphilis wing', and Gonne made a direct complaint about their location:

> the visiting justices came to see us and to inquire if we had any complaints. It turned out that I knew one of them. I had met him at dinner at my uncle's when I was staying with him some years before. He expressed regret at seeing me in such circumstances and asked if he could do anything for me. I said I thought it rather a strange thing for the British government to put us into a VD wing. He was evidently not aware of it. He got very angry and said that would be remedied at once. The next day the governor and matron came and apologised to us, adding that every precaution was taken to ensure us against infection. We were moved to other cells.[48]

Those were the cells in which the Irish women were housed when Clarke arrived in Holloway. She was unable to sleep on the beds there, and the prison doctor suggested she 'go into the hospital, where [she] would have a better bed':

> I said I would be glad to go if my friends could go too. [The doctor] said there was no room for them there. Then I said that I would stay where I was, that I did not want to be separated from my friends. He said I could sleep in the hospital and come back to my friends in the morning. No, I said, I would have no privileges that they did not have. ... Then one day he came into my cell, beaming: 'You are getting your own way at last', he said, 'I have got room for you and your friends in the hospital.' I thanked him, and said I would be very glad to go there now.[49]

Thus in this case, as in the cases of the prison diet and the hours of exercise, the 'little', 'insignificant', short Irish woman through her defiant insistence, won better material comforts for all three rebel women. Clarke is as proud of her negotiating skills as Gonne is of her valuable connection with powerful men.

In the early days of her imprisonment, Clarke walked alone in the exercise yard, 'eager for news from Ireland', while the other two women argued over their relative importance in a moribund society. Contrasted with the others, as she inevitably was when the two of them walked together, Clarke considered herself more 'Irish'. When she was leaving Holloway, the prison matron asked her why she had remained 'hostile' when 'We have done everything ... within the prison rules to make things easy for you. The other two ladies ... seemed to appreciate what we did, but you have not.' Clarke responded, 'I am Irish, purely Irish, and as such ... how can I be other than hostile to my country's only enemy, England? ... The other two ladies ... are of English descent, born in Ireland, and they belong to what we call there the Ascendancy, or English element.'[50] In Holloway, at least, Clarke defined status in terms of degrees of Irishness. Markievicz, in Clarke's view, defined status in terms of the length of her prison sentence: 'I had a feeling she was glad I was released before her, she considered herself too important to be released until the last. I told her once she was like all her class in Ireland, very arrogant and full of her own importance.'[51]

In prison, Clarke wrote, 'people are inclined to be irritable over trifles not worth bothering about normally'.[52] As she puts it in unpublished notes about the time spent in Holloway, 'We had many arguments, many hot at times. I suppose people in jail are never their normal selves. Little things that would pass unnoticed assume large proportions in jail, there is so little to occupy the mind.' Yet the sorority remained. The two read books to each other, and Clarke knitted, crocheted, and embroidered, while Markievicz sketched and water-coloured. In the only sentence of this period that manifests warmth towards Markievicz, Clarke wrote to her sister Madge, 'It's here only when one comes to jail with her one learns her value.'[53] Markievicz planned to spend Christmas 1918 with the Dalys in Limerick if the women were released by then, but they were kept in prison despite the end of the war. By 12 February, just before Clarke's release, she wrote to her sister Madge, 'Madame and I have planned to live together for a bit.'[54] In 1922, Clarke and Markievicz were among the anti-Treaty women TDs who were not elected to the Dáil. Her comment about that occasion sounds like Anderson's 'deep horizontal comradeship' – in this case a gendered comradeship: 'We were all women who had worked and suffered for the freedom of our country.'[55]

Although the conflicts over status and dominance in prison do not appear to have caused changes in the women's later friendships, they are nevertheless significant, because prison releases and makes visible conflicts in the larger society that are suppressed, or less visible, the rest of the time, when the women worked together in comradeship and collaborated on a common political project. The issues that surfaced among them in Holloway were obsolete: there was not going to be any more Dublin Castle social life, and the Ascendancy was not going to be ascendant anymore. Daughters of the Protestant Big House would not patronise the Limerick middle classes, or not for much longer. Other kinds of class fault lines would take their place. But it was 1918 when these three women were locked up together, and the hierarchies of the society they were trying to displace still persisted in their minds.

Chapter 3

Gendered Memories and Belfast Cumann na mBan, 1917–1922

MARGARET WARD

The historian Peter Hart, considering the conduct of the Irish War of Independence, recognised that the IRA 'required a constant support network of women, organised or informally active in their own homes, to survive.' His conclusion was that 'Revolutionary republicanism is likely the most female-dependent major movement in modern Irish history.'[1] Historians of women's involvement in Irish revolutionary struggle have provided empirical evidence for this over many decades; evidence that is now substantiated by the release of witness statements and applications for service pensions made by thousands of former activists. However, despite this greater accessibility of records, our knowledge of the contribution made by members of Belfast Cumann na mBan to this period remains fragmentary, limited to a few activists, with the contribution made by others still obscure. Given the far greater availability of male archival evidence, a key element of this chapter is an exploration of the extent to which testimonies of male activists can amplify the sparse records that exist of women's participation in military struggle. These male and female accounts provide the foundation not only for a gendered understanding of the nature of the guerrilla war in Belfast in the years before the Treaty settlement, but also provide us with evidence to enable preliminary reflections regarding the gendered nature of recollections of the past.

Some of the difficulties in constructing a detailed narrative of this period in the north can be attributed to the hazards of being an active republican in an environment where at least 70 per cent of the population – the unionist majority – was hostile. Many suffered loss of business, an inability to find employment, and even family homes being burnt to the ground. In consequence some who played particularly prominent roles in this period found themselves forced to leave their homes to make new lives in the south. Those who remained resident in a northern state that pursued a policy of active discrimination against the nationalist minority had little option but to maintain low profiles. These circumstances help to explain the brief note attached to the Military Service Pensions Collection regarding the Belfast Brigade of Cumann na mBan, dated 11 November 1939, 'In an interview with the Advisory Committee today Misses McCullagh and Valentine promised to have a Cumann na mBan "Bde" Committee established in Belfast which would send in the required organisation records without delay.'[2] No information was supplied and as a result no official list of Belfast members exists. The violence perpetrated during the years 1918–22 in Northern Ireland, where hundreds of people were killed and burned out of their homes, is also something that needs a gendered analysis and is noted here (also see Marie Coleman's analysis in Chapter 7 of this volume).

Studies that have been made of the role played by Belfast republicans in the War of Independence concentrate upon the efforts of the IRA, with little attention given to the participation of the women of Cumann na mBan.[3] Given the difficulties in carrying out operations in that environment, and with such small numbers of activists involved, one might have calculated that evidence of women's activities, if not easily obtained from their own testimonies, could be supplemented by the evidence of their male colleagues, as contained chiefly in the witness statements collated by the Bureau of Military History between 1947 and 1959. Unfortunately, Belfast was not well represented in the 1,773 statements given by male and female activists. The bureau was viewed with suspicion as a 'Free State project' by many of the anti-Treaty activists, who refused to cooperate. It was also heavily weighted to those active in Dublin.

I have identified forty-five witness statements of men who were either members of the IRA in the north or operating there at some period. Of these, twenty-nine did mention women's contributions or recalled a specific woman, but many centred on the Easter Week period. Of the 146 female statements, only four are by women active in Belfast – Nora and Ina Connolly, Elizabeth Corr and Kathleen Murphy – and their focus was entirely on the period up to 1916. In addition, we have military service pension applications made by sixteen members of Belfast Cumann na mBan covering the period up to 1922: Rose Black, Frances Brady, Winifred Carney, Elizabeth Corr, Elizabeth Delaney, Mary McClean, Teresa McDevitt, Margaret Fitzpatrick, Mary Hackett, Annie and Alice McKeever, Amy Murphy, Nellie O'Boyle, Mary Russell, Nora Quinn and Emily Valentine.[4] More applications will be released in the future, given the fact that 1,319 applications by former

Cumann na mBan members are included in the archives. This collection will be, in the words of Marie Colemen, 'one of the most detailed archival collections for charting the role of women in any national revolution that will cover the activities undertaken by women as well as the subsequent treatment of female veterans by the state.'[5] For the moment, however, the Belfast sources are limited, with key figures like Annie Ward, OC of Central Branch from 1919 onwards, omitted. Some information is available from other sources: the application of Sarah Crummey, wife of Frank Crummey (a headmaster and IRA intelligence officer and, from March 1921, staff member of the 3rd Northern Division) is cited by Jim McDermott, who quotes her, stating that her home was raided over 100 times – 'sometimes three or four times weekly … and lasted for hours.'[6] She and her daughter Cissie (who also applied for a pension), after Frank was forced on the run after July 1920, ensured that their house remained an IRA headquarters by dealing themselves with intelligence reports and the transferring of arms. One of Cissie Crummey's tasks was to take and receive messages between Michael Collins and her father and bring instructions to Volunteer officers.[7] Seán O'Neill, Brigade OC, used the Crummey home as his office until his arrest in early 1921. It was, as McDermott describes the impact of war upon family members, 'the closely knit nature of militant republicanism in the period [that] ensured that everyone became involved in the movement.'[8] Wives, sisters and mothers undoubtedly played a role, even if they did not formally belong to any organisation, as in this testimony from Thomas McNally, Brigade Quartermaster in Belfast in 1920 and Divisional Quartermaster for the 3rd Northern Division in 1921-2, 'My mother's house on some occasions was like a minor arsenal when it was being used as a sort of clearing house for arms.'[9]

Post-1916 Reorganisation

In County Antrim in the post-Rising period, the numbers of active republicans were minuscule. Twenty-four of the most prominent Volunteers had been interned in the aftermath of the Rising, while others were forced to go on the run. Belfast Cumann na mBan suffered significant losses in personnel. Nora and Ina Connolly never lived in Belfast again. Winifred Carney was not released from jail until December and she did not return to Belfast until the spring of 1917, when she was elected President of the Belfast branch, resigning the following year while remaining a branch member. Agnes Ryan, a teacher in St Mary's College, who had presided over early Cumann na mBan meetings, had returned home to County Wexford. Her sister Nell and brother James had both been imprisoned after the Rising and Agnes was supporting her family at home while also waiting for the release of her fiancé Denis McCullough, Belfast's leading IRB figure, whom she would marry in August. McCullough testified that his wife helped him with regard to smuggling guns.[10] She was a representative for the organisation at their 1918 convention but does not feature in any accounts of the period otherwise. Róisín Walsh from Clogher, a teacher in St Mary's who had helped the Volunteers hiding in the Tyrone hills over Easter 1916, left Belfast in 1919 and returned to County Tyrone because of political harassment. She moved to Dublin in 1922, unable to keep her job as she refused to take the Oath of Allegiance.[11] It became difficult for Belfast republicans to take a public role when they had easily identifiable occupations. Teachers were easy targets and Belfast Cumann na mBan before 1916 had at least five teachers as members. One, Kathleen Phelan, from Dublin, might have left the north during this time as she is not mentioned again. Elizabeth Corr, who together with her sister Nell, Nora and Ina Connolly, Eilís Allen and Kathleen Murphy, had accompanied the Belfast Volunteers to Coalisland (and later, when news came of the countermanding orders, travelled by midnight train to Dublin to warn the leadership of the disarray in the north, returning north with new mobilisation orders signed by Pearse), lost her job in Belfast Central Library after being absent from work without leave. Articles, published and unpublished, by Corr in the succeeding years are used to supplement these sources. However, they rarely reference other individuals and are confined to standard Cumann na mBan activities rather than operational support for the IRA.[12]

Corr's comment on the northern situation after 1916 – 'of course we never got a chance to fight in the North … I went around with a chip on my shoulder ready to snap at anyone … only to find that such an attitude wasn't necessary – a change had come over even the diehards'[13] – does not reflect the attitudes of the majority. Most Catholics supported the United Irish League and the Parliamentary Party. In West Belfast, which had the highest concentration of Catholics in Belfast, Joseph Devlin MP ruled supreme; some of his greatest supporters were the women who worked in the linen mills, whose cause he had espoused over many years. When republicans began to regroup, the focus was on arms training, lectures and wary manoeuvres in the countryside, keeping a very low profile. Nancy Wyse Power, a member of Dublin Cumann na mBan, whose mother Jennie had been a founder member, testified that she moved to Belfast after the summer of 1916 and 'assisted in getting Cumann na mBan going there again.' This was fairly common practice, with executive members travelling to other areas to provide support to weak branches. However, Wyse Power added that she represented Belfast at a small convention of Cumann na mBan, held just before Christmas in the Sinn Féin offices in Harcourt Street, with no more than twenty present, mostly from Dublin. She returned to Dublin in 1917.[14] Was this an indication that the Belfast women were still in a state of flux? In the spring of 1917 Winifred Carney returned to Belfast after working in the Transport Union offices in Dublin following her release from jail. Her comrades, so proud of the role she had performed, presented her with a Tara brooch at a ceremony on Divis Mountain. The Volunteers marched and trooped the colour and the women praised Winifred as 'the only one of our little band who did her duty like a woman on that never to be forgotten Easter Week, where the blood of our Irish heroes washed away the stain that dimmed the glory of Ireland for so long'.[15]

Shortly after this, in May 1917, Winifred Carney and Elizabeth Corr were asked by a Mrs Mary Harvey, whose husband was in B Company of Belfast IRA, to go to Longford to work on the by-election campaign. The fact that both women had been active during the Rising provided them with significant credentials. Carney said she was unable to go as she was working for the Transport Union and her colleague Cathal O'Shannon was in jail and another member of staff was ill. It is also possible that she preferred not to have so close an association with Sinn Féin as her political allegiances were much closer to Labour. Instead, Elizabeth travelled with May Wisely, a Cumann na mBan member who came, like herself, from the east of the city. Corr's memoirs portray a community spirit amongst those she met, with the added thrill of meeting people who had become revered figures in the movement: Arthur Griffith, Count and Countess Plunkett, Mrs Pearse, Grace Plunkett and Kathleen Clarke ('with whom May and I fell in love at first sight. She is exactly like a widow in a book – slender, sad and sweet looking'). It would be rare for Belfast activists to have occasion to meet such figures. The Irish Party had been strong in Longford but Sinn Féin just managed, by thirty-seven votes, to have the imprisoned Joe McGuinness elected.

Corr was also one of the Belfast Cumann na mBan members who took part in the Thomas Ashe funeral procession in Dublin in September 1917, staged for a Sunday so that there could be an all-Ireland presence. The 1917 Convention of Cumann na mBan remained Dublin-centred, but this changed the following year when the representation on the executive was enlarged to include three representatives from each province. Winifred Carney and Una McCullough were listed as county members on the executive, with S. Brennan the delegate from Belfast.

While Ulster featured strongly within the proceedings of the convention, Belfast did not. Alice Cashel, full-time organiser for Cumann na mBan, reporting on her work, talked about the task of re-organisation: 'The reasons for commencing in the Northern Province were twofold: firstly it was the Province in which we were weakest, and secondly we were requested by Éamon de Valera to join with the Irish Volunteers and Sinn Féin in a simultaneous effort to range the Ulster countries on the side of an Irish Republic.'

She had worked in the counties of Donegal, Tyrone, Cavan and Monaghan. Delegates were informed that the executive had made arrangements with another organiser, subject to the approval of the new executive, to complete the work of organising the north, 'by working up the Counties of Armagh, Louth and Down.' Work that they hoped would start the following month. What is significant is that County Antrim is not mentioned. The focus was only on counties with nationalist majorities. The one intervention by Belfast in the 1918 convention was in response to a motion by the Ranelagh branch, 'That the study of Irish be compulsory for every member of Cumann na mBan, such study to be pursued in the Branch or elsewhere.' An indication of the difficulties in learning Irish in Belfast at this time can be gleaned from the amendment proposed by Miss Brennan for Belfast, 'where there is no other Irish class, Irish to be taught in the Branch'. This was passed unanimously.[16]

Although there are scant records, northern women were organising and regrouping. Elizabeth Delaney was a founding member, in 1917, of a West Belfast branch of Cumann na mBan – Craobh Larthar – reflecting the fact that so many activists came from around the Falls Road area.[17] Central branch, A Company, still existed and in the intense 1921–22 period another branch, Lamh Dearg, was formed in the North Queen Street area in response to a request by the local IRA.[18]

In September 1918, the RIC reckoned Belfast Volunteers to be numbered as no more than 500 and referred to them as 'inactive'. Although Sinn Féin clubs were holding weekly meetings, their membership of 1,000 compares unfavourably with nearly 7,000 members of the United Irish League.[19] Seán Cusack, by 1919 OC of the Antrim and East Down Brigade of the IRA, reckoned there were less than 100 Volunteers in the East Down area at that time.[20] Even by 1921 the Sinn Féin membership in the whole of County Antrim was less than 1 per cent of the population.[21] While the RIC made estimates of Cumann na mBan's strength in some areas, it did not list either County Antrim or Belfast. However, neighbouring County Down was estimated as having one branch and eighty-four members, and Armagh, much more fertile territory for nationalists, two branches and 190 members.[22] Belfast probably fell in between these figures, although accurate statistics are not possible. Elizabeth Corr said Lamh Dearg had thirty to forty members, with around twenty-five by the time of the Truce, and Elizabeth Delaney calculated a membership of thirty for West Belfast.

Conscription, Prisoner Support and 1918 Election Work

Northern nationalists had to be extremely cautious. Although Sinn Féin in Belfast was active in the opposition to conscription, 'it was not considered good policy to hold public meetings ... as meetings organised by the nationalists were likely to lead to sectarian trouble.'[23] Efforts were instead directed at getting resolutions passed at meetings of public boards and other bodies such as the Ancient Order of Hibernians and the Gaelic League. This must have left women with very little to do as they would have had scant presence or influence with such bodies. Even Sinn Féin had few women. Elizabeth Delaney testified that she was the only woman member of the propaganda committee of their Belfast Executive. While Belfast did organise the signing of an anti-conscription pledge on the same day as everywhere else, this was confined to Catholic churches and did not have the public profile of elsewhere. There was no 'women's day' against conscription, unlike other parts of the country.

Support for prisoners was a key role for Belfast Cumann na mBan, particularly after the 'German Plot' arrests of May 1918, when there were, wrote Elizabeth Corr:

> Men from every corner of Ireland in the Belfast prison at that time and it was my task to organise the visits (each prisoner was allowed two in the week) so that none should be neglected. I visited Terence MacSwiney every week during his term and I visited scores of others as well.[24]

Many members participated in this work. Ernest Blythe, writing of his time in Crumlin Road Jail, stated there was a 'large branch of Cumann na mBan in Belfast' which meant that 'we sometimes had two or three visits a day' and 'between members of that Branch and people from outside, all prisoners had one visit a week at any rate.'[25] Nellie O'Boyle visited Terence MacSwiney and brought his wife, Muriel, to the jail to visit her husband. A number of Cumann na mBan women made contact with sympathetic warders. Nora Quinn knew three warders and they visited her house with messages to be passed on. Nora O'Boyle and Teresa McDevitt both mention Warder Leonard, who provided a reference for the latter, testifying to her work in getting out the news that gas and water supplies had been cut off by the authorities in retaliation for prisoner riots. Dublin Castle responded and conditions in Belfast improved. Martin McGowan, OC of the 2nd Battalion in Sligo, had Cumann na mBan arrange for him to visit the jail so he could meet with the Sligo prisoners.[26] Emily Valentine and her mother supplied daily meals to a number of the prisoners for a period of two to three months, provided accommodation to released prisoners and, with the support of a friendly warder, smuggled messages in and out of the jail. In supporting Valentine's application for a pension, James O'Brien testified that 'anyone who visited the prison surroundings was sure to meet Miss E. Valentine looking after the interests of many prisoners'.[27] Mary Hackett carried dispatches from the imprisoned Austin Stack, to Seán Cusack, and on behalf of the imprisoned Limerick man Seán Murphy. Winifred Carney testified that Nora Quinn gave her a message from Stack which she then had dispatched to Dublin. Carney herself not only liaised with Stack, who was OC of the prisoners, and with Michael Collins, she also worked with an IRA committee in planning an ultimately unsuccessful escape of prisoners from the jail. One of the few men in witness statements to mention a specific woman by name was Denis Houston, who was visited fortnightly by Mona Delargy when in jail and then brought home to her house for a meal before being escorted to the train station for his journey home to Donegal. His release was on 11 July 1921, a time of increased sectarian violence, and he described 'an orgy of destruction and violence' on his tram journey from the prison: 'at one stage all passengers in the tram had to lie flat on the floor to avoid flying bullets and glass.'[28] It could be dangerous work. In December 1920 Mary Russell, while taking the names of a new batch of prisoners arriving at the jail, was then asked to attend the trial of one of the prisoners. After refusing to answer questions about a letter in her possession she served a three-month sentence in Armagh jail.

During the general election of 1918, Belfast Cumann na mBan women were mostly active in the campaign against Joe Devlin in West Belfast, the only constituency in Belfast where Sinn Féin had a glimmer of hope in winning. Elizabeth Corr said that she acted as a 'leader in public meetings' and administered first aid when necessary as 'the opposition crowd was very violent'.[29] Newspaper reports testified to numerous clashes between Irish Party and Sinn Féin supporters. Cork man Patrick Whelan, working in Belfast at the time, was a part of the bodyguard formed by C company of the IRA for the election speakers. He was struck on the head and rendered unconscious, then brought to a first aid station on the Falls Road where a local Cumann na mBan member attended to him.[30] De Valera, the most senior survivor of the Rising, was the Sinn Féin candidate, but he was no match for Devlin, who received almost three times more votes.

For women, the significant election candidate was Winifred Carney, the first woman to stand for election in the north, standing for Sinn Féin in the Victoria ward in unionist East Belfast. She was supported by several prominent nationalist women: Róisín Walsh and three Brady sisters, all from Belfast Cumann na mBan; Eileen McGrane, originally from Cumann na mBan in Dublin and now working as a teacher in Armagh and as a Cumann na mBan organiser; Marie Johnson, former suffragist, labour supporter and close friend of Carney's; and Alice Milligan, poet, Irish language activist and former member of Inghinidhe na hÉireann. At an election meeting disrupted by followers of Joe Devlin, Alice Cashel, Agnes McCullough, Alice Milligan and Countess Plunkett all spoke on her behalf,[31] but Carney was highly critical of what she perceived as lack of support from Sinn Féin. Although Father O'Flanagan spoke at two meetings on her behalf and Seán T. O'Kelly at one, she had no agents, committee rooms, canvassers or vehicles. She wrote afterwards to a colleague, 'it was amazing to me to find that 395 people went to the ballot on their own initiative, without any persuasion'.[32] Her platform was defiantly socialist, calling for a Workers' Republic. Northern nationalists were so outnumbered that in the general election of 1918 the whole province of Ulster could only elect three Sinn Féin members. Carney was secretary of the Republican Prisoners' Dependant's Fund and later also worked for the White Cross. Her significance extended beyond Cumann na mBan, being 'an important figure in the development of an infrastructure of support for activists and their families'.[33] Documents seized from her home during a police raid revealed the range of her contacts while her careful notes regarding those who required support provides considerable detail on IRA membership as she also listed their status within the movement.[34]

Until the military campaign began Cumann na mBan branches were engaged in usual activities such as training, fundraising and general support, such as prisoner welfare. Cal McCarthy has analysed the amount of money raised by Cumann na mBan branches during the 1920–1 period, correlating the total amount raised with the numbers of branches in each province. By doing this, Ulster comes first, with £1.51 raised per branch, as compared with Munster, the most militarily active of the provinces, with £0.67. Republican women in Ulster, because there was less military action to support, devoted comparatively more energy into fundraising - an indication of the less active role played by the IRA in the north in comparison with places like Dublin and Cork.[35]

The Military Campaign and Male and Female Testimony

The IRA campaign in the north began in response to an order from GHQ in Dublin for units to carry out raids on unoccupied police barracks and government buildings. On 3 April 1920 the income tax office in the Custom House was burned down. On 12 May the income tax office at Scottish Providence Buildings was burnt and at the start of June RIC barracks in Crossgar and Ballinahinch were attacked. The conflict intensified with the IRA execution of Auxiliaries and Black and Tans and retaliation by both crown forces and loyalist groups. Cumann na mBan's focus now became the development of communications, intelligence, transportation of arms and other military support.

References in witness statements to activities by women in the guerrilla warfare of Belfast are few. Roger McCorley, recognised as the leading gunman in this period, OC of the Belfast Brigade in 1921 and a member of the IRA Active Service Unit, provides copious details of operations, from the burning of the income tax offices to bombings and assassinations of various key figures such as D.I. Swanzy in Lisburn, yet in fifty-four pages of evidence makes no mention of Cumann na mBan, in intelligence work, as providers of safe houses, movers of armaments, or even in first aid.[36] Seán Cusack, in two statements totalling sixty-six pages, refers only to Mrs Harvey providing a safe billet for a driver sent from Dublin by Collins to collect ammunition for Dublin.[37] Women are rarely mentioned by name. Liam McMullan from Ballycastle, an activist in the Antrim Brigade area, escaped arrest in 1920 when he was warned by a Cumann na mBan member that the police had just raided his house. She took his car and gave him her bike so he would not be so easily recognised.[38] Cavan man Thomas Fitzpatrick, who was OC of the 2nd Battalion in Belfast before being transferred to the Antrim Brigade in March 1921, paid tribute to the women who organised a series of houses connecting the different parts of the brigade area which at the time he described as 'three skeleton battalions stretching from Ballycastle in the north to Lough Neagh in the west'. They organised a system of houses 'with the Cumann na mBan girls connecting the different parts of the brigade area.'[39] Of course, with the distance of time, specific names might have been difficult to recall.

In May 1921 a flying column was formed in the Cavan area, mainly consisting of Belfast men who were on the run. It was decided by the Southern GHQ that it had to be equipped with rifles transported from Belfast. Several men testified to the work of Belfast Cumann na mBan in that dangerous task. Thomas McNally, Quartermaster for the 3rd Northern Division, acknowledged the 'dangerous mission'[40] and Thomas Fox, quartermaster for the Cavan Brigade, said of those who brought the guns by train, disguised by travelling rugs, 'No praise is too high for these ladies'.[41] Rather differently, Thomas Flynn, who recalled in detail the rifles being put into golf clubs and arms in Gladstone bags, asserted that his wife was responsible for making up all the parcels and taking all of them to the railway station: 'she made numerous journeys to Cavan with the rifles and ammunition before the men left Belfast.' His wife was obviously a brave and determined woman, as he gives other examples of her conduct removing explosives and removing documents during a raid. She was brought to court after one raid but eventually had her case discharged.[42] The Cavan transportation, however, was not a one-woman enterprise. Mary Russell testified that she helped to prepare the arms for transporting, but Seán O'Neill refused to let her travel. She was too useful an ally to be put in danger, being described by one of her IRA referees as 'an auxiliary to the Belfast Brigade', secreting raw material to make bombs from Mackie's foundry and transferring grenades, mines and other equipment from the brigade bomb factory in Chester Street – the only woman entrusted to act in this capacity.[43] Teresa McDevitt, Amy Murphy and Nellie O'Boyle were all couriers for the Cavan men. Seán O'Neill and Roger McCorley both signed an affidavit on O'Boyle's behalf: 'whilst in possession of rifles concealed in a golf bag Miss O'Boyle was trapped in a cordon of British troops, but with great coolness succeeded in bluffing the troops and got the arms safely through.'[44] The Cavan venture was a disaster as a tip-off led to an ambush at Lapanduff with one death and the capture of several activists. The loss of equipment almost bankrupted the poverty-stricken Belfast Brigade.[45] O'Boyle was sent back to Cavan, to see about funeral arrangements and make contact with the three men on the run. Those captured were under a death sentence and it was planning their attempted rescue that saw Winifred Carney liaise with leading activists Seamus Woods, Roger McCorley and Seán O'Neill, a fact testified by O'Neill in his support for Carney's pension.

On 26 November 1919 Sinn Féin, the Volunteers, Cumann na mBan and the Gaelic League were all being proscribed, a suppression which forced activists underground. Jim McDermott, a historian of the Northern Divisions of the IRA, comments: 'Anyone who did become a Volunteer in Belfast at this time needed to have a very strong personality.'[46] One could say the same about their female counterparts. It became increasingly difficult to maintain Cumann na mBan as an organisation with premises and regular meetings. In later years Corr reminisced that 'Between riots, and police and military raids, life was anything but pleasant.'[47] By July 1920 the Catholic minority was experiencing the impact of sectarian tensions, leading to riots, workplace expulsions, which affected women as well as men - and attacks on homes that left hundreds as refugees. It was soon being described as a pogrom. Altogether, Belfast accounted for almost half as many deaths as would occur in the twenty-six counties of the south and west during the whole of the War of Independence.[48] Over 450 were killed between July 1920 and June 1922, with over 1,100 wounded, 8,000 forced out of their homes and 650 homes and businesses destroyed. Eventually the riots became so violent that Cumann na mBan members could no longer reach the North Queen Street area of Belfast where the Lamh Dearg branch met, and their meeting place was closed by the police.[49] Catholics numbered 24 per cent of the Belfast population, yet they suffered 70 per cent of the casualties.[50] In those circumstances one would have expected that support from Cumann na mBan would have been not only welcome, but vital. Thomas Fitzpatrick described the 'considerable difficulty in keeping wounded men hidden and attended to', making no mention of any possible contribution by women.[51] This lack of any indication that women activists were involved in providing first aid is a common feature in many testimonies, particularly striking in ASU accounts, when one would have presumed that women's help would have been an important feature in their operations. Michael MacConaill, in spring 1921 a qualified doctor and medical officer for the Belfast IRA, organised first aid stations in nationalist areas and enlisted the help of medical students from the Mater Hospital as a means of improving mortality figures. He mentions only 'local people' in kitchen houses, and Cumann na mBan is not included, although they were evidently around.[52] When the Belfast bomb factory blew up in June 1920, seriously wounding the Volunteer inside, he was taken to the house of Mary Russell, who was then told by Seán O'Neill to move him to another location so that Dr McNabb could attend to his injuries.

Thomas Flynn, OC of D Company, stated that the ASU was composed of twenty-one men specially selected for full-time services and paid a weekly salary.[53] Robert Lynch has subsequently assessed membership of the Belfast ASU as numbering thirty-two men at the height of the conflict, eight from each of the four companies of the 1st Battalion, which was based in West Belfast.[54] It was a small, select group. As with the fifty-four page testimony of Roger McCorley, what exists regarding the activities of this group is predominantly a gender-free recollection of those years, encapsulated in the words of Flynn, 'it was the ordinary people (who) made their houses available to the IRA and helped us in every way possible. They fed us and made every possible provision for our comfort.' Joseph Murray, another ASU member, describes a number of activities, including developing frontier posts in nationalist areas in order to defend the inhabitants from attack (which entailed knocking holes in walls to facilitate the escape of these pickets), without any reference to help by women.[55] In the crowded streets of Belfast, surrounded by a hostile population, being able to dump arms quickly and get away was a key element in the planning of attacks. Flynn stated only that 'we had a number of friendly houses where arms could be safely dumped', but he is explicit in who did the work – and it was not women. The IRA did their own scouting in each company area, with about twenty IRA men detailed each day for unarmed scout work. However, somewhat ironically, Seán Montgomery's memoirs recall that after he and Flynn and a few other IRA members launched an unsuccessful attack on a police tender; he was told by Flynn that they needed to get someone to take away the hand guns and Montgomery 'went to Mrs Flynn and asked her to come up and take the lot, which she did – a great Irish woman.'[56] Liam Gaynor, another teacher who served as intelligence officer, recalled that in 1922, at the height of the pogrom, he arranged for confidential files to be 'transferred to a young girl in Smithfield markets', who had them taken home and then handed over to the divisional OC,[57] so evidence for women's assistance exists. Women's pension testimony and the corroboration of their verifiers reveals a much fuller picture of their participation.

Women's Pension Applications

A strict demarcation between the less-regarded work of Cumann na mBan and that of providing military support for the IRA informed the attitude of pension assessors. Assessment was made on the basis of the contribution women made to the military campaign of the IRA, so their Cumann na mBan work, for example drilling, fundraising or support for prisoners, was not considered to be eligible.[58] Their claims had to be verified by senior IRA activists, and a distinction was drawn between 'routine Cumann na mBan activities', and 'useful service to the Brigade.'[59] One assessor noted it was difficult to assess the 'degree of intensity' of the work performed by Margaret Fitzpatrick so they would rely on the verifying officers to provide that information. In protesting against an initial rejection of her claim, Teresa McDevitt wrote to the board, 'in fact the only work I did not engage in was to take part in actual armed combat with the enemy. If this was part of the duty of Cumann na mBan I agree I am not a person to whom the Act applies but, otherwise I cannot understand the decision of the Referee.' She had a number of influential referees who testified to her work supporting prisoners, gunrunning and carrying dispatches. James Heron affirmed that she not only carried arms through cordoned areas when men were unable to, but when 'a continuous lookout was being kept for D.I. Ferris at the Falls Road it was Teresa McDevitt who took care of arms, delivered them daily and picked them up again.' It took two appeals before she received a pension based upon twenty-one and one-eighteenth years' service. Most women had pensions that amounted to one-and-a-half years, being mainly based around the period of 1920–21, when the conflict in Belfast was most intense.

The experience of Mary Hackett, who served with Cumann na mBan from 1917 to 1923, was typical of many of the Belfast women. Her first year was spent in first aid training and drilling, much as her male comrades were doing. Gradually, the scale of her responsibilities increased, to visiting prisoners and providing them with food and other necessities, fundraising, and transferring arms and ammunition. At the height of the war in Belfast in April 1921, she transferred rifles from the home of Roger McCorley to St Mary's Hall. The following month she transferred more arms to St Mary's Hall and carried arms and ammunition to another venue, on each occasion accompanied by the branch president, Elizabeth Delaney. She transferred other arms on her own to St Mary's Hall, and in July carried rifles between venues. She also carried communications to staff officers 'on the run' in Belfast and to other officers located outside the city. In May 1921 Hackett was discharged from work because fifty rounds of ammunition and a bomb were found in her place of work. She testified to the Pensions Board that she had been debarred from employment since that time and her health had suffered. While Hackett listed Seán Cusack and Denis McCullough as references for her application, neither made mention of her in their lengthy witness statements, nor supplied references for her. She received one and one-third years' pension, the assessors evaluating her support for the military campaign as limited to the period of April 1920 and July 1921; her Cumann na mBan work regarded only as 'routine activities'.[60] Mary Russell, a Cumann na mBan member since 1914, received a pension based upon two and one-sixteenth years' service, covering the period 1 April 1919–11 July 1921. Amongst her activities was carrying and removing arms used in the Ballinahinch and Crossgar attacks, removing materials following the burning of cars at Spence and Johnson's motor works, providing the raw material to make bombs, transporting explosives, conducting dispatch work and caring for wounded Volunteers.[61] Emily Valentine received a pension based upon three and one-twenty-fourth years' service, a longer time span explained by the fact that when her family home was burnt out she moved back to Dublin and continued until 1923 to provide support to republicans. Nellie O'Boyle's service was assessed as three-and-a-quarter years, reflecting a secondment to 'special services' for the IRA in 1920 when Frank Crummey ordered her to withdraw from her Cumann na mBan branch. She also had Civil War service until arrested in 1923 and interned in the North Dublin Union. David McGuinness, Intelligence Officer for the 3rd Northern Division, testified that she was to a great extent responsible for keeping communications open between the 3rd, 4th and 5th Northern Divisions, 'I know no other member of the Cumann na mBan whose record surpasses Miss O'Boyle.'

Rose Black from the Falls Road, a member of Cumann na mBan from 1919, stored arms, collected funds and housed men on the run, but her work was much more significant than this. Similarly to O'Boyle, she had orders not to associate with Cumann na mBan at meetings and parades in order not to draw attention to herself. The IRA obviously regarded her as an adjunct to their organisation, as eight officers connected with the 3rd Northern Division signed a letter on her behalf to the Pensions Board, attesting to Black as 'an outstanding character in the Physical Force Movement.' They testified to the fact that she stored large quantities of arms and explosives in her home; looked after significant amounts of gold and cash, acted as an intermediary in the purchase of armaments, was a courier between Belfast and Dublin and allowed her home to be used as a meeting place for brigade and divisional staff. In addition, she would guide IRA officers coming from other parts of the country, such as the members of Cork No. 1 Brigade who were in the north to assassinate Chief Inspector Swanzy in Lisburn, a revenge for his killing of Thomas MacCurtain, Lord Mayor of Cork. Her home was raided in June 1921 and she received a five-year prison sentence, being released from Armagh Jail during the Truce of September 1921 and forced then to go on the run. Those who testified on her behalf included Thomas Flynn, Seamus McGoran and Sam Heron. Joseph Cullen and Patrick Fox appeared on her behalf in person before the Pensions Advisory Committee on 5 June 1938 and Colonel Felix Devlin wrote to say that she 'gave us wonderful assistance in our activities in Belfast. She harboured Seamus Woods, Joe McKelvey, T. McNally and myself and others, took custody of arms after the principal "jobs", "held Brigade Divisional monies"', adding, 'If Woods has not already made a statement perhaps you would ask him to do so'. The board, when deciding the value of her service, mentioned Roger McCorley, Seamus Woods and Seán O'Neill as other men who could testify on her behalf. However, it was stated by Cullen and Fox during questioning that Black had 'run foul of Seamus Woods', the Divisional OC at the time, who 'would not help her to any degree'. She received a pension at Grade E, covering a period of four-and-a-half years – a significant period of time.[62]

Winifred Carney received a pension of five and 637th of 1,000 years' service. She objected to the initial decision to award this at Grade E (the grade most women were awarded), arguing that as aide-de-camp to James Connolly, a trusted confidante and member of the GHQ staff in the GPO, she should have received officer status for that period. She was later awarded a pension at Grade D, her officer status for the critical period eventually recognised. As a comparison, Seamus Woods and Roger McCorley, two of the foremost IRA activists in Belfast, both received pensions based upon 7.25 years' service.

Appearing before the advisory committee of assessors was not easy for those who found it difficult to remember events with precision, but even when precise claims were made, assessors were far from generous in their conclusions. Thomas McNulty, Quartermaster for C Company, listed numerous occasions when Nora Quinn removed and transferred arms, including one occasion when he was in a 'hostile locality' and she transported by handcart, concealed under a feather-bed cover, eleven rifles, six revolvers, and hundreds of rounds of ammunition. Quinn successfully appealed the original pension awarded, feeling they unfairly assessed her contribution during 1919–20, 'the last time I appeared before your referee he treated me like an imposter, or a criminal. If he treats me in such a manner again, I have no intention of letting him away with it.' Elizabeth Corr was awarded a pension based upon service of one and five-seventh years, relating solely to the work she performed during the period of the Easter Rising. None of her work during the War of Independence was considered of military significance.

The same few male names appear as referees in claims made by both men and women, reflecting the small number of key figures within the Belfast command structure of the IRA, and the smaller numbers still alive to testify. As several important figures, such as Seán O'Neill, Joseph Billings and Michael Price, did not supply witness statements, the references they gave on behalf of female claimants are invaluable in providing information about the hazardous work engaged in by Cumann na mBan activists. Michael Price, writing to pension officials in 1942, concerned about the long delay in considering the application of Emily Valentine, added, 'surely Seán O'Neill and Roger McCorley, both of whom are now in Dublin, can support these statements'.[63] O'Neill, as OC of the Belfast Brigade, provided several references, regretting 'that a record was not kept of the various services' given by the women.[64]

Carney referenced Seán O'Neill and Seán Cusack in her application. She said she reconnoitred buildings suitable for destruction by the IRA, a claim supported by O'Neill, who became first OC of the 3rd Northern Division.

He was specific in stating that Carney had assisted in plans concerning the burning of the tax offices, adding, 'Though well known to the authorities her home was always open to those of the movement.'[65] When Carney was questioned about her service she mentioned helping Seán Cusack to pack ammunition in potato bags for transporting to Dungannon. Significantly, Cusack does mention the removal of ammunition in sacks of oats in his witness statement. He was receiving regular supplies from a contact and reckoned that 80,000 rounds of ammunition were 'sent safely in this way to Dublin', but he does not mention who filled those sacks.[66]

Dubliner Catherine Byrne, who had been in the GPO during the Rising, travelled to Belfast in 1918 and 1919, her contact being Winifred Carney. She was shown the docks area by Carney and the building where she would collect the 'stuff' that she was to transport to Dublin. On Byrne's first visit she had to return to the venue alone as 'the police were watching (Carney) since 1916'. She was introduced to Seán Cusack and later tried, unsuccessfully, to obtain a certificate of support for her pension application from him, adding that she 'didn't know if he was still alive.'[67] Her statement was made in February 1952 and Cusack died two months later, on 13 April, aged 70. His own pension claim had been made in June 1950. Admittedly a large period of time had elapsed, but he was not particularly elderly, aged 68. An ex-British soldier and later Brigadier General in the Free State army, his recall of those times focused on military matters, remembering the names of many of the men and none of the women with whom he had worked. James O'Neill, who testified for Byrne during her pension application, described her role in bringing ammunition from Belfast 'at a very dangerous and critical period, and on that occasion she was the only one who succeeded in taking the ammunition through safely.'[68]

Two other Cumann na mBan members from Belfast were also awarded Grade D pensions – Frances and Kathleen Brady – although the majority of their work was outside Belfast. Frances, when working in the War Office in London, was engaged in espionage work for Michael Collins. When back in Belfast in July 1919 she performed what she described as 'the usual activities' of Cumann na mBan, 'carrying dispatches, conducting and harbouring IRA men in Belfast and ... Dublin with my sister'. Pádraig Thornberry testified that 'on at least one occasion hand grenades were brought by her from Belfast to GHQ Dublin.' Frances moved to Dublin in 1920, was paid a salary to work for the Belfast Boycott and was told she could also recruit for the Volunteers. In June 1921 she was found in the Boycott office with a revolver and incriminating documents, court-martialled and sentenced to two years hard labour, taking part in a hunger strike while in jail.[69]

The Truce and the Treaty

The Northern Ireland parliament was opened by George V on 22 June 1921. There were mixed views on the Dáil policy of enforcing a boycott of Belfast goods. Denis McCullough's musical instrument business was seriously affected and he went bust, moving with Agnes to Dublin.[70] The October Convention of Cumann na mBan, held under the conditions of the Truce, revealed the weakness of Ulster in comparison to other parts of the country. Ulster had forty-six delegates in attendance, with Elizabeth Corr the Ulster delegate, Kathleen Brady, May Wisely and Annie Ward representing central branch and L. ni Criac representing Lamh Dearg, the North Queen Street branch.[71] There is no indication why Craobh Larthar was not represented as a separate branch, although its president, Elizabeth Delaney, was inactive at this time because she had started a family. From this level of representation McCarthy calculated a total membership in Belfast of around 143.[72] There were 123 delegates for Leinster, 20 from Connacht and 156 from Munster. McCarthy, adjusting those figures according to the 1911 census, calculates Munster had one branch to 2,761 population, Leinster had one to 6,181, Connaught one to 6,569 while Ulster, with its large unionist population, had one to 34,385.[73] Cumann na mBan women were therefore massively outnumbered in the overall population of the north. Their need for additional support was very apparent in the proceedings of the convention. After a motion that full-time officers be appointed and trained to instruct branches in a range of activities, Kathleen Brady, for Belfast, called for an officer to be allocated to the north.

Truce conditions barely existed in Belfast, as the truce talks were accompanied by a sharp increase in loyalist violence.[74] Mary McClean was one member who continued her activities during the Truce period, as did Nora O'Boyle, who reckoned there was 'no truce in Belfast', continuing to transport arms to her sister's house in the country. The northern IRA used the time to increase their supply of arms. Amy Murphy went to Dundalk for arms seven times in 1922, using disguises of glasses, different hats and coats to get through the barriers at the station. Fear of partition was the overriding concern. In January 1922 Michael Collins met James Craig and agreed to end the boycott against unionist businesses. He had close links with a number of prominent Belfast IRA men, some of whom accepted officer posts from him, believing that Collins's anti-partition drive and secret arming of the northern IRA was the best way forward.

Cumann na mBan members in the north did not appear to be consulted on this shadowy strategy for the north. After the Treaty was debated and accepted by Dáil Éireann, their rejection was swift and unanimous. Belfast sent a number of delegates to a special convention of Cumann na mBan, held in Dublin on Sunday 6 February 1922, where all sixty-two Ulster branches rejected the Treaty. The numbers of northern branches in attendance were an increase on the forty-six branches attending the previous year. During the debate some mention was made of the north. Leslie Price Barry talked about 'the letting down of the north' and urged delegates not to 'hand the people of the north over to the enemies who tortured them. This is the main reason why I ask you not to support the Articles of Agreement signed in London.' A Belfast delegate declared that 'Mrs Wyse Power said she has seen the army of occupation leaving Ireland. It is not. It is being drafted into the Six Counties. We want a Republic. Nothing else.' Although the delegates attending the convention were named, those from Belfast and the border county of Louth remained anonymous.[75] Elizabeth Corr, watching from the gallery, described the scene:

> The counties were taken alphabetically, beginning with Antrim and our delegate's name was called first. Her 'Ní toil' was flung into the assembly in a voice that could have been heard at the Cave Hill. 'Up Belfast!' said my neighbour on the gallery. The other Belfast and County Antrim delegates were as emphatic ... Sometimes, a delegate, not sure of her Irish, said 'Against', but nearly all used the Irish.[76]

This conviction that the Treaty was disastrous for the north may help to explain the rupture between Rose Black and Seamus Woods, mentioned in the former's pension application, as Woods went on to become assistant chief of staff in the Free State army. Woods complained in a letter to Richard Mulcahy, 'The Cumann na mBan are all working for the Irregulars and are only attending to the Dependants of Irregular Prisoners', although that comment concerned the organisation as a whole, not its northern members.[77] Men were still being arrested and interned. The IRA launched an offensive across the north in May 1922, to be met with whole-scale internment. McCorley and hundreds of others fled south. Others were forced south, served with exclusion notices by the northern authorities. After the death of Collins on 22 August northern republicans, said Roger McCorley, 'gave up all hope.'[78] Winifred Carney was arrested on 25 August and all her documents were seized. The authorities in the north now had information on every member of the 3rd Northern Division who had ever received help from the White Cross, which was a severe blow to the organisation.[79]

It was a hard time also for female activists. Margaret Fitzpatrick, who had worked closely with Roger McCorley, Seán O'Neill and Seamus Woods, as her principal task had been the transfer of arms from the Rosemary Street dump to wherever the men of HQ and the ASU required them, said their preoccupation now was saving 'their own hides'. Amy Murphy dropped out after the death of one of her brothers, 'we had a lot of deaths'. Mary McClean said that after the 'big round up' of May 1922, their activities were confined to collecting funds for the prisoners. Mary Russell had been one of the delegates at the Cumann na mBan convention, but she took no part in the ensuing Civil War. Emily Valentine's family home had been destroyed in the pogrom of 1920 and the family returned to Dublin. She was on duty during the Croke Park massacre of spectators and later worked for the anti-Treaty side in the Civil War. Frances Brady, who was in Belfast when the Four Courts was attacked, returned to Dublin to give support to the anti-Treaty side. Following her sister's arrest in March 1923 she came back to Belfast, took over the position of secretary of the Irish Republican Prisoners' Dependants Fund and organised the distribution of anti-Treaty papers like *Eire* in the Belfast area.

Rose Black was rearrested in February 1923, to be released under doctor's orders in July, in poor health and almost blind. She was totally blind by the 1930s, signing her pension papers with an X and under the care of her sister. Annie McKeever, who had been a member of Belfast central branch since 1917 and whose home and shop had been used as an arms dump and meeting place, left temporarily for America in 1922. She said her activities 'caused me to have a nervous breakdown'. The family business was boycotted for twelve years and it collapsed, leaving her and her sister Alice with financial ruin. After spending eighteen days in police custody, Carney was spared internment in Armagh because of her deteriorating health.

With the IRA crushed and the Civil War not fought in the northern counties, Belfast Cumann na mBan no longer had a role to play. For a while, it appears to have ceased to exist, until in the late 1920s republicanism in the north, isolated from the south and outlawed in the north, began, slowly, to re-organise.

Conclusion

Louise Ryan, in analysing male narratives of the war, concluded that 'Nationalism, armed conflict, activism and the construction of masculinity and femininity are all closely connected and interlocking issues.'[80] Eve Morrison, focusing on the witness statements in the collection of the Bureau of Military History, describes how they illustrate 'the complexity of the relationship between nationalist women and prevailing notions of gender in Ireland's revolutionary period and after', as they reveal highly gendered activities, where women and men 'operated in separate organisations and were ideologically assigned roles and values according to what was deemed appropriate for their sex'.[81] What is fascinating about women's applications for service pensions is the fact that in order to succeed in obtaining a pension they had to prove that they had transgressed such gender norms and had in effect proven themselves the equals of men in military activities. As Ryan demonstrates, in the classic male texts of the period, 'attempts to contain, sanitise and depoliticise women's involvement in the war can be read as a strategy for reasserting the gender hierarchy'.[82] Most men did not, voluntarily, go out of their way to acknowledge the myriad ways in which their female comrades had worked alongside them, as the witness statements demonstrate. However, when called upon to provide testimony for service pensions, some gave generous recognition of the various roles played by women during this turbulent period of Irish history. These pension applications reveal a rare opportunity for some women to stake a claim that challenged a gender-based hierarchy of roles and in so doing, destabilised, albeit briefly, rigid notions of appropriate roles in times of revolutionary upheaval.

Chapter 4

Cumann na mBan, Martial Women, and the Irish Civil War, 1922–1923

JOHN BORGONOVO

One of the most welcome outcomes of the centenary of the Easter Rising has been the renewed interest in women's participation in the revolutionary movement. Exciting new work has broadened the literature, building on groundbreaking earlier contributions by Louise Ryan and Margaret Ward.[1] This chapter contributes an additional perspective pertaining to female involvement in the Irish Civil War (1922–23), specifically, expanding on the scholarship of Louise Ryan, Margaret Ward, Sinéad McCoole, Cal McCarthy, Ann Matthews, and others.[2] It will examine the military role played by the women's organisation Cumann na mBan in the anti-Treaty cause during 1922–1923, and contextualise that service within the evolving military conditions of the Civil War. Submissions to the Military Service Pensions Collection will also be used to illuminate the extent of Cumann na mBan's martial responsibilities. The chapter will argue that the gradual defeat of the anti-Treaty IRA created the conditions for Cumann na mBan to assume greater military responsibilities than it had during the War of Independence period, thereby transgressing gender boundaries and causing some discomfort among male republican leaders.

Cumann na mBan to the Truce of 1921

From its establishment in 1914, Cumann na mBan evolved rapidly as both a political and paramilitary organisation.[3] By 1921 it espoused an Irish-Ireland ethos, endorsed sovereign independence, and supported women's suffrage and political participation in civil society. Cumann na mBan echoed parallel mobilisations of women during the First World War, particularly military auxiliary organisations in the United Kingdom, United States, Canada,

Australia and elsewhere. By taking on the responsibilities of citizenship via military service in wartime, many feminists hoped to secure the full rights of citizenship in peacetime. Diane Urquhart showed that an estimated 3,000 Ulster women also participated in the paramilitary Ulster Volunteer Force, as nurses, signallers, couriers, and intelligence agents – similar roles to those later taken up by Cumann na mBan.[4] Irish historians have a less-developed understanding of parallel female paramilitary mobilisations by various contemporary revolutionary movements in Poland, Finland, the Baltics, Hungary, Russia, China, Mexico and elsewhere, which offer opportunities for comparative studies.

Cumann na mBan was run by women for women and maintained organisational independence throughout the Civil War. Senia Pašeta, in her book on Irish nationalist women in the earlier period 1900–18, suggests the organisation undertook significant political organising, electioneering and fundraising duties from 1917 on.[5] Non-violent activity continued during the War of Independence, through administrative support of the Dáil Éireann underground administration, street demonstrations, fundraising, and the dispersal of humanitarian assistance to political prisoners and victims of State violence. As a guerrilla war took shape in 1920, Cumann na mBan also actively assisted the IRA military campaign, willingly subordinating itself to the IRA in the process. Cumann na mBan members undertook many gendered duties, such as feeding fighters and washing their clothes, and nursing the sick and wounded. Other women took on covert military roles in IRA communications and intelligence gathering networks.[6] Active participation in the military campaign likely helped Cumann na mBan secure better female representation in the Dáil, with its number of women deputies rising from one in 1919 to six in 1921. While those deputies' connections to male republican 'martyrs' have been emphasised,[7] all six were also members of the Cumann na mBan Executive.[8] Three (Ada English, Mary MacSwiney, and Kate O'Callaghan) were selected to stand for election, at least in part, to represent Cumann na mBan.[9]

Margaret Ward writes that guerrilla warfare of 1920–21 'necessitated a complete transformation of the internal structures of Cumann na mBan'.[10] Like the IRA, Cumann na mBan organised itself geographically, establishing defined operating areas for each unit. The smallest unit was a branch, which could be further subdivided into a 'section'; Cumann na mBan tried to align these with a similar IRA formation called a company. That unit area typically encompassed a parish, village, or townland. A number of Cumann na mBan branches formed a 'district council', which corresponded (in theory) with an IRA battalion. Its operating area often centred around a large town, and was roughly the size of a parliamentary constituency or former 'barony'. However, the Military Service Pension Collection unit rolls for 1921 show uneven Cumann na mBan development, with only about one-third of IRA battalion areas paired with a Cumann na mBan District Council.[11] Many parts of the country seemed to have possessed no Cumann na mBan district councils at all. Munster possessed the most paired units (fifty-seven Cumann na mBan district councils against eighty-eight IRA battalions), followed by Leinster (eighteen out of eighty-eight), Ulster (twelve out of fifty-six), and Connaught (four out of sixty-two). It can be argued that areas with higher ratios of district councils to battalions (such as in Munster) had a more sophisticated Cumann na mBan organisation. It should also be emphasised that Connaught contained strong IRA membership but poor Cumann na mBan organisation. This might be explained by low household incomes and fewer opportunities for employment outside the home. Together these factors may have created less economic independence among women, who could not surmount the financial burden of Cumann na mBan membership.[12] Further investigation in this area is clearly needed.

Provincial Cumann na mBan units lacked organisational formations above the district council; there was no Cumann na mBan equivalent to an IRA brigade (encompassing a number of battalions) or division (encompassing a number of brigades, and introduced nationally during the Truce of 1921). The flat Cumann na mBan structure discouraged coordination across district council boundaries, prevented close governance of poorly functioning district councils, and produced a command bottleneck between the district councils and the Cumann na mBan national executive.[13] This structure limited Cumann na mBan's overall effectiveness.

Guerrilla warfare in 1920–21 created opportunities for women to become active, unarmed combatants. By the Truce of July 1921, military duties were the main focus of Cumann na mBan. At its October 1921 annual convention, the Cumann na mBan department of organisation called for organisers to instruct members in first aid, drill, signalling, and the care of firearms.[14] A programme of branch work listed seven recommended activities: (1) First aid (treating the wounded); (2) making first aid field dressings (usually carried by IRA Volunteers on active service); (3) dressing stations (safe houses for IRA wounded); (4) food and rest stations (safe houses for IRA columns, officers, and couriers); (5) dispatch carrying; (6) intelligence work; (7) study of Irish; (8) drill and signalling (Morse code and semaphore); (9) supporting Irish industry. While first aid and safe house functions were gendered roles, signalling, intelligence and dispatch work would be considered combat support roles in any army of the period. The organisation continued to prioritise military duties during the Civil War period.

The Treaty Split

The Anglo-Irish Treaty split solidified when the Provisional Government officials assumed Dáil governing responsibilities in mid-January 1922. The first open breach of the independence movement occurred within Cumann na mBan, before Sinn Féin or the IRA took a formal stance on the Treaty. Cumann na mBan's ruling executive overwhelmingly rejected the Treaty (twenty-four members opposed, two supported).[15] The decision was confirmed at a national convention held on 5 February 1922, which likewise produced a strong anti-Treaty majority of 419 delegates to 63 (86 per cent). Cal McCarthy and Ann Matthews have argued that anti-Treaty sentiment across the organisation was actually much weaker, owing to pro-Treaty branches at the convention abstaining from the vote, not sending delegates to the convention, or being unable to travel owing to a Munster railway strike. However, this conclusion is somewhat speculative, as many pro-Treaty branches did send delegates, and the area of Munster affected by the railway strike also largely rejected the Treaty. The Military Service Pensions Collection Cumann na mBan membership returns give branch figures on two dates, 11 July 1921 and 1 July 1922 (the latter representing anti-Treaty Cumann na mBan only), which provide a rough quantification of anti-Treaty strength in those reporting areas.[16] Rolls for 347 Munster Cumann na mBan branches show a drop of 26 per cent of their members (from 8,863 to 6,534) from the Truce of 11 July to the outbreak of the Civil War, which is slightly less than the national total decline of 28 per cent (from 17,119 to 12,248). Such figures suggest a strong but not overwhelming anti-Treaty majority of members. Like the IRA, some members opposed the Treaty but subsequently took a neutral stance in the Civil War. Republican women were also heavily involved in what I call the peace movement during 1922, which was especially active from March to July.[17] The Treaty split likely affected Cumann na mBan's branch leadership, which in some cases predated the Easter Rising, as it pushed out some of the more cautious and conservative elements. This could have facilitated the emergence of more aggressive and militant leaders, a radicalising process similar to that experienced by the IRA following the Easter Rising.

Geographically, Cumann na mBan's Treaty split roughly followed the IRA's territorial breakdowns, though not precisely. The 1922 Military Service Pensions Collection membership returns for the IRA and Cumann na mBan show some disparities, such as the Dublin city Cumann na mBan retention of 75 per cent of its 1921 membership compared with only 51 per cent by the Dublin city IRA.[18] Similarly, Longford Cumann na mBan units returned 34 per cent of members against 17 per cent for the Longford IRA; Mayo Cumann na mBan outperformed the IRA with 105 per cent of 1921 members against 81 per cent for the IRA. On the other hand, Cork city Cumann na mBan fielded 53 per cent of listed members, against an IRA retention of 71 per cent; and Carlow Cumann na mBan returned 33 per cent of its 1921 strength, against 71 per cent by the IRA. Internal organisational dynamics affected the Treaty split within Cumann na mBan just as they did within the IRA, with members of both organisations showing agency throughout the Treaty fallout.

Republican women TDs were prominent during the Anglo-Irish Treaty debates, and Louise Ryan has discussed pro-Treaty propaganda efforts to use their gender to undermine the republican position.[19] Outside of Dáil Éireann, republican women remained visible in the lead-up to the outbreak of hostilities in June 1922. During March and April, the republican leadership mobilised the IRA and Cumann na mBan to spread the anti-Treaty message.[20] Women participated in anti-Treaty public meetings and demonstrations, which often included processions of IRA and Cumann na mBan units.[21] Cumann na mBan members also helped disrupt pro-Treaty rallies with aggressive tactics like setting fire to speaking platforms and invading platforms to snatch tricolour flags.[22] Such episodes further linked Cumann na mBan to republican militancy within the public consciousness.

Cumann na mBan, Cumann na Saoirse, and the Contested Public Sphere

Cumann na mBan tried to rally opposition to the Treaty throughout 1922. However, the republican movement offered a much weaker civil presence compared to the War of Independence, as it lacked a counter-state alternative and faced hostile newspapers, public bodies, and Catholic Church officials.[23] Death rituals, particularly funerals, offered republicans an effective platform to assert their legitimacy.[24] During 1920–21 Cumann na mBan had often repurposed gendered mourning roles for political purposes, by leading public prayers during executions and hunger strikes or washing and dressing corpses in IRA uniforms for paramilitary funerals. Cumann na mBan continued these duties during the Civil War, but also took on additional funeral ceremonial responsibilities. While IRA units had participated in most War of Independence funerals, this was no longer possible during the

Civil War. In their stead, uniformed Cumann na mBan members took over marshalling and processional duties at the spectacle funerals of prominent anti-Treaty leaders like Cathal Brugha, Harry Boland and Liam Lynch, as well as numerous ordinary Volunteers.[25] Women marched in military formation, acted as the deceased's guard of honour, and often fired ceremonial volleys at the graveside.[26] As Louise Ryan has argued, this 'could be interpreted as a challenge to traditional gender roles and may explain some of the anxieties around the women's unnatural and unfeminine behaviour'.[27] The Cumann na mBan presence was even more noticeable to the public because, owing to their anti-republican sentiments, far fewer representatives of civil society attended IRA funerals in the Civil War. In this way Cumann na mBan became the public face of militarised republicans during the conflict.[28]

Cumann na mBan undertook most of the republican propaganda responsibilities. During the War of Independence, Cumann na mBan had assisted both the IRA and Sinn Féin in waging complementary propaganda campaigns. During the Civil War, the IRA dominated republican publicity, though its efforts were much less effective than its Sinn Féin predecessors or its National Army counterparts.[29] Cumann na mBan had established a publicity department, which was closely integrated with IRA propaganda efforts.[30] Brigid O'Mullane managed the IRA publicity office, assisted by three full-time Cumann na mBan members who helped her find a flat in Dublin and outfit it with commandeered typewriters and duplicating machines. As she later explained:

> and in my capacity of D/P [Director of Propaganda] C. na mBan was able to issue orders direct to all Cumann na mBan branches throughout the country and in Dublin for publicity distribution ... In addition to the issuing and distribution of pamphlets [sic], leaflets and posters throughout all Ireland, I edited and published an official War Bulletin weekly in Dublin, giving details of all IRA operations. I also had to keep records of all raids, arrests, and shootings and make arrangements for legal attendance at the latter inquests, to represent IRA interests. It was a day and night job of secret and dangerous activity against terrible difficulties, and all the time evading police and Free State troops' attention.[31]

Women distributed propaganda in the War of Independence, but during the Civil War they also appear to have been more heavily involved in its production.[32] The Cumann na mBan publicity department printed IRA notices to the civilian population, such as warnings against billeting of

National Army soldiers in homes, paying of income taxes, and attending public amusements.[33] The notices were placed as wall posters, and handed out as leaflets.[34] Cumann na mBan instructed units to distribute leaflets, 'at the church doors and any other places where people collect in numbers. They might also be dropped in the letter boxes of people who would likely be interested. A few might also be placed up in prominent places, such as market squares, near church doors etc'.[35] The painting of wall slogans was also organised by the Cumann na mBan publicity department. In Dublin, Brigid O'Mullane established ACU (Active Cumann Unit) 'painting squads' in each city district. She reported that occasionally Free State troops fired at them, and 'we were beaten up other times by the soldiers'.[36] Other women painting wall slogans also described danger from troops and hostile civilians.[37] Wall slogans like, 'Soldiers of the Republic are True to their Oath' or 'Into the Empire, over Cathal Brugha's Dead Body', were described by Ernie O'Malley as 'a very effective method of propaganda'.[38] Such visible engagement further associated Cumann na mBan with the unpopular republican war effort.

During the first weeks of the war, Cumann na mBan produced special editions of the IRA newspaper, under the titles of *War Bulletin*, *Special Bulletin* and *Official Bulletin*.[39] Máire Comerford helped publish, *Heads Up*, a bi-weekly newsletter put out by Cumann na mBan, and a newspaper called, *Boys of Wexford* during the June 1922 general election.[40]

During the autumn of 1922, Mary MacSwiney managed IRA publicity in the 'Munster Republic' with Erskine Childers.[41] Lily O'Brennan undertook national and international distribution of the IRA *War Bulletin*, setting up her own communications network and directing republican propaganda packages via Liverpool to destinations around the world.[42] The main anti-Treaty newspaper (and successor to the *Irish Bulletin*) was the daily, *Poblacht na hÉireann*. Cumann na mBan undertook its distribution, which reached foreign countries, appeared in many Irish newsagents and was sometimes delivered nocturnally to private homes.[43] In Glasgow, Countess Markievicz put out her own version of *Poblacht* called *Eire: The Irish Nation*, which was smuggled into Ireland.[44] Throughout the conflict, Cumann na mBan essentially fuelled and operated the republican propaganda machine.

Pro-treaty Cumann na mBan leaders Jenny Wyse-Power, Alice Stopford Green, Louise Gavan Duffy and others established a new women's organisation, Cumann na Saoirse, in April 1922. Vocally supportive of the government, it appeared strongest in Dublin (seventeen Dublin branches marched in Michael Collins's funeral) and Cork city, with branches also apparent in Wexford, Wicklow, Monaghan, Kilkenny, Tipperary, Leitrim,

Sligo, Meath and Kildare.[45] Members organised dances, concerts, travel hostels, and railway canteens for National Army troops. They also supplied wounded soldiers with comforts like cigarettes, fruit and playing cards. Cumann na Saoirse emphasised feminine tasks traditionally associated with auxiliary organisations rather than paramilitary duties. In doing so, it conformed with gender norms. At the same time, members quietly provided military assistance to the National Army, most commonly as searchers of women prisoners and detainees. Cal McCarthy has noted the organisation was dubbed 'Cumann na Searchers' by republicans.[46] Members also occasionally served as intelligence agents and covertly carried messages across IRA lines.[47] Pro-Treaty female military service was largely ignored by government propagandists, and was less common than in anti-Treaty Cumann na mBan. Margaret Ward has argued of Cumann na Saoirse, 'the organisation represented the aspirations of the emerging elite, and it looked with horror and distaste on the wild women of Cumann na mBan'.[48]

Cumann na mBan during Conventional Fighting

Military historians usually divide the Irish Civil War into two separate periods: a conventional phase, and a guerrilla phase.[49] The seven-week conventional phase saw the IRA and the National Army fight for territory, with numerous parts of the country experiencing set-piece battles, fortified positions, troop movements, ship landings, and artillery shelling. This phase concluded in mid-August 1922 with the National Army's seizure of major cities and towns and dispersal of large-scale IRA forces. It was followed by a second phase during which the IRA reverted to the guerrilla tactics honed during 1920–21. IRA units wore no uniforms and held no fixed territory, operated underground, and undertook hit-and-run attacks. This guerrilla phase lasted nine months until the IRA's final collapse in May 1923. Cumann na mBan was highly active during both phases.

The Civil War opened in June 1922 with a week-long engagement historians have termed 'The Battle of Dublin'.[50] Republican women were prominent throughout the Dublin fighting, which resembled the Easter Rising. Republican forces barricaded themselves inside strong city centre buildings, until artillery and flames forced them to give way.[51] The integration of Cumann na mBan with republican forces appeared smoother than during the Easter Rising. The Cumann na mBan Executive established headquarters at Tara Hall in Gloucester Street and at Bachelor's Walk.[52] Four women served in the Four Courts garrison until its surrender, and another thirty women joined seventy male republican fighters in 'the block', a collection of fourteen inter-connected buildings on O'Connell Street that was blasted by artillery and fire. Republicans defended many additional buildings around Dublin, with Cumann na mBan members operating kitchens and combat dressing stations in the Tramway Office, Moran's Hotel, Dobson's Pub, Hughes's Hotel, 44 Parnell Square, and business premises at Capel Street and Dominick Street. First aid stations were also located in Rathfarnham at St Enda's School, and in Leinster House.[53] The Irish Citizen Army (ICA) mobilised eighteen women alongside 125 men, with Countess Markievicz acting as second in command during the ICA's occupation of Barry's Hotel and pulling duty in firing posts.[54] It is unclear whether additional Cumann na mBan members or ICA women took up arms during the battle, but they certainly acted as unarmed combatants by running messages and moving arms and ammunition. Additional research is needed to determine if republican forces in 1922 contained a higher proportion of women fighters than in 1916.

Over the ensuing six weeks, the Dublin fighting was replicated on a smaller scale across the south of Ireland, with some clashes involving hundreds of fighters. Cumann na mBan units in those areas provided catering, medical and courier services in support of what I term the IRA 'field army'. Many women served in fortified IRA positions, feeding troops and carrying messages and ammunition during fighting in Kilkenny, Nenagh, Cork city, Carrick-on-Suir, Tralee and Limerick city.[55] Cumann na mBan members also set up first aid stations and joined mobile IRA medical units treating the wounded in Tralee, Blessington, Baltinglass (County Wicklow), Bruff, Cork, Enniscorthy,[56] Clonmel, and Limerick.[57] 'Active Service' units were formed to make members available for specific duties at short notice, such as the Dun Laoghaire branch's three active service groups: 'first aiders', dispatch couriers, and cooks (with Miss M. Broderick designated OC or 'officer commanding' of Cooking).[58] Similar formations were likely organised to assist IRA 'field units' operating throughout the south. At the same time, provincial Cumann na mBan mobilisations appear more ad hoc than those carried out during the Battle of Dublin by the organisation's national executive. This may be attributed in part to Cumann na mBan's flat structure, which, as mentioned earlier, largely lacked brigade formations to coordinate efforts across broader geographic areas. The transition from guerrilla force to conventional army during July and early August required clear centralised planning, which both the IRA and Cumann na mBan lacked. Better-defined roles for Cumann na mBan emerged when the IRA switched to familiar guerrilla tactics in mid-August 1922.

Cumann na mBan as Guerrilla War Combatants

By the time the IRA resumed guerrilla warfare in mid-August, it was much weaker than a few months earlier. Public opposition to the republicans became more intense as the war continued. The IRA's opponent, the National Army, was well financed and supplied, growing rapidly, and understood the IRA's underground structure. The IRA organisation in many places was decimated by arrests during the conventional phase, with junior and senior officers in Dublin especially hard-hit. Increasing numbers of demoralised anti-Treaty IRA Volunteers abandoned the struggle after the successive military defeats of July and August. Arrests mounted over the ensuing months, and IRA units in many areas stopped functioning.[59] Despite occasional successes, the republican forces continued to decline until the IRA Executive declared a ceasefire in May 1923.

As IRA units came under greater strain and continued to lose reliable personnel, tasks that had been carried out in 1920–1 by rank-and-file IRA members were increasingly taken over by women. In this way, Cumann na mBan Civil War service assumed more overtly military and thus less gendered duties than it had in the War of Independence. For example, senior IRA leaders instructed Cumann na mBan to bolster the faltering republican communications network, which connected units and departments across the country. Female couriers picked up and delivered messages at 'call houses', which were linked together like a stage coach.[60] These interconnected communication lines extended throughout the country, relied on synchronised delivery schedules, and were often established by senior Cumann na mBan organisers to incorporate branches for courier service.[61] Numerous Cumann na mBan Military Service Pensions Collection statements from different parts of the country detail this kind of dispatch service, which required hundreds (possibly thousands) of individual couriers and call house managers.[62]

During the guerrilla phase, the headquarters of IRA divisions, brigades, and battalions became even more isolated. Unlike the 1920–21 conflict, senior IRA figures could often be identified by their opponents or hostile civilians, so they tried to remain out of sight. Fugitives sometimes moved underground literally in rural areas by using 'dugouts' (hidden underground chambers lined with timber and covered with camouflaged tin roofs, which could accommodate a number of people without detection). In urban areas it was more common for republicans to hide in private homes, some with custom-built hiding places. Women predominately operated as special couriers, connecting IRA headquarters and high-ranking fugitives with their command apparatus by hand-delivering messages from call houses.[63] Messages could also be sent to unit headquarters at 'cover addresses' either by hand or via the government postal system. An outside envelope was addressed to a person at the cover address; inside was a second sealed envelope holding the dispatch, which was kept until a special courier collected it for the intended recipient. The IRA preferred to use women for cover addresses, as seen in a 1922 list from the IRA's Eastern Command area (Leinster and Ulster) which contained fifty-seven female names compared to twenty male ones.[64] Such service required discretion, tact, and sound judgement.

Women were also frequently chosen as couriers for sensitive missions outside of Ireland. For example, Kathleen Connolly Barrett connected the republican envoy in Britain, Art O'Brien, to the republican headquarters in Dublin, travelling to London and back multiple times.[65] She also went to Manchester and Liverpool to transmit and receive Austin Stack's telegraph traffic with the IRA's American network. These messages included money transfers, and she later claimed, 'our supplies of cash came from me'.[66] Another Cumann na mBan member, Maureen Ryan, was dispatched to Berlin to collect $50,000 wired from the United States, which she delivered to an IRA commander in London. Éamon de Valera later sent her to deliver copies of the May 1923 ceasefire order to republican contacts in Paris, London and Rome.[67] Seemingly innocuous and non-threatening, women used their gender as a cloak while navigating the shadowy world of subversives and spies.

While women were highly active in IRA intelligence operations during the War of Independence, such duty appears to have been less common during the Civil War. This reflected a general disruption of IRA intelligence networks, as the organisation's information-gathering methods and human assets were much better known to their new Irish opponents than their former British ones. A more common type of activity for Civil War women was that of scout and sentry for IRA flying columns (groups of armed fighters), fugitives, and passing fighters. Numerous female Military Service Pensions Collection applicants mention providing security to fighting groups. This might mean standing guard in a safe house to listen for approaching enemy troops or taking up a position to watch for road traffic or the movement of neighbours who could warn the National Army. Women on foot or bicycles acted as scouts for flying columns, fugitives, and attacking parties, guiding them away from enemy troops or hostile civilians.[68] This was dangerous, as Leslie Price later explained: 'If you came into an area where the flying column was going from one area to another and if they thought you would be useful as a kind of blind they would take you with them, and travelling with an armed body of men you might run into an ambush'.[69]

The inability of IRA officers to move about freely resulted in another common role for Cumann na mBan in the Civil War: holding, maintaining, distributing, and transporting weapons. Historian John Dorney has referred to these women as 'quartermasters', a military position found within every level of the IRA hierarchy.[70] Numerous Cumann na mBan members across the country claimed this kind of pension service, which necessitated maintaining secret weapons caches and transporting guns for use in IRA attacks.[71] Cumann na mBan proficiency tests from early 1923 feature questions on types of pistols,[72] while the head of the Free State government, W.T. Cosgrave, denounced the republicans for 'using women and little girls to carry lethal weapons and explosives, thus exploiting the chivalry of Irish troops to their own danger'.[73] The noted female republican activist Margaret Skinnider reported that she effectively ran the IRA's Quartermaster General's department for several weeks at the outset of the Civil War, performing the duties generally ascribed by IRA staff to an 'assistant quartermaster'.[74] Despite the clear military function of this kind of activity, women do not appear to have been formally recognised as quartermasters by the IRA either then or later.

The Civil War IRA was better armed than its 1920–1 predecessor, which allowed it to field many more 'columns' and active service units of armed guerrillas. Each guerrilla band created its own logistical structure, which was often maintained by Cumann na mBan. In this way, Cumann na mBan collaborated even more closely with IRA fighting units in the Civil War than it had in the War of Independence. To meet these challenges, Cumann na mBan formed several female active service units compromised of women who were available at any time for duties.[75] A member of the Wexford unit explained it was comprised of women from several branches, who 'could be depended to carry out immediately every order given them. Their activities consisted chiefly of dispatch work, including carrying ammunition and explosives to the column operating in the North Wexford area'.[76] Margaret Mary MacSherry served full-time with a Dublin IRA active service unit and later with the 'Plunkett Column' (led by Neil Plunkett O'Boyle), as it prowled about the Wicklow Mountains. For both guerrilla bands, she moved arms, maintained their supplies, and occasionally joined their attacks as a combat nurse.[77] The irrepressible Máire Comerford scouted for large republican columns during the conventional fighting and acted as a getaway driver for a Dublin IRA Active Service Unit during numerous raids and attacks. Also in Dublin, Kathleen Kenny distributed and collected arms for various

IRA street ambushes.[78] Hard-pressed, easily identified by their enemies, and suffering debilitating losses, IRA fighting units seemed more willing to directly involve women in their combat operations during the latter stages of the guerrilla conflict of late 1922 and early 1923.

Women generally participated in the Civil War as unarmed combatants. Their duties often exposed them to hostile gunfire, and sometimes they found themselves, in the understatement of one veteran, in 'a bit of a scrap'.[79] However, evidence suggests that during the Civil War it became more common for women to hold arms and join IRA attacks, though it was still rare for them to engage in gun battles. Armed women seized property even before the conflict began. Eithne Coyle achieved national notoriety after she undertook numerous armed train raids in Donegal, to capture material moving in defiance of the Belfast Boycott in the spring of 1922.[80] During the June general election campaign, armed Cumann na mBan members in Wexford (led by Máire Comerford) raided between nine and thirty post offices for stamps.[81] When the fighting began, women seized at gunpoint clothing for IRA fighters from drapery shops in Dublin and Wicklow town.[82] During the conventional fighting, some newspaper reports placed armed women with the republican forces, such as the description of the Cork city republican headquarters during heavy fighting in the Cork suburbs: 'One lady, wearing a trench coat, and armed with a revolver in holster, cycled up and spent a few minutes inside'.[83] Kathleen Kennedy Cleary helped burn down the Athenry military barracks, Margaret McSharry participated in the blowing up of bridges in Wicklow, while both Siobhán Lankford and Roseanne Boland cut telegraph wires to disrupt Free State communications.[84] In the republican redoubt of Kilnamartyra, County Cork, Nora O'Sullivan helped her brother Micheál man a machine gun during a Free State attack on their home.[85] In early 1923 Cumann na mBan members were arrested attempting to organise a mass breakout of IRA prisoners from Limerick Jail.[86] Julia Ryan-O'Leary claimed that during the removal of IRA Chief of Staff Liam Lynch's body from the Catholic Church in Mitchelstown (County Cork), the local canon refused permission to toll the church bells. At gunpoint she seized the belfry keys from the church clerk, locked herself inside, and rang the bells as Lynch's body was removed.[87] The taking up of arms by women likely reflected intensifying militancy within the organisation. Arms were also more plentiful in the Civil War and often under the control of women. It is likely that the full release of the Military Service Pensions Collection will produce many more examples of this kind of armed activity.

Direct engagement in combat operations transgressed gender norms and seems to have been discouraged by top IRA leaders. Cal McCarthy has reported how IRA Chief of Staff Liam Lynch intervened with Cumann na mBan headquarters to clarify military tasks, explaining: 'The conditions in this guerrilla war are so different to those of ordinary war that we do not wish women to take an active part in hostilities'.[88] This unease was also seen in the anti-Treaty press, as explained by Louise Ryan.[89] Republican propagandists, including female writers, downplayed female participation in military operations, and corrected false Free State reports of women engaged in combat. Such direct female involvement was perceived as damaging to the republican movement, which was as much an indictment of Irish public opinion as of anti-Treaty propagandists.

The evolution of Cumann na mBan as a military organisation can be seen by the increased Civil War fatalities of women participants and incarceration of Cumann na mBan members compared to the War of Independence. While a single Cumann na mBan member is known to have been killed in the War of Independence, at least four women died in the Civil War.[90] The losses show the diversity of Cumann na mBan activities in the conflict. The first fatality was Mary Hartney, who during July 1922 was killed while working in an IRA field hospital in Adare (County Limerick) when it was struck by a Free State artillery shell.[91] Dubliner Lily Bennett was shot down by National Army troops who fired at a republican demonstration on O'Connell Street in November 1922. In April 1923, Adrigole (County Cork) branch secretary Margaret Duggan was killed by Free State forces during a raid on the Beara Peninsula village. Newspapers reported that she was standing near the two IRA Volunteers when a gunfight broke out. Duggan's Cumann na mBan superior later reported that she was shot while carrying a warning of the raid to IRA fighters hiding 'up on the side of the mountain'.[92] Historian Pádraig Óg Ó Ruairc reports that East Clare Cumann na mBan leader Annie 'Nan' Hogan died after her release from Kilmainham Jail from the effects of a hunger strike.[93] There were likely additional fatalities among female republican sympathisers, such as Helena Barry, who lived in an IRA safehouse in Bantry (County Cork) and was killed after it was riddled with bullets by Free State soldiers angry at the loss of a comrade.[94] In Dublin, Elizabeth King McCarthy reported that her sister Anna King was deliberately shot dead by National Army soldiers while walking with another sister who was in Cumann na mBan (the latter was wounded).[95] It is likely more female fatalities will be identified by scholars in the future.

Perhaps the most striking indicator of Cumann na mBan activity in the Civil War was the incarceration of over 560 women by Free State forces, compared to roughly fifty in the War of Independence.[96] The National Army initially avoided detaining women, quickly releasing about fifty Cumann na mBan members captured during the Battle of Dublin to make room for male prisoners.[97] However, when the guerrilla war heated up in the autumn of 1922, the National Army decided to arrest women activists who were perceived as important to IRA operations. Cumann na mBan headquarters and personnel were specifically targeted in different parts of the country, which rapidly filled Free State prisons.[98] Space limitations here prevent a full discussion of female republicans' Civil War prison experience.[99] It can be said that republican women were jailed in harsh conditions, had their plight documented by republican propagandists and undertook prison resistance which generated shootings, beatings, hunger strikes, and attempted escapes. The full release of the Military Service Pensions Collection will provide more evidence of trauma experienced by those prisoners.[100]

Ending and Aftermath

The Irish Civil War ended for Cumann na mBan, as it did for the IRA, in demoralisation and comprehensive defeat. In May 1923, the IRA Executive unilaterally declared a ceasefire, disregarding the Cumann na mBan Executive's request that it be consulted first.[101] After the government emptied the prisons in 1923–4, some Cumann na mBan members returned to the organisation. However, many female activists transitioned to non-violent opposition to the Free State. After 1926 they could be found in both Sinn Féin and Fianna Fáil. Others moved to different forms of agitation or civil engagement and some withdrew from public life altogether. Female involvement in civil society was initially contained and then slowly rolled back, which was a bitter pill for first-wave feminists within the Cumann na mBan leadership.[102]

Cumann na mBan's contribution to the national struggle was not entirely forgotten, though that memory was reshaped by male anti-Treaty republicans after they gained political power. In 1932, the new Fianna Fáil government radically expanded the military service pension scheme by recognising anti-Treaty service and activity by other paramilitary organisations, including Cumann na mBan.[103] Marie Coleman has argued government recognition of female military service appears to have been unusual by contemporary European standards.[104] At the same time, under the 1934 Pensions Act, Cumann na mBan service was limited to the bottom two of five IRA service letter grades, omitting certain female activists whose responsibilities were equivalent to the higher IRA service grades. Some women who acted as IRA officers but had nominal Cumann na mBan membership were recognised only for their Cumann na mBan service. A few women who served as IRA officers without Cumann na mBan affiliation were officially designated as belonging to the IRA, but had their military rank either unstated or understated in their pension file.[105] In this way, the State both acknowledged and confined female military participation in the independence struggle by bureaucratically establishing limited, 'acceptable' military service by women.[106]

The Military Service Pensions Collection contains generous and sometimes moving testimonies by male IRA veterans describing their female comrades. For example, striking tributes were paid to Máire Comerford, the one-woman paramilitary dynamo for both Cumann na mBan and the IRA.[107] Thomas Derrig, a future Fianna Fáil minister, reported that Comerford carried out 'special missions which could only be performed by a person of greatest trust, resource, and fearlessness'. His cabinet colleague Oscar Traynor, wrote glowingly of Comerford's service during the Battle of Dublin:

> On numerous occasions during that week, under heavy rifle and machine gun fire, she made personal contact with the GHQ's personnel. How she accomplished this, to me, almost impossible feat only she can explain ... I can say without the slightest exaggeration that her general conduct in the carrying out of the duties entrusted to her was a source of inspiration to all who had the honour to be associated with her during that period.[108]

Comerford was one of the women who remained inside the Four Courts when it was besieged by the National Army during the Battle of Dublin. Their presence was described by IRA Executive leader Rory O'Connor in a communique: 'Cumann na mBan tend to the wounded and say the rosary in Irish'.[109] That message was most likely carried by Máire Comerford during one of her daring dashes through hostile gunfire to keep communications open to the Four Courts. Yet, Rory O'Connor deliberately positioned his Cumann na mBan comrades in the traditional female role of caregiver, even when their war service did not conform to gender norms.

Maryann Valiulis has discussed the emergence during the revolutionary period of 'the alternative masculine role of rebel hero, the IRA man ... acting outside of the contemporary conventional norm ... The rebel hero rejected the Victorian ideal of "the paterfamilias", the family man, businessman, staid political leader'.[110] Masculine identity was at the heart of nationalist formation, Aidan Beatty has suggested, as Irish separatists tried to forge a respectable European identity that would bolster their claim for full national independence.[111] Military recruiters deemed male republicans 'cowards' for refusing to enlist in the British Army during the First World

War. In 1920–1, British authorities portrayed the IRA's guerrilla campaign as cowardly, primitive, and degenerate.[112] As Gavin Foster has shown, Free State propaganda depicted the anti-Treaty campaign as mad, hysterical, ignorant, irrational, primitive, and feminine.[113] The direct involvement of women in the republican military campaign of 1922–3 was therefore highly problematic for male republicans because it posed questions about their masculinity and respectability.

Sikata Banerjee has suggested that the war service of Cumann na mBan members 'situated them in a borderland between normative womanhood and manhood … martial women were threatening the order of muscular nationalism by weakening boundaries between normative masculinity to create a space in the borderlands of gender as "manly women"'.[114] Cumann na mBan members had become more overtly martial in 1922–3 than in 1920–1. Female republican military activity was highly visible and widely publicised throughout the Civil War. After the war, this complicated efforts by male republicans to reclaim their respectability, legitimacy and masculinity. They responded by shaping republican memory of Cumann na mBan participation in the Civil War to better conform with independent Ireland's attitudes towards women. While the female military service was not entirely forgotten, it was pushed into the background of the independence narrative. In this way it replicated the experience of first wave feminists and other politically active women in the State during the first half-century of Irish independence.[115]

Chapter 5

Women's Political Representation in Dáil Éireann in Revolutionary and Post-revolutionary Ireland

CLAIRE McGING

This chapter outlines and assesses women's political representation in Dáil Éireann, the lower house of the Irish Parliament, in both revolutionary and post-revolutionary Ireland. It argues that the establishment of the Irish Free State and the onset of Civil War in 1922 represent a shift in the opportunities available for women to enter parliamentary politics. Although the first woman MP ever elected was from Ireland and six women TDs[1] were returned in the 1921 general election, Dáil Éireann following independence was a 'colder house' for women's representation. The outright opposition of women TDs (and Republican women more generally) to the terms of the Anglo-Irish Treaty in 1922 was a crucial factor in the decline of women's representation, as was the influence of various political, legislative and socio-cultural changes in the Irish Free State. Drawing on the parliamentary record and secondary sources, this chapter aims to reveal political women's agency as activists and politicians in the decades that followed the establishment of the Irish Free State and considers the gendered obstacles the first women TDs faced in their roles. In doing so, the chapter assists with an important reappraisal of women in politics over this period.[2]

Women's Enfranchisement and the 1918 General Election

After many years of mobilisation and struggle, the passage of the Representation of the People Act 1918 marked an important victory for suffragists and suffragettes in Britain and Ireland.[3] The legislation granted the right to vote to women over 30 who met minimum property or education qualifications and to all men over 21. The age restriction was to ensure that women did not become the majority of the electorate due to the loss of young men in the First World War. Gender was no longer an absolute barrier to women's electoral participation in Ireland, but formal restrictions related to class and age remained in place until 1922 when Irish women were enfranchised on par with men under the terms of the Constitution of the Irish Free State. Significantly, British women would not win this right for another six years. In terms of political representation, the Parliament (Qualification of Women) Act 1918 gave British and Irish women over 21 the right to stand as parliamentary candidates. This created a somewhat odd situation whereby women and men in Britain and Ireland were treated equally as potential candidates, at least formally, but not as voters. Thane,[4] however, shows that men had long run for election as MPs, some successfully, before they qualified to vote.

In Ireland, Cumann na mBan, the women's section of the Irish Volunteers (later the Irish Republican Army or IRA), had asserted a policy at their 1917 convention that members should participate in the public and political affairs of the nation[5]. Women activists urged the Sinn Féin party to recruit women candidates for the December 1918 general election (the first general election in more than eight years). Four women had been appointed to the twenty-four-member Sinn Féin executive in 1917 (although women activists had pushed for six representatives, citing the promises of gender equality as enshrined in the Proclamation of the Irish Republic in 1916) and the party was, at least on paper, supportive of women's equality. It was committed to women's suffrage on equal terms with men, and the final clause of the party's constitution from 1917 onwards read: 'That the equality of women and men in this organisation be emphasised in all speeches and pamphlets'.[6] This resolution, proposed by Dr Kathleen Lynn and seconded by Jenny Wyse-Power, was passed by general agreement. However, nationalist women were disappointed when Sinn Féin selected only two women candidates to run in 1918, Constance Markievicz (Dublin St Patrick's) and Winifred Carney (Belfast Victoria). It was assumed that women prisoners, like men, would be included among the list of Sinn Féin candidates. Hanna Sheehy Skeffington, founder and chairwoman of the Irish Women's Franchise League (IWFL), had turned down an unwinnable seat in Antrim North (the unionist candidate ultimately received 78 per cent of the vote). Kathleen Clarke, imprisoned in Holloway Jail at the time of the election, was disappointed to learn that she had not been selected to run in either Dublin North City or her childhood home of Limerick City – internal male-gendered party politics in Sinn Féin had resulted in the selection of two men.[7] Louie Bennett, a suffragette and labour activist, was nominated as a candidate by the Labour Party but she declined to stand (in the end, Labour did not contest the 1918 election to prevent a split in the nationalist vote).[8] Across the islands, there was confusion as to whether women candidates could legally stand for election in 1918, and the one-page Parliament (Qualification of Women) Act was hurriedly passed in November 1918 to clarify their candidacy.[9] Ryan points to Sinn Féin's 'somewhat uncharacteristic concern for British constitutional rules' as the party was not sure 'whether it would be according to the law' for women candidates to run.[10]

Markievicz, who was Cumann na mBan President in 1918, was in Holloway Jail when selected as a Sinn Féin candidate. On learning the news she wrote to the IWFL to express her hope that the Dublin St Patrick's constituency would become a centre for women's political participation.[11] Women of all political hues undoubtedly understood the significance of having at least one woman candidate elected, but not all were prepared to concentrate their efforts solely on Markievicz – political ideology trumped gender. Cumann na nBan and IWFL activists did come together very effectively to work on Markievicz's campaign, but the IWFL was disappointed with the lack of support afforded to her by the Sinn Féin organisation and by the level of campaigning Cumann na mBan did for male candidates instead of their President.[12] Candidates across the island were in prison so women's participation was vital for Sinn Féin nationally.

Meanwhile Winifred Carney, a committed socialist, was very disappointed with the campaign in Belfast Victoria. A majority unionist constituency, she was selected for a totally unwinnable seat and received just 395 votes (3 per cent). Local Sinn Féin activists were not enthusiastic about campaigning for a socialist woman who insisted on having her own election programme about a 'Workers' Republic', and Carney would later join the Northern Ireland Labour Party, unhappy with the lack of a class perspective in the Sinn Féin platform.[13]

The IWFL was not pleased with the lack of women's representation in the 1918 general election and instructed their members to 'keep the flag of sex equality flying' in their 1918 annual report.[14] Sinn Féin understood the electoral importance of women as a new group of voters and emotionally appealed to them directly for support, but the party was less willing to accept women as candidates.

Seventeen women candidates, including Constance Markievicz and Winfred Carney, ran in the 1918 general election. Markievicz was the only woman elected and became the first woman ever to be elected to Westminster, but refused to take her seat in line with Sinn Féin's policy of abstentionism.[15]

In January 1919 she became part of the first Dáil Éireann, the parliament of the revolutionary 'Irish Republic', and was made Minister for Labour (which included responsibility for social welfare) by the President of the Dáil, Éamon de Valera. This made her the second woman cabinet minister in the world. However, Kathleen Clarke documents how Markievicz did not receive this groundbreaking appointment without a struggle – a further illustration of Sinn Féin's dubious attitude towards women's participation in politics, despite a party platform that outwardly espoused gender equality:

> I asked her how she had managed it, as I had noticed that the present leaders were not over-eager to put women into places of honour or power, even though they had earned their right to both as well as the men had, having responded to every call made upon them throughout the struggle for freedom. She told me she had to bully them; she claimed she had earned the right to be a minister as well as any of the men, and that if she was not made a minister she would go over to the Labour Party.[16]

The department operated under difficult circumstances and Markievicz spent much of the period in prison. She was demoted from cabinet following a restructuring during the period of the Truce in 1921. She was later re-appointed to the role and held it until 1922, but it was no longer a full cabinet post. This move largely symbolised the ultimate exclusion of women from senior political positions. It would be almost sixty years before another woman would hold cabinet rank in the Republic of Ireland, when Máire Geoghegan-Quinn, a Fianna Fáil TD, was appointed Minister for the Gaeltacht (the Irish speaking communities) in 1979.

The 1921 General Election

The 1921 general election was held under the terms of the Government of Ireland Act 1920, which established separate Home Rule Parliaments in Northern Ireland and Southern Ireland (although this was never enacted in the south). All 128 candidates in the south were elected unopposed: 124 Sinn Féin and 4 Independent Unionist. The 124 Sinn Féin TDs constituted themselves as the second Dáil Éireann.

Disillusioned with how few women were selected by Sinn Féin in 1918 and by the lack of support given to the two women who had been nominated, feminists advocated for the selection of more women candidates in the 1921 election and called on women and men to vote for them. Meg

Connery, Vice-Chairwomen of the IWFL, wrote to the *Cork Examiner* three days before the election, reminding the nationalist and labour movements of the promises they had made in relation to women's equality in politics.

> At the general election of 1918 the women of Ireland were accorded one woman representative. It is up to Irishwomen and progressive Irishmen to see that the country is not treated to another example of political 'equality' of this kind. Republican and Labour forces have now a fresh opportunity of giving practical expression to their pledge of equal rights.[17]

Significantly, Sinn Féin selected and elected six women candidates. Constance Markievicz was returned, this time in Dublin South, and she was joined by Kathleen Clarke in Dublin Mid, Mary MacSwiney in Cork City, Dr Ada English in the National University of Ireland (NUI) constituency, Kathleen O'Callaghan in Limerick City and Limerick East, and Margaret Pearse in Dublin County.

Historians have emphasised that four of the six women TDs elected to the Second Dáil were relatives of dead Republican heroes.[18] Kathleen Clarke's husband, Thomas Clarke, and Margaret Pearse's two sons, Pádraig and William Pearse, were all executed for their role in the 1916 Easter Rising. Mary MacSwiney's brother Terence MacSwiney, Lord Mayor of Cork and Sinn Féin TD, died while on hunger strike in prison in 1920. Kathleen O'Callaghan's husband Michael O'Callaghan, a former Lord Mayor of Limerick, had been shot in her presence by British forces just two months before the election.

If they are mentioned at all, historians have tended to regard the women of the Second Dáil as 'the guardians of the revolutionary traditions and surrogates of memory'[19] – essentially as male replacements[20] – largely because of their unified opposition to the Anglo-Irish Treaty (as discussed in detail below). Importantly, the women themselves disputed this claim during the debates on the Treaty. A feminist analysis examining these women TDs as individuals and detailing their agency counterbalances the historical work that views these women primarily through the lens of their late husbands, brothers or sons.[21] They entered the Second Dáil for a myriad of political, ideological and personal reasons and not solely because of family. Though the connection these women had to deceased high profile men was undoubtedly important in the candidate selection process, few researchers have acknowledged that each had been involved in political and social causes prior to their election as TDs[22] and three had been imprisoned for

Republican activities. They were also well educated relative to ordinary Irish women of the day.[23] Furthermore, as Kathleen O'Callaghan argued during the Treaty debate, nationalist women had influenced the politics of their male relatives: 'It was the mother of the Pearses who made them what they were. The sister of Terence MacSwiney influenced her brother, and is now carrying on his life's work.'[24]

From a Fenian household in Limerick, Kathleen Clarke was an active campaigner prior to 1921. She had formed the first Committee of the Republican Prisoners' Dependent Fund in the aftermath of the 1916 Rising. Significantly, the Irish Republican Brotherhood (IRB) selected Clarke to be entrusted with plans for what should happen after the Rising. They felt she could be trusted to carry on with the work in the event of their arrest or death.[25] Clarke was a founder member and Vice-President of Cumann na mBan and became a member of the Sinn Féin Executive in 1917. She served as a district justice in the republican courts in Dublin during the War of Independence and was also chairperson of the judges. She was arrested for alleged involvement in the 'German Plot' in 1918 and was imprisoned in Holloway Jail with Constance Markievicz and Maud Gonne MacBride between June 1918 and February 1919. She also had electoral experience before serving as TD, being elected as an Alderman for Dublin Corporation in 1919.[26]

Mary MacSwiney's first political association was with the suffrage movement. After training and working as a teacher in Britain, she returned to Cork in 1904 and became a committee member of the Munster Women's Franchise League.[27] Partially but not exclusively because of her brother's influence, MacSwiney's interests shifted from women's equality to the nationalist cause and she was an ardent republican for the rest of her life.[28] She was a founder member of Cumann na mBan in Cork, holding the inaugural meeting of the branch in the MacSwiney home, and became the organisation's national vice-president in 1921. She joined Sinn Féin in 1917 and was active in the Gaelic language revival movement. She was also involved in the anti-conscription movement in 1918 and campaigned for her brother in the 1918 general election. McCoole notes that MacSwiney's republican sympathies were well known to the authorities and she was arrested and jailed after the Easter Rising.[29] She lost her job as a teacher as a result, so she established a girls school in her own home. After her brother's death in 1920, MacSwiney travelled to the United States to give evidence before the American Commission about conditions in Ireland during the War of Independence.

A professor in Mary Immaculate College until her marriage, Kathleen O'Callaghan 'took a distinguished part in the cultural, antiquarian and charitable life of Limerick'.[30] O'Callaghan was a founder member and Vice-President of Cumann na mBan in Limerick, where she was also a founder member of the Gaelic League. She collected money for the Prisoners' Dependents' Fund in the aftermath of the Easter Rising.[31] As she would later tell the Second Dáil, she was also active in the campaign for women's suffrage.

Of the four women TDs with familial connections, Margaret Pearse comes closest to being a 'token representative'. Pearse has been described as 'ill-equipped to cope with the prominent position her sons' fame had bequeathed her'.[32] She had, however, protected many men on the run, been a committee member of the Irish Volunteers' Dependants' Fund in 1916 and an honorary member of Cumann nBan between 1917 and 1918.[33] Pearse's biography suggests that she was an independent thinker of a strong nationalist background and greatly influenced the political views of her children.[34]

The charge of being symbolic representatives could not be made against the other two women, Constance Markievicz and Dr Ada English, as they had not experienced a close personal loss in the conflict. Nonetheless, they were often generalised in the same light. A letter to the editor of the *Irish Independent* in February 1922 for example described all six women TDs as 'bereaved women'.[35]

From a privileged background in County Sligo, Constance Markievicz was drawn to the cause of Irish independence through cultural nationalism and was active in various nationalist, socialist, labour, and suffrage campaigns.[36] As a member of the Irish Citizen Army, Markievicz was second-in-command at the St Stephen's Green and College of Surgeons garrisons in the Easter Rising. She was court-martialled and sentenced to death for her part in 1916, but later had her sentence commuted to penal servitude for life on account of her sex.[37] She was released under the general amnesty in 1917 but was re-arrested in May 1918.

Dr Ada English was one of the first women doctors in Ireland and pioneered much-needed reforms in psychiatry. She was a founder member and executive member of the Cumann na mBan branch in Ballinasloe, County Galway and also active in Sinn Féin.[38] Dr English was Medical Officer of the Irish Volunteers from the organisation's establishment in 1913 and was in Athenry during the Easter Rising (which was one of the few cases of activity outside of Dublin that week). She was close with many leading nationalist figures and was arrested and imprisoned for nine months in 1920 for possession of Cumann na mBan literature.[39]

Women TDs and the Anglo-Irish Treaty

The six women TDs elected in 1921 were, therefore, experienced political activists and held strong political and ideological beliefs.

We now turn to the significant contribution these women made to the Anglo-Irish Treaty debates in 1921 and 1922. The Irish War of Independence came to an end when a truce was called in July 1921. Irish women had paid a price: fifty women were jailed over the two- and-a-half years of war, and many women suspected of republican sympathies experienced domestic raids and physical and sexual violence at the hands of British forces.[40] A delegation was sent to London in October 1921 to negotiate the terms of a treaty, which included Arthur Griffith as head of the negotiating team and a reluctant Michael Collins. There were a number of women secretaries.[41] Some members of Cumann na mBan regretted the fact that no woman plenipotentiary was sent. They felt that, of all their high-profile members, Mary MacSwiney would have been a particularly good match for Prime Minister Lloyd George. MacSwiney herself claimed that she had asked de Valera to include her in the delegation, but he had refused because she was 'too extreme'.[42] MacSwiney was famously uncompromising and would not settle for anything else than an Irish Republic – which de Valera knew was not on the cards. She would thus have stalled the negotiations from the first day. Meanwhile, as the Treaty was being debated in the Dáil, an unnamed TD sarcastically asked Constance Markievicz why she did not go over to London instead. She replied, 'Why didn't you send me?'[43]

In December 1921, a treaty was signed by the plenipotentiaries. It required members of Dáil Éireann to take an Oath of Allegiance to the British Crown. It also provided for the division of Ireland into north and south and required the south to pay land annuities to Britain. The document was signed without consulting the cabinet. It was considered to be far from the Irish Republic that so many, including Mary MacSwiney, had wanted and made sacrifices for. The delegates knew this, but it was as much as they were going to get from the British negotiators. Furious, MacSwiney sent each of the Irish delegation a letter to tell them that they had made a grave mistake and urged them to reject the Treaty.[44] MacSwiney had made her lasting judgements on Griffith and Collins who (in her singular worldview) she now regarded as ideologically enslaved by the British.[45]

Debate over the Treaty began in the Dáil on 14 December. What ensued was weeks of acrimonious and deeply personal debate over the terms of the document, with the cabinet and Dáil deeply divided. The partition of the island and the fate of nationalists in Ulster were mentioned only in exceptional cases. Most opponents focused on the unacceptability of the Oath of Allegiance, which they regarded as continued rule by a foreign power, while TDs in favour argued that the Treaty represented the first step towards full freedom. Throughout the debates, women TDs were small in number but highly visible. As well as making their own extensive contributions, Constance Markieivicz and Mary MacSwiney regularly intercepted pro-Treaty speeches with comments and questions.

Each woman TD spoke against the terms of the Treaty and they claimed to represent the majority of Irish women in doing so. For example, Mary MacSwiney claimed to 'know the women of Ireland'[46] and Margaret Pearse knew 'the hearts and sorrows of the wives of Ireland'.[47] The all-male pro-Treaty side also argued that they represented female opinion on the Treaty. Women were accused by pro-Treaty TDs of emotionally evoking the ghosts of dead male martyrs to justify their stance, motivated solely by grief and anger and not reason. Finian Lynch, for example, argued that 'Now we have a great deal of emotion here and a great deal of emotional speeches about the dead. I say for myself that the bones of the dead have been rattled indecently in the face of this assembly'.[48]

Margaret Pearse asserted her right and the right of others 'to speak in the name of their dead'.[49] Most of her contribution focused on the legacies of her two sons, particularly Pádraig Pearse. She feared being haunted by the ghosts of her sons if she supported the Treaty. After outlining her own reasons for opposing the Treaty, Kathleen Clarke brought up her late husband Tom Clarke in the second half of her speech. She described seeing him before his execution in 1916, where he told her of his belief that they had struck the first blow for Irish freedom: 'I still believe in them'. Kathleen O'Callaghan stated that she had been elected on account of her husband's murder; she had 'paid a big price for that Treaty and for my right to stand here'. Nonetheless, she denied that women TDs were opposed to the Treaty solely because of personal loss: 'The women of An Dáil are women of character, and they will vote for principle, not for expediency'.[50]

As Knirck argues,[51] there is no doubt that women TDs understood the symbolic importance of using their familial connections to the dead. There were many attempts to discredit them for doing this, even questions raised about their mental stability, but the discourse gave women TDs considerable sway over shaping the debates.[52] However, a gendered re-reading of the debates shows that not all women deputies were prepared to adopt this narrative. Mary MacSwiney, who spoke for four-and-a-half hours in total throughout the debates, refused to conjure the tragic image of her dead brother (even as others did do) and opposed the Treaty on her own ideological terms. Constance Markievicz, who had no martyred relatives, was one of only two TDs to represent working-class interests. In a lengthy speech of opposition, Dr Ada English stated that she had 'no dead men to throw in my teeth as a reason for holding the opinions I hold' and disputed the argument that other women TDs only had opinions because of personal grievances.[53]

The 1922 Franchise Debate

Despite the external confidence exhibited by pro-Treaty TDs that they were the 'true' representatives of female opinion on the Treaty, no one really knew how women would vote on the issue. The united stand taken by women TDs against the terms of the Treaty must have given the pro-Treaty side cause for concern in regard to the full enfranchisement of Irish women on equal terms with men.[54] Hostility was likely entrenched by the fact that Cumann na mBan was the first organisation to vote against the ratification of the Treaty: 419 against and 63 in favour.[55] In the aftermath of the Treaty split in March 1922, Kathleen O'Callaghan proposed that women over 21 should be given the right to vote at the next election, in accordance with the promises of equal suffrage made in the 1916 Proclamation. Hanna Sheehy Skeffington, in an article in the *Irish Freeman* in May 1922, estimated that women aged between 21 and 30 would account for about one-seventh of the electorate if enfranchised.[56] A former member of a suffrage society, Deputy O'Callaghan's reasoning for extending the vote to these women was primarily a nationalist one – young women had played their part in the struggle for Ireland and had earned their say in the country's constitutional future: 'During these last years of war and terror, these women in their twenties took their share in the dangers. They have purchased their right to the franchise and they have purchased their right to a say in this all-important question before the country.'[57]

Constance Markievicz spoke strongly in favour of O'Callaghan's motion, stating that the suffrage movement had been her first bite 'at the apple of freedom' and made reference to the 'young women and young girls who took a man's part in the Terror'.[58] The whole debate was a curious affair, so entangled as it was with the Treaty question. A number of male anti-Treaty TDs who had been less than enthusiastic about gender equality in the past now found themselves advocating for full suffrage rights, whereas pro-Treaty TDs who previously supported full enfranchisement were now arguing against it.[59] Pro-Treaty TDs accused Kathleen O'Callaghan and her supporters of trying to bring down the Treaty. O'Callaghan responded that the pro-Treaty faction had no reason to fear more women voters if they truly believed themselves to be representatives of female opinion on the Treaty – a large women's vote in favour would strengthen the ratification of the document and not threaten it, she pointed out. Arthur Griffith, himself a long-time supporter of votes for women, had advised an IWFL delegation that there was no time to update the electoral register before the general election and that the Dáil did not yet have the power to update the franchise. To the disappointment of feminist campaigners, Griffith pledged that his government would fully enfranchise women voters after the next general election. O'Callaghan's motion was lost, with thirty-eight votes in favour and forty-seven against.

All six women deputies ran in the general election when it was held in June 1922, but only Mary MacSwiney in Cork City and Kate O'Callaghan in Limerick City were re-elected (O'Callaghan was unopposed), both in constituencies with strong anti-Treaty sentiment.[60] Pro-Treaty Sinn Féin TDs won 45 per cent of the vote and anti-Treaty Sinn Féin TDs 28 per cent. Pro-Treaty candidates received over 75 per cent of the vote in total. The results showed that, contrary to their claims, women TDs and Cumann na mBan were not reflective of the opinions of ordinary women voters (at least those under 30 who met minimum property or education requirements). Women voters wanted peace and sided with the Provisional Government. Anti-Treaty Sinn Féin TDs refused to take their seats in the third Dáil, which never assembled due to the outbreak of Civil War.

Women's Representation in Post-revolutionary Ireland

The Constitution of the Irish Free State in 1922, which formally ratified the Anglo-Irish Treaty, had a largely liberal-democratic ethos and dropped women's voting age to 21 (Article 12). Article 3 also made reference to wider citizenship rights and responsibilities 'without distinction of sex'. Many suffrage campaigners were initially optimistic about the constitutional rights being guaranteed to women and hoped that women's full enfranchisement would further improve the position of women in Irish society.[61] However, the statute book shows that a gender-based definition of citizenship was envisaged by the Free State government, one which ascribed different roles and functions to women and men. In spite of feminist opposition, a series of legislative changes were introduced by the Cumann na nGaedheal and Fianna Fáil governments during the 1920s and 1930s which severely restricted women's participation in the public, economic and social affairs of the new State.[62] A rigid division was created between the public and private spheres, although the government, the Roman Catholic Church and even most women saw the primary role of women in independent Ireland as a wife and mother. As had been the case before independence, feminists were concerned that 'a woman's domestic role appeared to undermine her rights as an equal citizen'.[63] Despite women's activities in the nationalist, labour and feminist movements and their participation in early Dáil elections and the establishment of all new political parties, there was now a clear sense that women should undertake their duties as citizens in the home and not in the public domain. The growing dominance of the Roman Catholic Church, and its nexus with a more conservative generation of political leaders relative to the 1916 signatories, heavily impacted on the gender ideology of the Irish Free State. While gender roles in the revolutionary period were relatively fluid, in the post-revolutionary period they were very rigid.[64]

The position that women TDs and Cumann na mBan had taken on the Anglo-Irish Treaty is fundamental to understanding the subsequent role of women in political life in Ireland.[65] Their fervent opposition to the document – which was interpreted by pro-Treaty factions as outright opposition to peace after many years of bloody conflict – constructed a discourse among male political elites, the Roman Catholic Church and wider society that women were too inflexible, bitter and emotional for politics. Republican women were seen as 'abnormal individuals'.[66] Pro-Treaty historian, P.S. O'Hegarty wrote that republican women were 'practically unsexed'[67] and 'the implacable and irrational upholders of death and destruction'.[68] When Mary MacSwiney and other republican women campaigned against W.T. Cosgrave's re-election as President of the Free State in 1923, *The Irish Times* reported that the President argued that they 'should have rosaries in their hands or be at home with knitting needles'.[69] The 1922 election had illustrated that republican women were not representative of 'ordinary women' and this gave the Free State further armour to suppress them. The aforementioned legislative changes introduced by the Free State, which essentially bound women's lives to the home, created further socio-cultural obstacles to women's participation in politics. These pieces of legislation were likely introduced, at least in part, to symbolically and literally control and punish republican women. It was also the case that, by opposing the Treaty, women TDs had self-excluded themselves from serving in politics at a time when the norms of parliamentary democracy in Ireland were being established.[70] They were also deprived of first-hand political experience. As a result of all these factors, women were significantly under-represented in Dáil Éireann for many decades after independence. The political system[71] was dominated by two parties, Cumann na nGaedheal-Fine Gael and Fianna Fáil, and neither was sympathetic to women's political equality[72] – but were content with party women to work 'in the background'.[73]

Five women TDs were elected to the Fourth Dáil in August 1923. Constance Markievicz, Mary MacSwiney and Dr Kathleen Lynn were all re-elected as republican candidates. They were joined by Caitlin Brugha in Waterford, a widow of Deputy Cathal Brugha, who was killed by Free State troops a month before the election. Sinn Féin deputies refused to take their seats in the Fourth Dáil. The only woman to take her seat was Margaret Collins-O'Driscoll, a sister of the late Michael Collins, who was elected as a Cumann na nGaedheal TD in Dublin North.

During the short-lived Fifth Dáil (June–August 1927), Collins-O'Driscoll was joined by Constance Markievicz (who was too ill to participate and died in July), Kathleen Clarke and Caitlín Brugha. The three women TDs then took their seats in Dáil Éireann (in Markievicz's case symbolically) as members of the new Fianna Fáil party. Meanwhile, Mary MacSwiney, Dr Kathleen Lynn and Caitlin Brugha had stayed with the now-struggling Sinn Féin (MacSwiney became the party's 'de facto' leader and vice-president). The party could only run fifteen candidates in June 1927 and elected six TDs – all men. MacSwiney and Dr Lynn both saw their share of the first preference vote half, relative to the 1923 general election (illustrative of the loss in Sinn Féin support nationally) and neither would serve as parliamentarians again. Brugha, meanwhile, had retired from electoral politics after one Dáil term.

Cumann na nGaedheal's Margaret Collins-O'Driscoll was the only woman TD elected to the Sixth Dáil, which sat between September 1927 and 1932. Kathleen Clarke unsuccessfully ran for Fianna Fáil in the same constituency as her, Dublin North, in the general election, and an independent woman candidate, Kate McCarry, ran in Donegal (receiving just 164 votes). As a bearer of the much-respected 'Collins' name and its intimate associations with the establishment of the Irish Free State, and as Cumann na nGaedheal vice-president between 1926 and 1927 – in addition to being the only woman TD for five years – Collins-O'Driscoll was undoubtedly placed in a difficult situation when faced with legislation strongly opposed by the women's movement, and she rarely spoke on women's issues.[74] Her contribution to the 1925 Civil Service Regulation Bill, which confined State examinations for senior civil service posts to men, was cautious. While 'by no means in love with it'[75] and accepting that it did place some limitations on women, Collins-O'Driscoll did not believe that it infringed on women's constitutional rights. She argued that she was elected to represent a wide community, not because of her sex, and that women voters in the next election could elect women TDs to amend the legislation if they wished. Collins-O'Driscoll also supported 1929 censorship legislation banning access to written information about birth control.

Although various women's organisations attempted to break the 'male monopoly' of Irish electoral politics, the 1930s through to the early 1970s was a bleak period for women's representation in Dáil Éireann. No general election returned more than five women TDs at a time. In a party recruitment system that was highly male-gendered and increasingly localised, most women TDs had to rely on political dynasties as an entry route to politics.[76] Many men elected to the Dáil over the twentieth century also succeeded a relative. However, in proportional terms women TDs were historically more reliant on these connections in such a conservative climate. The vast majority of women deputies elected between the 1930s and the 1970s were widows (or sometimes daughters) of deceased male TDs. By-elections were particularly important for this phenomenon as political parties attempted to capitalise on the 'sympathy vote' after a local TD's death.[77] It should be emphasised that while women relatives were advantaged relative to other women, they were not guaranteed an easy route to selection or election, and some faced gendered resistance in their attempt to enter public life.[78] Ireland was not alone in electing widows to office in this period. The term the 'widow's mandate' or the 'widow's succession' was first coined in the United States, such was the prevalence of women succeeding their deceased spouse in the Congress.[79]

Like the first generation of women TDs, the election of women from the 1930s to the 1970s was often linked to personal tragedy and death. A number of authors have minimised their role as political representatives. For example, McElroy describes them as 'honorary men'[80] and Manning similarly concludes that:

Thus, in the half century of independence, the impact of women on Irish politics in both numerical representation and quality of that representation has been slight. Indeed, it is difficult to ignore the judgment of one leading feminist and historian, Dr Margaret MacCurtain, who wrote in 1978: 'Irish women in post-revolutionary Ireland did not make political traditions; they inherited them from fathers, husbands and brothers.'[81]

That women TDs over this period nearly 'always placed party before sex' and rarely made feminist contributions to parliamentary debates, at a time when women's rights were being eroded, has been lamented.[82] However, their efforts in politics must be placed 'in a context of a social and political life that was inimical to the participation of women'.[83] Most of these women TDs focused on constituency-related matters as opposed to national issues but so did male TDs.[84] The main role of a backbench TD was to provide local representation and this was, and still is, the driving factor for electoral success. As a result, most women TDs of this 'wave' had long-established political careers (in many cases longer than their husbands) and impressive results at the polls. They provided a service that was expected of them by constituents. The parliamentary record also suggests that a number of women TDs did speak to women's everyday concerns, even if the discourse was not 'feminist' in tone.[85] Through their constituency work women TDs were almost certainly aware of issues and difficulties specific to women in Irish society, but the nature of the political climate meant that many social issues could not be placed on the parliamentary agenda.[86]

Conclusion

Despite the political gains made by women in the 1918 and 1921 general elections, this chapter has shown that women were soon 'faded out' of national politics in the post-revolutionary era. It would be the 1977 general election before the number of women TDs matched what was achieved in 1921. This is at odds with numerous democracies in Western Europe, where the proportion of women representatives increased, if slowly, in the decades following suffrage. The united position that women TDs took on the terms of the Anglo-Irish Treaty (one that appears to have been at odds with ordinary women voters), in addition to the rigidifying of gender roles in the post-revolutionary period, acted to suppress opportunities for Irish women to enter public life. The consequences of this historical under-representation remain to this day.

Importantly, this research also offers a reappraisal of the early generations of women parliamentarians in the Republic of Ireland. Previous scholarship analyses the selection, election and political priorities of these women largely through their connections to dead men – they are often characterised as surrogates. This discourse persists in relation to the republican women TDs of the early 1920s and the 'widows and daughters' elected from the 1930s onwards. This chapter puts forward a more critical, feminist reading of the history of women's representation in Dáil Éireann. It emphasises early women TDs as individuals with political agency but also illustrates the institutional constraints of the male-gendered political culture that they entered into. Familial connections to national revolutionaries or local TDs undoubtedly gave these women an advantage in the candidate selection process and election contests relative to other women. However, the politics of most historical women TDs likely came from a myriad of influences, including their own personal backgrounds and records of political activism, and not solely out a sense of duty to men.

PART II

Chapter 6

Towards a Further Understanding of the Sexual and Gender-based Violence Women Experienced in the Irish Revolution

LINDA CONNOLLY

During armed conflicts women's bodies become battlefields. Was the 'Irish revolution' an *exception*, however, in this regard? Peter Burke has stated that anthropologists became aware of the problem of 'collective amnesia'

> in investigating oral traditions, while historians encountered it in the course of studying events such as the Holocaust or civil wars of the twentieth century in Finland, Ireland, Russia, Spain and elsewhere. The problem is not a loss of memory at the individual level but the disappearance from public discourse of certain events ... These events are in a sense 'repressed' not necessarily because they were traumatic, though many of them were, but because it has become politically inconvenient to refer to them.[1]

Serious and destructive forms of violence perpetrated against women during this phase of Ireland's revolution certainly disappeared from public discourse for decades after the Civil War ended. Conservative attitudes to women, sex and sexuality in the new State combined with a desire to forget the worst atrocities of the War of Independence and Civil War, and the absence of a subsequent truth or reconciliation process, ensured any violence perpetrated against women during the revolution was not addressed. Recently it has come to light that investigations into atrocities against women and trials for violence, rape and sexual assault did take place in this period but they remained closed and hidden in military archives (British and Irish) and other sources for many decades. Documentation in relation to compensation claims and pension applications for select groups of women (southern loyalists and republican activists, for instance) also highlights numerous incidences of violence perpetrated. Newspaper reports and other documents also contain valuable evidence. As contemporary Ireland enters the final phase of a decade of centenaries, further consideration of some of the more horrific aspects of the War of Independence and Civil War is anticipated. Women's experience must be equally considered and explained.

The international journal *Feminist Review* published an early, seminal study of the violence women experienced in the War of Independence in 2000 by sociologist Louise Ryan that was informed by long-established theories of gender-based violence. Similar work in this area appeared much later in the discipline of modern Irish history, with some scholars recently focusing on counting the number of reported rapes, concluding the Irish revolution may have experienced exceptionally low rates of sexual crime in particular. The framing of transgressive violence as predominantly perpetrated by men against men combined with 'collective amnesia' about women's experience was the established framework for decades in Irish revolutionary studies, and this perspective has some continuity in the field. Ryan's research revealed both cases of forced hair cutting (endemic during the War of Independence) and sexual assaults, primarily reported in the *Irish Bulletin* periodical and newspapers.[2] Although her findings were largely met with silence for some time in the discipline of history, sophisticated archival and documentary research on gender, war and violence was developing in other fields internationally, including in European history, war studies, the social sciences and feminist theory.[3] Research on hair cutting in Ireland's revolution is therefore not 'new' or novel as can be frequently inferred in commentary.

Some ten years later in 2010, Ann Matthews drew more sustained attention to these issues in Irish historical studies in her study of republican women:

> One aspect of the war missing from the historiography of the War of Independence is the issue of 'the war on women' (by both sides) in the form of physical and sexual abuse. This has not been adequately addressed and has never been discussed in a historical context, perhaps because public discussion of sexual assault and rape in war is a modern phenomenon. While being careful not to place the context of the modern world onto this period, it is necessary to record that women and their families suffered a terror that was not confined to armed

conflict. Caught between the violence of the reprisals perpetuated by the IRA and the Black and Tans, the lives of women within the population descended into a living nightmare.[4]

In 2013, Charles Townshend subsequently noted:

> Women were targeted less often, though dozens of members of republican families or of Cumann na mBan had their hair cut off with scissors or razors – in mirror images of Volunteer assaults on women who were seen with policeman or soldiers. Many more were verbally abused and intimidated, usually deliberately, though of course any night raid was inescapably alarming to the women who experienced it.[5]

The figure of 'dozens' is not verified, however, and no evidence is provided to back up the claim that republican women were targeted less than men. The excavation of new evidence from across a range of sources suggests the incidence of this kind of violence, across different groups of women, was initially underestimated. Other scholars have recently started to identify the coercive practice of forced hair cutting and/or sexual assault in new archives.[6] Forced hair cutting is now generally accepted as a known and widespread gender-specific practice in the Irish revolution and in particular the War of Independence, twenty years after Ryan had established this in Irish sociology, but different conclusions have been arrived at on the incidence, scale and wider definition of sexual violence, including rape.[7] Hughes, for instance, concluded from a snapshot of RIC data that rape seemed to remain relatively rare during Ireland's revolution while the most common act of violence carried out against women by the IRA was the cutting of hair:

> There are no reports of rape or sexual violence against women among the précis and, notwithstanding reticence in reporting such crime, it seems to have remained relatively rare during the Irish revolution.[8]

In a review of Gemma Clark's study of surviving compensation claims specifically made by 'southern Irish loyalists' to British and Free State governments in three counties – Limerick, Waterford and Tipperary – Charles Townshend likewise concludes that Ireland 'did not suffer the use of rape as a weapon of war'.[9] However, the full examination of a wider range of sources that can document more comprehensively how other groups or categories of women also experienced violence during the War of Independence and Civil War period (British, Free State and anti-Treaty) requires greater consideration before such a definitive conclusion can be arrived at.

Sexual and gender-based violence in the Irish revolution was a serious problem that can be increasingly identified in sources across all counties in Ireland. As this chapter demonstrates, at least nine serious cases of military rape and sexual assault (two of them gang rapes and another an attempted gang rape) can be identified for the Civil War period alone, including in Moate, County Westmeath (rape), Kenmare, County Kerry (two women assaulted and a rape allegation made), Foxford, County Mayo (gang rape), Dromitee, County Armagh, (two women raped or sexually assaulted), Dromineer, County Tipperary (gang rape), County Roscommon (rape) and Tankardstown, County Meath (rape and attempted gang rape).[10] Such attacks took place during raids on private houses (including two public houses, where the women resided) involving at least twenty anti-Treaty, Free State and B-Special combatants in total in the overall violence. A new research agenda is increasingly uncovering some evidence of other possible cases, including in Irish language sources and institutional records previously unavailable.

Different definitions and understandings of rape as a weapon of war are also informing debates about the true scale of sexual violence in Irish history. Sexual violence in the Irish revolution is by definition going to be different to large wars in terms of structure and incidence. The phenomenon of rape 'as a weapon of war' does not, for instance, always mean 'mass' rape or rape-focused units on expansive battle fronts.[11] Rape as an asymmetrical war tactic, crime and injury to women is not just genocidal – it can occur on a more isolated and individual basis, depending on the extent and structure of a conflict, as this chapter demonstrates. The Irish revolution was obviously not conducted as a 'world war' with a front between two expansive armies, nor did it produce genocide. Guerrilla tactics instead influenced very serious attacks made on Irish women that cannot be diminished. As Goldstone states: 'Whereas conventional warfare relies on fighters who are massed in large-scale military units in regular formations … guerrilla warfare relies on smaller numbers of mobile fighters, in irregular-sized units, living off the land or blending into and supplied by the local population'.[12]

A tendency to treat cases of hair cutting and rape as entirely separate activities is also evident in Irish revolutionary studies. However, an interconnected spectrum of gender-based violence perpetrated is evident both in numerous studies of gender and wartime violence internationally and in how individual women actually experienced violence during the Irish revolution. The cases addressed in this chapter demonstrate a range of incidents that encompassed some or even all of the following, to varying degrees: (1) 'sexual harassment' (for instance, a woman was labelled a 'soldier's totty' and 'molested' if she walked on the same side of the street as British soldiers in Dublin)[13] and rough searching; (2) hair cutting, cropping, shearing, pulling or 'bobbing'; (3) hair cutting assaults combined with other physical injury/assault/harassment; (4) physical attack and injury (such as a beating or assault with a rifle/implement/fists/belts); (5) assault and sexual attack involving rape or gang rape; (6) and murder or kidnapping combined with some or even all of the above.

The legal and cultural premise throughout Irish history, that a woman was culpable in her rape unless she could prove otherwise, is a consideration in terms of ascertaining the scale of sexual violence. Women under-reported sexual crimes (or 'hushed them up') and perpetrators were often acquitted or not charged in many cases. Furthermore, there was little incentive for a woman to publicise or subsequently pursue and risk documenting a violation – her future safety, respectability, reputation and future marital prospects were at stake. Women who lost chastity were 'fallen' and blamed for the condition, irrespective of the circumstances. In agreement with D'Cruze therefore, 'Consequently historical study of this topic (perhaps more than most others) is necessarily a discourse on and around the surviving evidences, not an unmediated description of "what happened".'[14]

This chapter provides an analysis of 'surviving evidences' of gender-based violence and sexual violence in the period covering the War of Independence and Civil War in Ireland.[15] The incidence of sexual and gender-based violence is a 'hidden history' that requires in-depth research and recovery work across different sources.[16] Case studies explored suggest that the assertion that sexual assault was 'rare' both during the War of Independence and Civil War, and the years between, has not been adequately proven yet. More in-depth research across a wider range of sources, rather than singular sources or collections focused on just some regions or groups of women impacted by conflict, is required first. The case for a more expanded perspective on female sexuality, the policing of women's bodies, sexual violence, physical violence, psychological trauma and harassment of women in the Irish revolution is made. Deleterious sexual and sexualised assaults on women in Ireland (involving hair cutting, rape and other forms of violence) occurred in the context of a wider cultural and symbolic system of power, sexuality, gender and violence that did not discriminate. Republican women, women associated with the Crown and the RIC, and women engaged in private relationships and friendships with British soldiers were all targeted. Sustained analysis of both non-State and State violence in the revolution cannot be confined to just well-known and very shocking events or to one type of violence. Women from all backgrounds were impacted in different ways. As Marie Coleman has demonstrated, women also experienced psychological violence, caused by ongoing harassment, fear and intimidation, or from witnessing killing or transgressive violence towards others, including loved ones and other women.[17] The cases referred to in this chapter demonstrate how physical violence, sexual violence and psychological violence interacted. In short, evidence exists to suggest that women were labelled, humiliated, disciplined, policed, stigmatised, controlled, hurt, abused and in some cases killed in different ways throughout this period. Any study seeking to fully understand the violent history of the Irish revolution must acknowledge, investigate and explain why this occurred and why it was ignored for so long.

Hair

Forcibly cutting hair is a symbolic and bodily violation that involves unwanted physical contact between aggressors and victims. Moreover, it is intrinsically *sexual*. Historically, a woman's hair has long been regarded as a potent symbol of her sexuality. Throughout history adulteress women, for instance, had their heads shaved as a punishment. Forcibly cutting and taking hair by attacking a woman's head also physically breached her bodily autonomy and consent, as the woman was often 'taken', escorted, captured, pulled, tied up, blindfolded, gagged and/or physically held down and hurt by (predominantly) men in the process. Women's hair is remarkably significant in understanding how gender and sexuality shaped the Irish revolution. Forced cutting, shaving, cropping or shearing of women's hair was practised widely. Reference to it crops up in numerous archival and popular sources. Conor Heffernan describes such a scene from Ken Loach's 2006 film, *The Wind that Shakes the Barley*:

> Troops storm into the house and forcibly evict those inside. Screams of terror emanate from the house, growing louder and louder with each moment. Soon the house will be set on fire. In the melee that ensues, troops single out a woman known for collaborating with the enemy. Held down at gunpoint, her head is shaved. In the distance, fighters from the other side look on as she wails.[18]

Similarly, in an earlier cultural reference, the fictional character of Rose in the 1970 film *Ryan's Daughter* had her hair cut to the scalp with a clippers by a woman in front of an angry village crowd, for having an extramarital affair with a British officer.

Removing and taking women's hair is a deep-rooted practice in many cultures over time and place. Forcible shearing of hair also occurred with some regularity later during 'the Troubles' in Northern Ireland, often combined with 'tarring and feathering' in the early 1970s, and reportedly in agrarian conflicts in the nineteenth century. Coerced hair cutting was and is a serious assault. Frequently, it hurt because of the force involved in cropping or shaving a woman who may be dragged and held down. Mary or Mollie Alleway,[19] for example, active in the Youghal branch of Cumann na mBan, described how she was beaten by British troops and had her hair cut off, while her house was raided several times during the War of Independence. The public marker or humiliation of having a visibly scalped head within the community followed. For instance, Madge Daly, first President of the Limerick branch of Cumann na mBan in her witness statement, stated, 'We were raided regularly, our business place was set on fire, and our furniture seized for unpaid fines imposed by courts martial. My sister was dragged out of the house one night, her hair was shorn off and her hand cut with a razor'. Mrs Geraldine Dillon from Galway (a sister of Joseph M. Plunkett, executed in 1916) remarked in her statement that in County Galway in 1920: 'Certain houses had practically daily raids … Four girls had their hair cut off, which was more of a tragedy then than it would be now'. Seán Broderick, also from Galway, stated 'my sister Peg was taken out by Black and Tans who cut off her hair to the scalp and attempted to burn down our home after doing a considerable amount of damage'.[20] The hair could also be pulled and roughly handled with other injuries inflicted at the same time (such as cuts from razors or shears combined with physical assault, beatings, shouting, touching, blind-folding and mob behaviour by perpetrators). The violence of some of the attacks widely reported nationally in Ireland, and the number of often masked men who typically participated in them, is disturbing. On 28 July 1920, *The Irish Times* reported that two girls in Granard, County Longford were overpowered by 'a dozen young men and their hair was cut off, because it was alleged they spoke to soldiers. The girls had been previously warned'. A public court case in Galway involving an outrage near Tuam was reported in detail in the *Westmeath Examiner* on 15 May 1920. Bridget Keegan's hair was cut off when seven masked men entered her father's house at 12.45 a.m. on 30 April. Members of the family testified, and Jack, Frank and William Jordan (three brothers) were sentenced to six months, hard labour for the offence, with another man discharged. Brandishing revolvers, they took the girl, who had fainted and was unconscious, out to the yard in her nightdress and cut the hair off with shears, telling her sister 'that is what she got for going with Tommies'. While one of the men was cutting her hair he sang 'We are out for Ireland free'. Mr Golding C.S. said in court that it was a 'blackguardly action': 'Having attempted to free Ireland ... by cutting off the girl's hair, to complete the freedom of Ireland they proposed to cut off her ears but they didn't do so'. Dr Thompson from Tuam said the girl was suffering from shock and was still under his care. Likewise the *Belfast Newsletter* on 30 June 1920 reported 'Rebel gallantry Girls' Hair Cut Off in County Kerry': 'about 1 a.m. on the morning of 26 [June] a party of men, fifteen to twenty in number, armed and disguised, called at a house in Tralee and forcibly dragged two girls into the roadway. They knocked them down and in other ways brutally assaulted them, and then, whilst two men held their heads, a third cut their hair off with a pair of shears, and, not content with this outrage, they poured tar over the girls' heads'.

Why is hair attacked in wars? Pergament explains how hair on the head is not just a physiological phenomenon, it also has important social functions that are gendered.[21] Hair, she writes, is an object of intense elaboration and preoccupation in almost all societies and cultures throughout time. In many cultures hair played an important role in the development of social constructs of the body, power and sexuality. Past uses of hair as a means of social control and dehumanisation have influenced the meaning of 'hair taking' by states.[22] Pergament shows some cultures believe that a link remains between the individual and the severed hair, allowing the person who gained possession of the locks to exert power. Hair also often serves in different cultures as a symbol of women's virginal state – power and sexuality are implicated. Pergament notes that, in keeping with this symbolism, when legislating for damage to different parts of the body, the *fueros* (local codes of law and custom in the Iberian Peninsula) listed penalties for seizing a woman by the hair. These codes suggest that the 'violation' of hair was seen as a violation of the woman's honour.[23]

Enforced cutting of hair in the dehumanisation and sanctioning of women was conducted by both sides in the War of Independence in Ireland – crown forces and IRA. Hair taking was systematically used to sanction and dishonour Irish women who were considered overly familiar with the enemy or informers, and it was also inflicted by both sides to assert power and dominance. Women's hair therefore served as a site of symbolic power and acceptable violence that could be widely transgressed and abused by all sides in the conflict.

How did the Irish situation compare to the practice elsewhere? Hair cutting or shaving on a systematic scale is prevalent in later, much larger historical and contemporary conflicts. At the end of the Second World War, over 20,000 French people accused of collaboration with Germany endured a particularly humiliating act of revenge – their heads were shaved in public.[24] Nearly all those punished were women and this episode in French history continues to provoke shame and unease. In 1944–45, photographers like Robert Capa and Carl Mydan documented the terrible brutality to women accused of sexual collaborations with the Germans. The question has arisen, would historians have subsequently believed this happened if it was not photographed so extensively? According to Duchen, 'les femmes tondues', or 'the shorn women', were paraded through the streets bald and stripped to their slips with swastikas painted on their chests and foreheads, oftentimes with their own lipstick.[25] Thousands of women were reported to have committed 'collaboration horizontale'. Sadly, she writes, what is absent from these reports is whether or not these women consented to their crimes – meaning that many women may have been punished and shamed for their own rapes.[26] Stiles describes the public spectacle involved:

> The community gathered in French towns and villages to shear her head with animal clippers and then smear the sign of the swastika in soot on her bald forehead. The citizens judged her a 'horizontal collaborator' for having sex with German soldiers during World War II. Denigrated and denounced as a whore, she was even stripped naked sometimes before being paraded through town, a token of the emblematic territories, defamations, and controls of war. She remained solitary amidst the molesting, persecuting assembly, exiled in a particularly sordid historical moment in a throng of her countrymen and women.[27]

Forced head shaving is also widely documented in other civil wars that occurred after the civil war in Ireland, including the Spanish (1936–39) and Greek Civil Wars (1946–49) for instance, and in other more contemporary wars.[28] In Spain, female relatives of executed socialists also suffered the humiliation of public soiling by being forced to ingest castor oil, as well as head shaving and rapes. Julia Eichenberg also demonstrated that the cutting, shearing and shaving of hair was a form of violence frequently used in both Ireland and Poland, especially following accusations of alleged sexual and political betrayal:

> Similar excesses occurred in Belgium, where head-shaving was used to punish women who had become involved with Germans. After the Second World War shearing was taken up in several countries to humiliate and punish women 'traitors'. One significant distinction in Ireland and Poland lies in the category of victims. In Ireland,

the victims were almost exclusively women. Women were shorn on suspicion of spying, passing on information and betraying the new state. It was sufficient to be seen with the wrong men (members of the crown forces, sons of well-off Protestants, or ex-soldiers of the British army) ... The shearing of women therefore bears an explicit gendered, if not sexual connotation. Since women symbolised the fertility and the future of the young nation, their liaisons with the 'enemy' could not be tolerated.[29]

Reports in newspapers and other sources record systematic evidence of Irish rebels and crown forces inflicting this punishment in the War of Independence. Eileen Barker, for instance, had her head shaved at gunpoint by members of the IRA – for allowing British troops to stay in her hotel. According to Heffernan:

Head shaving was a deliberate violation of victims' femininity. Whilst the cutting itself was painful, the aftermath could be worse as the shaved woman became a symbol of betrayal and a warning to others. Newspaper reports suggest that in most instances the attack took place at night, as was the case for Julia Goonan who was taken at midnight by her attackers, hung up by her hair and shaved. Occasionally shavings took place in fields, when, finally exhausted from fleeing her pursuers, women were run to ground. Spurred on by the cheers of their compatriots, the attackers shaved the women's heads as punishment for their perceived indiscretions.[30]

Swithin Walsh refers to a case in Castlecomer, County Kilkenny. John Curran, a miner, brought a successful case to a Kilkenny court requesting compensation for the forced haircutting of his daughter Mary and his niece Julia Tobin, who were taken far away from the home through fields on 25 May 1921:

The girls were accused by the local IRA of 'keeping company with the Black and Tans'. On the night in question, at home around 11.00 p.m., 19-year-old Mary was sitting at the fireplace of her home with her two brothers and sister when a knock was heard at their door. There were around twelve armed men outside who told Mary's parents they 'wanted her for a moment'. They took her down the road where she was joined by her cousin Julia, who had been required to get out of bed to go with the men. Both women were then blindfolded and brought 'a considerable distance' through fields. At a location that was unknown to them, they were informed of the charge and penalty ... their hair was cut. Both women were brought back to their homes at around 1.00 a.m.[31]

Witness statements in the 'Bureau of Military History' also indicate that unlike later instances of hair cutting in Europe, including those that occurred in public in France after the Second World War, terrifying head shavings in Ireland were often performed in isolated locations away from the masses and those who could intervene. The public–private divide in the performance of such violence during Ireland's revolution is therefore an important issue in understanding its scale and nature compared to other wars. The more private nature of these attacks suggests there was also the potential for inflicting additional, unspoken-about violence.

The sexual justification for 'bobbing' the hair of women considered fraternising with British soldiers was described in the witness statement of Leo Buckley, a member of the Cork No. 1 Brigade, IRA, 1918–1922:

> I remember at the time, young girls from Cork going out to Ballincollig to meet the British soldiers. We curbed this by bobbing the hair of persistent offenders. Short hair was completely out of fashion at the period and the appearance of a girl with 'bobbed' hair clearly denoted her way of life.[32]

Whether or not the women bobbed were working prostitutes or just labelled for befriending soldiers is not clear but the 'way of life' remark suggests policing women's 'suspect' sexuality motivated the hair shearing. Women were also targeted as suspected collaborators or informers. In another incident, a young woman had her hair reportedly cut off for passing on information to an RIC man. Michael Higgins of Belclare, County Galway (a member of Sylane Company, Tuam Battalion, 1917–21) recalled:[33]

> I remember (although I cannot remember the date or the year) going to Barnaderg Company area with Thomas Hussey and Brigade O/C Con Fogarty and shearing the hair off the head of a young girl. She had written to an RIC man giving him information about Volunteer activities and the letter was captured in a raid on the mails. We brought the letter with us and Brigadier Fogarty read it for the girl and her people when we arrived at the house, which we were shown by one of the Dunleavy brothers of Barnaderg who were all officers in the Volunteers. The girl admitted writing the letter. Brigadier Fogarty gave them a lecture on

the gravity of the offence and said she was being treated leniently in having her hair cut off. There was a scene. The girl was crying and her people were sprinkling holy water on her and on us. She was a very beautiful girl before her hair was sheared and I pitied her, although I knew I should not in the circumstances.

Hair cutting is mentioned in numerous witness statements submitted by men and women in the military archives. Elizabeth Bloxham, a Cumann na mBan activist, for instance reported in her statement of 1951, 'These were the days when girls were roughly searched and had their hair cut off by British soldiers'.[34] Peg Broderick-Nicholson from Galway, a well-known republican, described how she was called out from her bed and her hair was cut 'to the scalp with very blunt scissors'.[35]

RIC reports also contain numerous references to hair cutting during the War of Independence alongside a range of other punishments perpetrated, such as kidnapping and assaults:

> CO SLIGO. At 11 p.m. on 18-05-21 twelve armed and disguised men entered the residence of Mrs. Feeney, Cliffoney, Sligo district, a woman in poor health and cut off the hair of her two daughters, owing to having spoken to some members of the Cliffoney Constabulary. The Feeney family were warned they would be shot if they reported the matter to the authorities.
>
> ...
>
> CO CLARE. At 2 a.m. on 9-7-21 Miss B. Burke was kidnapped from her mother's home 2 miles from Kilrush by a number of I.R.A. raiders. Miss Burke who is a typist in the Victoria Barracks, Cork, was home on holiday and intended to return on 10th instant. So far her whereabouts are unknown, but a letter was received to the extent that she is not in danger and she will be released soon.
>
> ...
>
> TIPPERARY S.R. At 7 p.m. on 27-6-21. Miss G. Slattery Chemist's assistant, Carrick-on-Suir, was held up by a party of masked and armed men at Ballinderry, Carrick-on-Suir District. She was assaulted and her bicycle taken from her. This was done by the I.R.A., to terrify her as she is friendly towards the police.[36]

The correlation of this reported assault with a statement in the Bureau of Military History suggests it was in fact a sexual assault transgressing her 'inside garments', which underlines the importance of reading across different sources to understand and document sexual violence in Ireland's revolution. Wider cultural assumptions about female sexuality, sexual assault and women's right to a private and intimate life within the context of the IRA are evident in Seamus Babington's witness statement, as is the violation that appears to correlate with the Slattery report above:

> At that time, a rather wild sort of young woman, a native of Kilsheelan parish, was employed in Turner's chemist shop and, like many other girls, had a grádh for men in uniform. She ignored warnings and, most dangerous at that time, used visit the barrack after the shops closed and then proceed home. This had to be stopped, so two Volunteers from the Kilsheelan end of the town were ordered to be on the Kilsheelan road anytime about 7 p.m., remain there until she arrived, fully search her and warn her that her clothes would be taken off her if she went into the barrack again. The two volunteers, Thomas Torpey and Paddy Colleton (latter long since dead, R.I.P.), swore that she did not know either of them. They went as far as Brunswick's, and were instructed to go to the river bank or railway and remain there until she approached ... they carried out the order and without over-description gave the lady a thorough searching from head to foot without missing any of her inside garments. It was so thorough and minute that she did not dare call on the barrack again, but lost no time in reporting.

For decades, historians of the Irish revolution either completely omitted discussion of hair cutting or considered it 'lenient' punishment. This is in stark contrast to the histories of obviously much larger wars conducted in Belgium, France and Germany but also smaller scale civil wars elsewhere, where the shaving of women's hair has sparked immense debates about the sexual, gender and power relations exhibited by this form of punishment and violence. A body of literature examining this practice in other European civil wars exists,[37] yet Ireland's contribution to this form of debate internationally has been sparse in contrast, with the received analysis of the Irish revolution focusing mainly on the deaths and fate of male combatants. Prominent texts on the War of Independence and Irish Civil War by Bill Kissane, Peter Hart, David Fitzpatrick and others did not give sustained attention to such attacks on women in the period.[38] Kissane developed comparative theories of civil wars and has analysed the historical amnesia characteristic of many civil wars, including in Finland, but no detailed analysis of this kind of gender-based violence in the Irish case is provided – a significant omission when one considers how gendered and familial civil wars often are.

The widespread shearing and taking of women's hair was not a benign act at the individual or collective level – it constituted a systematic and frequently terrifying form of symbolic, physical *and* sexualised violence that singled out women as sexual transgressors and traitors. As demonstrated in the next section, hair cutting could also be combined with other forms of transgressive violence inflicted on women in a single event, and it cannot be therefore considered lenient, completely separate or distinct from other kinds of gendered violence performed in the Irish revolution, including sexual violence.

Other humiliating and destructive acts of violence involving the tarring of hair and use of paint is evident throughout the period. The *Irish Independent* for instance reported 'Girls Painted Over Shocking Kerry Outrages'. On 14 August 1922, six 'young ladies' in Killarney known to have sympathy with the Irregulars had their bodies painted with green paint by armed and masked men. Brigadier Paddy O'Daly of the National Army, who was accused of another prominent violent attack that destroyed the hair of two sisters, known as 'the Kenmare Incident', 'promised to mete out extreme measures to the culprits'. Sources that document State violence perpetrated against anti-Treaty and other civilian women during the revolution must also be examined in equal measure alongside the compensation claims of loyalists and other civilian women, as the next section demonstrates, to build up a more complete picture.

Sexual Violence in Ireland's Revolution

An 'Irish exceptionalism' view apparently exists when it comes to sexual violence in this period. As suggested above, a paucity of statistical or documentary evidence has been cited to confirm there was very little rape in the 1919–23 period, especially when compared to the many thousands of rapes that occurred during other large-scale wars or civil wars in other parts of Europe.[39] Townshend, however, submits:

> There must also have been sexual violence, though it was much less well attested. There were undoubtedly cases of rape, probably more than the few that were formally reported – which may indeed be 'surprisingly few', certainly by the depressing standards of the contemporary world

... The truth remains obscure: as the Cork Gaelic Leaguer Caroline Townshend said, 'it is very difficult to get facts about such cases'. In November 1920 Lady Gregory heard from her doctor in Galway that 'the family of the girls violated by the Black and Tans wish it to be hushed up,' and 'another case of the same sort in Clare' was also 'to be kept quiet'.[40]

Rape has always been under-reported or never reported in Irish history – and this remains the case even today. It is by definition a *hidden* crime 'to be kept quiet' and covered up. Reporting rape could also risk further violence and intimidation from perpetrators, especially where regular law enforcement had broken down. Local doctors and hospitals often quietly dealt with the physical injuries and psychological impact of such attacks on women and girls, as in the case of Maggie Doherty in Foxford in May 1923, Eileen Biggs near Dromineer in June 1922 and Mary Doyle near Kells in September 1922, which suggests the techniques of social history, medical history, legal history and women's history must be combined with sources in military history to better understand the incidence of sexual violence. The shame of being a fallen woman or a single mother after a rape or considered a woman of dubious morality would have taken precedence over seeking justice and accountability. As D'Cruze points out 'a woman forfeited her respectability merely by the fact of having been raped'.[41] Research on sexual violence in Ireland's revolution is complicated by the fact that rape often 'crops up' or is briefly mentioned in the middle of an otherwise, seemingly unrelated source – there is no 'rape archive' that can be readily searched. Sources and evidence can be disparate and complicated, and contain euphemisms. In agreement with D'Cruze, 'If questions as to the historical incidence of sexual violence prove so difficult to answer, other ways of using such sources must be devised which can nevertheless yield a meaningful interpretation of sexual violence in the past'.

T.K. Wilson recorded and compared the level of rape in one region in Ireland (Ulster) with another partitioned region in Eastern Europe (Upper Silesia) in 1918–22, which overall experienced on a different scale more intense violence.[42] Acts of violation such as rape or mutilation were noticeably more common in Upper Silesia than in Ulster. This 2010 study is still used to inform a view that there was little or no rape in Ireland's revolution as a whole. However, Wilson's comparative method preceded the subsequent emergence of new quantitative and qualitative evidence documenting individual and hidden cases of sexual violence and attacks on women in Ireland from this period, which merit further consideration.

Qualitative sources including first-hand accounts or statements by women during trials need to be further interpreted from the perspective of social history, women's history and feminist perspectives on gender and violence, alongside any available quantitative data (however limited) in order to advance research and knowledge in this field.

Recently released Bureau of Military History witness statements, for instance, contain numerous references – direct and veiled – to alleged sexual violence. Liam A. Brady, active in Derry-Ulster, recalled in his witness statement:[43]

> On the 19th October 1920, the Irish Catholic Bishops at Maynooth passed a resolution condemning the present British Administration in Ireland as characterized by terror and failure. They declared outrages had been connived at and encouraged, if not organised, not by obscure or irresponsible individuals but by the Government. They alleged that men had been tortured with barbarous cruelty and that there are cases where young women were torn undressed from their mothers at the dead of night.

The transgression of gender norms that occurs during all revolutionary outbreaks produces different outcomes, in a given context, and can encompass different levels and kinds of humiliating, damaging and patriarchal practices (such as hair cutting), apart from and in addition to the extremity of mass or genocidal rape as a weapon of war. Rape in the context of smaller scale, guerrilla wars involves more private transgressions than episodes of mass rape. Additional focus on understanding more about the known cases that did occur instead of emphasising those that apparently did *not* represents a more fruitful way of understanding the particular context in which gender-based violence occurred during Ireland's revolution.

Some rape cases were of course fully investigated, publicly or in closed trials, but these could also be suppressed during the revolutionary period and some have only recently been discovered, hidden in archives. In particular, military investigations into alleged perpetrators (British, Free State and republican) were typically marked 'secret' and closed in archives for many years, with no punishment or sentence indicated.[44] Evidence is also emerging that alleged perpetrators were also investigated in secret IRA courts with women present and cross-examined. The case of Sarah Jordan, for example, is referred to in the breaches of the Truce papers for County Wexford.[45] The Irish Republican Police kidnapped a man near the Tombrackwood area of Ferns for an alleged sexual assault in 1921. Robert Nolan, the 27-year- old son of a mill owner, was 'brought up at a Sinn Féin Court at Ferns' by the IRA on a charge of 'seduction of Sarah Jordan'. Seduction was a widely used term for rape in the courts and newspaper reports. The document 'Kidnapping, Robert Nolan Tombrackwood, County of Waterford, Enniscorthy 10.10.21' states, 'it was rumoured that Robert Nolan had got a girl named Sarah Jordan 15 years in the family way'. Sarah was examined and in a cross examination by Mr Dunbar, Solicitor Enniscorthy, said she made a statement to Sargent McNamara, RIC, Ferns in which she stated that 'Nolan never interfered with her'.

Context and culture are extremely important in arriving at a better understanding of the scale of rape during the Irish revolution. In agreement with Joanna Bourke, 'Rape and sexual abuse are common, even if we do not actually know how many women and men are raped every year. Sexual assault eludes statistical notation. It is not simply that the statistics are collected in a consistent or reliable manner. They cannot exist'.[46] Society and culture put an inordinate burden of proof and blame on victims. As Bourke points out: 'there is no crime more difficult to prove than rape and no injured party more distrusted than the rape victim'.[47] Any suggestion that there are only a handful of cases in military archives or other public sources (such as, the press) therefore appears premature as the definitive reading of the true scale of sexual violence in Ireland's revolution.[48] Cover up or failure to report criminal assault and suspicion of female culpability was the default position. Calling out or reporting a rape in public or among combatants could involve significant risk of reprisal or further violence.

Conflict-related rape cannot be considered insignificant in the period 1919–23. A 'Return showing no. of serious crimes reported to the Gardaí during the six months from 1st July 1923 to 1st December 1923 in Saorstat Éireann', for instance, records five verdicts of 'guilty' for rape, three of 'indecent assault' and five of 'other sexual assault' in the National Army:

Table 6.1 Return showing no. of serious crimes reported to the Gardaí during the six months from July 1st 1923 to 1st December 1923 in Saorstát Éireann[49]

Nature of Crime:	No. reported:	Cases in which members of the National Army were:	
		Guilty	Suspected of being Guilty
Rape	9	5	1
Indecent Assault	9	3	-
Other Sexual Assault	6	5	-

Claims made by male combatants in witness statements are instructive and require further investigation. James Maloney from Bruff, County Limerick, for instance, stated, 'IRA men's sisters and other girls had to go "on the run" fearing rape. The IRA gritted its teeth and showed little mercy to the tans after such outrages'.[50] The women's movement at the time also reported incidents. The *Irish Citizen* reported on hair cutting 'outrages' and Hanna Sheehy Skeffington issued a 'Statement of Atrocities against Women'.[51] Historians increasingly recognise that sexual violence in Ireland's revolution may have been hidden. Brian Hanley, for instance, has remarked:

> It has been generally believed that instances of sexual violence were rare in this period but they may in fact have been understated. I know of at least two more, one involving the Free State army in Kerry and the Special Constabulary in Armagh … In June 1922, B-Specials raided a pub in south Armagh, seeking its owner, republican activist James McGuill. During the raid, women were beaten, McGuill's wife raped and a servant sexually assaulted.[52]

Women's own narratives of violence are coming to light in new sources and require detailed and appropriate analysis. Other potential sources, such as the records of doctors who treated sexual assault victims for injury or trauma, are also being identified and examined. Lindsey Earner-Byrne uncovered in a letter a first-hand account of a rape perpetrated during a robbery in Moate, County Westmeath by a group of republicans in 1923.[53] The rape, which had a 'dangerous' effect on the health of 'Mary M.' and badly injured her, was buried for decades in an institutional record. The letter she wrote documented her associated concealed pregnancy and secret child given to an orphanage. Further hidden evidence of the history of sexual violence in the revolution may also lie in other institutional records.

Reports of other rapes or attempted rapes in the military archives are evident. Séamus Fitzgerald from Cobh, a TD in the First Dáil, recalled:[54]

> I have been asked if I had collected any evidence of rape by Crown Forces. I regret to say that I had two such cases. One, an already middle-aged pregnant woman was raped in Blackpool by Black and Tans, and in the same locality another middle-aged woman successfully resisted a similar attempt.

The contention that women suffered less brutality in Ireland than in other conflict zones must therefore be considered with caution – it is premature given the need for further micro historical research on previously unexamined sources.[55] Arguments about the limited scale of sexual violence in Ireland cannot detract from the lived experience and voice of women who did actually step forward, report an assault or document it in a private letter or document, for instance – it is *they* who were the exception rather than the rape.

Much of this abuse is by definition hidden and covered up, including sometimes in archival collections that do not release such records to the public for fear of traumatising relatives of the woman in later generations. In the context of revolutionary Ireland its scale was inevitably going to be under-reported and indeed kept 'secret', as is noted on the top of a file released in 1980, containing a 'Court of Inquiry in lieu of Inquest' report of 1921.[56] Kate Maher was found almost dead in Dundrum, County Tipperary on 21 December 1920 after spending an evening in the local pub with a group of British soldiers from the Lincolnshire Regiment, including a Private Bennett. Kate was an 'unmarried mother' of one, aged 45 at the time of her death, and she worked as a servant for a local farmer. Extensive vaginal wounds were recorded in the investigation file, and nobody in her company that night was found guilty for her 'manslaughter':

Secret
Finding
The court declares ' …
(3) That the cause of death of the said deceased was fracture at the base of the skull accelerated by haemorrhage from and around of the vagina
…
(5) That such wounds were caused by some person or persons unknown … and that such person or persons unknown are guilty of manslaughter
…
I concur. There is no direct evidence to connect Pte Bennett or any other soldier with this woman's death except that he was found near her and other officers had been seen in her company. Signed … 5/1/21'.[57]

Another case of sexual assault involved pregnant Norah Healy in Cork city, who was raped by a drunk British soldier in her home in April 1921.[58] When she went to report the case the next day to a Sergeant Normoyle, he encouraged her to say nothing when she encountered head-on the perpetrator at the local barracks – 'never mind, don't say anything now'. Her husband had himself served as a soldier in the British Army during the First World War and was present in the house when the attack occurred.

An incident that interconnects hair cutting and rape was written into a diary of activities of the Manchester Regiment (based in Ballincollig, County Cork) entry for 29 November 1920:

> A young woman was held up by two uniformed men near Ballincollig at 21.00 hrs and raped. As she had been threatened with 'bobbing' (hair cut short), this is thought to be the work of the rebels.[59]

Other examples of how hair cutting was sometimes deployed as a warning that more severe violence would follow exist. Bridget Noble from Castletownbere, for instance, was shorn before she was ultimately killed by the IRA in March 1921.[60]

Several recently released online files from the Military Service Pension Collection document more generally some of the more dangerous 'outrages' women experienced.[61] Katherine Collins's application in February 1939 documents her activities in County Clare from 1917 to 1923, and the file refers to 'the outrage' she suffered in February 1921 as well as other raids and incidents. Rape, gang rape and sexual assault are explicitly named in some files and sources. A National Army case documented in a Military Service Pension application released in May 2018 is that of Margaret Doherty in Foxford, County Mayo, a victim of a gang rape on 27 May 1923.[62] Three Free State officers who appeared before a court martial in Ballina, chaired by Austin Brennan on 27 July 1923, were also dealt with in 'secret' and attained an 'honourable acquittal'.[63] The later 1933–37 pension application file relates to Catherine' Doherty's receipt of a partial dependents' gratuity of £112/10 (112 pounds ten shillings) sterling in 1937 under the Army Pensions Acts in respect of her daughter, Cumann na mBan intelligence officer Margaret Doherty. Margaret's death on 28 December 1928 'in the Mental Home' in Castlebar was deemed attributable to her service with Cumann na mBan. It is stated, with accompanying medical evidence, that on a night in May or June 1923 Margaret Doherty was taken from her family home, dragged outside by three masked National Army members and stripped naked, away from the house. Her hands were tied, she was held at gunpoint and 'outraged' (raped) by them in succession. In this file, the word rape is explicitly used. Margaret (Maggie) died prematurely, a young woman in 1928.[64] According to a letter signed by Maggie's brother (Patrick) dated 16 September 1935, a sworn enquiry by 'Officers of the Free State Army' was held into the attack.[65] The detailed report of the associated court of inquiry that was held on 18 July 1923 and remained closed in the Irish Military Archives until 2019 suggests this was an attack that was clearly planned and premeditated and it was not a random act by 'undisciplined' or 'rogue' soldiers. Rape could be weaponised and targeted rather than just opportunistic or caused by 'errant' sexual violence. The opening statement in the trial by Dr Kiernan described the internal injuries Maggie had suffered when he examined her after the attack. Other files and evidence documenting such transgressive violence are being found in additional sources.

Gang rape is extremely violent. The causes of wartime rape, including in relation to patriarchy, sexuality and gender, have received little analysis in studies more focused on proving and concluding that the number of rapes was low in Ireland. John Horne and Alan Kramer have observed that wartime rape was a 'three-way relationship' – between the perpetrator, victim and the victim's male compatriots. The 'them and us' opposition in military conflict is subverted by the common or shared violent treatment of women on both sides when this occurs.[66] Group rapes, it is argued, tend to increase during war. Joanna Bourke and others reiterate that such gang rapes in militarised contexts can be particularly violent because the leader of the gang normally has to continually prove he is more powerful than the others, often ending in the death of the victim as a result (reminiscent of the horrific death Kate Maher experienced and the internal injuries documented in other cases).[67]

In another case during the Civil War, four men from Kells, County Meath claiming to be 'Irregulars' (Patrick Morgan, James Connell, George Connell and another unnamed) were released from Mountjoy Prison and acquitted of two charges of robbery in Trim Circuit Court. Two of the men (brothers) were consequently not tried on a third and separate charge involving the alleged rape of a 17-year-old servant girl, Mary Doyle, during the masked robbery of a public house owned by Mrs Elizabeth Finegan, a widow, in Tankardstown in September 1922. The girl was examined by Dr Gavin, who attended on that occasion and prior to that in a packed parish court held in Kells where Mary was cross-examined in detail about her ordeal after the crowd was asked to leave the room.[68] Another public house nearby in Greetiagh owned by the sister-in-law of Mrs Finegan, also a widow, was robbed on the same night and the women in the household (including her young daughters) were treated in a violent manner. A verdict of *nolle prosqui* was returned by the jury on the charge of the robberies and the separate rape charge consequently did not proceed.

Another additional more widely documented attack in June 1922 involved the horrific gang rape of a Protestant woman, Mrs Eileen Mary Warburton Biggs, in Dromineer, County Tipperary by four young local, anti-Treaty IRA men.[69] Eileen subsequently went to England with her husband Samuel and was awarded a large sum of compensation, documented in an Irish Grants Committee file.[70] Her husband had a nervous breakdown after the incident, in which she was reported to have been 'outraged' on eight or nine different occasions, and Eileen Biggs's mental and physical health never recovered.[71] Eileen ultimately returned to live in Dublin and died in St. Patrick's Psychiatric Hospital in 1950. She is buried in an unmarked grave with her sister Hilda V. Robinson in Mount Jerome cemetery. As Marie Coleman reveals in her analysis of compensation claim files in Chapter 7, one of Eileen's sisters seemingly ended her life as a consequence of the atrocity perpetrated. Mo Moulton suggests there are other cases of sexual assault 'in veiled language' in Irish Grants Committee files, which require further investigation, such as the case of Thomas John Day Atkinson and Mrs Cicely Helen Burrington–Atkinson (assault, possibly sexual) and Mrs. Margaret Fox (sexual assault, County Roscommon).[72]

Numerous references to very frightening and humiliating raids where women were injured and roughly treated (often dragged from their beds in darkness and in nightclothes) are evident in different sources.[73] Three masked Free State army officers beat two young women, Flossie and Jessie McCarthy, with their belts and rubbed dirty motor oil in their hair (known to cause hair to fall out), in an attack in Kerry on 2 June 1923 that became known as 'the Kenmare incident'.[74] One source in Ernie O'Malley's Kerry diaries alleges rape was also implicated in this attack.[75] A major row was caused in the cabinet and it led to the resignation of the senior officer Major General Paddy O'Daly, who had escaped any official sanction when eight republican men were horrifically executed when they were tied to a mine that was detonated at Ballyseedy. The two girls, daughters of a local medical practitioner, Dr Randal McCarthy, were dragged out of their beds, and were found very badly beaten, whipped and with their hair and faces covered in dirty grease.[76] Two investigations undertaken by both the Gardaí and a Dublin Military Court of Inquiry into the assaults recommended court proceedings. Neither was acted upon by the Minister for Defence, Richard Mulcahy, and the President of the Executive, W.T. Cosgrave. Dominic Price suggests, 'The way in which the Dublin Guards and National Army GHQ dealt with the Kenmare scandal followed the same procedural cover-up used in the aftermath of the Ballyseedy atrocity'.[77] Ernest Blythe in his witness statement referred to the young women as 'tarts' and downplayed the terror and injuries caused:

> Apparently, the girls were dragged out of their beds and beaten with belts. No great harm was done to them and the outrage was more an indignity to them than anything else … I did not agree personally with O'Higgins

in feeling particularly revolted, at what seemed to me to be merely a case of a trouple of tarts getting a few lashes that did them no harm.[78]

The witness statement of Mary Walsh from Kilbrittain illustrates the wider spectrum of violence and threat that could occur in one incident (sections of the original statement were typed in capital letters):[79]

> Victim's Statement
>
> On Monday morning, May 9th, about 7 a.m., fifty soldiers, under an Officer, surrounded our house. A number of these rushed upstairs, entering the bedrooms of my father and sister, who were both in bed. The Officer asked them to get up, but my father was unable to do so. They then searched the rooms.
>
> My mother and I were having our breakfast in the kitchen, and one solider seized my cup of tea and drank it off immediately. The other soldiers were moving about, and my mother noticed one taking eggs from a box in the dairy. We went towards the dairy door and saw some of them drink and spill cream, and they also took about six pounds of butter. My sister called the attention of the Officer in charge to the looting and he denied it. Just then a soldier came along with a capful of eggs; the cap dropped from him as he was passing the Officer, and the eggs got broken. That was sufficient proof, and the officer said: 'If you will keep your b......... mouth shut I will pay for them'.
>
> THE OFFICER THEN TOLD ME TO GO UPSTAIRS AND GET MY CLOTHES ON AS I WAS UNDER ARREST. I DID THIS AND WAS FOLLOWED BY TWO SOLDIERS, AND FOR THAT REASON I CAME DOWNSTAIRS AGAIN WITHOUT CHANGING MY CLOTHES …
>
> My sister went to work as usual outside, and when feeding the pigs was held up by two soldiers who twisted her arms behind her back. They told her they wanted her up the road for some time; but she told them they should take her as she refused to go willingly with them …
>
> WHEN MY SISTER SAW MY MOTHER UNCONSCIOUS IN THE YARD SHE RAN TO HER ASSISTANCE. SHE ALSO SAW ME BEING CHOKED BY A SOLDIER: SHE CAUGHT HIS ARM BUT WAS BEATEN BY ANOTHER WITH SOMETHING HARD

In recently available records, there also appears to be a further unexplored link between violence, women, institutionalisation and the revolution – asylums, institutionalisation and nervous breakdowns feature in a number of pension applications made on behalf of women. Three examples include the files relating to Mollie O'Shea (from Kilflynn, County Kerry),[80] Margaret Doherty (referred to above) and Delia Begley (from Ennis, County Clare).[81] Delia suffered a nervous breakdown after attending men who were wounded while making explosives in 1919 and which later saw her in the care of the Sisters of Charity religious order. 'Miss Begley had no estate, in fact, she was destitute, she fought bravely for her country, but when she became helpless no one wanted her, not even her relations', Reverend Mother Sr Paschaline wrote in support of her pension application.[82]

Mollie O'Shea, another vibrant young woman in the Cumann na mBan Kerry No. 1 Brigade, suffered lifelong insanity after the revolution. Mollie suffered a nervous breakdown after her brother was killed in what is considered to be the Civil War's worst atrocity, the blowing up of eight anti-Treaty prisoners by Free State troops in Ballyseedy, County Kerry in 1923.[83] A number of executions took place during the Irish Civil War and a cycle of atrocities developed. From November 1922, the Free State government embarked on a policy of executing republican prisoners in order to end the war. Many of those killed had previously been allies, and in some cases close friends, during the War of Independence. Such executions left a lasting and bitter legacy.

The guerrilla campaign was notably intense in Kerry during the Civil War. Mollie O'Shea was an active agent in the major incidents at that time. Yet a pension application submitted by Mollie's brother in 1952 referred to her as 'a person of unsound mind' and a ward of court. The file details the trauma suffered by Mollie during the Civil War, including an 'outrage', as well as the psychological impact of the dangerous work she did in very risky conditions:

April 1921 to May 1921
   Did scout work for IRA. Carried dispatches regularly. Was in line of fire at Shannow ambush. Helped to dress wounded. Was alone at home one evening Tans raided my house. They beat her and stole gold watch and chain and books. Applicant was very ill after this outrage. This actually happened on the day of the truce.

1 July 1922–31 March 1923
   Carried dispatches frequently. Did useful intelligence work with regards to the movement of Free State soldiers. Cooked and washed for those in the flying column. Collected and supplied smokes and comforts as well. Had charge of supplying dugout where wanted men were. Jack Shannahan, George Shea (her brother who was killed at Ballyseedy), Jim

Twomey (also killed at Ballyseedy), Leo Lyons and Stephen Fuller. The dug-out was at Glena Ballysna Wood. These men were kept in supplies by applicant and she had to go there each night after dark. The journey was long and lonely. Her sufferings about this time were very great her worst could not be estimated. Subsequent events at Clashmullen and Ballycudy unnerved her. She was taken to a mental home late in 1923. Her brother Dan brought her home a harmless lunatic in 1925 and has kept her at home since. She is harmless but all the time mentally affected and hopelessly insane.

Mollie was 'very ill' after the 'outrage' of May/June 1921. Likewise Maggie Doherty did not recover from the sexual abuse and associated injuries (physical and mental) she suffered in 1923 until her premature death in 1928. The Doherty pension file states Maggie 'was totally incapacitated from 31/5/23 until death' and she was never ill prior to this event.

Conclusion

Did Ireland of the 1920s lock away, conceal and institutionalise the trauma of the revolution suffered by women? Is this where some more stories of the hidden history of atrocities experienced by women in the revolution lie? Was institutionalisation for life and mental illness not a 'lethal' outcome for living women who were victims of assault or life-altering trauma in the revolution – or just a product of 'lenient punishment' considered to be exclusively meted out to women? The widespread incarceration of 'fallen' women and children in institutions is documented in recent State inquiries and related scandals involving abuse – which is an issue that also arises in relation to the period encompassing the Irish revolution and its aftermath. The documented impact of trauma on women that is currently emerging provides a very different kind of narrative to the analysis of sectarianism, ethnicity and community conflict which has dominated the masculinist historiography that has prevailed to date. The war against women in this period is therefore a matter that merits due recognition if the forthcoming State commemorations in Ireland are to seriously address the most difficult questions of the past, inclusively understood.

Men and boys can also of course be victims of sexual violence in conflict situations. Evidence of the incidence of sexual violence against males in wars and conflicts is not equivalent to the more widespread, systemic violence perpetrated against females recorded in history. But research into sexual violence against men and boys in conflict zones has been conducted in some contexts.[84] We might consider how placing sexual violence and sexual humiliation against men and against women in the same analytical frame could complicate and advance future research in Ireland should any new evidence come to light on this issue. Such an analysis will also broaden the analysis of violence between men beyond mere focus on guns, warfare and killing to looking at the other kinds of bodily punishment, torture, terror and humiliation performed.

As this chapter has demonstrated, gender-based violence and sexual violence was a serious occurrence in the specific context of Ireland's revolution. Women suffered and experienced a range of transgressive violence that was gendered and sexual. Difficult questions demand difficult histories and the final stage of a decade of commemorations should present an opportunity for a full debate about such erased narratives in Irish revolutionary history. This includes recognising the still-unfolding legacy of violence as it applied to women's lives in the period 1919–23.

Brett Shadl argues, however, that studying the history of sexual and gender-based violence against women continues to have real political reverberations.[85] Evidence that suggests Irish republicans and National Army soldiers may have turned on their fellow Irish women in this way as well as on other men/their 'brothers' during the Civil War is bound to generate discomfort. In the 1970s, in establishing rape crisis services, the women's movement in Ireland transformed public and academic knowledge of how hidden gender-based violence and rape was and is in society.[86] At that time, rape was not considered to be a real or serious problem by the political, legal, academic and religious establishment in Irish society. Yet further research and later scandals, including abuse perpetrated in Church and State-run institutions since the foundation of the State, suggested sexual violence was and is an ingrained question in modern Irish history.

There is strong evidence that sexual and gender-based violence occurred during the Irish revolution and that this is an element of its history. My aim in this chapter has been to write back into the received narrative some of the recovered stories of Irish women directly impacted by this violence. Additional court martial trial reports that remain closed, first hand testimonies, memoirs, diaries, letters, political documents, medical records that document the full range of physical and psychological injuries after attacks, and institutional records (including for asylums and mother and baby homes), hold more evidence. Further examination of all these sources carefully combined will build up additional evidence-based insights into an important issue that was hidden, silenced, suppressed, diminished and denied for too long.

Chapter 7

Compensation Claims and Women's Experience of Violence and Loss in Revolutionary Ireland, 1921–23

MARIE COLEMAN

The 'decade of centenaries' has been a boon to historians as archival repositories have released new and valuable material relating to the Irish revolution and its immediate aftermath. The level of destruction to property and the extent of personal injury suffered by combatants and civilians resulted in significant compensation schemes being introduced by the Irish and British governments to provide restitution to those who suffered loss. Archives relating to compensation are among the most valuable currently being released and will help to expand knowledge, not just of the activities which took place during the revolution itself but also on the afterlives of those involved and the efforts to restore landscapes and streetscapes and repair infrastructure. This chapter will introduce the principal archival collections available relating to post-revolution restitution, focusing on their significance as evidence for the experience of women during and after the revolution. One such collection, the Irish Grants Committee, a valuable source for the experience of southern loyalists after the Truce, will be considered from a specifically gender perspective.

The Military Service Pensions Collection

The largest and most significant collection dealing with post-revolution financial restitution is the Military Service Pensions Collection (MSPC), encompassing approximately 300,000 files. Not only is this in the process of release to the public for the first time, but the majority of files are also being made freely available online, enabling easy access for scholars and researchers.[1]

This collection includes applications (successful and unsuccessful) for service pensions from combatants as well as disability pensions for those who were wounded. In this regard it is a particularly rich source of detail on the activities of Cumann na mBan, providing a much wider perspective on women's involvement than the Bureau of Military History, which contains only 146 transcribed witness statements from women.[2]

As a source for the activities of women who played an active part in the conflict, through membership of Cumann na mBan, or the Hibernian Rifles and Irish Citizen Army during the Easter Rising, the Military Service Pensions Collection underlines the significant role that they played in intelligence gathering, communications and gun-running.[3] Pensions were also awarded for Civil War service, unlike the Bureau of Military History, which largely did not stray beyond 1921. Therefore, the collection is a uniquely valuable source for the experience of female republican prisoners, who had a much harsher experience at the hands of Free State jailers than with the British authorities in the preceding conflict.[4]

An extensive collection of administrative files governing the adjudication of pension applications also contains many insights into the state's attitude towards women in the period after the conflict and the way in which the status and contribution of female veterans was assessed relative to those of men. In order to assist in verifying the service of applicants, former IRA brigades and Cumann na mBan branches were requested to compile lists of their membership during the revolutionary period. This series is extremely valuable for estimating how many women were members of the organisation in all areas of the country. There are 165 Cumann na mBan nominal rolls available.[5]

The most problematic and controversial aspect of the pensions process, throughout the thirty-four years of its operation from 1924 to 1958, was providing an adequate definition of what constituted active service in either the Easter Rising or the guerrilla campaigns of 1919–21 and the Civil War. The guerrilla nature of the war could make it very difficult for all applicants, male and female, and especially those from the least active areas, to prove the merit of their claims. As no legislative definition of active service was provided, different assessors used different criteria at different times. Both the legislation and the subsequent assessors' interpretations valued the role of women considerably lower than that of men, so that under the principal pension legislation introduced in 1934, Cumann na mBan were restricted, along with the republican boy scouts, Fianna Éireann, to the two lowest ranks for pensions, 'D' and 'E'.[6]

Compensation Claims and Women's Experience of Violence

The Fianna Fáil Minister for Defence, Frank Aiken, had been reluctant to include Cumann na mBan in the 1934 legislation, making his views of the inferiority of women's contribution and slim chances of pension success known in the Senate when the amendment to include Cumann na mBan was proposed:

> I want to point out, however, that the same test of service will be applied to women as was applied to men and that that will result, in my opinion, in very few being granted an active service certificate ... while members of Cumann na mBan are treated equally with men, they will not be treated better. If the officers of Cumann na mBan of nominal high rank were treated in the same way as officers of the Volunteers there would be a very big discrepancy, because their responsibilities were not as great ... no member of Cumann na mBan will be graded higher than Rank D. I think it is only fair to say that while Cumann na mBan had a national organisation, they acted as auxiliaries to the local units of the Volunteers or I.R.A.[7]

A similar interpretation was formulated by Aiken's close associate, John McCoy, a member of the advisory committee that assessed pensions, and one of the most influential figures in the pensions process during the 1930s and 1940s:

> It would be unwise to adopt a standard of service for the women less exacting than what will be applied to men who are classed as 'key men' ... On the other hand, it would be most ridiculous to expect women to have taken part under arms in engagements with enemy forces. As the act makes no distinction in favour of women claimants it is essential that the service recognised should be service of a military nature. Activities such as collecting and distributing funds, propaganda, classes, cannot be considered without other important activities of a military nature as a qualifying asset.

McCoy did not see how Cumann na mBan service could be equated with that of the IRA, rejecting a claim by Cork IRA officers that some of the Cumann na mBan applicants were 'of such an outstanding character that their value to the I.R.A. was greater to the I.R.A. than the best of the I.R.A. men' and complaining that that they had taken 'an exaggerated view ... of the military value of the work done by the Cumann na mBan.'[8]

This effectively ruled out accepting many of the principal activities undertaken by Cumann na mBan as evidence worthy of a pension, making it more difficult for women to get recognition. Effectively, Cumann na mBan applications were judged by a standard drawn up to reflect the activities of the Irish Volunteers. This was based on a 1924 definition of 'Acts of War' that included 'Attack on enemy forces or position … Destruction of enemy property … Manufacture, purchase or disposal of munitions … Collection of information … [and] … organising and training for above activities', the first of which were the most significant and in which very few, if any, Cumann na mBan women participated in during the War of Independence.[9]

Cumann na mBan was not even included in the first pension legislation, introduced in 1924, because it was reserved for pro-Treaty veterans who had also served in the Irish national army, from which women were excluded, with the notable exception of Dr Brigid Lyons. Lyons received a 1924 act pension largely due to her family's close political links to Cumann na nGaedheal, in spite of the army's reluctance to award it to her. This reluctance mirrored in part the failure to award a disability pension to the 1916 veteran, Margaret Skinnider. While the stated reason for Skinnider's rejection was that she was a woman, and as such did not conform to the definition of 'soldier' in the 1923 Army Pensions Act, I have argued elsewhere that gender was used as a cover to deny a pension to a republican opponent of the government, and that the real significance of gender in her case is that her sex, rather than her political views, was a more acceptable pretext for the denial.[10]

In addition to pensions for actual 'military service', the collection also includes applications for wound and disability pensions, which will allow for a critical examination of the impact of revolutionary activity on the subsequent physical and mental health of combatant women. On the basis of modern-day estimates for the numbers of combatants who suffer from Post-Traumatic Stress Disorder (PTSD), it has been estimated that 'Approximately 300 of the veterans of 1916 would have suffered from undiagnosed and untreated PTSD'.[11] Files currently available in the Military Service Pensions Collection show that traumatic injury resulting from revolutionary activity was in fact diagnosed, under the all-encompassing term of 'neurasthenia'. Kate Greaney, who was active in intelligence gathering for the IRA in Kerry during the War of Independence and Civil War, was awarded a partial disability pension in 1947 following a medical diagnosis of 'neurasthenia or general Neurosis'.[12] In some cases such diagnoses were linked directly to a woman's experience during the revolution; Margaret Clancy's 'depression', diagnosed in 1933, was attributed by her doctor 'to the strain she underwent during the Black and Tan regime'.[13]

In Greaney's case, the diagnosis included the rider that: 'This lady is generally neurotic'.[14] These files provide the material for a more focused analysis to investigate whether there was a gendered approach to diagnosing PTSD among revolutionary veterans. A more detailed examination of the medical assessments of applicants for disability pensions could be undertaken to scrutinise the diagnostic nomenclature for gendered stereotypes; was the description of Kate Greaney as 'generally neurotic' unusual, and were such descriptions applied also to men? In short was 'neurosis' seen as a 'female malady'?[15] Detailed comparative work exists on diagnosing traumatic injury in soldiers after the First World War. However, these deal almost exclusively with male soldiers.[16] The Military Service Pensions Collection offers a unique opportunity for students of conflict and its impact to consider its traumatic impact on both men and women, due to the richness of the material now available in disability pension files.

Evidence of gendered conceptions that reflected wider societal attitudes is to be found throughout the Military Service Pensions Collection. The administrative files governing the award of pensions and gratuities to the children and spouses of National Army soldiers during the Civil War show how 'un-married wives' who were co-habiting with deceased soldiers without being married to them presented a specific problem: 'as a general principle we cannot recognise dependency claims in regard to un-married wives'.[17] As a result, when Private Patrick Perry was killed in action in Cork city in April 1922, the only one of his dependants to receive a compensation payment was his mother, Mary, who was awarded a gratuity of £50 under the 1923 Army Pensions Act. Initially following his death, a payment of £2-5s-6d was paid to his 'unmarried wife', Rose, and their two children, as the army deemed them to come within the definition of the dependant of an unmarried soldier as 'such members of the family or household as were wholly or in part dependent upon the earnings of the soldier for a reasonable period before enlistment ... A woman who has been dependent on a soldier for her maintenance and who has been supported regularly by him on a *bona fide* permanent domestic basis comes under this definition'.

After the Civil War, regulations governing payments to dependants were superseded by the 1923 Army Pensions Act. At this point a tussle arose between Mary and Rose Perry as to who was Patrick Perry's rightful dependant, with Mary informing the Department of Defence that her son 'was not legally married to the woman he was living with, as her legal husband was & is still alive'. Rose Perry's legal husband, named Mooney, appears to have deserted her and their two children on enlisting in the Royal Dublin Fusiliers in 1915. Patrick Perry had also served in the First World War, with the Irish Guards, and had gone to Scotland after the war, where he met Rose. By 1922 they were living in Dublin and had two young children together, born in 1919 and 1921. In 1925 the Army Pensions Board was prepared to provide maintenance allowances for Rose Perry's two children, her son up to the age of 16 and her daughter up to the age of 18, under the provisions of the 1923 Army Pensions Act.[18]

At this point their illegitimate status became problematic. The Treasury Solicitor ruled out any payment to Rose Perry: 'I can find nothing in the above Act which would authorise the admission of a claim on behalf of the woman who lived with Perry'. Consequently, this affected the legal right of her children to dependant's allowances: 'Neither can I find any authority for payment to illegitimate children of a member of the National Army'. There was evident sympathy for the plight to the two children, who were then being maintained in the Eccles Street orphanage. The Treasury Solicitor recognised that the case was 'a cruel one as on the face of it there seems no good reason why helpless children should suffer for their parents' error'. The army authorities appear to have been willing, on the basis of the solicitor's advice, to take a broad interpretation of the term 'child' as it appeared in the 1923 Army Pensions Act, following a similar British precedent: 'I am under the impression that the British Army made allowances in such cases and I think that a broad view might be taken of the case so as to enable the expression "child" to be read in its natural sense as opposed to its strictly legal sense'. However, the final say lay with the Minister for Finance, the notoriously parsimonious Ernest Blythe, who decided in 1925 to adhere to the strict legal interpretation of 'child' as 'legitimate' and as a result was 'precluded from consenting' to the proposed award for the Perry children.[19]

The case of Rose Perry highlights the value of Military Service Pensions Collection in providing significant new evidence on non-combatant women, especially the wives, mothers, children and other dependants of combatants who died during the period, allowing for an assessment of the revolution's impact on women who have been largely hidden to date. While the stories of some of the more prominent 'Easter widows', such as Kathleen Clarke, were already quite well known,[20] the Military Service Pensions Collection has facilitated the stories of many others to emerge. Examples include the experiences of Roger Casement's sister, Agnes Newman, who was left in a precarious economic position after the death of her brother, who had been supporting her financially following her separation from her husband and subsequent widowhood, or Margaret Geoghegan, who was left widowed with a young family to support after the death of her husband, George, a member of the Irish Citizen Army who was killed during the Rising.[21] The collection also includes details of pensions and gratuities provided to the Irish soldiers who served in the British Army, in the Connaught Rangers, and who mutinied in India in 1920 in response to stories of crown force atrocities in Ireland, and in many cases includes details of payments to women, including widows of deceased pensioners.[22]

Compensation Collections in the National Archives of Ireland

A number of new and forthcoming releases in the National Archives of Ireland (NAI) will also enhance greatly the ability of historians to recount and analyse the experience of women, and in particular non-combatants, whose lives were affected in different ways by the events in Ireland between 1916 and 1923. To mark the centenary of the Easter Rising, the Property Losses (Ireland) Committee claims were released online by the NAI. These papers relate to the workings of a committee that sat over the summer of 1916 to assess the extent of damage to property in Dublin during the Rising. While the majority of the 6,567 digitised files relate to claims from men, business owners especially, there are a number of claims from women for personal losses that shed fascinating light on the minutiae of women's lives in inner city Dublin a century ago.[23]

Fanny Abbot was employed in the Public Record Office, then based in the Four Courts, and received £3 compensation for the loss of a silver watch and some items of clothing.[24] A number of women claimed for property held by businesses such as jewellers or silversmiths, when such premises were destroyed.[25] Approximately eighty women, including the artists Sarah Purser and Estella Solomons, claimed for the loss of their work when over 500 works of art that were on display in the annual exhibition of the Royal Hibernian Academy were lost when the RHA building on Lower Abbey Street was destroyed.[26] Hanna Sheehy Skeffington was awarded £44 of a claim for £49 for the loss of and damage to personal effects removed from her home during a raid on 28 April.[27]

The most significant compensation for damage to property during the revolutionary period was that paid out by the Irish Free State government under the 1923 Damage to Property (Compensation) Act for destruction caused during the Civil War. The claims are held in the NAI's Department of Finance, Finance Compensation (FIN COMP) series, which were made available for all counties between 2014 and 2015. Women, and especially loyalist women, figure prominently in these files. They are particularly useful for charting the experience of Protestant and loyalist women whose property was targeted by the IRA during the Civil War, and for evidence of whether or not this led them to leave Ireland, contributing to the ongoing debate about the reasons for Protestant depopulation between 1911 and 1926. This appears to have been the case with the Neill family – John and Mary and their daughter Annie – who had moved from Edgeworthstown, County Longford to Portadown, County Armagh, by 1923. Their claim for damage to property in a raid on their home in Longford by the IRA in May 1921 was rejected because it took place before the period covered by the legislation. A similar claim made to the British Irish Grants Committee (see below) was equally unsuccessful for the same reason.[28] While these claims did not succeed, they remain as valuable evidence for the experience of female loyalists in Ireland during the revolutionary years.

In an effort to prevent successful claimants from simply taking their compensation and leaving Ireland, the legislation included re-instatement clauses which required the applicant to use the compensation to restore or re-build the damaged premises, although exceptions were allowed where a convincing case for impracticality was made. These awards were made through the local courts and the administration of the Act fell to the Office of Public Works (OPW).[29] Since the transfer of the archives of the OPW to the NAI, many of the files, in particular sub-series OPW6, have not been available to the public but are undergoing conservation in preparation for release in the near future. These will complement FIN COMP and similarly serve as an important source for examining how women coped with the aftermath of the revolution and the efforts to return to as normal a life as possible. They will be of particular value in examining the experience of loyalist women and why some left Ireland but, more specifically, why so many chose to remain, in spite of violent attacks on their property resulting from opposition to their political ideology, links to the British administration, or religious affiliation.

The Free State government prioritised compensation for damage to property over that for personal injury suffered; between 1923 and 1939 the government paid £12,527,942 for property losses and £772,528 for personal.[30] The bulk of this was for damage caused during the Civil War. While these new archival releases offer enormous potential for expanding our knowledge of the experience of women from various backgrounds in revolutionary Ireland, greater use can also be made of collections which have been in the public domain for some time but have yet to be analysed in detail from the perspective of gender. This is especially the case with the archives of the Irish Grants Committee, held in the United Kingdom's National Archives at Kew.

Women and the Irish Grants Committee

Through the mechanism of the Irish Grants Committee (IGC), which operated between 1923 and 1928, the British Government made financial restitution to 2,237 southern loyalists (just over half of the 4,032 claimants) for injuries suffered between the declaration of the Truce on 11 July 1921 and the end of the Civil War on 24 May 1923.[31] Geographically, there were claimants from all counties, though the largest numbers were from Cork, Tipperary and Clare, with the fewest from Ulster and especially the six counties of Northern Ireland.[32] While the records have been utilised for specific geographical and occupational analysis, such as Brian Hughes's examination of the claims from County Cavan and Paul Taylor's examination of claims by ex-servicemen,[33] their value as a source for evidence of the experience of women specifically has yet to be fully realised.

Gemma Clark's study of *Everyday Violence in the Irish Civil War* examined the incidence of gender-specific violence, and in particular sexual violence, in a sample of compensation claims.[34] As Linda Connolly has also demonstrated (see also Chapter 6 of this volume), the collection contains details on one of the most notorious cases of rape during the revolution, of which a written record exists. Mrs Eileen Biggs,[35] wife of a Protestant (Church of Ireland) market gardener from Dromineer, County Tipperary, was 'outraged altogether on eight or nine different occasions', when her family home 'was raided by about a dozen armed men who stated that they were the IRA', on the night of 15–16 June 1922. Her husband was attacked physically, and while the assault upon his wife was in progress he 'was kept fully informed by these raiders of what they were doing'.[36] The details in the IGC report, which dates from 1926, are similar to those reported to authorities by her husband on the day following the assault:

> The men locked up Mr Biggs and another old man, an invalid, in a room. They ransacked the house, consumed a quantity of whiskey, and then two of them seized Mrs Biggs while another man outraged her. The men warned Mrs Biggs that if the matter were reported they (the Biggs's) would be shot.

A number of items of jewellery and clothing were also stolen during the raid. Such was the extent of the physical and mental trauma experienced by Mrs Biggs, it was considered 'not inconceivable that the guilty party may be charged with manslaughter'.[37]

The only motive that Samuel Biggs could suggest for his wife being mistreated was that she 'did not associate with the "lower-class" neighbours'.[38] The attack appears to have been part of a wider series of threats made against Protestants in the area at that time. A week before the incident, the local Church of Ireland Bishop of Killaloe and Clonfert, Thomas Sterling Berry, brought concerns regarding the safety of Protestants in Tipperary to the Minister for Home Affairs: 'There is scarcely a Protestant family in this district which has escaped molestation'. In addition to property being damaged, cattle driven off land, and a prominent member of the gentry being shot at on his way to church, 'Protestant families have been warned to leave the neighbourhood. Altogether a state of terrorism exists'. The situation appears to have been confined to an area around Nenagh and was not replicated elsewhere in his diocese.[39]

These attacks appear to have been carried out by the local anti-Treaty IRA. The nature of the raids as described by the bishop was consistent with the guerrilla tactics adopted during the War of Independence and Civil War: 'A range of hills runs south of this district and I believe the perpetrators of these acts of violence come down from the hills where they have many places in which to conceal themselves'.[40] Four local men who were arrested soon after the attack on Mrs Biggs and appeared in a local court in early August had links to the IRA. Patrick and Edward Hogan were the younger brothers of a prominent anti-Treaty IRA activist, Martin Hogan, who was later shot dead in Dublin in April 1923, towards the end of the Civil War, apparently by the Free State forces.[41] James Grace, of Annabeg, appeared in court in a military uniform. The fourth accused, Michael Grace, was from the same townland as the Hogans.[42] Nominal rolls produced in the late 1930s for the purpose of verifying Volunteer membership for military service pensions list Edward Hogan and Michael and James Grace as being members of E Company (Ballycommon), 3rd Battalion, Tipperary No. 1 Brigade as of 1 July 1922.[43] A witness, Thomas Webb, who was locked in another room during the incident, indicated that another man described as 'thickset', who was not among those brought to court, was also involved.[44]

While the euphemism of 'outrage' was used throughout Mrs Biggs's account and the few State documents that relate to her case, the charge subsequently brought in court against four of her alleged assailants was that they did 'rape' Mrs Biggs.[45] A memo summarising the attack that was prepared by the IGC investigators also referred to her being 'outraged and raped by the raiders'.[46] Recognised as 'one of the hardest cases' the IGC had to deal with, the couple were awarded £6,000 to cover the medical treatment for Mrs Biggs's physical injuries, subsequent psychological trauma, loss of property and substantial expenses incurred in moving to live in England.

The files reveal starkly that this was more than a case of rape and led to the abandonment of the couple's home and livelihood in Ireland, and had an adverse effect on the health of both from which they probably never fully recovered. The shame of being a victim of a crime of that nature still resonated deeply with Mrs Biggs four years later, when she explained that 'We cannot hold up our heads amongst our friends and acquaintances. My sister, Mrs Peacock has since died from shock as a result of the incident and the stigma to the family'.[47] Mrs Peacock, who was Eileen Biggs's elder sister, Margaret (Daisy) and was married to a former RIC medical officer, Dr Pryce Peacock, appears to have committed suicide in October 1924, illustrating further the extent of the trauma experienced by the wider family circle as a result of the assault on Mrs Biggs. The civil record of her death indicated that the cause of death was 'laceration of the brain and haemorrhage caused by throwing herself out of the window' at her home in 26 Upper Pembroke Street, Dublin.[48]

While the Biggs's were living in England at the time of their claim to the IGC in 1926, they obviously returned to Ireland subsequently. Samuel died in Monkstown, County Dublin in February 1937. Eileen survived him by thirteen years, dying in St Patrick's Hospital Dublin on 8 June 1950. Her death in a psychiatric hospital suggests that she never recovered fully from the trauma of her ordeal thirty years previously.[49]

The fate of her alleged assailants is unclear. At the time of their court appearance in early August they had been in custody for six weeks. They were released on sureties of £200 each on condition that they 'be of good behaviour towards all subjects of the realm, and Mrs Biggs especially, for a period of twelve months; or in default to go to jail for four months'.[50] In a follow-up enquiry by the Department of Home Affairs in July 1923, no further record of court proceedings was found, and there was confusion over which Dáil court had jurisdiction over the case, as the men seemed to have appeared in a district court, which did not have criminal case jurisdiction.[51]

The upheaval surrounding the start of the Civil War in mid-1922, the establishment of a new Free State police force and questions over the future of the revolutionary era republican courts contributed to a situation in which it appears that no further action was taken against the accused men. In 1933 when Patrick and Edward Hogan's mother, Catherine, applied for a dependants' gratuity as compensation for the financial loss resulting from Martin's death, she noted that she had a 32-year-old son, who was married, working as a carpenter and living at home, and a 30-year-old son who was a labourer in the USA. While not named, these ages correspond to Patrick and Edward respectively, who were aged 10 and 7 in the 1911 census.[52]

Feelings of shame on the part of victims explain why it can be difficult to ascertain evidence of actual rapes and sexual assaults in compensation claims such as the IGC. William McKenna did not believe that his 75-year-old wife would ever 'recover from the outrage committed on her' when their home in Roscrea was raided in August 1922. As Clark points out, the term '"outrage" has sexual violence connotations and the description of the ordeal as one from which Mrs McKenna "would never recover", does suggest rape'.[53] The account given by Margaret Fox, the wife of a disbanded Royal Irish Constabulary (RIC) sergeant living in Roscommon, of an attack on her in April 1922 is also suggestive of a rape: 'a few of the party pushed me into my bedroom and treated me very roughly. I was pregnant at the time and as a result of their cruel treatment I took a haemorrhage which led to a miscarriage'.[54]

In addition to rape and sexual assault, the instances of which are not very frequent within the claims, other forms of personal assault for which women sought compensation included more minor physical injuries and psychological trauma consequent on witnessing physical assaults, usually of close male relatives. In the former category, Elizabeth and Angela Gorman from King's County (Offaly), claimed for unspecified consequences of a car accident that occurred 'on account of the trench made in the road during the troubled times'. As this took place prior to the Truce their claim was outside the scope of the IGC, but it is highly unlikely that they would have been awarded much, if anything at all, as they 'could not describe the loss' and made a highly exaggerated claim for over £800. They had previously been awarded £5 for the damage to the car by the Compensation (Ireland) Commission, chaired by Lord Shaw, which assessed claims for damage and injury during the War of Independence.[55]

The claims of Margaret McCormack (Roscommon) and Delia Reidy (Clare) for the traumatic impact of witnessing fatal physical assaults on close family members were also ruled outside the scheme's scope because the events in question took place during the War of Independence. Nevertheless, even though such claims did not succeed, the details contained in them remain an excellent source of evidence for the experience of women during the conflict. Reidy claimed unsuccessfully for the death of her mother in a reprisal attack by the crown forces on their home, which she believed was a case of mistaken identity. She alleged that her mother's death was a consequence of her bed being 'sprinkled with petrol and set on fire'.[56]

Margaret McCormack's husband died in 1926 as a result, she believed, of being 'beaten and bruised' by the Black and Tans in March 1921. Even if the alleged assault occurred within the timeframe covered by the IGC, it is unlikely that the claim would have succeeded in view of the time lapse between it and his death.[57] In seeking to distribute their resources as fairly as possible among genuine cases of hardship, the IGC was suspicious of those claiming consequential loss some years later. The investigators were clearly highly dubious of the 'professional ingenuity' of Mrs Essie Taylor's doctors, who managed to attribute her 'shock' to events which occurred in 'the precise period covered by the Committee's references'. Expressing a lack of surprise 'that any person resident in certain parts of what is now the Irish Free State during a period of intense severe disturbances would receive shocks', it was considered 'unlikely … to produce Graves disease'. In spite of this, and the fact that some of the period for which the Taylors's claims for damage to property fell outside the chronological remit of the commission, it remains unclear how an award of £1,420 was recommended.[58]

In cases where the committee was keen to help, the distinction of pre- and post-Truce events could be blurred if the traumatic impact could be shown to have occurred during the period covered by its terms of reference. This appears especially to have been the case where the claimants' loss was directly attributable to having been in the service of the Crown. Thomas and Cicely Atkinson were compensated for expenses incurred in moving to England and the breakdown of their health, consequences of an attack on their home in Killiney, County Dublin, in March 1921, which was attributed to Thomas Atkinson's 'service at [Army] General Headquarters Ireland attached to Intelligence Branch and Courts Martial'. He was shot and wounded, and shots were fired at his wife but she was unhurt. Mrs Atkinson's doctor found that by July 1921 'she was in a state of complete nervous breakdown'. The state of her health in 1921 and the danger inherent in returning to Ireland made it impossible for her to lodge a claim for criminal injury compensation in Ireland itself. In spite of the committee's reluctance to concede much of the claim based on the pre-Truce timing of the principal events and the desire not to duplicate awards where compensation had already been granted (in this case to Thomas Atkinson), sufficient latitude was found to make them an *ex gratia* payment of £750.[59]

In a similar manner, Elizabeth Doyle from Longford, was awarded £150 when she was boycotted by her neighbours and unable to hire labour to save her crops during 1922, as a consequence of events that occurred prior to the Truce when she 'rendered some slight assistance to the wounded' Auxiliaries after the Clonfin ambush in February 1921. The support for her claim from the local Church of Ireland rector, Archdeacon Henry Johnson, helped her claim, as a reference from him was given considerable weight by the committee where the Longford county cases were concerned.[60]

Margaret O'Dowd, the deserted wife of a disbanded RIC officer, was awarded £200 for her own personal economic loss when she was forced to abandon her job as a maternity nurse after her family home was destroyed by the IRA in March 1921 and she was forced to leave, in spite of the fact that this event took place prior to the Truce, and she received £450 compensation for the loss of her home from the Compensation (Ireland) Commission. Perhaps the committee's sympathy stemmed from her husband's abscondment – he was described by the committee as 'a waster' who 'dissipated what money he had' on arrival in England in 1922 – although they appear to have been reconciled by the time of her claim four years later.[61]

The most extreme, though rare, cases involved the murder of the women claimants' husbands. One of the most notable cases in this regard was the £500 paid to Mrs Margaret Robertson Moore, whose husband, Henry, was shot dead at their home in Stillorgan on 9 October 1922. As Henry Moore was a land steward for Sir Henry Guinness, who was a member of the Irish Free State Senate, this appears to have been part of the IRA's deliberate targeting of the homes of senators. The award from the IGC was to make recompense for the loss of income since the death of her husband.[62]

Cases for personal injury, either direct or consequential, were not reflective of the overall nature of claims made by women to the IGC, which tended to focus more on the financial implications of damage to property or economic loss through boycotting or loss of business from forced migration. A significant number of these were from women associated with the crown forces, either as wives of policemen or businesspeople who traded with them. The incidence of claims from families of disbanded RIC reflects the findings of the British Labour Commission that visited Ireland during the War of Independence and reported that among the categories of women subjected to considerable violence and intimidation were 'Policemen's Wives and Barrack Servants'.[63]

Some RIC wives, who were in paid employment of their own, were also at a financial loss as a result of having to give up their jobs and leave Ireland. Bessie Churchill was appointed as principal of Kilclonfert National School in King's County in 1909, where her sister (Mrs Mary O'Sullivan) was also employed as an assistant. Both were married to policemen, and because of the republican boycott of the RIC, the school was boycotted from 1920 and 'to all practical purposes the school had ceased to exist owing to the boycott', which was 'attributed solely to the fact that the two teachers were policemen's wives'. The government continued to pay her salary until 1921, and her husband was disbanded the following year on a pension of £148, after which they moved to Liverpool. He also received compensation in the form of a disturbance allowance from the RIC tribunal.

In her claim, Bessie Churchill referred to seeking her old job back from the new Irish government but that another teacher was appointed in her stead, even though the school had still not re-opened by September 1923. The committee was sympathetic to her plight, which it considered to be 'undoubtedly a case of considerable hardship', but her claim for £2,000 was considered excessive, as the committee were of the opinion that there was never any realistic prospect of her remaining in her post after 1921: 'the claimant would probably on the disbandment of her husband from the Constabulary have herself elected to accompany him to this county [England] and resigned her appointment ... it was unlikely, even had Mrs Churchill remained in the country [Ireland], that she would have been appointed to the post [as school principal]'. Her loss was more significant because of her relatively young age; she was only 33 in 1921 so too young to qualify for a pension, but the sums she had already contributed to her pension appear to have been reimbursed. Taking account of the hardship she suffered but acknowledging that some compensation had been given via the RIC tribunal, the committee awarded her £500.[64]

By contrast, Ellen Wilkinson, who also had to surrender her employment as a teacher in Galway on the disbandment of her husband, who had been a sergeant in the RIC, had her claim for loss of earnings rejected. They moved to County Down, where he joined the new Royal Ulster Constabulary and she eventually found employment in January 1923, which appears to have been interpreted by the committee as adequate mitigation of their losses.[65]

Awards to RIC wives and dependants were not substantial, presumably because many of them also benefitted from disturbance allowances made by the RIC tribunal. Sarah Jane Heuston, the wife of a Dublin Metropolitan Police pensioner, who had a good claim but did not present it very well, was awarded £75, for economic loss and the detrimental impact on her health of frequent raids on her home. Kathleen Fitzgerald's father was ordered out of Ireland following his disbandment from the RIC. She remained in Ireland for a few more months but claimed the impact of the upheaval on her health prevented her from being able to hold down a job as a teacher; the committee awarded her £100. A more substantial award of £300 was made to Kate Hayden, whose RIC pensioner husband had died by the time she made the claim in 1926. While the committee was unwilling to concede the principle of making a personal injury award based on the claim that her husband's death 'was accelerated by the injuries and fear which he suffered in 1922', there was an evident desire to provide some restitution for her 'hardship and loss'.[66]

Businesswomen who had continued to serve the crown forces in spite of the boycott of the RIC decreed by Dáil Éireann, and who resisted intimidation to cease, are a notable group within the women who made applications to the IGC. Some suffered doubly, as they lost the local custom but then were also deprived of the custom of the crown forces when they withdrew from Ireland in 1922. In Skibbereen, the prominent loyalist solicitor Jasper Wolfe, and a local Justice of the Peace, Angus Swanson, attested to the loyalty of a local hotelier, Annie O'Shea, who provided accommodation for the army during 1920 and into 1922. Her decision to do so in spite of threats and boycotts may have arisen in part due to the fact that one of her daughters was married to an ex-soldier. The committee awarded her £250.[67] Also in Cork, Nora O'Mahony received £150 for the loss of business through a boycott for serving the crown forces in her public house.[68]

Even where the losses incurred to business were deemed more likely to have ensued from British withdrawal than boycotting during the revolution, awards were still made, in recognition of the owners' willingness to continue serving the police in the context of the Dáil boycott. Margaret Colohan, the widow of an RIC constable who ran a pub and grocery at Church Street in Listowel, County Kerry, and claimed to have traded with the RIC for twenty-five years, was awarded £200.[69]

The committee was more dubious of the claim made by Bridget Ryan of Tyrrellspass, County Westmeath, that an economic boycott cost her to lose 80 per cent of her custom, equivalent to an annual financial loss of £350. The committee felt she was exaggerating the extent of her business to begin with: 'The village of Tyrrellspass contains 236 inhabitants, the nearest railway line is six miles distant, there is no bank. Even assuming that claimant had a virtual monopoly for the trade of surrounding farmers, the trade cannot have been really substantial. A loss of £350 per annum suggests a drop in turnover of say £3,500, doubtful in a district such as this'. While conceding an element of boycott, they viewed her loss was more likely attributable to prevailing economic circumstances: 'by far the greater loss is caused by the economic state of the country. Farmers suffering years of heavy losses could not meet their accounts and left, or curtailed their purchases to a minimum'. In spite of these reservations, the poor state of her accounts ('the existence of two accounts by a small trader keeping no business books might call for comment') and the view that her case should be regarded with 'more than ordinary suspicion'. She was given a substantial award of £2,800. This case highlights the difficulty in ascertaining the basis for a decision from the evidence in the files. In this case there are strong objections to the veracity of her claim, yet a seemingly inexplicably large award was made.[70]

A particularly vulnerable group who suffered an economic loss through their services to the crown forces were barrack servants and generally less well-off women who performed domestic tasks for local police barracks. Agnes O'Halloran, a widow, resisted threats from 'Sinn Féiners' to stop her work as a washer-woman for the local RIC in Ennistymon, County Clare, because she had 'no [other] means of livelihood'. As a result, her home was raided and property damaged. Her case was probably not helped by her re-marriage to an ex-soldier in 1922. In spite of her pleas that 'I have not got a day's work since the British forces left' and her only income was the children's allowance, her claim was rejected, and there is no evidence on file to explain why.[71] A similar claim was made by Mary O'Brien, also from Ennistymon, who stated that she had worked for thirteen years 'doing laundry & scrubbing for RIC in Ennistymon' and was unemployed since their disbandment, but because of her prior association was unable to get alternative work. This was ruled outside the scope of the committee, presumably because much of her alleged loss had been during 1920 and 1921.[72] Two claims from women in the same town to have been doing effectively the same work might have aroused the committee's suspicions, although this is not stated in either of the files.

The IGC files are a valuable source of evidence for the economic lives of women in revolutionary-era Ireland, as many claimed for losses to their commercial or agricultural businesses. These included financial losses from enforced billeting by republicans during the Civil War, as in the cases of Anne Jones and Alice Bevan in Cork; boycotts of business due to extended family members' connection to the crown forces or British administration in Ireland (Mary Sheridan, Cavan, and Walpole, Roscommon); enforced sale of land below market value (Jesse Hunter, Sligo); and the abandonment of commercial businesses due to intimidation (Rachel Honner, Queen's County).[73]

Many claims were unsuccessful, often because they fell outside the scope of the terms of reference because they took place prior to the Truce. Nevertheless, the substance of the claims is evidence of how the revolution also affected women who were not involved in indirect ways. Emma McManus claimed for consequential loss because the disturbed nature of County Mayo prevented her from running a nursing home. While the committee sympathised with the fact that revolutionary Mayo 'was not a suitable place to send patients suffering from epilepsy and various nervous disorders', her claim was not for damage caused directly by revolutionary violence and as such was outside the committee's scope.[74]

The value of many of the claims was relatively small, but there were some substantial payments made to female landholders of large estates. Mrs Waller-Sawyer was awarded £6,775 for damage to her residence and the dereliction of her land at her estate, Hunstanton, in King's County (Offaly). Much to the committee's despair she was 'Unfortunately … a voluminous letter writer, who simply did not … seem to have the least idea of how her affairs stand, or how they stood before the troubles in Ireland'.[75]

Conclusion

The Irish revolution is unusual for the significant role played by women in its various military phases. Up to 300 women are estimated to have been involved in Easter Week 1916, and the nominal membership of Cumann na mBan was approximately 20,000 at the time of the Truce in mid-1921.[76] Access to newly released archival collections and further examination of existing ones from a specifically gender perspective present exciting new opportunities to expand considerably our knowledge of the activities of women during the revolution. Constructing the afterlives of revolutionaries is now possible through an examination of the pension files, which detail the attitudes of the State and former male revolutionaries to women, and allow for an assessment of the long-term physical, psychological and economic effects of their revolutionary activity. Not all of the women referred to in the Military Service Pensions Collection were combatants, and the revolution's wider impact on the widows, mothers and children of the men who died fighting for Irish independence is a story that can now be told 100 years later.

Many women in revolutionary Ireland opposed the campaign for independence, and their continued loyalty to British rule, either through their own political ideology or the service provided by their families to the State through the crown forces or public service, frequently attracted the unwanted attentions of either the IRA during the War of Independence, its anti-Treaty successor, or criminal elements exploiting the breakdown of law and order under the guise of republican sentiment. Attacks on property, and less often on their persons, are detailed comprehensively in the Irish Grants Committee, which has yet to receive a thorough analysis from the perspective of gender. The experience of these southern loyalist women, some of whom joined the Protestant exodus but many of whom stayed in the Free State after 1922, is largely absent from the studies of both the Protestant minority between 1911 and 1926 and the lives of Irish women in the Irish

Free State. Complementing and enhancing the evidence in the Irish Grants Committee, the Finance Compensation and OPW collections now present the opportunity to fill this lacuna in modern Irish history. The release of archival collections dealing with post-revolution compensation is opening up many new avenues for exploring the holistic experience of all Irish women during and after the revolution, and will contribute significantly to our understanding of the revolution and of women in this formative period of modern Irish history.

Chapter 8

Female Fatalities in County Cork during the Irish War of Independence and the Case of Mrs Lindsay

ANDY BIELENBERG

Despite the chaos that prevailed during the Irish War of Independence, as the administrative machinery of the old regime became increasingly untenable, the business of recording deaths continued, albeit with some reluctant British military assistance in relation to conflict-related fatalities in more disturbed areas. As a consequence, it is possible to roughly track the rising trend of female homicides recorded in Ireland in these years.

These figures imply that while women had not achieved parity in the incidence of murder (with the notable exception of 1917), they still accounted for almost 39 per cent of registered homicide victims between 1910 and 1918. Yet, when registered homicides mounted progressively during the course of the War of Independence, the female share declined to merely 6 per cent in 1920 and a low of only 5 per cent in 1921.[1] Although this starkly reveals a dramatic gender imbalance during the conflict, the absolute number of female homicides still registered a progressive rise from merely 11 in 1918 to 59 by 1921.

This chapter examines female, conflict-related fatalities in County Cork during the War of Independence. The victims have been identified and isolated from an ongoing project on all conflict-related fatalities in County Cork between 1919 and 1923, a work in progress, jointly written and researched with Prof. J.S. Donnelly, which is nonetheless sufficiently advanced to identify most female fatalities and discern both wider patterns and certain exceptional cases. One of the more important outcomes of this project is that it has brought greater focus to the issue of *civilian* fatalities, by far the largest category in the case of County Cork (the other three categories being combatant fatalities among the Royal Irish Constabulary (RIC), the British Army and Irish Republican Army (IRA) Volunteers).

Random Violence and its Consequences

County Cork recorded the highest number of conflict-related deaths among all counties in Ireland in absolute terms as well as somewhat more than 20 per cent of total fatalities in Ireland between the beginning of 1919 and the Truce in July 1921, revealing its position as a core conflict zone and an important case study of revolutionary violence. Our County Cork death register has captured thirteen female fatalities (all civilians) so far, which is merely 2.5 per cent of the total fatalities identified, again revealing a strong gender imbalance. Far less women than men were killed during this period. However, what happened to those women who were actually killed and what do these cases tell us about the conflict, in general?

A notable feature of the conflict was the small scale of most engagements. Very few episodes in this 'war' could be described even as 'battles'. A majority of the victims lost their lives in incidents where only one person was killed; most of the female fatalities in County Cork also conform to that pattern. The first was Ella Wood, who was killed when the Soldiers Home at Ballyvonare Military Barracks, Buttevant, was burnt to the ground by unidentified arsonists on the 14 February 1920. She was a sister of the owner.[2] Mary Parnell, a war widow with two children, was accidentally shot near Kyrl's Quay in Cork city on 26 June 1921 by crown forces when they were trying to recapture an escaped IRA prisoner.[3] Josephine Scannell, aged 19, was shot through the heart while working at a sewing machine just inside the window of her family residence at 12 French's Quay in Cork city on 23 June 1921, in a bout of random gunfire from the RIC following an IRA bomb attack on the RIC barracks on nearby Tuckey Street.[4]

Mary Ward died in the course of an IRA raid and arson attack on the Cat Fort on Tower Street in Cork city on the night of 11–12 July 1920. She collapsed with a heart attack when they were awoken and ordered to vacate the barracks. The attack occurred at a time when the IRA were destroying a number of RIC barracks in the city.[5] In somewhat similar circumstances, Sarah Medalie died from a heart attack when she was awakened by British soldiers who had broken into her premises searching for IRA men.[6] Harriet O'Meara on the other hand, an elderly lady, had the misfortune to be hit by an auxiliary division Crossley tender while crossing the road on the Grand Parade in Cork city, near the corner of Augustine Street, on 8 December 1920 and later died in the Mercy Hospital.[7]

In Cork city, the proximity of the civilian population to conflict episodes between crown forces and the IRA posed dangers, evident in all these instances. This was also the case in the garrison towns of the county; Nellie Carey of Fermoy, the 19-year-old daughter of a labourer, was mortally wounded on 18 March 1921 when in the company of British soldiers, one of whom she was engaged to, at a fair on the Mill Road in Fermoy. They were both shot at from behind a wall by a man in a soft brown hat and another with a cap, and she and her fiancé were hit. She was eventually taken to the local military hospital, where she lingered until her death at 5.30 p.m. the following day. She had been hit with a single bullet in the abdomen, fatally damaging her intestine. Although the military inquest returned a verdict of wilful murder against some person unknown, it was later claimed that the Castletownroche Battalion of the IRA carried out this attack as reprisals for some IRA executions in Dublin and the soldiers were the intended target. Her coffin was covered in the Union Jack, and both the military and police marched behind it as the Buffs regiment band played a dead march.[8]

Likewise, following a successful IRA arms raid on Mallow Army Barracks, in which a British soldier was fatally wounded defending the barracks (dying a few hours later), about ninety British soldiers were transported to Mallow from neighbouring garrison towns later that night (27–28 September 1920) to carry out an orchestrated reprisal, sacking and burning of parts of the town, including Cleeve's Condensed Milk Factory (which put 500 to 600 people out of work). Terrified civilians took refuge in the graveyards in the middle of the town that night. Frank Dempsey, a witness to the American Commission on Conditions in Ireland (who was chairman of the Urban District Council of Mallow) when questioned on this episode recalled:

> One woman, Mrs Connolly, who had a baby about three days previous to this, – she had to get up out of bed with her baby, of course. She got up, with nervousness and shock, and took her baby and remained out in the graveyard with her baby all night, with the result that she died two or three days after this. The baby is alive yet. Another old woman who went to the graveyard –
> Question; What was her name?
> Answer; Mrs. Quirk. She got sick and lost her head, and died about a month afterwards.[9]

These fatalities collectively provide examples of the tragic outcomes of the deployment of violence by both sides, in which female fatalities were usually unintentional. In similar circumstances, Mrs Alice King was fatally shot at the west end of the town of Mallow near the rail station on 31 January 1921, when returning to lodgings with her husband, the RIC county inspector William King. The IRA flying column of the Mallow Battalion were responsible for this attack. While it has generally been assumed that the county inspector was the target, a subsequent witness statement testimony from a participant, Jeremiah Daly, (given decades later) alleges the IRA believed they were attacking RIC men and were not specifically targeting either the county inspector or his wife. The RIC at the nearby barracks then carried out a reprisal attack on the railway workers at Mallow Railway Station resulting in a host of casualties, some fatal.[10]

While commemoration has been an important source for this project, invariably this was highly selective, leaving out civilian fatalities, including all the female victims noted above. Perhaps the most extreme example of this is the Upton ambush, on 15 February 1921, when the IRA attacked a train travelling from Cork city, targeting British military personnel. They had not taken into account the possibility that additional soldiers might join the train at Kinsale Junction (the stop prior to Upton station).[11] When this transpired, the IRA were significantly outgunned and suffered three fatalities, while none were recorded on the British side. This botched attack resulted in many needless civilian fatalities. While a memorial was subsequently erected at Upton station to the three republican dead (and a song even written in their memory), little consideration was given to the eight civilian fatalities. Among them was Mary Hall, who the *Irish Examiner* noted was killed in one of the carriages during the exchange of fire. She was a domestic servant working in Cork city, who came from Castletownbere, the only daughter of Richard and Mary Hall. She was travelling home to have a holiday, where she also assisted on the farm and sent money home regularly. She worked as a cook for David Desmond of Ballycureen House. Her parents were granted £400 in compensation. Here we get a small glimpse of grief, loss and broken survival strategies.[12]

Most of the female deaths recounted above have been long forgotten and 'hidden' in history. There were two fatalities in County Cork, however, which survived longer in popular memory. Both were intentional killings of suspected informers carried out by the IRA, making them somewhat untypical of the wider pattern.

Female Disappearances Carried Out by the IRA

One of the more notable features of fatalities in County Cork was the exceptionally high level of disappearances carried out by the IRA relative to other counties during the War of Independence; forty-seven disappearances have been documented so far, of which twenty-three were crown forces, while twenty-four were civilian suspected spies and informers, which included two women.

An IRA General Head Quarters (GHQ) directive forbidding the death penalty for female suspects had been issued in November 1920,[13] which was seldom broken, but in County Cork it appears to have been disregarded on more than one occasion. Bridget Noble's abduction from her home at Ardgroom on the Beara Peninsula on 4 March 1921 by members of the Castletownbere Battalion of the IRA was one such case. Her Scottish-born husband was obliged to work as a cooper in Grimsby so he was away. Her associations with the local RIC brought her into conflict with the IRA, more especially since she had alleged that the perpetrators of an agrarian murder in May 1920 were both in the IRA (and included the commandant of the 5th Battalion). Subsequently when local Volunteers cropped her hair, she informed the local RIC and was afterwards abducted. This gave rise to queries from her Grimsby-based husband, who wrote to de Valera in July and September 1921 requesting information on the fate of his missing wife.[14] De Valera raised the issue with GHQ in Dublin, and the IRA chief of staff sent a letter to the 1st Southern Division on 21 September 1921 demanding a report.[15] A response was finally submitted to the Cork No. 5 Brigade, from the headquarters of its 5th Battalion (Castletownbere) on 21 October as follows:

> I received your dispatch re Mrs. Noble asking for further particulars. I have been looking up these particulars for the past three or four days which accounts for delay. The following details are all that are available:
> No 1. Officers responsible for executions: The battalion staff of that time.
> No 2. The then Batt. Comdt. was of course responsible for everything that happened in the Battn. Area.
> No 3. Evidence and source from which obtained:
> (a) She was seen by some of the men of C. company (or Bere.) going into the police sergeant in a private house in C.T. Bere on two occasions.
> (b) When she came home from hospital she was bobbed by order of Battn. After a military raid in the district, in the course of which her house was visited by two officers, a search of her house was made by order of the O/C. H. Coy (Ardgroom) and the following were found: – Part of a letter from the H. Constable, Castletown,

five half torn letters from other members of the R.I.C. and two photos of R.I.C. men.

Information reached us from the R.I.C. that Mrs Noble told them that Liam Dwyer and Pat Crowley were the men who shot William Lehane. This man was shot for land grabbing in Febr. 1920.

After having been 'bobbed' Mrs Noble went into the police barracks in company with another girl – Nora Sullivan who, on being questioned afterwards told Pat Crowley, Jerh. Connor, James Malvey, Con Crowley and Tim Rahilly that she saw Mrs Noble handing a letter to the Head Constable containing the names of seven volunteers and stating that these were the men who bobbed her.

On the 4th March, in a raid on her house a letter was found addressed to Mrs Noble from the Head Constable asking her to meet him in C. Town on that evening. She was arrested on her way to the police barrack.

No 4. Date of arrest   4/3/1921.
Date of trial   13/3/1921.
Date of execution   15/3/1921.

No. 5. What resulted from the information which Mrs Noble gave to the police was not too serious as any of the 'murderers' were not caught, but were kept on the run. The district was constantly raided for them up till the truce.

One of the men, Ml. Sullivan, whose name was given by Mrs Noble as having taken part in the bobbing was arrested in the month of May and interned. Another man, John Dwyer, who was arrested on 4th March, was charged with having bobbed Mrs Noble and got six months imprisonment for same.

No 6. Mrs. Noble admitted guilt on all the charges. She was fortified with the rites of the Church before being executed.

Commandant.[16]

The 'commandant' of the 5th Battalion, Cork No. 5 Brigade in this instance was Liam O'Dwyer, who took full responsibility. In a further communication on the matter the following day from the 'commandant' of the Cork No. 5 Brigade to the adjutant of the 1st Southern Division, it was pointed out that 'As these reports were sent in to the old Cork No. 3 Brigade some time ago I had some difficulty in getting them again. I have nothing to add to the information contained in the reports from the battalion concerned.'[17]

It was clear from correspondence between Travers Wolfe, Solicitors, Skibbereen and the Minster for Defence that Mrs Noble's husband had still not been informed of her fate until after 22 March 1922, when the solicitor finally received notification from the Minister of Defence that 'records go to show that this woman was arrested on the 4th March 1921, on a charge of espionage, court-martialled by a duly authorised authority. Found guilty and executed on the 15th March 1921'.[18] This put a somewhat brave face on matters, even by the standards dictated by IRA procedure. Firstly, female suspects were not supposed to be killed; moreover, no evidence so far has emerged to indicate that the brigade had even been consulted (as required by the GHQ directive of November 1920 on women spies), though a report was alleged to have been sent subsequently. Moreover, Alexander Noble provided testimony in late January 1922 at a court hearing when he was making a claim for compensation that conflicted with other elements of the battalion commandant's report, since he pointed out she was actually going to visit her 80-year-old father when she was abducted (as opposed to going to the barracks). However, he did admit she went a number of times to the police barracks and must therefore have been suspected. At this stage he stated he had given up hope and assumed she was dead. After breaking down and weeping openly in court, he was awarded compensation of £1,500 by the judge.[19] GHQ's suspicions that the Cork brigades were not always following protocol in the matter of handling female spies were not entirely misplaced.

It is unclear from documented evidence precisely where Bridget Noble's death took place. Eve Morrison's work on revolutionary memory, combined with documentary evidence, has turned up a taped interview which touches on this case; Eva Sullivan, who had been a member of the Ardgroom branch of Cumann na mBan, recalled that Noble had been in touch with the British Army in the area on a few occasions (it was actually the RIC), that she was abducted and kept a prisoner for a period and then taken to Collorus (by boat up the Kenmare River just across the county bounds in Kerry) and then shot and buried. This interview also included some comment on the case by a man who had heard she was taken out in a boat and thrown overboard.[20] This case was largely kept out of the limelight, getting limited coverage in the press. As such it provided something of a contrast to the case of Mrs Lindsay, probably the most notorious female fatality of the Irish revolution.

The Case of Mrs Lindsay

Mary Lindsay was a well-connected loyalist living in Leemount House, Coachford. She had entertained General Strickland (the commander of the 6th division of the British Army in Ireland), who went occasionally to her house for lunch, or tea in 1920. She had been suspected of passing information on a few occasions.[21] However, when she intervened to avert bloodshed by preventing an IRA ambush on crown forces near Dripsey, on the main Macroom to Coachford road to the north of the River Lee on 28 January 1921, her stated intentions had precisely the opposite effect. On learning of the planned ambush, she met the Catholic priest, Father Shinnick, and agreed that he would send word to the flying column that their position was known and they should clear out (a tip-off which was ignored). Lindsay for her part immediately went with her chauffeur, James Clarke, at breakneck speed to the police station in Ballincollig, thus fully revealing the IRA's position. This information was promptly passed on to the British Army stationed at Ballincollig, who immediately mobilised a unit to engage the ambushers, who were thus surprised and routed. Ten arrests were made and five of the ambushers were court-martialled and earmarked for execution. Despite being warned by the British military authorities of the potential dangers, she remained in the area.[22] Of this, she was evidently well aware; General Strickland recorded in his pocket diary that on 2 February 1921, when he returned from his office, he 'found [text heavily redacted] here, in a great state – apparently she gave the information about ambush, & thinks they know it'.[23] Her fears regarding IRA suspicions were well founded since both Lindsay and Clarke were subsequently picked up by armed members of the 6th Battalion of the Cork No. 1 Brigade and were held as hostages under heavy guard at Gowlane North, Donoughmore.[24] Her sister later filed a report which gave further details:

> Mrs Lindsay was forcibly removed from her residence by members of the IRA about 1 a.m. on the 17th February last, her butler, James Clarke, was also taken. A few days afterwards a note came from her asking for some clothes to be sent to the Railway Station at Coachford. A fortnight later a party of armed men came to the house in charge of the same leader, who had carried out the abduction. He showed to the house keeper Miss Eakin, a few lines written by Mrs Lindsay on a leaf of his note book asking to have some papers taken out of her desk which the leader permitted Miss Eakin to obtain. Afterwards the party sprinkled petrol & and burned down the house. They took away with them all blankets and eider-down quilts, but refused to allow any of Mrs Lindsay's clothes or furniture to be saved. The leader stated when asked that Mrs Lindsay was then "fairly well and very plucky." A week or so later a large party of armed men came and towed Mrs Lindsay's motor car away, they also removed a boil engine and dynamo &c. At later dates

farm implements, tools, stable fittings, iron gates, donkey and cart, and 11 cows were taken.[25]

Reports in the press indicate that Leemount House was burnt to the ground at around 1 a.m. on the night of 12–13 March 1921.[26]

To avert the impending execution of the five IRA prisoners, letters were drawn up by the 6th Battalion leadership of the Cork No. 1 Brigade (accompanied by a note signed by Mrs Lindsay), and dispatched to General Strickland (stationed at Victoria Barracks in Cork city), indicating that her life would be in danger if the executions went ahead. Tragically, Strickland's diary entry for 28 February 1921 (the day of the executions) revealed that her letter only arrived after the executions had already been carried out.[27] Revolutionary and military justice meted out by both sides was certainly ruthless, uncompromising and inhuman. The bodies of the five executed by the British Army were never returned to relatives, but instead were transported to Cork Jail and buried on grounds which are now part of the campus of University College Cork, marked by a memorial.

Mrs Lindsay's sister, Ethel Benson, wrote to de Valera on 6 July 1921 requesting that he issue orders for her release:

> or if this will not be conceded that she should be permitted to communicate with her relatives, which as you know is allowed to all prisoners in any civilised country; or if she has died I ask that I should be definitely informed with the date of death & place of interment, such information is likewise not refused. I also request the release of her man James Clarke or similar information about him.[28]

This finally elicited a response from Cathal Brugha, Minister for Defence, on 29 July 1921, as follows:

> Madam, in accordance with instructions from the President, I have made inquiries from our local commanders into the case of Mrs Lindsay. The information sent us is that she was executed as a spy some months ago. The charge against her was that she was directly responsible for conveying to the enemy information which led to the execution of five of our men by the British authorities, to the death of a sixth, from wounds received in action, and to a sentence of twenty-five years' penal servitude passed upon a seventh. Mrs Lindsay wrote a letter to General Strickland pointing out the consequences to herself should our men be executed. They were executed, nevertheless. Five days after

their execution in Cork Barracks the sentence which had been passed on Mrs Lindsay, and suspended pending General Strickland's reply, was duly carried out. We regret the circumstances and the stern necessity to protect our forces which necessitated this drastic action by our local commanders.[29]

This implied they had been shot and buried on 5 March 1921, but it has been argued they lived longer, and there is evidence to support this contention.[30] A second letter from Mrs Lindsay to Strickland appears to have been drawn up around 8 March as follows:

Dear Sir Peter,
I am told that 2 more men of the Dripsey Ambush, Denis Murphy and James Barrett, are to be tried tomorrow – Will you please for my sake spare these two men – I beg of you to do so, as if these men are spared I shall be allowed to go home and if not I cannot say what will be my fate. Yrs very truly,
M. LINDSAY.

This letter was subsequently published in the *Morning Post* on 23 March 1921.[31] It remains possible that this is why greater clemency was shown in these cases; Denis Murphy got twenty-five years penal servitude instead of the death sentence, while James Barrett had been too badly wounded at the ambush, was not fit to stand trial and subsequently died in custody on 22 March 1921, but his body was at least returned to his relatives. This second letter implies she was still alive after 5 March. Brugha may have misconstrued the report from the OC Cork No. 1 Brigade, which appears to have indicated instead that the five executions in Victoria Barracks (on 28 February) took place five days after Lindsay's first letter was drawn up.[32]

When Mrs Benson published Brugha's response in the press, the matter was subsequently raised in both houses of the British Parliament, and Mrs Lindsay was increasingly lionised as an exemplary loyalist citizen. In the House of Lords, the Earl of Selborne in response to the allegation that she was a spy declared that:

all that can be alleged against Mrs Lindsay by her murderers is that in the normal experience of daily life she obtained some information which she passed on to the police – information against criminals or likely to lead to the apprehension of criminals. If that is what she did, she did nothing but that which every honourable and loyal citizen ought to do, and nothing more than everybody would wish to do who was proud to be terrorized by the Sinn Féin organization. If that is the story, as I am informed it is, then throughout the whole of the English-speaking world Mrs Lindsay's case will run on parallel lines with that of Nurse Cavell, and she will be nothing less than a martyr in the eyes of the whole Empire.[33]

Following this unwelcome exposure, Brugha adopted a harsher tone with Ethel Benson, pointedly noting that the statements in the Commons in early August 1921 conclusively indicated that Lindsay had indeed passed information to crown forces.[34] Yet her execution remained controversial even within the IRA. General Crozier (who had resigned from the Auxiliary Division in March 1921) indicated that in a subsequent conversation with Michael Collins, he (Collins) expressed remorse about this execution, alleging that it was not referred to him for the final decision, which it should, and that he was unlikely to have sanctioned it on account of her age.[35] While the typist in Richard Mulcahy's office clearly recalled the report on the execution, she could not remember any advice being sought regarding Lindsay's treatment and observed that Cork tended to act independently and send reports after.[36] In Cork it was alleged that GHQ had been informed by word of mouth, but this had not been put in writing. At a Cork No. 1 Brigade meeting held near Blarney, Seán O'Hegarty stated he had been in communication with GHQ who were not in favour of the killing and recommended another course of action.[37] What is absolutely clear is that Collins had been informed in writing on 15 March 1921, in a communication signed by the Brigade Adjutant of Cork No. 1 Brigade, Florence O'Donoghue, that James Clarke had been dealt with 'in the usual way', and that Mrs Lindsay, who was too old for deportation, was dying and the local battalion commandant proposed to hold her until she died. The communication sought approval for this course of action from GHQ, thereby appearing to comply with the women spy directive.[38] However, this is somewhat at variance with the subsequent report on her death by Seán O'Hegarty, which implies that they were both dead at this point, since Lindsay and Clarke had been shot at the same time and buried in the same grave - a more likely scenario, since it was corroborated by the testimony of Frank Busteed, the battalion flying column leader who supervised the executions at Rylane, Donoughmore.[39] The communication from the Brigade Adjutant written on 15 March 1921 implies that the Cork No. 1 Brigade leadership was probably covering up her execution, because it did not follow GHQ protocol in the matter of killing women spies.

Unsurprisingly, there was consequently some confusion on her fate in Dublin. Between late May and early July 1921, communications indicate that Erskine Childers, the Dáil director of publicity, was still unaware of her death, and the editor of *An t'Óglach*, Piaras Beaslaí, was also unaware if she was alive or in custody and was informed quite incorrectly that she had been released and was in hospital.[40] The same day a letter was sent to the Divisional Commandant of the 1st Southern Division from the IRA Chief of Staff seeking 'an early report of the circumstances concerned with her decease. Also the President asked for a written statement as to what her offence was'.[41] At this stage GHQ was becoming concerned with the adverse propaganda the case was generating. *The Morning Post* (which had championed her case) declared on 10 August that it was a long time since anything had so moved their readers as the exposure of the facts on the foul murder of Mrs Lindsay.[42]

The northern Irish unionist press was also following the case with more than a little interest, more especially given the connections of her late husband with the linen industry in Banbridge, County Down – where James Clarke came from, having been employed by the Lindsay family all his working life. The *Newsletter* noted, that while no charge had been revealed against him, he (Clarke) was a Protestant.[43] If Lindsay was guilty (by IRA definitions) of passing information to crown forces, Clarke was clearly innocent, and it was unlikely he was killed for sectarian reasons, but simply because if released he knew too much. Moreover, having communicated the intention to execute both hostages if the five prisoners were executed, the IRA leadership felt it was necessary to follow through, and just like the British military leadership had done in the case of Mrs Lindsay, they were equally unwilling to compromise.

Despite extensive correspondence and investigations to recover her remains, which were disinterred and then made irretrievable, the Office of the Director of Intelligence at Parkgate, Dublin informed the secretary to the Ministry of Defence in February 1924 that 'the Die-Hards are determined that the body will never be recovered'.[44] Though Mrs Lindsay was denied a Christian burial, the Manchester Regiment did not let her memory fade. On 28 January 1922, exactly a year to the day after the foiled ambush (rather than her actual death), a memorial service was held in Ballincollig Garrison church, to acknowledge her role in this successful military operation. The Commanding Officer recalled that 'after she had received information of the impending ambush her informant was afraid to pass it on and asked Mrs Lindsay to do so.' It was also noted that 'this was the first occasion on which the tables were turned on a rebel ambush party', thus making it a significant event from a crown force perspective.

Furthermore, in relation to her death it was alleged (somewhat improbably) that information was received:

> from a source believed to be absolutely genuine (quite likely *The Morning Post*) and confirmed from a different quarter that she was murdered with revolting brutality, so many shot guns and revolvers being emptied into her body that some of the limbs were detached. At the time of her death she was in a state of collapse having been dragged across country night after night with insufficient food and clothing. The body lay in a ditch near Blarney for four days but how it was subsequently disposed of is not known.

The final stages of the address noted:

> The courage required was of a very high order and Mrs Lindsay knew the risk she ran. All the more reason, therefore, should we be proud of the fact that there has been an instance in which duty has been placed before self. Mrs Lindsay showed devotion to duty of a very high standard and we have every reason therefore to pay respect to the memory of a very devoted and self-sacrificing lady more especially as she gave information which undoubtedly saved some of our own regiment and the local police force from running in to this very ambush. The ultimate result of her action [was] also that our area was cleared of a large number of rebels and it certainly put an end to any desire on their part to lay similar ambushes in future … the Manchester regiment should not lightly forget her bravery.[45]

In addition, at this time a larger public memorial service 'was held at St Mary's Cathedral Limerick. Detachments from the Welsh and Oxford and Bucks regiments, ninety men of the RIC and many members of the general public were present. The Dean of Limerick and other clergymen officiated at the service, which concluded with "The Last Post".'[46] Her commemoration evidently had a strong military aspect, normally reserved for fallen members of the crown forces. This, combined with the failure to return the five IRA prisoners' bodies, may explain why the leadership of the 6th Battalion refused to return her body and wished to avoid any prospect of a funeral, thus removing the possibility of any further ostentatious military displays in her memory.

Conclusion

As the records of the Irish revolution become more fully available, other female fatalities may yet come to light. The correspondence relating to Mary Lindsay's disappearance suggests as much, revealing that investigations were made into allegations that her body had been buried either near Ballinhassig or in the Knockraha-Little Island area. While both these regions had witnessed a number of secret burials, in the case of Mrs Lindsay the reports were merely rumours. Nonetheless, the crime branch investigating the Lindsay case shortly after the Civil War learned from persons who were in close contact with the IRA of the Knockraha district that while she was not buried there, 'two women were shot at a place called Reinslaugh'.[47] Another account, (based to a large extent on oral testimony gathered half a century later), asserted that the IRA 'had shot several women, mainly prostitutes, for giving information to the authorities, but these women were of the lower class'.[48] As yet these tentative references have not been corroborated and remain part of the unresolved history and memory of the revolution.

Although no female conflict-related fatalities have been located during the Truce period in Cork, during the Civil War twelve have been identified in the county so far in our study, eight of whom were killed between mid-August 1922 and the end of that year, and the other four in 1923 (encompassing the whole year). The fact that almost as many women were killed in the Civil War as in the War of Independence in Cork is remarkable, given the fact that the total number of civilian killings in the county was markedly lower in the Civil War than during the War of Independence – which might imply that there was relatively more of the kind of random violence in the latter conflict, which gave rise to female fatalities.

If Cork was no different to the rest of the country regarding the cause of most female fatalities in the War of Independence, the deliberate targeting of two women, Bridget Noble and Mary Lindsay, was quite untypical of the wider pattern. Both cases transgressed the so-called IRA code of honour in relation to killing women and broke with GHQ directives. As such, both gave rise to enquires from the next of kin to de Valera, which in turn gave rise to demands from GHQ for explanatory reports at brigade level in Cork. Both deaths occurred during an intense phase of the War of Independence when fatalities were particularly high on both sides. The differences between the two cases are equally instructive.

The case of Bridget Noble drew relatively little attention in the media, but that of Mary Lindsay became a major story. This was connected to several factors. Lindsay's higher social status, her sister's tenacity in seeking answers and boldly confronting the revolutionary government and communicating with the press, Lindsay's steadfast loyalism supporting crown forces, her social networks and connections (including those with British military leadership in Cork), and the fact that she was a Protestant, all drew further attention to this case. This was evident in the House of Commons in the way a question was framed on 4 August 1921 by Colonel Newman, who asked the British Prime Minister Lloyd George 'whether his attention has been called to the confession of the murder of two Protestants residing in County Cork, Mrs Lindsay and her manservant, James Clarke … and if the murder of these two British subjects in the South of Ireland is to be left without an effort to bring the parties responsible to justice?'[49] Lindsay and Clarke constituted two of the twenty-two Protestant suspected spies and informers killed in County Cork in the War of Independence out of a total of seventy-one suspects, but the circumstances set out in this chapter provide no support for the contention that they were killed for sectarian reasons. The fact that she had passed information, on the other hand, was incontrovertible, but Lindsay's action also had far worse consequences for the local battalion of the IRA than in the case of Mrs Noble.

The tragedy of the Lindsay case, including all of the other lost lives that resulted, was that her intervention in an attempt to save lives led firstly to five British military executions of IRA prisoners, followed quickly by six fatal IRA reprisals on British soldiers and a further crown force reprisal on an IRA member, while another IRA volunteer did not recover from the injuries received at the ambush. If we include her own death and that of Clarke, this needless and tragic train of killings arising out of this single episode, exemplified the extent to which neither side was willing to back down or compromise in the deployment of violence. Yet in Cork, and other parts of Ireland, females constituted a remarkably small share of total fatalities. The circumstances that led to most fatalities in the county broadly conform to the pattern identified by Marie Coleman, who concluded that many female deaths were a result of 'non-targeted or random acts of violence'.[50] In other words the deployment of violence by both sides resulted in many unintentional fatalities and these accounted for most female fatalities in County Cork.

Female fatalities in County Cork during the War of Independence

Ella Wood, 14 February 1920, perished in an arson attack on soldier's home in Buttevant.

Mary Ward, 11–12 July 1920, heart attack during IRA raid or arson attack on Cat Fort.

Mrs Connolly, 28–29 September 1920, died of pneumonia shortly after the sacking of Mallow by Crown forces, having taken refuge in graveyard overnight.

Mrs Quirk, died a month after the sacking of Mallow having taken refuge in graveyard overnight.

Harriet O'Meara, 8 December 1920, died as a result of a traffic accident when she was hit by an Auxiliary Division Crossley Tender, subsequently dying in Mercy Hospital Cork.

Sarah Medalie, 10 December 1920, heart attack during British military raid of premises.

Alice King, 31 January 1921, shot by IRA near Mallow Railway Station.

Mary Hall, 15 February 1921, shot in Upton train ambush when the IRA attacked military.

Mary Lindsay, 17 February 1921, abducted from her home, near Coachford and held captive, having passed on information about the Dripsey ambush. She was executed and disappeared by 6th Battalion, Cork No. 1 Brigade.

Bridget Noble, 4 March 1921, abducted near her home at Ardgroom, and subsequently executed and disappeared by 5th Batallion, Cork No. 5 Brigade.

Nellie Carey, 18 March 21, shot by IRA in attempted reprisals on military, Fermoy.

Josephine Scannell, 23 March 1921, shot by RIC gunfire following barrack attack at French's Quay.

Mary Parnell, 26 June 1921, shot by crown forces recapturing a prisoner at Kyrl's Quay.

Chapter 9

THE HOMEFRONT AS BATTLEFRONT:

Women, Violence and the Domestic Space during War in Ireland, 1919–1921

MARY McAULIFFE

In the July 1921 edition of the *Irish Bulletin*, a republican newspaper, funded by Dáil Éireann, most specifically by the Department of Propaganda, a headline reads 'The war on women and children'. The author of the piece wishes to make known 'the real nature of the war which the British premier (Lloyd George) expresses his earnest desire to terminate'.[1] The investigator from the *Bulletin* had spent twenty-nine days in the Southern Martial Law area, namely in Cork city and district, Limerick city and district, Macroom, Mallow, Bantry, Tralee, Ballymacelligott, Ennis, Dungarvan and Waterford. His report stated, 'the lot of women living in the Martial Law areas is a most unenviable one, but at the same time is of a character difficult to measure in concrete terms'. The *Irish Bulletin* never had widespread circulation in Ireland, but by the time the article detailing the investigator's results in the Southern Martial Law region was published, its new editor, Erskine Childers, was determined that one of its aims was to incite civilian opposition in Britain to the continuation of the war in Ireland by the British government. If the war persisted, he wrote, 'it would corrupt and eventually ruin not only your Army, but your nation and your empire itself'.[2] In publishing details of violence and atrocities carried out on the civilian population in Ireland, the *Irish Bulletin* was attempting to shock British and international readers into withdrawing support for the war and the terror tactics used by the crown forces in Ireland, tactics which had the tacit support of the British government.

Despite its obvious propaganda purpose, the *Bulletin* did demonstrate, in its reports, the vulnerability of the civilian population during what was a guerrilla war. Burning and sacking of houses and farmsteads, attacks and assaults on women, midnight raids and searches, insults to families of men on the run, and families reduced to 'absolute want' were part and parcel of the experience of raids by the crown forces. Examples given noted that it was

> Women and Children [who] suffer very greatly from these operations, which were extensive and of frequent occurrence all over the South ... Burnings at Ballymacelligott, Co. Kerry, where a number of farmhouses were destroyed, families of young children had to be roused from sleep and carried, partially clothed, through scenes of terror, into the darkness of the night and the fields.[3]

As Louise Ryan has argued, guerrilla warfare in Ireland, which was fought in the countryside and isolated villages, meant that 'women [and children] were easy targets'.[4] Frustrated with the ease with which armed flying columns could melt into the countryside, the crown forces carried out revenge attacks on 'soft' targets, the remote farmhouse, the undefended village, the small communities, and, most particularly, the home. In those homes, in the privacy of the domestic sphere, it was women and girls who bore the brunt of attacks.

The last four decades have seen an upsurge in interest in, and research and writing on, women's experience and involvement in the revolutionary decade. While the recent decade of centenaries has certainly increased public appetite for histories of women's involvement in this period, scholars, mostly women, have been researching and writing on this since the 1980s.[5] These publications, along with many other journal articles, edited collections, and biographies of individual women activists, have advanced our knowledge of women's political and militant activism in the early decades of the twentieth century and transformed the usual narrative, which had generally marginalised or ignored the very important and integral role of women in the socio-political histories of the period.

Other publications have looked at the military campaigns and the impact of the war, violence and use of terror as a tactic, on communities during the War of Independence and Civil War. Works from scholars such as Joost Augusteijn, David Fitzpatrick, Gemma Clark, Peter Hart and Anne Dolan, have studied the impact of the military campaigns, terror and violence of the War of Independence and Civil War.[6] Despite these publications however, the question of gendered violence during this period, 1919–1923, is still a contested, and relatively under-researched one. There has been some excellent work done by Louise Ryan (one of the first scholars to write about this), Marie Coleman, Sarah Benson, Linda Connolly and Lindsey Earner-Byrne, among others.[7] Now, with the newly accessible archives, especially the Bureau of Military History witness statements, and the Military Service Pension Collection, as well as collected papers of activist women in UCD Archives, the National Archives, access to online digitised newspapers and other materials, as well as materials in British archives, we have access to sources that can broaden our knowledge of all events, and histories of this period, including the political, social and gendered experiences of women.

Cork Cumann na mBan member and activist, Lil Conlon, in her book, *Cumann na mBan and the Women of Ireland, 1913–25*, described the activities of the crown forces, comprising the Black and Tans, the Auxiliaries, and the Royal Irish Constabulary (RIC) during this period, as visiting a 'reign of terror' on Ireland. This reign of terror, she wrote, 'had swept throughout the whole country, the Black and Tans co-operated with the Auxiliaries in perpetrating atrocities which were unparalleled in the annals of civilisation'.[8] She recalled that raids were 'made at night, entries were forced', in order to intensify the terror.[9] This is borne out by the fact that in 1920 alone the crown forces raided almost 50,000 homes (as reported by the Interim Report on the American Commission on Conditions in Ireland) while the IRA also raided thousands of homes. In writing the history of the War of Independence, these numbers make it imperative that we look beyond the narrative of the British crown forces against the IRA, and those usual histories of attacks, ambushes, spies, informers, assassinations, negotiations and other military and political histories. There are other narratives and histories of the period that need research.

A report from a British Labour Party Commission sent to Ireland in November 1920 to see conditions for themselves gives an indication of the violence experienced by civilians, particularly women. The Commission stated that, unfortunately, the crown forces, 'in their work of hunting down people ... often act in a way which is terrifying to women'.[10] According to the report, attacks on women in their homes, particularly women living in isolated, rural communities were commonplace. However, as newspaper reports and other archival material demonstrates, it was not only the crown forces who were attacking women in their homes and communities. Constant raids on communities, searching and looting of homes, mistreatment of women by both sides in the conflict starkly reveals that there was a real blurring of lines between 'home front' and 'battlefront'.

In traditional narratives of war, the home front is conceived as a feminine space, where women are safe, protected and supportive of the masculine space of the battlefront. Within British mainstream narratives of the First World War, when the term 'home front' was popularised, there was a clear delineation between home front (feminine) and battlefront (masculine). The home front, a protected, domestic, feminised space, served to support and reinforce the needs of the battlefront. As Joanna Bourke has observed, for the Victorians, 'the womanly woman was gentle, domesticated and virginal; the manly man was athletic, stoical and courageous'.[11] Virility, athleticism, courage, militancy and protection of 'his' women and children were the mark of a true man. With the outbreak of the First World War in 1914, gendered propaganda was used to entice men to enlist to protect the nation and the home front.

Masculinity and militancy were inimically intertwined, while femininity, patriotic motherhood and domesticity were celebrated by war governments and the press. While the war did create upheavals in the lives of men and women, traditional assumptions about gender roles remained fairly consistent throughout the period. Women could and did take the place of men on the factory floor and on farms. But on the home front, they could contribute by 'doing their bit for the duration', with the expectation that this was temporary. Women would keep the home front intact and running while men went off to war, and on return, gender roles would revert to their normative practices, with women back in the domestic. One of the most effective war propaganda posters was one that called on British (and Irish) men to protect the women of 'little' Belgium, who were being violated in their homes by the dastardly 'Hun'. On the poster it states that British homes 'are secure, our mothers and wives safe, our children still play and fear no harm', while in Belgium homes 'are destroyed, their women are murdered and worse, their children are dead or slaves'. Women, it said, 'back up the men who have saved you'.[12] This propaganda, as Lisa Todd writes, was about motivating men to protect women and children and the domestic space.

This concept of home front and battlefront, however, becomes very blurred when a different type of warfare brings the battle to the front door. Guerrilla warfare was very different to the usual type of trench warfare that the British had fought on the Western Front during the First World War. The inability to tell the difference between combatant and non-combatant, to be unable to see and identify the enemy, created the conditions in which men who had fought trench war on the Western Front against a uniformed and recognisable enemy, were now facing an invisible enemy who could be anywhere and anyone. One of the causes and effects of the tactics of the War of Independence was, therefore, to blur the distinction between soldier and civilian, between enemy and friend, and between where conditions of war did or did not prevail. These conditions caused the crown forces to, as Leeson writes, 'behave in ways that [violated] their pre-existing moral and ethical standards', and 'to fight terror, as they saw it, with terror'.[13] In this type of guerrilla warfare, with the IRA active service units often 'on the run', it was up to the women's militant republican organisation, Cumann na mBan, to provide the support to the men. They ran safe houses, protected arms dumps, carried dispatches, provided intelligence information of the movement of the crown forces, and provided provisions and first aid for IRA Volunteers.

Most of these activities were conducted from their own homes, so for Cumann na mBan women, their homes were, most often, their battleground. As Ryan notes, 'women within this "home front" took grave risks … providing shelter for IRA men "on the run", which was for the women a demanding, risk-filled task'.[14] Julie Peteet, writing about the 1948–49 war in Palestine, notes 'the home as front' where the 'continuous violations of the home – the violent entries, searches and demotion (or burnings in Ireland's case) … casts aside the notions of the home as a space distant from conflict'.[15] 'Blurring of home and front', she notes, 'further collapsed distinctions between feminine and masculine, between who experienced terror and who did not'.[16] In Ireland during the War of Independence and Civil War, Anne Dolan notes 'certain repetitions' which are revealed in the raids on homes in this period. These are, as Dolan writes, the patterns of how the violence works:

> there are disturbances associated with the strange and the familiar, building up to the moment of violence and in themselves an integral part of how the violence terrifies, of how the terror works. The sound of the knock echoing through the house in the middle of the night seems to be the place where most witnesses begin. It is the sound that tolled all sorts of dangers – raids for arms, demands for food or shelter, the coming of the Crown forces in their many forms, the spectre of the Black and Tans firing their rifles and frightening our wives and daughters, murdering … in the middle of the night.[17]

The home front becomes, therefore, not a safe space, but a battlefront, a space of gendered violation and terror. This violation of the intimate, feminine, domestic space reflects, as Ryan, notes, 'the intensely political work which was going on inside many Irish homes' in this period.[18] This is the collapsing of the traditional spaces of masculine and feminine in war - war is now everywhere. The Irish revolutionary war was, as Justin Dolan Stover writes, 'intimate', 'where British security forces and the IRA routinely attacked private spaces'.[19] Violated 'intimate' spaces, during the War of Independence, included the rooms in private homes where intelligence agents working for the crown forces were assassinated by the IRA, the homes of RIC men whose wives and children were terrorised, and the homes of IRA men on the run, whose families were often targeted for counter-reprisals. Women were also specifically targeted for reprisal within these intimate spaces.

In this chapter I will look at the private spaces occupied by Cumann na mBan women targeted by the crown forces, some of whom were related to IRA men and involved in militant activism themselves. In addition, I will look at those women who were targeted by the IRA, most often in their own homes. Why and how this gendered targeting of violence against women, within their homes, was conducted by both sides will be considered. Often these private spaces were not occupied by militant men, members of active units of the IRA or flying columns who were 'on the run'. Both British Army soldiers and RIC men also withdrew to barracks as the war progressed, while women associated or thought to be associated with them were vulnerable to assault and attack, as they remained living within their communities. While the men withdrew from these spaces as they became unsafe, for the women and children (and non-militant men) there was little or no choice but to remain in their homes, so the domestic was the space where women and children most often encountered the brutalities of both the crown forces and the IRA.

It was often acknowledged by IRA men that women had it hard in their homes. As Michael Hynes, a member of the Galway IRA, said, women had it difficult as they had to remain 'in their homes, and there, along with their parents, meet the midnight raiders who came to threaten and bully and burn them out'.[20] Even in their ordinary, domestic, familial, and communal activities, doing the shopping, going to schools with children, or to Mass, there was a threat of constant violence. In evidence given by RIC member John McNamara, to the American Commission on Conditions in Ireland he described an attack by the crown forces on women and children coming from evening Mass, in Ballylongford, County Kerry:

> the two Black and Tans from the barracks went to a church in the village at about seven o'clock in the evening when two or three hundred

residents were at evening devotion. They stationed themselves at the gate of the church with batons and beat the people as they came through the gate. There were many women and children beaten upon this night. The two Black and Tans who perpetrated this outrage boasted about it at the barracks, but no official investigation was ever made and they were not reprimanded by their superior officers.[21]

Again, as Stover suggests, the 'acknowledgement of women who had borne the brunt of the raids and interrogations … suggests that some of the most vital contributions to the independence movement took place away from the ambush site'.[22] Rather for women and girls, it takes place in the intimacy of the domestic space, in the home, or adjacent to the home, in the village, in the community, or in the church.

This focus on the different experiences of violations in the domestic spaces, and attacks on women in that domestic space, during the War of Independence, allows us to come to a closer understanding of the motivations for these attacks, and the differing outcomes and impacts on women, emotionally, psychologically, and societally. The reasons behind the raids, the type of violence visited on women, the emotional and psychological experience of that violence, differed according to the motivations and the make-up of the raiders. Some similarities do occur, however; these were always raids led by men, on family homes, in which women were mistreated. Most happened late at night after the occupants of the house had retired to bed; women and girls were often dragged out of bed, clothed only in their night attire, and often they were isolated either within or just outside the home by masked and armed (sometimes drunk – although, most often, this fact is stated in relation to raids by the crown forces) men. These groups could range in number from three to five men, to large groups of fifteen to twenty men, always armed and masked. Descriptions in the sources of these raids show that certain received narratives need to be revisited. Not all raids were undertaken by 'drunken Tans' on respectable, loyal Irishwomen, who were probably members of Cumann na mBan or in the families of men on the run. Not all raids, either by crown forces or the IRA, were violent. Some women report the kindness of soldiers, and not all women appeared to have been terrified. In the *Leitrim Observer*, September 1920, one young girl who was having her hair sheared in her home, during a midnight raid by the IRA, for 'keeping company' with soldiers, asked that they 'Cut it nicely so that it will not be noticed'.

However, as the war continued into 1920 and the frustrations of the crown forces at fighting a guerrilla war boiled over, the violence in many parts of the country, especially in the south-west, escalated, and the raids and reprisals on homes increased. As Gemma Clark writes, house burning for example, a viciously destructive yet common tactic, employed throughout 1919–23, directly affected these groups who would have otherwise avoided serious violence'.[23] Lil Conlon acknowledged the period 1920 into 1921 was when the British authorities began to recognise the importance of Cumann mBan women to the guerrilla war effort. She said:

> The going was tough on the female sex, they were unable to 'go on the run', so were constantly subjected to having their homes raided and precious possessions destroyed. To intensify the reign of terror, swoops were made at night, entries forced into their homes, and the women's hair cut off in a brutal fashion as well as suffering other indignities and insults.[24]

It was during this period that active Cumann na mBan members began to experience the worst of the raids and reprisals, when 'masked raiders could come to threaten, bully and burn out their homes'.[25] Descriptions in sources such as the Military Services Pension Files, the Bureau of Military History and other archival materials detail the escalation and intensity of violence perpetuated on women in their domestic space. Attacks on homes affected women militants more than men, and many of the Cumann na mBan women who later applied for military pensions detail raids and burning at their homes. The interim report from the American Commission on Conditions in Ireland also details some of the violence visited on women during raids on their homes. Women had the 'privacy of their bedrooms … invaded in the dead of night, and their hair cut off'. Such was the terror of the population that it reported, 'in some places, those who were not "on the run," and the infirm and aged, the women and children, would appear to feel safer in the fields than in their homes'.[26] However, despite the imminent possibility of terror, Cumann na mBan women remained at work for the cause, in their homes.

In their military service pension applications, we have first-hand accounts of the violence visited on them because of their work. For example, Julia Duffy, Ballinalee Cumann na mBan, County Longford, recorded that 'her house was raided several times by the Black and Tans and on one occasion they brought her outside and beat her about the head mostly, they broke nine teeth. I had to get my teeth extracted three days after'.[27] Duffy was involved during the war in carrying dispatches for the local IRA, transporting ammunition to ambush sites, providing first aid and any other work demanded of her by her local commandant. There is no doubt she and her home were deliberately targeted because of her membership of Cumann na mBan, her relationship with members of the local IRA (the North Longford ASU in particular) and suspicions about the work she was doing; as she herself stated, 'they [the Black and Tans] would be silly not to know one so prominent, they would know my brother was adjutant [of the local ASU]'.[28] Because she continued with her work, in December 1920, after another raid, she and her mother and sister were burnt out.

In County Limerick, Bridget O'Donnell, a member of Ballylanders Cumann na mBan whose house was a known safe house used by the IRA, stated that it was no surprise after an attack on Kilmallock Barracks, where she was involved as a scout, in May 1920, 'her home was bombed by the Black and Tans, at about 2.30 a.m. in the morning. All the shop windows and the goods in the windows were shattered … two weeks later the house was burned down'.[29] O'Donnell was an integral part of IRA militant actions in Kilmallock and surrounding areas. She worked with IRA leaders Seán Hogan and Dan Breen, reporting on RIC movements and helping her brother make ammunition. The burning of her house did not prevent O'Donnell for continuing her work for the IRA. After it was burned, she lived with a Fr Humphries in Knocklong, County Limerick and continued transporting arms, helping the men on the run, helping with the coordination and scouting with ambushes and other actions. She was, she said, 'always on the alert for the movements of the Black and Tans and kept in touch with the column all the time'.[30]

In another pension application, Cumann na mBan member, Mary O'Neill of the Mid-Clare Cumann na mBan noted 'hard days that followed for her family and herself' after raids on their home. Her brother, Patrick Lehane, Vice-Commandant of the 4th Battalion, Mid-Clare Brigade of the IRA, had been killed the night of the Rineen Ambush (in which several RIC men were killed). The two Lehane brothers (Patrick and Dónal) had taken part in the ambush, as had Mary O'Neill's husband, Ignatius O'Neill. In revenge, several homes were attacked and burnt. Mary O'Neill's brother Patrick was among the reprisal victims. His charred body was found the next day in the ruins of Michael Howard's house, which had been burned as a reprisal by the British forces.[31] The Lehane home was also attacked and set on fire, and their father Dan was shot dead at his own front door. As Mary O'Neill wrote in her pension application, 'They shot [my] father dead at his own door, robbed and plundered, and … [her] young helpless family escaped by a hairbreadth … her mother was later a physical and mental wreck after the house was looted and burned'.[32] This did not stop O'Neill in her work, as noted, 'The family took up abode in another house on the farm, and Mrs O'Neill was as determined as ever in her help to the active service unit'.[33] In 1921 she was still active and supplied the local IRA active service unit with information before the ambush at Miltown Malbay.

The traumas the women suffered because of their raids could be severe. Even if their homes were not burned, the attacks served to terrorise women. In Ennis, Cumann na mBan woman Katherine Collins spoke of how, after her home was raided, she 'suffered cruel ... I had to leave home and the lodgers that were staying with me – they had to leave the house'.[34] In Castleisland, County Kerry, Ellen McGillicuddy, a member of the local Cumann na mBan, kept rifles, arms and ammunition for the local IRA. Her place, her home and pub was frequently targeted by the crown forces, sometimes raided twice a day, and she was eventually burnt out in May 1921. Christina Ahern of the Middleton branch of Cumann na mBan had her home burned out in January 1921, and she had to live with a neighbour, until outbuildings were converted into a living space.[35] Later in May 1921, the crown forces raided this new domestic space, found her brother Michael there and shot him dead. Margaret Brennan of Meelick Cumann na mBan in Limerick had 'her comfortable home ... subjected to raids several times every week', and eventually, in October 1920, it was burnt out. She and her mother 'were brutally hustled out on the roadside in night attire and were compelled to seek shelter from neighbours'.[36] In order to terrorise the women even more, the crown forces threatened to burn out anyone who gave them shelter. It was also noted by many of the women that the raiders who came to their homes were fully armed. A raid on the house of Dr Kathleen Lynn in Dublin, described in a newspaper report on 1 March 1920, mentioned the 'half company of soldiers with glittering bayonets, and a dozen policemen' who surrounded the house.[37] In February 1921, the home of Cumann na mBan member Annie Murphy of Kilmyshal, County Wexford was burned 'on the occasion of the burning her mother was dragged out ... they [the Black and Tans] left about nine grenades around the house and after they left she picked them up and put them in a bucket'.[38]

The accounts by women of these raids follow a similar pattern. Kathleen Clarke and Kathleen McDonnell, both activists in Cumann na mBan, and well known, like Dr Lynn, to the crown forces, described 'houses occupied by women and children raided at night by armed men – the terror of the situation underlined by the fact that the men were rude, insulting, threatening and undisciplined'.[39] Clarke described a terrifying raid by crown forces, on her mother's home on an occasion when she was visiting Limerick. The raid was conducted by 'seven men, all drunk … [and] one never knew what drunken men could do'.[40] These raids, the *Irish Bulletin* noted, were a 'source of sleeplessness, nervous breakdowns, and in the case of expectant mothers, produce grave results for mothers and children'.[41] However, these incidents as reported by the women of Cumann na mBan came as no real shock to them. They were working for a cause and the dangers of that work included coming to the attention of the crown forces. In most cases the women, stoically, continued their work for the republican cause until the Truce, and many continued into the Civil War. While some women later wrote that the raids on their homes left them as 'nervous wrecks', oftentimes they sought to deflect the trauma of the experiences on to their female relatives, speaking of their mothers or sisters who were left with nervous conditions, while they themselves continued with their 'work for Ireland'. Their seeming stoicism, and their emotional and psychological recovery from violence, is in stark contrast to the experience of women not associated with Cumann na mBan or actively involved in the war.

These other women who experienced raids, reprisals and mistreatment in their homes, were women and girls accused of 'keeping company'. While the reason for the raid might be different, the pattern of the raid was the same, and similarly designed to terrorise. The knock on the door late at night, armed and masked men entering and demanding to see a young girl of the house, dragging her from her bed in her night attire, isolating her and then shearing off her hair, often with a statement of warning to stop keeping company with soldiers or police. Head shaving, shearing or bobbing, as it was often called, was a deliberate violation of victims' femininity, within or adjacent to what was considered the safe space of the home. As Linda Connolly has demonstrated, while the cutting itself was painful, the aftermath could be worse, as the shaved woman became a symbol of betrayal of her community, her family and her nation, and a warning to others.[42] Contemporary newspaper reports give us a flavour of the method and intent of these raids, and add to the ignominy of the treatment, as the unfortunate young women are often named in these reports. In Tuam, County Galway, in May 1920, a Miss Anne Devine was dragged from her bed by five armed and masked men, accused of keeping company with an RIC constable, told that the men would 'make Irish girls have nothing to do with Ireland's 'sworn enemies'.[43] Her hair was cut off with a shears, one man holding her … a hair cutting machine was used to complete the job with her hair being cut almost to the skin'.[44] Another case near Tuam was Bridget Keegan, whose house was raided by armed and masked raiders (see chapter 6).[45]

In Newport County Tipperary in July 1920 a young woman 'who was keeping company with a policeman … was attacked by four disguised men who cut her hair off remarking "You won't be seen going to the creamery for a while"'.[46] The implication of this of course is that the very public marker of shame, a cropped, bobbed or shaved head on a woman or girl, would be visible to all. This shame of the shaving could confine her to the domestic, where she, it was presumed, could not continue with her unacceptable relationship with an RIC man. This is one of several cases in which revenge was taken by the crown forces on the local community, after one of 'their' women was attacked by the IRA. The same report states:

> The girl and her father reported the outrage to the police. Soon afterwards the [local] creamery and cheese house, together with all the valuable machinery, as well as two dwelling houses were completely destroyed by bombs and fire caused, it is said, by men in uniform.[47]

Here, in the same community the Black and Tans and the RIC were terrorising women in their homes and communities, as were the IRA. While some of the crown forces raids were carried out looking for men suspected of being in the IRA, and some were reprisals on Cumann na mBan women for their own militant activities, there were quite a few carried out in revenge for raids undertaken by the IRA on girls accused of keeping company. On the other side, many young women were attacked by the IRA, most often in their homes, on suspicion of betraying the cause of freedom, of passing information to the RIC or crown forces, of keeping company with the enemy. Those who delivered their punishment were young men who would, potentially, be the leaders in the new Ireland. They delivered gendered judgements of bodily regulation and moral control, and gendered punishment of shame on these young women. As IRA man James Maloney stated in his witness statement:

> Some young girls created a problem. The British uniform was an attraction for them, as indeed would any uniform. They could be a real danger to the movement and gave bad example by consorting with the enemy. They were warned repeatedly and stronger measures had to be resorted to. No Volunteer liked the job, but on occasion these girls' hair had to be cut.[48]

Years later, fashion he said, was to dictate bobbed hair 'but at this period … it was deemed shameful'.[49] Witness statements from several ex-IRA men mention the need to conduct this type of terror on young women for 'keeping company'.

In July 1920, Mr Justice Samuels of the Cork Assizes, condemned the 'most detestable crime of assaulting young girls, attacking them in their homes, dragging them from their beds and shaving their hair, the object being to intimidate them, because they had been friends with soldiers or police'.[50] This form of violence by the local community on its own, conforms to the idea of 'insider violence', deployed, as Marie Coleman notes, 'as a method of disciplining women, including those who were, or expected to be, on the same side as the perpetrators'.[51] This tactic was also used to send a message to the men in a family. In November 1920 an attack on a young woman in Listowel, County Kerry, was carried out, and her hair cut, because 'one of her brothers had passed an examination for entry' into the RIC.[52] Even reporting on non-militant activities to the police could bring retribution. In Derrybeg, Belfast, a woman, Mary Gallagher, was attacked in her home by raiders, as 'she had reported a neighbour to the crown forces for having poisoned her dog'.[53] In Killorglin, County Kerry, the IRA raided the cottage of a poor woman, as an RIC constable had called in there to repair his bicycle. During the raid the men 'wrecked all of the furniture and damaged the building … and also cut out the tongue of a donkey belonging to the woman'.[54]

The crown forces and the IRA used similar terror tactics on women in homes and communities. In those cases, it was one group of men sending another group of men a message though the bodies of women. The *Skibbereen Eagle* of September 1920 had a report on a Miss Madden of Galway, who described her experience of a crown forces raid on her home, late one September night. This was a revenge raid, as a woman close to the Black and Tans had had her hair cut earlier in the week. As Miss Madden described:

> They brought me outside and closed the door, leaving mother inside in a terrified condition. They had shouted 'hands up' in the first instance and held revolvers on me but when I went outside they told me that it would be alright if I would be quiet … Mother was locked in during this ordeal and as she thought they were going to shoot me after what had happened a week ago, she felt the whole thing much more than I did. When they cut my hair they let me go. They spoke with English accents but I was too upset to notice what uniforms they wore.[55]

Because the raiders sometimes wore disguises, women were often only able to distinguish which group of men had attacked them by their accents. Miss Madden stated she heard English accents during the raid on her home, but a report in the *Belfast Newsletter* of 21 October 1920 noted that it had become known to the authorities that 'unauthorised persons posing as soldiers have raided houses in the Dublin district'.[56] At times, it would have been impossible to know which group of armed, militant men was raiding and visiting terror on women in their homes, and for whatever reason. Indeed, the IRA was also not above using the threat of raids on homes and violence against women as a subterfuge, demonstrating a knowingness of the effect their threats had on people. In Listowel, County Kerry, one of their most important spies was a Mrs Amelia Wilmot, who worked in the local RIC station as a cleaner. When they became aware that the RIC were becoming suspicious of her activities, the local IRA commandant, Denis Quill, sent Mrs Wilmot a letter, warning her 'to leave Listowel Barracks at once'.[57] To receive a warning like this was not always an empty threat or a ruse. In Ballyshannon, County Donegal, a woman who cleaned the local RIC station was attacked in her home by the IRA. Four or five men came to the house, 'took her to the Big Meadow and made her swear not to go back to the police again'. She was, they said, 'a traitor to her country and her religion'.[58] In the case of Mrs Wilmot, the ruse worked, and she continued working for the RIC and spying for the IRA, now getting an armed RIC escort to and from work every day. It is perhaps ironic that Quill used what was a common tactic to control women during this period attacks by the IRA, on girls and women suspected of consorting with the RIC or crown forces, to keep Mrs Wilmot safe in her position, where the IRA needed her. In Ballyshannon, the frightened young woman, who was attacked by the IRA for just this reason, spent nine weeks living in the RIC station, in fear of her life.

The evidence and knowledge of constant raids and the terror experienced by civilians, especially women, was becoming a major issue for the crown forces and the British government. The propaganda effect of the articles in the *Irish Bulletin* and its 'war on women' articles was substantial. As early as March 1920, Erskine Childers was describing, in articles in the *Daily Mail*, the awful effects these raids or home invasions had on the occupants, especially the women. This series of articles published between March and May, 1920, and reproduced in a pamphlet entitled 'Military Rule in Ireland', outlined the effects of terror. His vivid depictions of night raids were to bring the horror of the war in Ireland into British homes. 'A raid', he wrote, 'begins with a thunder of knocks; no time to dress (even for a woman alone) or the door will crash in. On opening, in charge the soldiers, literally charge, with fixed bayonets and in full war kit … in many recent instances even the women occupants have been locked up under guard while their own property is ransacked … is it any wonder that gross abuses occur; looting, wanton destruction, brutal severity to women'.[59]

Through his articles he outlined raids on homes and on women, telling personal stories of horror and terror. A raid on the house of Una Brennan was entitled 'A young mother's ordeal'. Mrs Brennan was roused by knocking on her door; 'running down in her nightdress' she heard a voice shouting 'damn you, open the door or we'll smash it in – one soldier is drunk and uses foul language and in spite of her passionate supplication to be allowed go to her children, she is kept apart under guard while the rooms are searched and the search is conducted with the roughness and insolence worthy of veritable Huns'.[60] This, he concludes, at the end of the description of the Brennan raid, is 'not a civilised war'.[61] Robert Brennan was hiding out in a house nearby when one of the raids occurred and felt, keenly, his inability, as a marked man, to do anything to help his family. On seeing his wife after the raid, he was shocked at her condition:

> I had never seen her so near a break. She had been crying. They had kept her downstairs all night away from the children and they had grilled her and our eldest child, Emer, aged 9, for hours, on my activities and whereabouts … The two younger children, Maeve … and Deirdre … were hysterical, which was not to be wondered at.[62]

This had all the typical patterns of 'terror' raids on homes, conducted late at night, the women at home alone, or isolated once the raid began, the drunkenness of the soldiers, foul language, abrasive and rough treatment. Childers cleverly references 'the Huns', the German invaders in Belgium, who terrorised and mistreated the women of 'little' Belgium. This depiction of terrorised Belgian civilians, particularly women, was, of course, one of the main propaganda tropes to encourage recruitment in the British Army when war broke out in 1914. Propaganda at that time concentrated on how Germans mistreated civilians in Belgium, most specifically how the 'Hun' mistreated and visited terror and outrage, on the women of Belgium. Here Childers presents propaganda evidence that the British soldiers were similarly mistreating Irish women.

Terror, fear, violation, degradation were all elements of the violence perpetrated on women and girls within the domestic sphere. The home was regularly the front line, as women, particularly Cumann na mBan women who lived in these communities, had become conduits of aid and information for the IRA, and enemies to be stopped for the crown forces. On the other hand, young girls, also living in these communities who 'kept company' with soldiers or police were considered to have betrayed their communities and had to be terrorised and controlled by the IRA. Julia Eichenberg writes, 'women symbolised the fertility and the future of the young nation, their liaisons with the enemy could not be tolerated'.[63] Families of men on the run or men suspected of involvement in republican activism, girls and women who were perceived as collaborating with the crown forces, were all fair game in a war in which the enemy could not be seen or identified. This meant that girls, women and families were vulnerable to raids, mistreatment, violence, sexual assault and degrading treatment, from both the IRA and the crown forces. The psychological strain on women, families and communities was immense. Women seemed to deal with the trauma of terror in different ways. Cumann na mBan women often talk about how they just continued with their work, despite sometimes experiencing homelessness after being burnt out, as well as injury and assault. Young women who were assaulted by the IRA were less well able to exhibit such stoicism, if they had been marked as deviant, dishonourable, potential traitors.

However, the trauma experienced by all these women remained a hidden subject in the histories from the 1920s onwards. While the subject of the 'war on women', terror attacks in homes and communities, head shaving and attacks on women by the IRA and crown forces were regularly reported in the newspapers during the period, 1919-21, it soon became an invisible subject in the historical narratives. The use of violence in the intimate domestic space of the home front was difficult to rationalise, post-independence. In the new Free State, the narrative constructed was of the vicious Auxiliary and the drunken Black and Tan, who alone had visited terror on the women of Ireland. The virtuous army of liberation, the IRA, some of whose leaders were afterwards the political masters in the new State, would not to be judged in a similar fashion as the drunken Tan. As Eichenberg notes, any violence which had been visited on civilians by the IRA was an expression of 'a para-state or a pre-state justice'.[64] These were the power brokers in waiting, who delivered gendered judgements on women considered moral miscreants. Now, with access to new sources and materials, the types and methods of gendered violence used by both armed forces in Ireland, 1919–21 and the reasons for that violence, during the War of Independence can be fully studied. The crown forces, fighting a guerrilla war it could not win, took its frustrations out on a civilian population, and from late 1920, on women suspected of aiding the enemy. The IRA, fighting for the cause of freedom, used gendered violence as a way of disciplining 'its' women. Not only was the War of Independence fought over the power, land and property of Ireland, it was fought, in their homes, in what was considered a safe space.

PART III

Chapter 10

'WHEN WE'VE LICKED THE
WOUNDS OF HISTORY':

Literary Representations of Women's Experiences of the War of Independence and Civil War

AILBHE McDAID

What use is literature in reconstructing and representing the past? In *The Politics of Language: Beyond the Gender Principle*, Nelly Furman observes that '[t]he literary text is the space where writer and reader, narrator and narratee engage in dialogue, and where a specific literary piece enters into the literary system and inscribes itself into a network of intertextual relationships with other literary works'.[1] In the Irish context, and in particular in relation to the period of conflict during the revolution, literary production not only inscribes itself into literary relationships but also engages with (and is engaged by) the wider historical, political and socio-cultural environment. As Furman goes on to note, traditional forms of discourse are encoded by existing cultural values, responding to and out of a wider context that informs the creation of and response to literary practice. The close intertwining of literature and history in Ireland is well established and much work has been done on literary representations of class, religion and politics during the revolution; however, the specifically gendered experience of women as represented in literature written in and about the period remains, to date, seriously under-explored.[2]

Given the relatively recent rehabilitation of women into the historical narrative of the period, it is perhaps unsurprising that little literary-critical attention has yet been paid to this dimension. The ongoing necessary attention to women's roles in the Rising, the War of Independence and the Civil War is reshaping our collective understanding of women's experiences by filling the many gaps in the historiography of the period. A literary-critical approach offers the opportunity to perceive the period from another perspective, to recognise and restore women's experiences of the time through the medium of literary rather than historical practice. Literature has the unique capacity to expand the restrictive contours of official remembering to represent different levels of unrecorded experience, thereby, as memory theorist Cathy Caruth claims, 'resituating it in our understanding'.[3] In pushing at the limits of embedded memory confined in witness statements and pension applications, literature revivifies dimensions of the past that are forgotten by the archive. Literary practice can retrieve voices not recorded, stories not told, experiences not deemed worthwhile since they fall outside the specific criteria. As poet Rita Ann Higgins articulates, literature accesses another, alternative but nonetheless legitimate past to which the poet is obliged:

> To get to the poetic truth it is
> Not always necessary to tell the
> What-actually-happened truth;[4]

Recognising the distinction between the 'what-actually-happened truth' and the 'poetic truth', Higgins points to the central crux of literary 'remembering'. Literature is not restricted to the strict representation of the recorded past and indeed as Higgins observes in another poem, the recorded past does not always present a complete picture: 'And we saw / what we saw / and we didn't see / what was hidden'.[5] Literature does, however, bear an ethical responsibility to the complex conflicted truths that necessarily are found beyond the margins of the recorded past. The literary construction of memory is not a literal retelling of the past – rather it is the product of cultural conditions resulting in a particular version of the past, as mediated through the prism of the present.

The role, and the dilemma, of art as witness to conflict is the subject of theoretical consideration throughout the twentieth and twenty-first century, from Adorno's reflection on poetry after Auschwitz to Sontag's treatise on *Regarding the Pain of Others*.[6] The tensions of witnessing, recording and responding to cultural trauma, and the ethics and aesthetics of necessarily-mediated literary representation, are the essential characteristics of conflict literature. Application to the Irish context of the model traced out by Gerd Bayer in 'Trauma and the Literature of War' would allow for an illuminating interrogation of how Irish literature has responded to the moment of historical crisis, both contemporaneously and retrospectively.[7] In its long-term mapping of the circumstances and consequences of conflict, and within its various implications as representative, imaginative and repudiative, literature takes its position as a concomitant site of negotiation. Works by writers directly involved in the revolutionary movement engage explicitly with the 'contrastive emotional fields of revulsion and curiosity', inhabiting a 'grey zone between the didacticism of educating readers about the horrors of the battlefields, and the enticement that stems from drawing on extreme emotions'.[8] Retrospective representations of conflict tend to move beyond the seduction of the moment of engagement to reflect more profoundly the reverberations of conflict across social, familial, intergenerational, gendered and class contexts, as demonstrated in this chapter.

This chapter is primarily concerned with how three contemporary poets represent the period of revolution in their work, and specifically, their attention to women's experiences of the conflict. The widespread academic and media attention to the roles of women undoubtedly influences how, as citizens as well as artists, poets respond to a changing historical narrative undergoing a public, and at times fraught, renegotiation. A more comprehensive analysis of how the representation of women in works about this period in Irish history can be seen to reflect the existent cultural conditions is the subject of a larger research project, but given the limitations of space here, it is possible only to mention some key examples of earlier works and their representations of women, before moving on to consider poems by Paula Meehan, Éiléan Ní Chuilleanáin and Martina Evans in some detail. In tune with the historical narrative that, up until recently, remained largely undisturbed, the works written around the period of the conflict have women speak quietly, if they speak at all. The canonical texts of the period are the stories of men, and those that feature women give them little narrative space. Resistance to women's voices in this literary period manifests itself in various ways – it can be as explicit as Johnny's exclamation in response to the women's efforts to witness their own and other's suffering in Seán O'Casey's *Juno and the Paycock* (1924): 'What sort o' talk is this to be goin' on with? Is there nothin' better to be talkin' about but the killin' o' people? My god, isn't it bad enough for these things to happen without talkin' about them!'[9]

In O'Casey's play, the women assert their right to mourn, even if they are met by an urge to silence. Another canonical text of the period, Frank O'Connor's short story 'Guests of the Nation' (1931), is equally dismissive of the old woman in whose home the action occurs, another of what Ryan describes as one of the 'many ... stock nationalist images of women and home' in O'Connor's fiction.[10] There is little recognition of the transgression of the domestic space enacted by the military men on both sides, and the cantankerous old woman is a broad-stroke caricature who remains nameless and, significantly, almost entirely voiceless throughout. In a story that is sensitive and nuanced in many ways, the gendered blind spot is particularly striking. Despite the old woman being described as having 'a great warrant to scold' and wont to give the guests 'a lick of her tongue', until the penultimate paragraph, O'Connor allows her just a single utterance in the story. The effect of limiting the narrative space rather than investing the old woman with the kinds of emotional depths afforded to the other main characters in the story has the effect of not only marginalising the old woman's experience of the war but also of stripping her of the ability to represent it in her own voice. When she finally speaks, it causes a shock, both within the narrative and on a textual level: '"What did ye do with them?" she says in a sort of whisper, and Noble took such a mortal start the match quenched in his trembling hand'.[11]

The moving final paragraph of the story is a sharp glimpse into the processes and effects of grief, as well as a symbolic reflection on the profound traumatic effect of the period on a national level but it is only Noble and the narrator whose perceptions are recorded. The old woman is once more recessed into the background of the story's set, with the birds, the stars, the hearth and all the other paraphernalia that supports rather than participates in the story.

> Noble says he felt he had seen everything ten times as big, perceiving nothing around him but the little patch of black bog with the two Englishmen stiffening into it; but with me it was the other way, as though the patch of bog where the two Englishmen were was a thousand miles away from me, and even Noble mumbling just behind me and the old woman and the birds and the bloody stars were all far away, and I was somehow very small and very lonely. And anything that ever happened me after I never felt the same about again.[12]

A less well-known but important novel of the period, Peadar O'Donnell's *Adrigoole* (1929) presents the corrosive collective trauma experienced by local communities during the conflict. The insidious damage to community bonds brought about by the war is another hidden dimension of this period's history but, like the other texts of the time, the specifically female dimensions of this are only briefly alluded to. In *Adrigoole*, the loss of community support due to divided loyalties during the Civil War garners far more narrative exposition than the representation of the experience of the female protagonist Brigid, particularly her emotional experience. The common theme of a refusal of narrative space to mourn emerges repeatedly in literary representations of women in the period. This excerpt demonstrates the minimal textual space allowed to Brigid's response to the death of her great-uncle and the shooting of her husband: 'Brigid held the basin for the doctor; her heart beat in her throat. The doctor stood up and Brigid stood tall and pale in front of him and the agony in her eyes reached him. "Oh, he'll live" the doctor said decisively. It was only then that Brigid found tears.'[13]

A thorough exploration of the literary texts of the Irish revolution and their representations of women requires far more space than can be offered here, but as the above examples suggest, women are afforded minimal narrative opportunity to articulate the experience of the invasions of their homes and the violence imposed on the domestic space; whether through omission, resistance, hesitation or absence, the result is the same – canonical texts written immediately in the period present women as voiceless, peripheral characters whose experiences of conflict remain unarticulated, unremembered and, implicitly, unimportant. The dialectic of 'memory and forgetting' as evidence of the 'multi-layered traumatic experience' provides a broader theoretical framework for a reconsideration of the representation of this period of conflict in twentieth- and twenty-first-century literature, but this chapter can only gesture towards a more ambitious project that explores the complex intertwining of memory and silence in literature of the Irish revolution.[14]

While this chapter is concerned with literary representations of women's experiences, the evidence from the archives as explored in other chapters in this collection undoubtedly supports the fact that civilian women came into close contact with conflict during the period and that exposure to violence had serious consequences for women and children.[15] Publications by Louise Ryan, Linda Connolly, Justin Dover Stolan, Marie Coleman and Gemma Clark have contributed to a burgeoning body of work on the physical and psychological impacts of this period not just on those participating as military volunteers but, on civilians, namely women and children.[16] The emerging archival material demonstrates the pervasive nature of domestic disruption while the personal statements of women in recently digitised files from the Bureau of Military History and the Military Service Pensions Collections testify to the impact of conflict on their mental, physical and domestic situations, reinforcing the need for a reconsideration of the 'truth' of the dominant historical narrative of this period. The ways in which this period of traumatic collective experience has been represented in literature can help us to understand the workings of a collective memory process, opening different avenues to apprehend the past not preserved in official histories of the time.

While the literature written immediately out of the period is produced in the turmoil and distress of the time, later literary reflections of the conflict respond to different contemporaneous cultural conditions. There has been a great deal of research on memory, collective trauma and commemoration on an international level, and this has been well applied to the Irish context, with much more surely to come in the decade of the centenaries.[17] The idea of 'postmemory', defined as the memory of events not witnessed first-hand but rather inherited or absorbed through familial, cultural or collective memory processes, is of particular interest in the context of how contemporary literature responds to the events of the revoluiontary period. As memory theorist Marianne Hirsch notes, the 'bodily, psychic and affective impact of trauma and its aftermath' reverberates long after the event has passed, especially in circumstances of unrecorded or unacknowledged trauma.[18] The complex coming-to-terms with this period of history has had some mid-century literary reflections, most significantly in the work of William Trevor, whose representations of intergenerational and postmemory build powerful pictures of how families, especially women and children, are profoundly affected by their experiences of violence.[19] In works such as Trevor's, it is evident that literary articulations that register trauma can 'interrupt and splinter historical narrative in a productive way', challenging the ways in which the legacies of the conflict are recognised and recorded.[20] The act of bearing witness in literature is an ethical imperative, and in the case of the three contemporary poets on whom the remainder of this essay concentrates, this ethical imperative is realised in the ways their work bears witness to the memory-trace of unclaimed or subjugated experience that implicitly and explicitly challenges existing historical narratives.

Caitríona Clutterbuck observes that 'Irish women's poetry not only suggests that a causal link exists between the silencing of women's lived reality and the trauma of national history, but that the silenced woman can speak most clearly for that trauma exactly in her own voice as woman'.[21] The intertwining of the personal with the public, and of the received and the interrogated, in these works confirms Clutterbuck's insight, and the poetry considered here strikes at the heart of Caruth's argument that '[l]iterature, like psychoanalysis, is interested in the complex relation between knowing and not knowing'.[22] The poetry explored here underpins the broader argument that the varied literary responses to this traumatic period call for 'different ways of thinking what it means to understand and what kinds of truth we are looking for' in literary representations of this period.[23]

In recent publications, Paula Meehan, Martina Evans and Éiléan Ní Chuilleanáin have addressed the hidden legacies of women's experiences of the Irish revolution in poems that challenge not only those inherited narratives but also push at the boundaries of poetic representation. Here it is explored how these poets approach their centennial representations, pursuing different kinds of 'poetic truth', to use Rita Ann Higgins's phrase, in order to represent this period of trauma in Irish history. What instigates the impulse of these three poets to interrogate and complicate the received past? Wider historiographical movements towards retrieving the role of women in the period of the revolution are undoubtedly influential, but the writers in question have always prioritised marginal narratives in their poetry. The urban eco-poetics underpinning Meehan's poetry might seem like a contradiction in terms but her poetry is possessed of a prescience that increases in relevance over time, while her commitment to the unrepresented is demonstrated from her very earliest works. Evans's work challenges any kind of master narrative through her careful, intimate and often darkly humorous work that reverberates long after the joke is over. Ní Chuilleanáin is well established as a poet of the hidden spaces of Irish history, shining a light on women's experiences through imaginative reconstructions of forgotten pieces of the past. In the poems discussed here, there is a shared emphasis on the resistance of dominance, and each poet builds this resistance through distinctive poetic techniques. Elaine Showalter observes that the female literary tradition comes from 'the still-evolving relationship between women writers and their society', and the way these poems interrogate received narratives (familial, communal and archival) while agitating at the boundaries of memory is particularly significant in a culture whose national identity has long been intertwined with the constructs of its literary imagination.[24]

Paula Meehan's 'Them Ducks Died for Ireland' is part of a sequence entitled 'Six Sycamores' published in her 2009 collection *Painting Rain*.[25] The volume is thematically underpinned by the frailties of memory and shared heritage, with Meehan's characteristic ethical commitment to 'emphasising the fragility of local stories in danger of disappearing or being forgotten in modern times'.[26] This imperative to witness stretches across Meehan's work, whether in response to recording ecological devastation, class injustice, the erosions of capitalism or the female experience. The 'Six Sycamores' sequence hooks itself on the sycamore trees of St Stephen's Green and is composed of twelve short poems – six explicitly linked to the sycamores and six that offer a snapshot of Dublin city and its various inhabitants past and present. It is the fourth segment of the sequence that is of particular relevance here, drawing its title and its topic from the park superintendent's report on the damage to St Stephen's Green during the Easter Rising. The poem opens with a quote from the report: 'six of our waterfowl were killed or shot, seven of the garden seats broken and about 300 shrubs destroyed'. Meehan's initial instinct to gesture towards the innocent avian and arboreal victims of the events of the Rising expands into a poetic undertaking to bear witness to the other hidden human experiences of those events.

The poem recognises the necessary processes of traumatic memory that are bound up in the dialectic of remembering and forgetting and sets these human traits alongside the cyclical processes of nature that continue unperturbed by the temporary dramas of revolution and bloodshed. The opening image poses time and, by implication, history as omnipresent and sticky as it 'slides slowly down the sash window/puddling in light', suggesting the way in which the past becomes enmeshed in the present, complex as both 'summons and antidote to pride'. The park itself, St Stephen's Green, acts as a silent witness to all that has crossed its path, while it quietly continues to nourish the city with its presence.

> The Green
> is a great lung, exhaling like breath on the pane
> the seasons' turn, sunset, moonset, the ebb and flow
> of stars.

Set against the natural shifts of tides and seasons, the image of the 'wounds of history, the wounds of war' is jarring, yet the poem recognises the need to allow those wounds to heal before moving into the next stage of remembering that can accommodate a wider perspective on a shared history. The strategic break between stanzas approximates the necessary distance while nevertheless bridging the gap between past and present through the enjambment, a deft poetic representation of the dialectic between remembering and forgetting.

The final two stanzas of the poem directly address those figures who have been forgotten in the struggles of commemoration, and who to date have spent their afterlives as unnoticed marginalia in a dusty archive.

> we'll salute the stretcher-bearer, the nurse in white,
> the ones who pick up the pieces, who endure,
> who live at the edge, and die there and are known
> by this archival footnote read by fading light;

Meehan's careful recognition and presentation of those quiet outsider figures is in stark contrast to the striking image of the countess's stride which embodies 'A Republic's destiny' in the earlier stanza, and yet it is effective for the way it recovers the past from the confines of the archive. The implicit distrust of an official, bombastic narrative that consigns the ordinary to the margins of the historical is clear in the poetic space afforded to these hidden individuals. Ultimately, Meehan finds a way to equalise past and present, remembered and forgotten, in the final image that recognises the mutual fragility (and significance) of 'a breathmark on the windowpane or the gesture/of commemorating heroes in bronze and stone'.

As a poet whose imagination hones in on unspeakable silences and voided spaces in irretrievable pasts, Éiléan Ní Chuilleanáin's work connects with many of the threads unpicked in Meehan's 'Them Ducks Died for Ireland'. In Ní Chuilleanáin's poem 'On Lacking the Killer Instinct' from her volume *The Sun-fish* (2009), remembering is bound up in multiple traumatic events of personal, familial and communal experience.[27] Triggered by the photograph of a hare pursued by greyhounds on the front of a newspaper, the poem winds back to an earlier sighting of a hare in the Dublin mountains on the occasion of the death of the speaker's father, which in turn evokes the father's recollections of fleeing a lorry of soldiers during the War of Independence. The three narratives recreate a layered palimpsest of memories that intertwine with each other across time, complicated by omission and forgetting.

The binding symbolism of the hare is significant in Irish folklore, as a shapeshifter or as one who can pass from human to otherworld. Ní Dhuibhne sees the hare as a symbol in folktales that are balanced on binaries, between male and female, young and old, sexuality and repression, between open spaces and domestic sphere, between violence and guile.[28] In Ní Chuilleanáin's poem, the hare is both the memory trigger and the binding symbol. In the archetypal folktale, the hare eludes its pursuers by 'leaping through a hole or a broken window pane' into a house.[29] In Ní Chuilleanáin's version of this folktale, the refuge sought by the father in the safe house restages the actions of the shape-shifting hare, the young man transforming from a rebel on the run to become a drowsy family member '[d]rying his face, dazed-looking, the towel / Half covering his face'. By invoking the heritage of the folktale, Ní Chuilleanáin signposts the narrative unreliability of inherited stories, a concern she probes further by pushing at the boundaries of the family story. The image of the shape-shifting hare leaping into a house connects with the conventions of the folktale but differs in one crucial factor: in the folktale, the hare returns to its own home and regains its human (and usually female) form. In Ní Chuilleanáin's version, the pursued enters a home not its own, and this violation of the domestic space defines civilian women's experiences during this period in Irish history, to which the archives testify.

At the heart of 'On Lacking the Killer Instinct' is an awareness of the ethical imperative of witnessing – a duty recognised in the speaker's obligation to witness her father's passing and the poet's obligation to witness the hidden dimensions of an inherited narrative. As Clutterbuck observes, '[b]oth interrogation and change are offered in the self-reflexive interwoven witness offered by Irish women to their own and the nation's history', and 'On Lacking the Killer Instinct' merges personal and national narratives in a poem that seeks to expose both the flaws and the possibilities of memory.[30] Ní Chuilleanáin's poetry is underpinned by a commitment to the act and the art of witnessing, and is always alert to the tensions involved in that act, whether on an individual or a collective basis. In 'Bearing Witness Or the Vicissitudes of Listening', Dori Laub highlights that listening is an act of witness, and that in itself is a participatory act: 'the listener to trauma comes to be a participant and a co-owner of the traumatic event: through his very listening, he comes to partially experience trauma in himself ... He or she must *listen to and hear the silence*, speaking mutely both in silence and in speech, both from behind and from within the speech'.[31] Ní Chuilleanáin's aesthetic of recording silences is a distinctive technique of her poetry – as demonstrated in 'Ballinascarthy', also from *The Sun-fish*, the silenced past is presented in the image of 'the secret monument / to the dead of the battle of Kilnagros'; the quiet whispers 'where spruces whistle to each other and the carved stone is lost' are still heard. 'On Lacking the Killer Instinct' similarly seeks out the silences that surround the inherited narrative of the father's story.

> The lorry left,
> The people let him sleep there, he came out
> Into a blissful dawn. Should he have chanced that door?
> If the sheltering house had been burned down, what good
> Could all his bright running have done
> For those that harboured him?

In asking unanswered (and unanswerable) questions, the poem gestures towards the historical silence without attempting to fill it. Instead it recognises the gap in cultural, intergenerational and traumatic memory in the way it tentatively tests out the limits of the narrative inherited from the father. In reaching back through memory, the poem briefly glimpses the unremembered past before recognising that it lies beyond recovery.

In the literature of the Irish revolution, the stories from this side of the threshold are rarely told. In conflict literature, the domestic space is the female space and it is always ancillary to the main events, a backdrop to the 'real' action as conducted through the military men. Recent international scholarship on women in war increasingly recognises the home space as a conflict site that requires critical, historical and theoretical attention.[32] The domestic space in war is also seen as a contested site in which gendered norms, often under negotiation in the emergence of a new State, are challenged, reinforced or subverted. As Louise Ryan has pointed out, the crude dichotomy between home front and battlefront is particularly problematic in the Irish context, given the involvement of women and the use of the domestic space as a weapon in the arsenal of resistance.[33] The resonant questions within the poem shift the focus obliquely, whereby the poem brings the central conceit of a filial responsibility to attend and witness a father's death to bear on a wider question of ethical obligation to the remembered and the unremembered past.

Where Ní Chuilleanáin cracks the façade of the domestic front as constructed in conflict narratives, Martina Evans breaks it down completely in *Facing the Public* (2009), a collection that directly addresses this period of the contested past from the perspectives of various first-person narrators.[34] Evans's poems open spaces to explore cultural anxieties around how to represent and remember the fraught and divisive past. These poems expose the complex workings of cultural memory, in which acts of omission are as significant as the selective preservation of the past, and in which memory can often be coercive. The opening lines of 'The Boy from Durras' indicate the destabilisation of communal memory that is predicated on the assumption of shared knowledge, while its retelling asserts the very process of memory, which is formed unconsciously through repetition.

> Yes, that's right, the Tans picked up children
> and you know why of course, don't you?
> They were looking for information.
> I'll tell you something now on the quiet
> and you'll get no one round here
> to talk about it.

The implication of secrecy, that 'no one round here' will talk about it, underpins the reality of a hidden but uninterrogated traumatic past, which remains unexplored. *Facing the Public* is engaged in the interplay between telling and not-telling, an exchange that mirrors the construction and conservation of memory and history. Evans's poetry invests in the power dynamic between authorised and subversive narratives, the distinction between true and invented/adapted memory, and the purposes and practices of remembering and forgetting. While the narrator of 'The Boy from Durras' insists on recounting the collective memory, he is equally adamant that the story remain suppressed. The phrase 'You'll get no one round here to talk about it' becomes a refrain in the poem, repeated three times in thirty lines. In a society continuously exercised by versions of its past, time consolidates rather than recuperates silence in this particular reproduction. '[S]eventy years on', memory is diffused only in whispers by anxious anonymous narrators in a practice that rests somewhere between remembering and forgetting, as per the poem's final line – '[a]nd don't forget that you never heard this from me'.

In addition to the literary depictions outlined earlier in this chapter, many of the foundational documents of the period of revolution are autobiographies or memoirs. Ryan's exploration of these texts highlights the extent to which women are sidelined or silenced in these narrative reconstructions of the period.[35] In *Facing the Public*, Evans addresses one such foundational text, Ernie O'Malley's *On Another Man's Wound*, in a number of poems that complicate the one-dimensional, first-person narrative of O'Malley's memoirs.[36] The closing set of poems of Evans's *Facing the Public* approaches cultural memory through the memoirs of IRA commander O'Malley, and direct excerpts from *On Another Man's Wound* preface 'Mallow Burns, 28 September 1920' and 'Wooden Horse', while the poems themselves directly re-state O'Malley's exact words from his memoir. It is a curious act of appropriation, not least because O'Malley's own version of personal and collective history was itself also a deeply literary gesture. As *lieux de memoire*, O'Malley's memoirs now stand as part of the cultural (and historical) memory of the War of the Independence, yet the memoirs themselves are carefully constructed literary works, reinventions of personal and political memory. Evans's appropriation of O'Malley's carefully constructed version of the past has the effect of distancing history by further blurring the boundary between narrative and fact. The fluidity and unreliability of memory, as mediated through narrative, is at the heart of Evans's evocation of O'Malley's memoirs, as the poems attempt to go about putting what Evans describes as 'the flesh and blood' onto what O'Malley called 'the wooden horse of Mallow'.

Evans's poems here are invigorating pieces of writing, as she engages her characteristic technique of genre manipulation, a stylistic imperative that imitates a commingling of sources and modes within the O'Malley memoirs themselves. At the level of form, the poems engage a prose poem narrative similar to Evans's earlier volume *Petrol* which straddles the boundaries between poetry and prose just as O'Malley's books reside somewhere between history, memoire and literature. 'Mallow Burns, 28 September 1920' drifts through the dying thoughts of Sergeant Gibbs, the RIC officer killed in the IRA raid on the Mallow Barracks that led to the infamous sacking of the town by the Black and Tans. The stream-of-consciousness style brings the prose poem from beginning to end without a full-stop, gaining momentum as the town burns and 'the sun goes finally / down on two hundred years of loyalty to the Crown' in Mallow, 'long a garrison town' – as the quote from O'Malley states at the poem's outset.

The difficulty in pinpointing the distinction between inherited memory and original statement is brought into full relief in 'Wooden Horse', which undertakes a comprehensive restaging of O'Malley's exact words. The epigraph quotes O'Malley on the IRA siege of the Mallow Barracks: 'We're like the Greeks in the wooden horse, here in the belly of the town, I thought, and laughed'. While the poem progresses to navigate between memory and quotation, the extent to which the poem draws on O'Malley's original words is demonstrated by relevant extracts:

> The column was drawn up. They smiled joyfully when they were told we were going to seize the barracks. At two in the morning, behind our scouts, we moved into the town. The advance guard was told to make prisoners of anyone they met and blindfold them. There were no lights in the houses, no people on the streets ... Our approach up to higher ground brought us through back yards, barbed wire and across high walls. We used ladders on the high walls. When I looked down on the house, I saw a toy town, blurred and misty with half light.[37]

Read alongside Evans's poem, the conflation is clear:

> If you meet anyone, blindfold them, they were told that and the men were smiling at the thought of seizing the barracks where an officer was starting to write a letter Mallow is a quiet town, nothing ever happens here. And it was true, – at 2 a.m. on the twenty eighth, there was no one on the streets, everything pitch as they navigated back-yards and barbed wire, put their ladders up against the high walls. Up there Ernie saw a toy town wrapped in mist[.]

O'Malley's original is evidently lyrical in its own right, but Evans's use of the original material surely invokes questions of authorship and ownership, not only of the words in question here but more broadly of the past itself. Importing O'Malley's writings into her own work through a process of iterative poetics, Evans draws attention to questions of ownership, representation and memory. When the final lines of the poem diverge absolutely from O'Malley's narrative, the ethical dimension of representation emerges in a powerful mythical image:

> but
> Mallow wasn't made of wood, it was flesh and blood, like Achilles' horses, Bailius and Xanthus, who dragged their shining manes along the ground when they wept for the death of Patroclus.

Evans turns from memory to myth to find a mode of accommodating the past, and the flawless segue from O'Malley's memoir to Greek mythology signals a narrative synchronicity between those two pre-existing texts that signals a further unease with the historical truth of *On Another Man's Wound*.[38] Evans picks up O'Malley's analogy of his column as being 'like the Greeks in the wooden horse', where myth is deployed as validation, and offers an alternative tragic myth drawn from *The Iliad*. Bailius and Xanthus, the horses who are defined by their grief at the death of their charioteer, embody sorrow rather than hubris, as Evans's poem reinvents O'Malley's use of myth to emphasise the effects of the burning of the town with its 'flesh and blood' inhabitants. This alternative version of events in Mallow underlines the difficulties of narrating the past without recourse to myth, and ultimately suggests that cultural memory itself is a kind of myth, another means of assembling the fragments of the past. 'Wooden Horse' serves to complicate the ways cultural memory is transferred by problematising ideologies of remembering encoded in the appropriated narrative.

The centrality of memory in Evans's poetry, in spite of its fragility, speaks to a fundamental misgiving about permanence and authority. In the constant rewriting of codes of legitimacy, history and belonging, *Facing the Public* demands a reconsideration of the substance and structures of remembering around this period. 'Knock', the final poem in *Facing the Public*, is a commitment by Evans to restore the private voice to one of the many women hidden in the margins of the archive and the documents of official remembering. Once again, Evans draws on the inherited narrative of O'Malley's memoir in which he recalls the humour of a former colleague:

> Coughlin ... helped to keep all in good humour, and his droll sayings were repeated. He had been billeted in a house which had a reputation for being stingy. One morning the woman of the house asked him how he liked his eggs boiled. - With a couple of others, ma'am,' he replied.

The story presented by O'Malley in the prologue to the poem is promptly and effectively recalibrated in terms of the 'woman of the house' being attributed her own voice in the poem proper. Rather than playing the supporting role like O'Connor's old woman or O'Donnell's Bridget, Evans affords the woman full narrative authority over the poem, the final poem in the collection. The narrator's entirely human, if slightly irreverent, response to the ongoing disruptions of her domestic space is an astute approximation of the real lived experiences of women who opened their homes, by choice or by obligation, during the War of Independence and the Civil War. All the complexities of loyalty, of selfishness, of duty and of resentment inwrought in that period are present in this unique presentation of the perspective from the other side of the domestic threshold:

> Coughlin, the first as usual, to smell the brown cake. It wasn't that I wasn't wishing them the best of luck the whole time and you might think I'd be worried if we were caught out by the Tans and burned to the ground and I'm not saying that I wasn't worried about that too, but to have to turn around and serve a crowd of men and make up beds and to have to pretend to be laughing away at their jokes. Oh God almighty, I was pure sick of them all then.

Whether in literal or abstract representations, literature offers a mode of listening to the past in a way that can bear ethical witness. Caruth advocates for a 'new mode of reading and of listening that both the language of trauma and the silence of its mute repetition of suffering profoundly and imperatively demand'.[39] In pausing to consider the peripheral movements around the edges of inherited memory, as demonstrated in these poems by Meehan, Evans and Ní Chuilleanáin, it is possible to restore voices to those silenced or ignored by institutional and official memory processes. Literature, and specifically poetry, can expand the restrictive contours and representational limits of official remembering, which embeds memory in witness statements and pension applications, to more profoundly understand the occluded foundational violence that involves fundamental violations of the female space that lies at the heart of the Irish revolution.

Chapter 11

COMMEMORATING THE
IRISH REVOLUTION:

Disremembering and Remembering the Women and Children of the Tuam Mother and Baby Home

SARAH-ANNE BUCKLEY AND
JOHN CUNNINGHAM

On Sunday morning, 10 April 1932, twenty members of the IRA marched from the Market Square, Tuam, to the old workhouse building on the Dublin Road, a distance of about half a mile. On arrival, they were greeted by matron Sister Hortense[1] and several others of the Bon Secours congregation, which had operated a mother and baby home in the building during the previous six years. The IRA men were commemorating six of their comrades who had been shot in the same workhouse by Free State forces in April 1923, in the final weeks of the Irish Civil War. Leading the marchers was Tom Maguire, recently an abstentionist member of the Dáil (Irish parliament), whose younger brother Seán had been among those shot. Hortense led her visitors to the place of execution, which they were pleased to see had been 'kept ... in perfect preservation' by her. Next, all went to the institution's chapel, where a decade of the rosary was recited for 'those soldiers of the IRA killed in action and executed', with Maguire placing a laurel wreath on the altar steps. Before their departure, Sister Hortense gave permission to a deputation of the marchers to erect a small monument at the site of the executions, 'bearing the names of the dead heroes'.[2]

This encounter between a nun and group of republicans directly impacted by the violence of the Irish Civil War resonates as a legacy of the past today. Two distinct monuments are located less than 100 metres from one another on the site of the former workhouse in Tuam. One, erected in 1985, commemorates the six executed rebels. The other, in 'loving memory of those buried here', remembers the deceased, *forgotten* infant children of unmarried mothers admitted to the Tuam Mother and Baby Home over several decades. This monument was prompted by the revelation since 2012 of the extremely high infant mortality rate in the home and the burial of the infants in a sewage area.

What is the significance of these two proximate monuments? During the 'decade of centenaries' in Ireland, questions over what or who we choose to commemorate and memorialise, in the context of the violent and traumatic foundation of the State, and how we do so politically and culturally, have come to the fore.[3] The sensitivity of remembering a divisive, internal civil war has been examined in key texts.[4] Institutions that incarcerated women and children have also been the focus of recent studies and debates about memory, commemoration and cultural trauma.[5] The two monuments currently located on the Tuam Mother and Baby Home site raise provocative questions about 'selective remembrance', trauma histories and heroic commemoration at the current conjuncture in Ireland. Of the three different groups invariably 'remembered' on the Tuam site, the memory of the infants who died at the home was treated with disrespect for decades while the Sisters of the Bon Secours and deceased IRA men were given decent burials on repeated occasions and memorialised in several places. This raises questions for us not only about the relationship between republicanism and Catholic institutions in the newly independent State, but also the harsh treatment and suppressed memory of marginalised women and children seen to be outside the acceptable strictures of society.

The first part of this chapter examines the social and political background to the institutionalisation of unmarried mothers and their infants in Tuam, in the early decades of the twentieth century. While the 1927 *Report into the Commission on the Relief of the Sick and the Destitute Poor, Including the Insane Poor* is often cited as the document that reflected attitudes to unmarried mothers in independent Ireland and how they should be treated, a home for unmarried mothers was being discussed in County Galway as early as 1904. The circumstances that led to the commemoration of the 'Tuam martyrs' on the site of the Tuam Mother and Baby Home/Children's Home (1925–1961) is addressed in the next section. The relationship between female religious orders, republicanism and gender in post-independence Ireland is explored in detail. The chapter will conclude with the question – *who do we commemorate?*

'... no great acquisition to the community': Refashioning the Welfare System

The building in which the April 1932 encounter took place had opened as part of the Poor Law system in 1846. In 1890, the Sisters of Mercy were invited to take over nursing duties at the workhouse, reflecting a general incursion into the system during the previous decades by Catholic religious orders, spearheaded by Catholic Poor Law Guardians.[6] In this instance, the sisters struck a hard bargain, rejecting the quarters initially offered them because of their proximity to a 'cesspool', and insisting that a new house be built for them on the grounds.[7] With declining demand for its pauper accommodation – especially after the introduction of the Old Age Pensions Act in 1909 – there was much contemporary discussion about the rationalisation of the poor law system. A Viceregal Commission on Poor Law Reform reported in 1906, while Myles Keaven, a veteran officer of several boards of guardians, had proposed a major reconfiguration for County Galway as early as 1904. Keaven urged that all but two of the county's workhouses be closed, and that dedicated social services, under religious management, be provided in the vacated buildings. 'The one given to the sisters would be for fallen women', he wrote, 'and I would have strict rules attached to this and not allow poor girls who were led astray under false pretences to mix with poor unfortunates'.[8]

Despite many such rhetorical interventions during the first two decades of the twentieth century, there was little actual change. With one minor exception, the opportunities for reform and consolidation provided by the Local Government Act of 1898 were not taken up by boards of guardians in any part of Ireland, and the system continued to stagnate.[9] In the immediate aftermath of the 1916 Rising, a special committee of Galway County Council and the ten Poor Law Unions of the county adopted a scheme that was quite similar to the earlier Keaven proposal.[10] It was not taken any further. But larger changes loomed and, increasingly, from the cabinet of the revolutionary Dáil down, members of the rising Sinn Féin movement virulently denounced the Poor Law system. Largely an aspirational document, the Democratic Programme of the First Dáil had, however, included a firm commitment to set about 'abolishing the present odious, degrading and foreign Poor Law System, substituting therefore a sympathetic native scheme'. William Cosgrave, the Dáil's local government minister from April 1919, was an advocate of radical change in the system but evidently was not sympathetic to those who had relied upon it. In May 1921, he stated in the Dáil:

People reared in workhouses ... are no great acquisition to the community, and they have no ideas whatsoever of civic responsibilities. As a rule their highest aim is to live at the expense of the ratepayer. Consequently it would be a decided gain if they all decide to emigrate.[11]

Under the emerging order the ratepayers' interest loomed large in such discussions, just as it had in the old one. These were the circumstances in September 1921, when Galway County Council adopted and set about implementing a scheme of institutional reform, similar to, but even more far-reaching than those discussed previously. All workhouses in the county were to be closed, the Galway facility to be a central hospital serving the whole county. One of the vacant workhouses, Glenamaddy initially, was to be set aside for orphaned/abandoned/neglected children and unmarried mothers.[12]

The Bon Secours sisters had been in the town of Glenamaddy, eighteen miles from Tuam, since 1903. They had taken over nursing duties at the workhouse and were soon seen to have greatly improved the condition of their charges.[13] A dramatic interruption of routine came in mid-1921, when the local IRA paid a visit. Over thirty years later, Martin Ryan, the officer in charge of the operation, described what happened:

In June 1921, I took charge of the burning of Glenamaddy workhouse ... to prevent the occupation of the building by British forces ... It was a big operation for which I drew on about 40 Volunteers ... The workhouse buildings covered a big area and all were burned with the exception of the hospital and the fever hospital. Fortunately for us, we had the help of the Bon Secours Sisters, under whose charge the hospital was, and of Fr Fergus, now Most Rev Dr Fergus, Bishop of Achonry. The Master of the Workhouse also assisted.[14]

Most of the details of Ryan's account were consistent with the contemporary report of the night's 'startling operations' in the *Connacht Tribune,* though remarks attributed to the workhouse master did not give the impression that he 'assisted' with anything.[15] Likewise with the future bishop, who later wrote his own account of the night's events.[16] And it may be surmised that any cooperation from the sisters in the burning of the building in which they worked was likewise not voluntary.

However, like many other religious of their generation, the younger Bon Secours sisters were drawn towards the revolutionary milieu. In their case this meant taking a special interest in the consolation of republican prisoners.[17] In Cork prison, for example, they ministered to hunger strikers, and on the night of 13 March 1921, six members of the congregation spent some hours in Mountjoy with six young men who would be hanged on the following morning.[18] As a young sister, it is quite likely (though not possible to confirm) that Hortense was involved in her congregation's prison visitation work. Either way, she must have been affected by its particular mission to republican prisoners.

Sister Hortense arrived in Glenamaddy in December 1921, when she took charge of the children's home recently announced by Galway County Council.[19]

'... a wonderful country for producing heroes': The Tuam Martyrs and their Remembrance

The six men commemorated at the Tuam workhouse in 1932 were among the last of seventy-seven republican prisoners officially executed by the Free State in reprisal for the activity of anti-Treatyite 'irregular' forces during the Civil War.[20] Of the six, five were part of a contingent surprised by Free State forces in Cluide, half-way between Tuam and Headford, on the morning of 19 February 1923. All were taken to Galway Jail, where they remained until 10 April.[21] As for the reason for the trouble taken to move the prisoners for execution to Tuam, a consideration would have been the impact of locating the executions in an area where several of the men were well known and where the anti-Treaty IRA remained active.[22] Following a perfunctory court martial, all were convicted of possessing a rifle and ammunition 'without proper authority', and sentenced to death. Two Tuam priests were summoned to pray with the condemned men, and a Mass was arranged for the morning of their execution, at which two of them acted as altar servers.[23]

The executed were Commandant Frank Cunnane (23), brother of a Tuam Mercy nun, Volunteers Martin Moylan (24), Mickey Monaghan (22) and Séamus O'Malley (25), and Lieutenants Seán Newell (32) and Seán Maguire (19).[24] The latter was the younger brother of Tom Maguire, who had been wounded at the celebrated Tourmakeady ambush, and who returned unopposed in the 1921 general election. Taking the anti-Treaty side, he became General Officer Commanding of the 2nd Western Division of the IRA, with the rank of Commandant General. It has been hypothesised that Seán was selected for execution by way of punishing his brother.[25]

Following the executions, the authorities took care to assure the public that the initial burial place of the six in the Tuam workhouse grounds was 'consecrated'. At the following meeting of the Tuam District Council, nonetheless, there was support for a proposal that the bodies be handed over to relatives.[26] Ahead of the withdrawal of troops from the Tuam workhouse, the remains were reinterred in the Custume Barracks in Athlone, provoking widespread outrage, including from Councillor Alice Cashel, who had the following resolution adopted by Galway Hospital Committee: 'That we view with horror the desecration of our dead by the disinterment and removal of patriotic Irishmen from their graves in Tuam'.[27] The politicisation of burial, commemoration and memorialisation would remain to the fore over the coming years in regard to these six men.

The Free State responded to public feeling, heightened by outrage at the Tuam exhumations. On 28 October 1924, the seventy-seven bodies were exhumed and given over to the custody of their families.[28] The remains of the Tuam six, together with five comrades from the 2nd Western Division were taken west from Athlone. Thousands gathered in Headford for a concelebrated mass, many marching from the Maguires' native Cross before proceeding to Donaghpatrick cemetery.[29] Among the speakers at the graveside, representing Sinn Féin, was Dr Kathleen Lynn, who consoled the bereaved as follows: 'It is not a day really for sadness, but of great joy ... Those boys, not more than twenty-four years of age bravely faced their death for the freedom of Ireland ... There would be pilgrimages to those graves for all generations, and they would never be forgotten'.[30]

Commencing at Easter 1926, there were annual commemorations at the 'republican plot' in Donaghpatrick, with clerical and political participation.[31] Complications would arise from the break-up of the anti-Treaty 'family' with the establishment of Fianna Fáil in 1926, though these took time to manifest themselves. Tom Maguire, the principal custodian of the republican plot, was one of those not reconciled to the Free State, continuing to regard the Second Dáil as the last legitimately elected Irish parliament, and he was one of the 'faithful' members of that assembly that voted to hand over their authority to the IRA Army Council in 1938. Until his death in 1993, he would hold iconic status among a section of republicans – through splits in 1970 and again in 1986.

The division of 1926 was copper-fastened by de Valera's ban on the IRA in 1936 and rendered very acrimonious by republican prison deaths during the 'Emergency' of 1939–45, including that of Tony D'Arcy, from a republican family in the Headford area.[32] In 1952, D'Arcy's name was inscribed along with the others on the striking republican monument unveiled by Tom Maguire in the presence of 650 people at Donaghpatrick. Six priests offered prayers, and, remarkably, TDs from Fianna Fáil and Clann na Talmhan attended the ceremony which was organised and marshalled by revolutionary republicans, including members of the illegal IRA.[33] The memory of the Tuam executions still resonated so powerfully in the area as to grant a measure of public legitimacy to the revolutionary underground.

In Tuam, the other site of memory, there were occasional mobilisations of Old IRA men at the workhouse gates.[34] Behind the gates, Sister Hortense did her best to remember the sacrifice of the six. By tradition in her community, she was distressed when she first visited the workhouse to see footprints outside the chapel, believing these to have been left by the executed men. It was said that 'the memory of the shooting was always in her mind'. She had the site blessed and placed a wooden crucifix there. Prayers were offered continually by the community and Mass celebrated annually on the site.[35] On the closure of the home, the county manager assured councillors that provision would be made for the 'removal and re-erection' of Sister Hortense's cross.[36]

A 'ramshackle habitat': the Glenamaddy Children's Home, 1921–1925

In November 1921, the decision had been made to locate the new children's home in Glenamaddy, in a section of the fire-damaged workhouse. The home would be placed in the charge of the already resident Bon Secours Sisters at a flat rate of 10s per head per week. The home's committee would be responsible for repairs and for medical care.[37] In 1922, the function of the Glenamaddy Home was set out by the Galway Board of Health as follows: 'For the care of children and the retrievement of unmarried mothers'. With regard to the type of unmarried mothers that would be 'retrieved', it restricted these to 'first offenders'.[38] This was five years before the *Report into the Sick and Destitute Poor Including the Insane Poor,* which is often cited as the official stance on this. While the contractual arrangements and expectations may have been clear, when Sister Hortense and her sisters opened the home in the burnt-out remnants of the former workhouse, it was not at all fit for habitation. Within a year, the Galway County Homes and Home Assistance Committee was expressing concern about the 'very high' mortality rate in the institution, for which the 'bad' windows, the 'defective heating' and the generally unsanitary conditions were held to be responsible. An inspection of 1922 found a variety of hazards:

> Baths and Water Closet – Additional baths should be provided, and also some water closets. The dry earth closet there should be closed.

> Kitchen – The drain passing under the kitchen … is an open trap into which all kitchen waste is thrown. A wooden cover is placed over it to prevent any person falling into it.
>
> The apertures (doors and windows) in the wall at the other side of the staircase and opening into the burned building are dangerous and should be closed to prevent accidents.[39]

There was a cesspit that was 'rather too near' the building, but for financial reasons the committee did not recommend it be taken further away.'[40]

Beyond the committee, the state of the building did not go unnoticed and there were a number of startling reports in the *Connacht Tribune* on the 'ramshackle habitat'.[41] In June 1924, in a decisive intervention, the paper published an investigation of the conditions endured in the home by 'the waifs and strays, the orphans and the abandoned, the nameless little ones of the county', and by those who cared for them. The writer continued:

> Upstairs in the rambling house … there are thirty-three babies … One day these little mites, if they survive the rigours of life in such a house, will be projected into life. They will have to start with a heavy handicap. That handicap should be lessened as much as it is humanly possible.'[42]

For those in officialdom, there appeared to be more concern with the conditions for the sisters working there than for the children. The medical officer of the Glenamaddy home, Dr O'Malley, certified it as insanitary and 'detrimental to the health of the officers'.[43] Very quickly, conversations about alternative buildings took place. Of the alternatives, the workhouses in Tuam and Portumna, the *Tribune*'s anonymous 'special correspondent' recommended the former, on the basis of its good transport links.[44] There were powerful voices in Tuam opposed to the move, on the grounds that the workhouse would make a suitable factory building. The opponents included for a period Archbishop Gilmartin. However, rather than see the facility relocated outside his own bailiwick when Glenamaddy became indefensible, the Archbishop became an advocate for Tuam.[45] Even after the decision was taken to relocate, however, the military continued to occupy the Tuam workhouse building, notwithstanding the exhumations of August 1924 and letters of protest from the Board of Health and the Bon Secours sisters.[46] Eventually, the sisters took over the Tuam premises on 11 May 1925. At that time, there were eighty-seven infants and children (up to the age of 9 years) in their care, and twenty-six mothers. On 2 June

1925, the children travelled the eighteen-mile journey in three ambulances and a motor car.[47]

Given that the army had only recently evacuated the building, conditions were not much better than Glenamaddy. In August 1925, the Galway Board of Health received a letter from Sister Euphemia, Bon Secours Superioress in Dublin, in which she threatened to withdraw her sisters from Tuam: 'it is impossible for the sisters to carry on as things are, and after five months of drudgery, trying to save the lives of small children, they feel their responsibility too keen to continue'.[48] Three months later, in October 1925, the Commission on the Relief of the Sick and Destitute Poor made similar points:

> It was arranged that the Board of Health put the Home in order, but … this had not been done, and signs of dilapidation and decay were painfully evident. Its continuance in the condition in which we saw it would be a grave injustice to the Sisters and militate very much against its usefulness for the purpose to which it has been allocated.[49]

An official opening of the Tuam Children's Home took place in 1927, at which point there were thirty mothers and 118 children – ninety-six of whom were classed as 'illegitimate'. In the fifth report of the Mother and Baby Homes Commission of Investigation, the commission acknowledged that a total of 973 children from the children's home died either while it was located in Glenamaddy, in Tuam itself, or in a hospital or institution soon after they were transferred there from Tuam. Of this figure, seventy-nine died in Glenamaddy between late 1921 and mid-1925.[50]

'… the advantages of being brought up under the care of nursing sisters'

In December 2012, Catherine Corless first published her research on the Tuam Mother and Baby Home in the *Journal of the Old Tuam Society*. The article, 'The Home', did not get attention outside County Galway, so, after collecting the death certificates for the 796 children who died between 1925 and 1961, she contacted a reporter from the *Irish Daily Mail*. The front-page story that followed would receive widespread attention internationally and nationally.[51] From that moment, Tuam became a site for remembrance, anger and investigation. In 2015, the Mother and Baby Homes Commission was set up.[52] Its final report was expected in Spring 2020, after being postponed for a further year, but it was again delayed. Its findings to-date form part of this analysis, but prior to the commission there were already historians, journalists and survivors who had written about Tuam and other homes such as Bessborough in Cork city.[53] Limits on access to Bon Secours records has placed restrictions on research for this chapter, but the authors have been able to draw on the death certificates of the children who died while in the home, on the minutes of the Galway Board of Health, and on available minutes from the Homes and Home Assistance committee. We have also drawn extensively on newspaper coverage and contemporaneous accounts of the home. In regard to the question of whether the remains of these children and infants were buried in a septic tank, both the fourth and fifth interim reports of the Commission of Inquiry into the Mother and Baby Homes are relevant. In a statement issued in March 2017, the commission stated:

> The Commission has completed its test excavation of the Tuam site ... One structure appears to be a large sewage containment system or septic tank that had been decommissioned and filled with rubble and debris and then covered with top soil. The second structure is a long structure which is divided into 20 chambers ... significant quantities of human remains have been discovered in at least 17 of the 20 underground chambers which were examined ... The Commission is shocked by this discovery and is continuing its investigation into who was responsible for the disposal of human remains in this way.[54]

This was reiterated in the Commission's fifth interim report in March 2020.[55]

So who were the women and children that entered the home? If the death certificates and the other available records for the earlier years may be relied upon, the overwhelming majority of the mothers were 'domestic servants'.[56] There were exceptions. In 1926, P.K. was described as the 'Son of a Farmer's Daughter', while another child was the 'Son of a Tailor'. Death certificates from 1926 and subsequent years show a wide dispersal throughout County Galway, as well as some children from County Clare. Strikingly, the homes of several of the mothers were close to those of the executed 'boys' of 1923, indicating that they attended the same schools, and perhaps sat in the same classes as Frank Cunnane and Martin Moylan.

In 1925, the year of the transfer to Tuam, its catchment area was expanded, following an agreement between the Galway and Mayo Boards of Health that women from Mayo would be admitted. Detail of family circumstance is available for a small number. In 1926, M.C. and her three children were in receipt of home assistance when their house burned down.

All were initially admitted to the children's home, but subsequently the mother and one of the children were arrested and charged with the burning of their previous dwelling. In some instances, women were assisted in leaving. In 1925, for example, M.O. was allowed to leave for America. Others were not so lucky. In April 1924 the secretary of the Homes and Home Assistance Committee reported that Mrs W, whose husband was 'an Englishman resident in Galway for the past three weeks', was seeking admission of herself and three children to the children's home. The request was denied but her husband was pursued for child neglect and given two months, hard labour. Two of the children were placed in the home. While outside of the remit of this chapter, the linking of records such as the court records to those of the home and relating to the home will also provide a broader picture of the circumstances of individual women, children and families. In another case in 1924, a married woman, destitute with a 1-year-old child, applied to enter the home. They were admitted when it was established that she had been deserted by her husband. In 1923, a 9-year-old boy was transferred to Cabra School for the Deaf from the Tuam home – there were other similar cases.

Significantly, there are examples in the records of so-called adoptions, long before adoption was legalised in 1952. In July 1924, for example, the 'adoption' of E.G. by a woman in Connemara was recorded. However, when it was discovered that formal agreement was not reached, it was decided that Miss M would accept her as part of the boarding-out system.[57] The boarding-out system itself was first introduced under the Irish Poor Law Amendment Act (1862), which allowed Poor Law Guardians to board-out with local families – children that would otherwise be placed in the workhouse. The system was re-affirmed in 1924 under the County Boards of Health (Assistance) Order and the Public Assistance Act (1939). From 1922, responsibility for the system fell to the Department of Local Government and Public Health. Virginia Crossman has demonstrated that the policy was not followed uniformly.[58] For example, annual returns demonstrate that the total number of children boarded out in 1900 stood at 2,223, of whom 849 had been boarded out by Boards of Guardians in Leinster, compared to just 99 in Connacht.[59] Yet the Galway returns show an increase after 1900. In 1917, for example, in the Glenamaddy Union there were eighteen children boarded out, all 'satisfactory' bar one, and seven children 'hired out'. In November 1922, the Galway Board of Health and Public Assistance stated that boys aged 6 and over could be boarded out but 'they see no reason why they should be removed from the Bon Secours nuns'. This question of the tension between institutional care and that provided in families is central to the history of mother and baby homes and children's homes.

In October 1924, the board stated that children would be kept until 9 years for girls and 7 years for boys. Throughout the early years there are references to the board ignoring circulars rejecting calls for boarding-out stating, 'Children maintained in the home … have the advantages of being brought up under the care of nursing Sisters, their health properly attended to, well clothed and fed and sent to school regularly'.[60]

'… the smell and shine of Cardinal red polish … long lines of potties'

There are several memoirs and accounts of life in the home. These include articles by the late journalist John Cunningham, who spent some time there after the death of his mother. As he acknowledged himself, Cunningham's experience was unusual, because his father was employed in the home:

> One has to be careful of any impressions gained in childhood, though memories of The Children's Home can be extraordinarily vivid – long passageways in 'The Home' dominated by the smell and shine of Cardinal red polish on the floors, long lines of potties, of the inexplicably large numbers of young women, and the mysterious business of the arrival and departure of the same young women, and apparently endless numbers of babies and toddlers'.[61]

Not typical either, but poignant and quite remarkable, was the account of life in the home by Julia Carter (later Devaney), one of those who made the journey from Glenamaddy to Tuam in June 1925, and who remained in the home until its closure in 1961. Against the odds, she subsequently married a man that she had first encountered as a handyman in the home. By her own account, published in the *Tuam Herald,* she herself was always 'a square peg in a round hole'. She recalled, 'It never dawned on us that the nuns were wronging us or that we were entitled to our own lives'.[62] Of the mothers who passed through the home during her thirty-five years there, she said:

> The women had to have an admission ticket from the doctor to get in. There was no such thing as being signed in, but once they were there they would have to wait a year to look after their baby. One girl escaped, but she was brought back in again that night by the Guards. The gates were never locked as there were always milk vans and bread vans coming in … The mothers spoke only to each other about the fathers of their

children. They'd hate to face home ... An odd fellow would come in and take the girl out and marry her. I remember one case where the parents and the priest and the fella came in and he said he would marry the girl, but he would not take the child as it was not his.[63]

For the inmates, the boarding-out system terminated friendships without warning:

> Olive, I was very fond of in particular. She was boarded out. I lost touch with her. We never knew where they went, you wouldn't dare enquire after them. The nuns never kept in contact with the children. The Loughrea ambulance would come, and they would be marched up into it.[64]

Emotional connections such as that between Julia and Olive were not considered when decisions about their futures were being determined. Spanning her childhood in Glenamaddy and three decades of her working life in Tuam, Julia's association with 'the Home' was probably the longest of all, giving a particular value to her reflections on the conditions of the children there:

> The children had a language all of their own. They didn't talk right at all, nobody to teach them. When the children came home from school, they got their dinner, and then their hair was fine combed for nits and fleas ... Whatever they learned at school, they learned nothing up there: eating, to sitting on the pot, to going to bed. I think they spent most of their young lives sitting on them pots.[65]

Those who saw the children outside the home similarly remarked on an 'otherness'.[66] For Tuam songwriter, Pádraig Stevens, the daily parade to school of the 'home babies', which he witnessed as a teenager, was an 'alien spectacle':

> Two by two. Pale faces, snotty noses.
> Little kids, their scabby heads shorn.
> No socks, no smiles, no chatter.
> The only sound a scraping, and clattering.[67]

These accounts and other similar accounts such as June Goulding's *Light in the Window* and Patricia Burke-Brogan's fictional play *Eclipsed* demonstrate that there was an understanding in Irish society of the existence of

'... any infant born in any other circumstances appears to have a better chance of life'

On the very salient question of infant mortality, as the Commission of Inquiry into Mother and Baby Homes has recorded on foot of the pioneering work of Catherine Corless, 796 children died in the home during its thirty-six years, averaging 22.2 deaths per year but ranging from 1 in 1958 to 53 in 1947. Prior to the move to Tuam, in Glenamaddy the average number of annual deaths was almost exactly the same, but the cohort of children was smaller. Among the certified deaths, the causes of death that were given include debility from birth, congenital heart disease, respiratory diseases, meningitis, measles, congenital syphilis, influenza, marasmus, malnutrition, premature birth, skin diseases, whooping cough, ear infections, chicken pox, convulsions/epilepsy, cerebral haemorrhage and gastroenteritis. If there was concern about the high mortality rate (or indeed about an apparently unceremonious approach to the disposal of the mortal remains) there is little evidence of this in the contemporary record. The sisters were seemingly held in high regard in Tuam, with Sister Hortense patronising local charities, and perennially winning prizes in her own name for the produce of her institution's garden.[69] A private hospital established by the congregation in the town in 1946 was very successful, and continued in operation for almost four decades after the mother and baby home closed its gates.[70]

In the home's operational period, the matter of infant and childhood mortality was raised on occasion, but generally not treated as a matter of urgent concern. In 1928, for example, during a debate at a meeting of the Galway Homes and Home Assistance Committee, Dr Thomas Bodkin Costello, the medical doctor to the children's home, responded to a query by stating 'that half the children born in all countries die before the age of 5 years', to which the committee secretary added, 'the deaths in the Children's Home would not be 50 per cent'.[71] One who had a very different perspective was Alice Litster, Inspector for Boarded-Out Children in the Department of Local Government and Public Health, who wrote as follows in 1939 in the *Report on Unmarried Mothers in Ireland*:

> The chance of survival of an illegitimate infant born in the slums and placed with a foster-mother in the slums a few days after birth is greater

> than that of an infant born in one of our special homes for unmarried mothers. One exception is the Manor House, Castlepollard, in which the infantile death rate is comparatively low. In theory, the advantage should lie on the side of the child institutionally born. Pre-natal care, proper diet, fresh air, sufficient exercise, no arduous work, proper and comfortable clothing, freedom from worry, the services of a skilled doctor, the supervision and attention of a qualified nurse, all should be available and should make for the health of the expectant mother and the birth and survival of a healthy infant … I have grave doubts of the wisdom of continuing to urge Boards of Health and Public Assistance to send patients to the special homes so long as no attempt is made to explore the causes of the abnormally high death rate … We cannot prevent the birth of these infants. *We should be able to prevent their death.* [Authors' emphasis][72]

An estimate for the number of illegitimate births in County Galway given to the Homes and Home Assistance Committee in 1928 was twenty-five a year, which was so far below the national average as to raise a considerable doubt about its accuracy.[73] Looking at other debates surrounding the home in its early years, cost, ability to pay and class were central to the discourse. In May 1926, Sister Hortense was asked by the Galway Board of Health how many unmarried mothers had been reared in a workhouse, boarded out, or reared in an industrial school before they entered the home. The question demonstrates the mentality of the board at that time regarding these women. In August 1926, discussions began about the need for a maternity ward for unmarried mothers, 'as the admission of this class of patients to the Maternity Department of the Central Hospital tends to prevent respectable patients from seeking admission thereto'.[74]

The cultural and social stigma placed on women who became pregnant outside of marriage has been very well documented, and while it certainly pre-dated independence, the increasing Catholicisation of Ireland in the 1920s remains a factor in this debate.

In 1928, the committee debated whether the cost of £26 per year for a child and the same for a mother was too much to pay the Bon Secours order. On the responsibility to care for these women and children, the chairman stated:

> This is really the parents' responsibility and not ours. There must be cases where the betrayers of these unmarried mothers are well-to-do, and they should not be a burden on the rates. I think we should look

into every case and send those girls back to their parents who can afford to keep them.[75]

A similar concern had been expressed in April 1924, when the county solicitor reported that he would take necessary legal action against the 'putative fathers' of all illegitimate children born in the State since 1 January 1922 maintained in any of the institutions under the board's control. In May of the same year it was decided that in order to obtain a decree against putative fathers of illegitimate children there must be some corroboration of the mother's evidence, and that proceedings should be taken at first 'in the strongest cases'. Members of the Homes and Home Assistance Committee were appointed to accompany the solicitor to the Glenamaddy home with a view to getting the necessary statement. In January 1925, the first civil bills against fathers had been pursued in Galway and in Clare.[76] This was an approach that had precedents in the workhouse era, with fathers having been pursued since 1862. Proposing the prosecution of a putative father in 1919, a member of the Tuam board of guardians remarked, 'It is right to put down blackguardism; there is too much of it going on the county'. In 1920, the guardians referred a case of disputed paternity to the local republican court.[77]

Commemoration and Remembrance

In 1947, marking the Famine centenary, the Old Tuam Society raised a monument in the workhouse burial ground. The ceremony was conducted by the Catholic Archbishop Joseph Walsh, who stated, 'Some have said, "Why trouble about past events, and people who are so long dead?" ... We ought not forget that those who died during the Famine were our brothers, redeemed by the precious blood of Christ, and destined for a place in heaven'.[78] One might ask why similar consideration was not given to the 'departed brethren' who had been confined in the same building in more recent decades. Between 1925 and the date of Archbishop Walsh's speech, 679 children and infants had already died in the Tuam Mother and Baby Home.

Almost forty years later, on Sunday 21 April 1985, Tom Maguire unveiled a substantial monument on the remnant of the workhouse wall against which his brother and the other men had been shot almost exactly sixty-two years earlier. It was the culmination of efforts dating back to the early 1970s. The smaller monument raised many years earlier by Sister Hortense was retained. The principal speaker was the former Sinn Féin president, Ruairí Ó Brádaigh, who had been ousted from his position in 1983. Because of the party's decision to take its seats in Leinster House, it was a time of ferment in the party, and the Tuam ceremony was, in substantial part, a rallying point for the faction associated with Ó Brádaigh, which would become crystallised as the Republican Sinn Féin party in 1986. This was noted at the time, with Ó Brádaigh's party being accused by a Fianna Fáil figure of 'taking over the whole thing completely'.[79] The local controversy did not prevent the participation of the Bon Secours sisters, with Sister Kieran placing a wreath to the memory of Sister Hortense, and 'the other sisters who devoted their lives to caring for mothers and their children'.

The monument, dedicated to the 'six members of Óglaigh na hÉireann who were executed on this spot', named the six and their comrades shot in Athlone, but there was one other name: that of Hortense McNamara of the Bon Secours Sisters, who had preserved the site. Her name also featured in a commemorative booklet issued on the day, which highlighted a donation made years before towards the monument by 'Three Girls who wish to remain anonymous':

> I and my friends hope that you and your committee will accept our small donation. It is in honour of Mother Hortense, a great nun who raised us with love and understanding. We remember seeing the names outside of the Chapel of the six brave men, who were executed at the Tuam workhouse. We hope you succeed in erecting a memorial for those men. We are very grateful that you and the people of Tuam have not forgotten Mother Hortense. She will live forever in our memory. We hope that, by now, she is in Heaven, enjoying the fruits of her labour. God bless and God love you all for remembering Mother Hortense.[80]

By contrast with the executed 'boys' of 1923, to whom robust memorials were unveiled in 1952 and 1985, commemoration of the infants and children who died in the mother and baby home is at an early stage. Prompted by Catherine Corless's work, a small monument was erected in 2015 on the wall of the institution, across from a children's playground and the republican monument. Since 2014, Tuam has become a site of pilgrimage for many survivors of abuse and those angered at their mistreatment. In August 2018, in response to Pope Francis's visit to Ireland, over 1,000 people marched silently from the town of Tuam to a vigil at the site, following the route of previous marchers mentioned above. As women and men held up the names of those 796 infants who died in the institution from 1925 to 1961, it became apparent that their story will remain of critical importance to future generations.

Conclusion: Who Do We Commemorate?

The names of those executed on 11 April 1923 resonated through the decades in the locality. This was the case even as the remains of hundreds of children mouldered unacknowledged, very close to the place of their execution. Care was taken of the bodies of the six – even their sworn enemies ensured that they were placed in 'consecrated ground' – and they were reinterred twice, the second time so that that they might find a fitting final resting place. On two sites their sacrifice was dutifully commemorated. Coincidentally, the Bon Secours Sisters who died while based in the Tuam home were also reinterred twice – once in 1961 on the closure of the home, and again four decades later when the sisters closed their private hospital in the town. This was all appropriate, and consistent with the strictures of the Archbishop of Tuam in 1947 in relation to the Tuam workhouse casualties of the Great Famine: that commemoration and a marked burial place were positive mechanisms, which 'urge us in our charity to offer a prayer for our departed brethren who need our help'. Why then did the congregation that went to exceptional lengths to honour the memory of 'martyrs' of 1923, and which was properly conscientious in its respect for the remains of deceased sisters, seemingly show such scant regard for the bodies of the orphaned and 'neglected' children placed in its care? Was this common practice in the institutions of Ireland, many of which dealt with mothers and infants viewed as outside the norms of respectability? Did the question of their burial and re-interment emerge throughout the decades? Without access to the Bons Secours records this is not a question that can be answered. Whether the current Mother and Baby Homes Commission can do so remains to be seen, but what is certain is that during this 'decade of centenaries', who we chose to commemorate, memorialise and remember should continue to be challenged and explored.

Chapter 12

Brightening

DOIREANN NÍ GHRÍOFA

'and the fire brought a crowd in'

– Austin Clarke

When night stirs in me,
it brings no dream of sea, no quench,
no liquid reprieve. No. Night raises only
the old roar, sets the stench of petrol spilling once more.

O night. How polite, the strangers who pushed me
to choose heirlooms to send out to safety.
How their smiles grew shaky, when I chose
only the front door key. O Home.

Down in the night-damp grass, I stood alone.
Men watched me from the lawn;
I knew their mute gaze, grown grey, grown cold,
as I knew all the women huddled on the gravel,
how they folded whispers in their shawls.

I turned from them and watched it begin –
the brightening – our windows, lit one by one
from within: cellar, to hall, to kitchen.
How the ballroom shone. How the library blazed.

If brigade bells sang, they sang in vain, for flames
were already spilling up the drapes, licking

every hand and face from their gilt frames,
swiping china and ivory knives, fox-furs and silks,
tugging precious stones from each brooch's golden grip.

Ghosts, those flames, racing up the stairs,
sending smoke through slates,
a vast constellation of sparks to star the dark.
O paraffin splash. O Ash.

When the eaves creaked, one boy came to me,
shy grin twisting to jeer:
The house of the thief is known by the trees.
When I turned to leave, I could feel my back gleam.

Now, I may have no home of my own,
I may be alone, but I am not meek. No.
I am a stone released from old gold,
and oh, I blaze a Sunday through every week.

ENDNOTES

PREFACE

1. Lil Conlon, *Cumann na mBan and the Women of Ireland 1913–25* (Kilkenny: Kilkenny People, 1969), p. 1.
2. Ibid., p. 2.

INTRODUCTION

1. Jack Goldstone, 'Towards a Fourth Generation of Revolutionary Theory,' *Annual Review of Political Science*, 4 (2001), pp. 139–87.
2. For an extensive discussion see: Linda Connolly, 'The Irish Women's Movement: A Social Movements Analysis,' *Irish Journal of Feminist Studies*, 1 (1996), pp. 45–77; Linda Connolly, *The Irish Women's Movement: From Revolution to Devolution* (London/New York: Macmillan Palgrave, 2003), pp. 56–88.
3. Fanny Bugnon, 'Gender and Political Violence,' *Encyclopédie pour une histoire nouvelle de l'Europe* [online] (2016): http://ehne.fr/en/node/1219 (accessed 20 August 2020).
4. Valentine M. Moghadam, 'Gender and Revolutions,' in John Foran (ed.), *Theorizing Revolutions* (New York: Routledge, 1997), pp. 137–67; Valentine. M. Moghadam, 'Feminism and the Future of Revolutions,' *Socialism and Democracy*, 32, 1 (2018), pp. 31–53.
5. Foran, *Theorizing Revolutions*, p. 5.
6. Moghadam, 'Gender and Revolutions,' pp. 137–67.
7. Linda Connolly, 'The Limits of Irish Studies: Historicism, Culturalism, Paternalism,' *Irish Studies Review*, 12, 2 (2004), pp. 139–62.
8. Earlier pioneering work includes Margaret Ward, *Unmanageable Revolutionaries: Women in Irish Nationalism* (London: Pluto Press, 1983); Margaret Ward, *In their Own Voice: Women and Irish Nationalism* (Dublin: Attic Press, 1995); Margaret Ward, *Hanna Sheehy Skeffington: Suffragette and Sinn Féiner, Her Memoirs and Political Writings* (Dublin: UCD Press, 2017); Margaret Ward, 'Gender: Gendering the Irish Revolution,' in Joost Augusteijn (ed.), *The Irish Revolution 1913–1923* (London: Palgrave, 2002), pp. 168–85; Margaret Ward and Louise Ryan (eds), *Irish Women and Nationalism: Soldiers, New Women, and Wicked Hags* (Dublin: Irish Academic Press, 2004); Margaret Ward and Louise Ryan (eds), *Irish Women and the Vote: Becoming Irish Citizens* (Dublin: Irish Academic Press, new edition 2018); Cal McCarthy, *Cumann na mBan and the Irish Revolution* (Cork: The Collins Press, 2007); Sinéad McCoole, *No Ordinary Women: Irish Female Activists in the Revolutionary Years* (Dublin: O'Brien Press, 2003); Ann Matthews, *Renegades: Irish Republican Women, 1900–1922* (Cork: Mercier Press, 2010); Ann Matthews, *Dissidents: Irish Republican Women, 1923–1941* (Cork: Mercier Press, 2012).

9   David Fitzpatrick, *The Two Irelands: 1912–1939* (Oxford: Oxford University Press, 1998), p. 3.
10 David Fitzpatrick (ed.), *Terror in Ireland 1916–1923* (Dublin: The Lilliput Press, 2012). See John Borgonovo, 'Review: Revolutionary Violence and Irish Historiography,' *Irish Historical Studies*, 38, 150 (November 2012), pp. 325–31.
11 Bill Kissane, *The Politics of the Irish Civil War* (Oxford: Oxford University Press, 2005), p. 229.
12 Kissane, *The Politics of the Irish Civil War*, p. 227. See Caitríona Beaumont, 'Gender, Citizenship and the State in Ireland, 1922–1990,' in Scott Brewster, Virginia Crossman, Fiona Becket and David Alderson (eds), *Ireland in Proximity: History, Gender, Space* (London and New York: Routledge, 1999), pp. 94–108; Connolly, 'The Irish Women's Movement,' p. 45; Connolly, *The Irish Women's Movement*, pp. 56–88.
13 One example of the full inclusion of women's history in a recent book includes: Roy Foster, *Vivid Faces: The Revolutionary Generation in Ireland 1890–1923* (New York: W.W. Norton and Co., 2014).
14 See Linda Connolly, 'Sexual Violence and the Irish Revolution: an Inconvenient Truth?' *History Ireland*, 27, 6 (2019), pp. 34–39.
15 Moghadam, 'Gender and Revolutions,' p. 137.
16 For example see: Charles Townshend, 'Historiography: Telling the Irish Revolution,' in Joost Augusteijn (ed.), *The Irish Revolution 1913–1923* (London: Palgrave, 2002), pp. 1–16; Peter Hart, 'Definition: Defining the Irish Revolution,' in Joost Augusteijn (ed.), *The Irish Revolution 1913–1923* (London: Palgrave, 2002), pp. 17–33.
17 Ward, 'Gender,' pp. 168–185.
18 Joan Wallach Scott, 'Gender: A Useful Category of Historical Analysis,' *The American Historical Review*, 91, 5 (1986), pp. 1053–75.
19 Aidan Beatty, *Masculinity and Power in Irish Nationalism, 1884–1938* (London: Palgrave, 2016).
20 Françoise Thébaud, 'Understanding Twentieth-Century Wars Through Women and Gender: Forty Years of Historiography,' *Clio. Women, Gender, History*, 39, 1 (2014), pp. 157–82: https://journals.openedition.org/cliowgh/538 (accessed 20 August 2020).
21 Some book length examples include: Joost Augusteijn (ed.), *The Irish Revolution 1913–1923* (London: Palgrave, 2002); Gavin M. Foster, *The Irish Civil War and Society: Politics, Class and Conflict* (London: Palgrave, 2015); Gemma Clark, *Everyday Violence in the Irish Civil War* (Cambridge: Cambridge University Press, 2014); Marie Coleman, *The Irish Revolution, 1916–1923* (London: Routledge, 2013); Michael Hopkinson, *The Irish War of Independence* (Dublin: Gill and Macmillan, 2004); John Borgonovo, *The Battle for Cork: July-August 1922* (Cork: Mercier Press, 2011).
22 Examples of additional work in the developing arena of women's social, economic and political history include: Margaret MacCurtain and Donnchadh Ó Corráin (eds), *Women in Irish Society: the Historical Dimension* (Dublin: Arlen Press, 1978); Margaret MacCurtain, Mary O'Dowd and Maria Luddy, 'An Agenda for Women's History in Ireland 1500–1900,' *Irish Historical Studies*, 28, 109 (1992), pp. 1–37; Mary O'Dowd and Maryann Gianella Valiulis (eds), *Women and Irish History* (Dublin: Wolfhound, 1997); Mary E. Daly, 'Women and Work in Ireland,' *Studies in Irish Economic and Social History*, 7 (1997).
23 Ward, *Unmanageable Revolutionaries*; Ward, *In their Own Voice*; Ward, *Hanna Sheehy Skeffington*; Ward, 'Gender'; Ward and Ryan, *Irish Women and Nationalism*; Sonja

Tiernan (ed.), *The Political Writings of Eva Gore-Booth* (Manchester: Manchester University Press, 2016).

24 Ward and Ryan, *Irish Women and the Vote*. See also Connolly, *The Irish Women's Movement*, pp. 56-88 for an extensive review of the literature.

25 For a full discussion see Connolly, 'The Limits of Irish Studies'. Angela Bourke, Siobhán Kilfeather, Maria Luddy, Margaret MacCurtain, Gerardine Meaney, Mairín Ní Dhonnchadha, Mary O'Dowd and Clair Wills (eds), *The Field Day Anthology of Irish Writing Volumes IV and V: Irish Women's Writing and Traditions* (Cork: Cork University Press, 1999) was a response to the underrepresentation of women in previous Field Day volumes.

26 Fearghal Mac Bhloscaidh, 'Objective Historians, Irrational Fenians and the Bewildered Herd: Revisionist Myth and the Irish Revolution,' *Irish Studies Review*, 28, 2 (2020), pp. 204–34.

27 Elizabeth Jensen, 'History, Minus the Historian Herself,' *NPR*, 17 July 2019: https://www.npr.org/sections/publiceditor/2019/07/17/742821803/history-minus-the-historian-herself?t=1592587126815. Gender inequality in Irish academia is very well documented, especially at the senior academic level. See: *Report of the Expert Group: HEA National Review of Gender Equality in Irish Higher Education Institutions* (Dublin: HEA, June 2016).

28 Recent examples include: Lucy McDiarmid, *At Home in the Revolution: What Women Said and Did in 1916* (Dublin: Royal Irish Academy, 2016); Lauren Arrington, *Revolutionary Lives: Constance and Casimir Markievicz* (Princeton: Princeton University Press, 2015); Liz Gillis, *Women of the Irish Revolution, 1913-23* (Cork: Mercier, 2014).

29 Maeve Casserly and Ciarán O'Neill, 'Public History, Invisibility and Women in the Republic of Ireland,' *The Public Historian*, 39, 2 (2017), pp. 10–30.

30 Two books were republished: Margaret Ward and Louise Ryan (eds), *Irish Women and the Vote: Becoming Irish Citizens* (Dublin: Irish Academic Press, new edition 2018); Louise Ryan, *Winning the Vote for Women: The Irish Citizen Newspaper and the Suffrage Movement in Ireland* (Dublin: Four Courts Press, new edition 2018).

31 https://president.ie/en/diary/details/president-gives-keynote-address-at-the-centenary-commemoration-of-the-1st-dail/speeches (accessed 20 July 2020).

32 See Linda Connolly, 'Sexual Violence in the Irish Civil War: A Forgotten War Crime?' *Women's History Review*, published online 6 March 2020: https://doi.org/10.1080/09612 025.2020.1735613

33 Brett Schmoll, 'Solidarity and Silence: Motherhood in the Spanish Civil War,' *Journal of Spanish Cultural Studies*, 133, 4 (2014), pp. 475–89.

34 Diane Urquhart, *Women in Ulster Politics, 1890–1940* (Dublin: Irish Academic Press, 2000).

35 Ward, *Unmanageable Revolutionaries*, p. 2.

36 Benedict Anderson, *Imagined Communities: Reflections on the Origins and Spread of Nationalism* (London: Verso, 1983).

37 Justin Dolan Stover, 'Families, Vulnerability and Sexual Violence During the Irish Revolution,' in Jennifer Evans and Ciara Meehan (eds), *Perceptions of Pregnancy from the Seventeenth to the Twentieth Century* (London: Palgrave Macmillan, 2017), pp. 57–76; Jennifer Evans and Ciara Meehan, 'Introduction,' in Jennifer Evans and Ciara Meehan (eds), *Perceptions of Pregnancy from the Seventeenth to the Twentieth Century* (London: Palgrave Macmillan, 2017), p. 5.

CHAPTER 1

1. Nira Yuval-Davis, *Gender and Nation* (London: Sage, 1997); Sikita Banerjee, *Muscular Nationalism: Gender, Violence, and Empire in India and Ireland, 1914-2004* (New York: NYU Press, 2012).
2. Suruchi Thapar-Björkert and Louise Ryan, 'Mother India/Mother Ireland: Comparative Gendered Dialogues of Colonialism and Nationalism in the Early 20th Century,' *Women's Studies International Forum*, 25, 3 (2001), pp. 301-313.
3. M.R. Haque, 'Educating Women, (Not) Serving the Nation: The Interface of Feminism and Nationalism in the Works of Rokeya Sakhawat Hossain,' *An International Journal of Asian Literatures, Cultures and Englishes*, 7, 2 (2013), pp. 95-113.
4. Breda Gray and Louise Ryan, 'Politics of Irish Identity and the Interconnections Between Feminism, Nationhood, and Colonialism,' in Ruth Roach Pierson, Nupur Chaudhuri and Beth McAuley (eds), *Nation, Empire, Colony: Historicizing Gender and Race* (Bloomington: Indiana University Press, 1998), pp. 121-38.
5. Gerardine Meaney, 'Sex and Nation: Women in Irish Culture and Politics,' in Ailbhe Smyth (ed.), *Irish Women's Studies Reader* (Dublin: Attic Press, 1993), pp. 230-44; Sabina Sharkey, *Ireland and the Iconography of Rape: Colonisation, Constraint and Gender* (London: University of North London Press, 1994).
6. Linda Connolly, *The Irish Women's Movement: From Revolution to Devolution* (London: Palgrave Macmillan, 2003); Louise Ryan, *Gender, Identity and the Irish Press, 1922-1937: Embodying the Nation* (New York: Mellen Press, 2002); Caitríona Beaumont, 'After the Vote: Women, Citizenship and the Campaign for Gender Equality in the Irish Free State (1922-1943),' in Louise Ryan and Margaret Ward (eds), *Irish Women and the Vote: Becoming Citizens* (Dublin: Irish Academic Press, 2018), pp. 231-50.
7. Renata Siemienska, 'Women and Social Movements in Poland', *Women and Politics*, 6, 4 (1986), pp. 5-35.
8. Sumita Mukherjee, *Indian Suffragettes: Female Identities and Transnational Networks* (Oxford: Oxford University Press, 2018). See also Banerjee, *Muscular Nationalism*.
9. Louise Ryan, 'An Analysis of the Irish Suffrage Movement Using New Social Movement Theory,' in Linda Connolly and Niamh Hourigan (eds), *Social Movements and Ireland* (Manchester: Manchester University Press, 2006), pp. 40-57.
10. See for example, H.J. Kim-Puri, 'Conceptualizing Gender-Sexuality-State-Nation: An Introduction,' *Gender and Society*, 19, 2 (2005), pp. 137-59; the recent work of Nira Yuval Davis, with colleagues, has also reappraised the resurgence of national bordering – Nira Yuval-Davis, Georgie Wemyss, and Kathryn Cassidy, 'Everyday Bordering, Belonging and the Reorientation of British Immigration Legislation,' *Sociology*, 52, 2 (2018), pp. 228-44.
11. Senia Pašeta, *Irish Nationalist Women, 1900-1918* (Cambridge: Cambridge University Press, 2013); D.A.J. MacPherson, *Women and the Irish Nation: Gender, Culture and Irish Identity, 1890-1914* (London: Palgrave Macmillan, 2012); Ann Matthews, *Renegades: Irish Republican Women 1900-1922* (Cork: Mercier Press, 2010); Karen Steele, *Women, Press and Politics During the Irish Revival* (Syracuse: Syracuse University Press, 2007); Louise Ryan and Margaret Ward (eds), *Irish Women and Nationalism: Soldiers, New Women, and Wicked Hags* (Dublin: Irish Academic Press, 2004); Marie Coleman, *The Irish Revolution, 1916-1923* (London: Routledge, 2013).
12. See *Irish Times*, 15 Feb 2016: https://www.irishtimes.com/culture/heritage/women-of-1916-1.2535291 (accessed 9 September 2020); *Irish News*, 19 March 2016: http://www.irishnews.com/news/easterrising/2016/03/26/news/1916-close-to-250-women-were-involved-in-the-rising-443447/ (accessed 9 September 2020).

13 Linda Connolly and Niamh Hourigan, (eds), *Social Movements and Ireland* (Manchester: Manchester University Press, 2006); Louise Ryan and Margaret Ward (eds), *Irish Women and the Vote: Becoming Citizens* (Dublin: Irish Academic Press, 2018); Louise Ryan, *Winning the Vote for Women: the Irish Citizen Newspaper and the Suffrage Movement in Ireland* (Dublin: Four Courts Press, 2018).
14 Mary Cullen, 'Feminism, Citizenship and Suffrage: a Long Dialogue,' in Ryan and Ward, *Irish Women and the Vote*, pp. 1–20 and also Maria Luddy, 'Introduction: an Overview of the Suffrage Movement,' in Ryan and Ward, *Irish Women and the Vote*, pp. xix–xxviii.
15 Thapar-Björkert and Ryan, 'Mother India/ Mother Ireland.'
16 It is beyond the scope of this chapter to present a full analysis of the women's movement in India. That has been discussed at length elsewhere, see for example, Mukherjee's recent book, *Indian Suffragettes*.
17 Haque, 'Educating Women,' p. 96.
18 For an overview see Louise Ryan, 'Traditions and Double Moral Standards: the Irish Suffragists Critique of Nationalism,' *Women's History Review*, 4 (1995), pp. 487–503.
19 Joanna Liddle and Rama Joshi, *Daughters of Independence* (London: Zed, 1986).
20 Liddle and Joshi, *Daughters of Independence*, p. 37.
21 Haque, 'Educating Women,' p. 97.
22 Editorial, *Irish Citizen*, 23 May 1914.
23 Haque, 'Educating Women,' p. 96.
24 Tom Nairn, *The Break-up of Britain* (London: Verso, 1981).
25 Anne McClintock, 'Family Feuds: Gender, Nationalism and the Family,' *Feminist Review*, 44 (1993), pp. 61–80.
26 Thapar-Björkert and Ryan, 'Mother India/ Mother Ireland.'
27 George L. Mosse, *Nationalism and Sexuality* (London: University of Wisconsin Press, 1985), p. 18.
28 C.L. Innes, *Woman and Nation in Irish Literature and Society* (Hemel Hempstead: Harvester Wheatsheaf, 1993).
29 Banerjee, *Muscular Nationalism*.
30 Ryan, *Gender, Identity and the Irish Press*.
31 Rajagopalan Radhakrishnan, 'Nationalism, Gender and the Narrative of Identity,' in Andrew Parker, Mary Russo, Doris Sommer, Patricia Yaeger (eds), *Nationalisms and Sexualities* (New York: Routledge, 1992), pp. 77–95.
32 Radhakrishnan, 'Nationalism, Gender and the Narrative of Identity.'
33 Ketu Katrak, 'Indian Nationalism, Ghandian "Satyagraha" and the Representation of Female Sexuality,' in Andrew Parker, Doris Sommer and Mary Russo (eds), *Nationalisms and Sexualities* (New York: Routledge, 1992), p. 397.
34 Ibid., p. 400.
35 Liddle and Joshi, *Daughters of Independence*.
36 Ryan, 'Traditions and Double Moral Standards'; Margaret Ward, *Hanna Sheehy Skeffington: A Life* (Dublin: Attic Press, 1997); Ryan, *Winning the Vote for Women*.
37 Rosemary Cullen Owens, *Smashing Times* (Dublin: Attic Press, 1984); Clíona Murphy, *The Women's Suffrage Movement and Irish Society in the Early Twentieth Century* (New York: Harvester Wheatsheaf, 1989).
38 Paige Reynolds, 'Staging Suffrage: the events of the 1913 Dublin Suffrage Week,' in Ryan and Ward, *Irish Women and the Vote*, pp. 60–74.
39 Ryan and Ward, *Irish Women and the Vote*.

40 See Cullen Owens, *Smashing Times* and Murphy, *The Women's Suffrage Movement and Irish Society*. Margaret Ward's biography of Hanna Sheehy Skeffington is another important source: Ward, *Hanna Sheehy Skeffington*.
41 Cullen Owens, *Smashing Times*.
42 Ryan, 'An Analysis of the Irish Suffrage Movement Using New Social Movement Theory'; Ryan, *Winning the Vote for Women*.
43 Murphy, *The Women's Suffrage Movement and Irish Society*.
44 Lucy Delap, Louise Ryan and Teresa Zackodnik, 'Self-determination, Race, and Empire: Feminist Nationalists in Britain, Ireland and the United States, 1830s to World War One,' *Women's Studies International Forum*, 29, 3 (2006), pp. 241–54.
45 Jo Vellacott, 'A Place for Pacifism and Transnationalism in Feminist Theory,' *Women's History Review*, 2, 1 (1993), pp. 23–56.
46 Cullen Owens, *Smashing Times*; Ward, *Hanna Sheehy Skeffington*.
47 Senia Pašeta, 'Feminist Political Thought and Activism in Revolutionary Ireland, c. 1880–1918,' *Transactions of the Royal Historical Society*, 27 (2017), pp. 193–209.
48 Cullen Owens, *Smashing Times*.
49 *Irish Citizen*, 18 April 1914.
50 Ibid.
51 Cullen Owens, *Smashing Times*.
52 Louise Ryan, 'Women Without Votes: the Political Strategies of the Irish Suffrage Movement,' *Irish Political Studies*, 9 (1994), pp. 119–39; Ryan, 'Traditions and Double Moral Standards.'
53 Christine Bolt, *The Women's Movements in the United States and Britain from the 1790s to the 1920s* (London: Routledge, 2014).
54 Ward, *Hanna Sheehy Skeffington*.
55 For a discussion of suffragism amongst the unionist community see the work of Diane Urquhart, *Women in Ulster Politics, 1890–1940* (Dublin: Irish Academic Press, 2000); Myrtle Hill, 'Ulster: Debates, Demands and Divisions: the Battle For and Against the Vote,' in Ryan and Ward (eds), *Irish Women and the Vote*, pp. 209–30.
56 Ryan, 'An Analysis of the Irish Suffrage Movement Using New Social Movement Theory.'
57 Meaney, *Sex and Nation*.
58 Ryan, *Winning the Vote for Women*.
59 For more discussion see Ryan, *Winning the Vote for Women*.
60 *Irish Citizen*, 14 September 1912
61 Ibid.
62 *Irish Citizen*, editorial, November 1917 (monthly edition only).
63 Mosse, *Nationalism and Sexuality*; Radakrishnan, 'Nationalism, Gender and the Narrative of Identity.'
64 *Irish Citizen*, 18 April 1914.
65 *Irish Citizen*, April 1917.
66 Banerjee, *Muscular Nationalism*.
67 Margaret Ward, *Unmanageable Revolutionaries: Women and Irish Nationalism* (London: Pluto Press, 1989).
68 For a detailed analysis of this fascinating debate see Ryan, *Winning the Vote for Women*, chapter 5.
69 *Irish Citizen*, 2 May 1914.
70 *Irish Citizen*, 9 May 1914.

71 *Irish Citizen*, 23 May 1914.
72 Bannerjee, *Muscular Nationalism*.
73 Liddle and Joshi, *Daughters of Independence*.
74 Ward, *Unmanageable Revolutionaries*.
75 For a discussion see Ward, *Unmanageable Revolutionaries*; and Beth McKillen, 'Irish Feminism and Nationalist Separatism, 1914-23,' *Eire-Ireland*, 17 (1982), pp. 52-67.
76 Lil Conlon, *Cumann na mBan and the Women of Ireland* (Kilkenny: Kilkenny People Press, 1969).
77 Cullen Owens, *Smashing Times*.
78 Ryan, *Winning the Vote for Women*.
79 For more detailed discussion see various publications by Louise Ryan including 'Women Without Votes' and 'Traditions and Double Moral Standards,' as well as the recent book *Winning the Vote for Women*.
80 For a discussion see Ryan, *Winning the Vote for Women*; Louise Ryan, 'Publicising the Private: Suffragists' Critique of Sexual Abuse and Domestic Violence,' in Ryan and Ward, *Irish Women and the Vote*, pp. 75-89.
81 *Irish Citizen*, June 1919.
82 Ryan, 'Publicising the Private.'
83 *Irish Citizen*, 19 July 1913.
84 Ibid.
85 *Irish Citizen*, September 1919 (monthly edition only)
86 Katrak, 'Indian Nationalism.'
87 Mary Jones, *These Obstreperous Lassies* (Dublin: Gill and Macmillan, 1988).
88 Rosemary Cullen Owens, 'Votes for Ladies, Votes for Women,' *Saothar*, 9 (1983), pp. 32-47.
89 *Irish Citizen*, 28 December 1912.
90 *Irish Citizen*, 9 August, 1913.
91 *Irish Citizen*, November 1917.
92 Mosse, *Nationalism and Sexuality*.
93 Radhakrishnan, 'Nationalism, Gender and the Narrative of Identity'; Yuval-Davis, *Gender and Nation*.
94 Ryan, *Gender, Identity and the Irish Press*.
95 Sarah-Beth Watkins, *Ireland's Suffragettes* (Dublin: The History Press, 2014).
96 *Irish Citizen*, November 2017 - now published only as a monthly.
97 *Irish Citizen*, 4 September 1915.
98 *Irish Citizen*, July 1919, now published only as a monthly.
99 For a fuller discussion see Mukherjee, *Indian Suffragettes*.
100 For a description of gendered violence against women during the War of Independence see Louise Ryan, 'Drunken Tans: Representations of Sex and Violence in the Anglo-Irish War, 1919-21,' *Feminist Review*, 66 (2000), pp. 73-92. Many of the subsequent chapters in this book draw on newly available archival sources to further develop this account of gender-based violence during the war years.

CHAPTER 2

1 I would like to thank Linda Connolly for inviting me to the conference at which this chapter was delivered as a paper, and Helen Litton, Fionnuala Walsh and Margaret

Endnotes

Ward for help with primary sources. All quotations from Kathleen Clarke's Notebook (1918-1919) in the Clarke Papers are cited here by courtesy of the National Library of Ireland. Quotations from Kathleen Clarke's letters to her sister Madge Daly in the Daly Papers are cited by courtesy of the Special Collections and Archives, Glucksman Library, Copyright of the University of Limerick. Thanks to James Harte, Ken Bergin, and Helen Litton for help in authorizing the use of these materials.

2 Margaret Ward, *Hanna Sheehy Skeffington: Suffragette and Sinn Féiner, Her Memoirs and Political Life* (Dublin: UCD Press, 2017), p. 24.
3 The women's prison terms overlapped but were not identical. Kathleen Clarke was arrested in late May 1918 and released on 18 February 1919; Maud Gonne MacBride was arrested on 17 May 1918 and released at the end of October, probably 31 October; Constance Markievicz was arrested on 17 May 1918 and released on 10 March 1919; Hanna Sheehy Skeffington spent 8–9 August 1918 in the Bridewell in Dublin and 10–12 August in Holloway.
4 Benedict Anderson, *Imagined Communities: Reflections on the Origin and Spread of Nationalism* (London, New York: Verso, 1991 edition), p. 7.
5 Kathleen Clarke, unpublished letter to Madge Daly, 14 June 1918.
6 Helen Litton, Kathleen Clarke's grand-niece, 'Class is such a difficult thing to define. If anything, [the Daly family] would probably use the term "lower middle class", as factory workers and shop assistants, "blue-collar" as opposed to "white-collar" – office workers, accountants, etc.' (private message).
7 Edward Moane, BMH WS 896; Frank Drohan, BMH WS 702.
8 Frank Drohan, BMH WS 702, p. 35.
9 Ibid., p. 36.
10 Frank Drohan, BMH WS 702, p. 37.
11 Eamon Ó Duibhir, BMH WS 1474.
12 Robert Brennan, *Allegiance* (Dublin: Browne and Nolan, 1950), pp. 230–3.
13 Ibid., pp. 212–15.
14 Eamon Ó Duibhir, BMH WS 1474.
15 Helen Litton (ed.), *Kathleen Clarke, Revolutionary Woman: An Autobiography* (Dublin: O'Brien Press, 1991 edition), p. 163.
16 According to Rose McNamara, the Inghinidhe na hÉireann branch of Cumann na mBan, the first to be founded, 'was the only one that had military ranks at this early date,' 1914 (BMH WS 482).
17 According to Gonne: 'In that prison I found my two friends, Constance Markievicz and Kathleen Clarke. The latter had been taken from a sick bed and looked very ill. We were allowed to associate at exercise. I told them that I intended to go on hunger strike, but unfortunately they said "If you do, we will." I knew it would kill Kathleen and I tried to dissuade her, but they resolved that we would all do the same thing. I therefore gave up on that occasion.' (BMH WS 317).
18 Clarke, *Revolutionary Woman*, p. 148
19 Ibid., p. 161.
20 Constance Markievicz, *Prison Letters of Countess Markievicz* (London: Virago Press edition, 1987); Kathleen Clarke, unpublished letters to her sister Madge Daly (Daly Papers, Glucksman Library, University of Limerick).
21 Clarke, *Revolutionary Woman*, p. 166.
22 Constance Markievicz, *Prison Letters of Countess Markievicz*, p. 196.
23 Ward, *Hanna Sheehy Skeffington*, p. 26.

24 Kathleen Clarke, unpublished letter to Madge Daly, 1918 (date illegible).
25 Clarke, *Revolutionary Woman*, p. 159.
26 Ibid., p. 160.
27 Ibid., p. 234. The quotation is from a letter Markievicz wrote to Clarke on 18 February 1919; the letter is in the Kathleen Clarke Papers, Glucksman Library, University of Limerick.
28 Markievicz, *Prison Letters of Countess Markievicz*, p. 194.
29 Kathleen Clarke, Notebook (1918–19), Kathleen Clarke Papers, National Library of Ireland.
30 Ibid.
31 Lucy McDiarmid, *At Home in the Revolution: What Women Said and Did in 1916* (Dublin: Royal Irish Academy, 2015), p. 57.
32 Clark, *Revolutionary Woman*, p. 160.
33 Maud Gonne MacBride, BMH WS 317: http://www.bureauofmilitaryhistory.ie/bmhsearch/browse.js
34 See 'Hunger and Hysteria: The "Save the Dublin Kiddies" Campaign, October–November 1913,' in Lucy McDiarmid, *The Irish Art of Controversy* (Ithaca: New York: Cornell University Press, 2005), pp. 130–1.
35 Ward, *Hanna Sheehy Skeffington*, p. 25.
36 Maud Gonne MacBride, BMH WS 317.
37 Gonne's arrival in Dublin precipitated the notorious encounter with W.B. Yeats, when he refused to let her in to her own house on St Stephen's Green. He was living there with his pregnant wife, who also had flu and pneumonia. Yeats was concerned not only about the danger of military raids if Gonne moved in but also about the possibility of more germs. The Yeats family soon moved to another house, but the Yeats-Gonne *contretemps* on that occasion was epic. See Roy Foster, *W.B. Yeats: A Life. II. The Arch-Poet* (Oxford: Oxford University Press, 2003), p. 135.
38 Clarke, *Revolutionary Woman*, p. 155.
39 Ibid., p. 157.
40 Ibid.
41 Kathleen Clarke, Notebook (1918–19), Kathleen Clarke Papers, National Library of Ireland.
42 Kathleen Clarke, unpublished letter to Madge Daly, 15 October 1918.
43 Kathleen Clarke, Notebook (1918–19), Kathleen Clarke Papers, National Library of Ireland.
44 Ibid.
45 Ibid.
46 Ibid.
47 Clarke, *Revolutionary Woman*, p. 163.
48 Maud Gonne, BMH WS 317.
49 Clarke, *Revolutionary Woman*, p. 158.
50 Ibid., pp. 165–6.
51 Kathleen Clarke, Notebook (1918–19), Kathleen Clarke Papers, National Library of Ireland.
52 Clarke, *Revolutionary Woman*, pp. 161–2.
53 Kathleen Clarke, unpublished letter to Madge Daly, 30 September 1918.
54 Kathleen Clarke, unpublished letter to Madge Daly, 12 February 1918.
55 Clarke, *Revolutionary Woman*, p. 196.

CHAPTER 3

1. Peter Hart, *The IRA at War 1916-23* (Oxford: Oxford University Press, 2003), p. 16.
2. Military Service Pensions Collection, Belfast Brigade, MA/MSPC/CMB/143. Both women lived in Dublin and it is not clear why Belfast women were not asked to compile the roll.
3. Jim McDermott, *Northern Divisions: The Old IRA and the Belfast Pogroms 1920-22* (Belfast: Beyond the Pale, 2001); Robert Lynch, *The Northern IRA and the Early Years of Partition* (Dublin: Irish Academic Press, 2006).
4. Rose Black, MSP34REF23258; Frances Brady Cooney, MSP34REF57744; Winifred Carney, MSP34REF56077; Elizabeth Corr, MSP34REF10854; Elizabeth Delaney, MSP34REF26212; Mary McClean, MSP34REF27555; Teresa McDevitt, MSP34REF10778; Margaret Fitzpatrick, MSP34REF26214; Mary Hackett, MSP34REF23258; Alice McKeever, MSP34REF51358; Annie McKeever, MSP34REF51359; Amy Murphy, MSP34REF16261; Nellie Neeson, née O'Boyle, MSPREF3411037; Mary Russell, MSP34REF24769; Nora Quinn, MSP34REF24338; Emily Valentine, MSP34REF56551. Nell Corr, MSP34REF10855, withdrew her application, saying she was unable to travel to Dublin for interview. In her application, in addition to her 1916 contribution, she stated she was section commander for the Lamh Dearg branch. Unless providing additional information, I shall not give reference number on each occasion the contribution of an individual woman is referenced.
5. Marie Coleman, 'Compensating Irish Female Revolutionaries, 1916-1923,' *Women's History Review*, 26, 6 (2017), pp. 915-34.
6. McDermott, *Northern Divisions*, p. 256.
7. Ibid., p. 70
8. Ibid. Application lent to McDermott by the nephew of Cissie Crummey.
9. Thomas McNally, BMH WS 410.
10. Denis McCullough, MSP34REF55173.
11. Evelyn Conway and Deirdre Ellis-King, 'Róisín Walsh', *Missing Persons in the Dictionary of Irish Biography*, Royal Irish Academy, December 2015.
12. With thanks to the May family for providing access to the Elizabeth Corr archive held by the family.
13. Elizabeth Corr, 'Highlights of a Long Life', 13 pp. unpublished radio script.
14. Nancy Wyse Power, BMH WS 587.
15. Elizabeth Corr, 'Up Longford', unpublished journal, 1917.
16. Cumann na mBan Convention Report, 1918, P2188, NLI.
17. Elizabeth Delaney, MSP34REF26212.
18. Elizabeth Corr, 'Highlights of a Long Life'.
19. Austen Morgan, *Labour and Partition: The Belfast Working Class, 1905-23* (London: Pluto Press, 1991), p. 286.
20. Seán Cusack, BMH WS 402.
21. David Fitzpatrick, 'The Geography of the War of Independence,' in John Crowley, Dónal Ó Drisceoil, Mike Murphy, and John Borgonovo (eds), *Atlas of the Irish Revolution* (Cork: Cork University Press, 2017), p. 536.
22. Cal McCarthy, *Cumann na mBan and the Irish Revolution* (Dublin: Collins Press, revised edition, 2014), p. 157.
23. Seán Cusack, BMH WS 402.
24. Elizabeth Corr, 'I remember Terence MacSwiney', 8 pp. script for radio broadcast, August 1958.

25 Ernest Blythe, BMH WS 98.
26 Martin McGowan, BMH WS 1545.
27 Emily Valentine, MSP34REF56551.
28 Denis Houston, BMH WS 1382.
29 Corr, 'Highlights of a Long Life'.
30 Patrick Whelan, BMH WS 1449.
31 *Irish News*, 10 December 1918.
32 Carney to Joe McGrath, quoted in Helga Woggon, *Silent Radical – Winifred Carney, 1887-1943: A Reconstruction of Her Biography* (Dublin: SIPTU, 2000), p. 20.
33 Ibid.
34 McDermott, *Northern Divisions*, p. 121.
35 McCarthy, *Cumann na mBan*, p. 164.
36 Roger McCorley, BMH WS 389.
37 Sean Cusack, BMH WS 9 and BMH WS 402.
38 Liam McMullan, BMH WS 762.
39 Thomas Fitzpatrick, BMH WS 395.
40 Thomas McNally, BMH WS 410.
41 Thomas Fox, BMH WS 395.
42 Thomas Flynn, BMH WS 429.
43 Mary Russell, MSP34REF24769.
44 Nora O'Boyle, MSP34REF11037. This is significant as it was one of the few occasions McCorley provided a statement, despite numerous request by many of the Belfast women. However, he only signed his name to the statement presumably drafted by Seán O'Neill, who was a generous endorser of many claims.
45 Lynch, *The Northern IRA*, p. 62.
46 McDermott, *Northern Divisions*, p. 17.
47 Corr, 'Highlights of a Long Life'.
48 Robert Lynch, 'Ulster', in John Crowley, Donal Ó Drisceoil, Mike Murphy and John Borgonovo (eds), *Atlas of the Irish Revolution* (Cork: Cork University Press, 2017), p. 621.
49 Statement by Elizabeth Corr in MSP34REF10854 and in 'Highlights of a Long Life'.
50 Lynch, *The Northern IRA*, p. 62.
51 Thomas Fitzpatrick, BMH WS 395.
52 Michael MacConaill, BMH WS 567.
53 Thomas Flynn, BMH WS 429.
54 Lynch, 'Ulster', p. 634.
55 Joseph Murrary, BMH WS 429.
56 McDermott, *Ulster Divisions*, pp. 83-4, quoting a memoir by Seán Montgomery, n.d. Montgomery did not provide a witness statement or make a claim for a military service pension.
57 Liam Gaynor, BMH WS 183.
58 There were a number of criteria that applicants had to demonstrate: dispatches had to be in an ASU area or in dangerous areas; services had to be rendered in connection with places used as HQ; arms dumps had to have a considerable supply, be used frequently; responsibility for documents had to be demonstrated by having them in claimants' own house, etc. See Catriona Crowe, *Guide to the Military Service (1916-1923) Pensions Collection*, 2012: https://militarypensions.wordpress.com/dissemination/. These criteria went far beyond routine Cumann na mBan work. See also Coleman, 'Compensating Irish Female Revolutionaries'.
59 Mary Russell, MSP34REF24769, statement made by O'Seanasein (?) handwritten statement, name difficult to read.

Endnotes

60 Mary Hackett, MSP34REF23258. Her references were supplied by Elizabeth Delaney, Edward McEntee and J. Regan.
61 Mary Russell, MSP34REF24769.
62 Rose Black, BMH WSP34REF22470. In files W34E567 on 4 November 1934, writing from the family home in Clowney Street, Black's sister Elizabeth wrote a letter on behalf of Rose, Maggie and herself wanting to make a claim for a pension. The files available deal only with Rose Black.
63 Emily Valentine, MSP34REF56551.
64 Seán O'Neill, 13 November 1937, in supporting the application of Amy Murphy, 'who repeatedly rendered service to the movement at personal risk to herself'. Amy Murphy, MSP34REF16261.
65 Seán O'Neill, 18 July 1940, Winifred Carney, MSP34REF56077.
66 Seán Cusack, BMH WS 402.
67 Catherine Rooney, née Byrne, BMH WS 648.
68 Catherine Rooney, née Byrne, pension application, MS34REF3935. Her pension application was made in 1935 and finally settled in 1941 when she was awarded six and one-third years' service.
69 Frances Brady Cooney, MSP34REF57744. Kathleen's pension file has not been found but the records indicate she received a Grade D pension for five and seven-ninths years, much of her work involving the use of her home in Dublin as a meeting place for Michael Collins and Richard Mulcahy.
70 Morgan, *Labour and Partition*, p. 292.
71 Report of the 1921 Convention in Erskine Childers Papers, MS 48,063, NLI.
72 McCarthy, *Cumann na mBan*, p. 244.
73 Ibid., p. 162.
74 McDermott, *Northern Divisions*, p. 108.
75 Minutes of Cumann na mBan Convention, Sunday, 6 February 1922, MS 49,851/10, NLI.
76 Elizabeth Corr, 'A Belfast Visitor's Impression', Cumann na mBan Convention, newspaper article dated Tuesday, 7 February 1922 (newspaper name obscured in archive).
77 McDermott, *Northern Divisions*, p. 275.
78 Quoted in McDermott, *Northern Divisions*, p. 266.
79 Helga Woggon, *Silent Radical – Winifred Carney, 1887–1943: A Reconstruction of Her Biography* (Dublin, SIPTU, 2000), p. 22; McDermott, *Northern Divisions*, p. 267.
80 Louise Ryan, 'In the Line of Fire: Representations of Women and War (1912–23) Through the Writings of Republican Men,' in Louise Ryan and Margaret Ward (eds), *Irish Women and Nationalism: Soldiers, New Women and Wicked Hags* (Dublin, Irish Academic Press, 2004), p. 60.
81 Eve Morrison, 'The Bureau of Military Activity and Female Activism', in Maryann Gialanella Valiulis (ed.), *Gender and Power in Irish History* (Dublin: Irish Academic Press, 2010), pp. 77–8.
82 Ryan, 'In the line of fire,' p. 61.

CHAPTER 4

1 Margaret Ward, *Unmanageable Revolutionaries: Women in Irish Nationalism* (London: Pluto Press, 1983); Margaret Ward, *In their Own Voice: Women and Irish Nationalism* (Dublin: Attic Press, 1995); Margaret Ward, *Hanna Sheehy Skeffington: Suffragette and Sinn Féiner, Her Memoirs and Political Writings* (Dublin: UCD Press, 2017); Margaret Ward and Louise Ryan (eds), *Irish Women and Nationalism: Soldiers, New Women, and*

Wicked Hags (Dublin: Irish Academic Press, 2004); Margaret Ward and Louise Ryan (eds), *Irish Women and the Vote: Becoming Irish Citizens* (Dublin: Irish Academic Press, 2018); Louise Ryan, 'In the Line of Fire: Representations of Women and War (1919–1923) Through the Writings of Republican Men,' in Margaret Ward and Louise Ryan (eds), *Irish Women and Nationalism: Soldiers, New Women, and Wicked Hags* (Dublin: Irish Academic Press, 2004), pp. 45–61; Louise Ryan, *Winning the Vote for Women: The Irish Citizen Newspaper and the Suffrage Movement in Ireland* (Dublin: Four Courts Press, 2018).

2 Ward, *Unmanageable Revolutionaries*; Cal McCarthy, *Cumann na mBan and the Irish Revolution* (Cork: The Collins Press, 2007); Sinéad McCoole, *No Ordinary Women: Irish Female Activists in the Revolutionary Years* (Dublin: O'Brien Press, 2003); Ann Matthews, *Renegades: Irish Republican Women, 1900–1922* (Cork: Mercier Press, 2010); Ann Matthews, *Dissidents: Irish Republican Women, 1923–1941* (Cork: Mercier Press, 2012).

3 Senia Pašeta, *Irish Nationalist Women 1900–1918* (Cambridge: Cambridge University Press, 2016), pp. 219–46.

4 Diane Urquhart, *Women in Ulster Politics 1890–1940* (Dublin: Irish Academic Press, 2000), pp. 63–5, p. 109.

5 Pašeta, *Irish Nationalist Women*, pp. 219–46.

6 John Borgonovo, '"Codename G": The Women Spies of Cork 1920–1921,' *The Recorder: The Journal of the American Irish Historical Society*, 19, 2 and 20, 1 (2007), pp. 129–48.

7 For example, see Jason Knirck, '"Ghosts and Realities": Female TDs and the Treaty Debate,' *Éire-Ireland*, 32 and 33, 4 (1997), pp. 170–94.

8 See Bureau of Military History (BMH): Eilís Uí Chonnaill, BMH WS 568, NLI.

9 See Eilís Uí Chonnaill, BMH WS 568; Madge Daly, BMH WS 855.

10 Ward, *Unmanageable Revolutionaries*, p. 157.

11 See the IRA Membership Series, Nominal Rolls, RO/1–611; and the Cumann na mBan Nominal Rolls, CMB/1–165, Military Service Pensions Collection, Military Archives, Cathal Brugha Barracks, Dublin.

12 Besides the free time needed, members also paid a small weekly subscription fee, and were responsible for their own uniform.

13 Cumann na mBan brigade structures could be found in East Clare, South Tipperary, Kilkenny, Wexford, Galway, and Kilkenny, but these were the exception rather than the rule. See Brigid O'Mullane's explanatory statement in Máire Comerford's pension application: Máire Comerford, MSP34REF60668.

14 Cumann na mBan Annual Convention Report, 22–3 October 1921, MS 48,063, Erskine Childers Papers, NLI.

15 Ward, *Unmanageable Revolutionaries*, pp. 156–7.

16 Many Cumann na mBan branches did not submit membership figures for the Military Service Pensions Collection, which is apparent when comparing that data with the branches represented at the October 1921 convention.

17 For details of the Women's Peace Delegation in Dublin, the Irish Women's International League, and the Women's Peace Meeting in Cork, see Pádraig Yeates, *A City in Civil War: Dublin 1921–24* (Dublin: Gill and Macmillan, 2015), pp. 97–8; John Borgonovo, *The Battle for Cork: July-August 1922* (Cork: Mercier Press, 2011), p. 58; Bill Kissane, *The Politics of the Irish Civil War*; Ward, *In their Own Voice*, p. 126; *Irish Independent*, 13 July 1922; *Nationalist and Leinster Times*, 29 July 1922.

18 Military Service Pensions Collection, IRA Membership Rolls, RO/1-611; Cumann na mBan Nominal Rolls, CMB/1-165, MA.
19 Louise Ryan, 'Splendidly Silent: Representing Irish Republican Women, 1919-23,' in Lubelska Gallagher and Louise Ryan (eds), *Representing the Past: Women and History* (London: Longman, 2001), pp. 23-43.
20 See Éamon de Valera's message to 'Irish young men and women,' *Cork Examiner*, 17 April 1922.
21 For Lismore, see *Freeman's Journal*, 17 March 1922; for Dublin, see *Irish Independent*, 18 March and 3 April 1922; for Carrick-on-Suir, see *Cork Examiner*, 18 March 1922; for Killarney, see *Sunday Independent*, 19 March 1922; for Knockroe, see *Waterford News and Star*, 24 March 1922; for Ballina, see *Western People*, 1 April 1922.
22 *Irish Independent*, 6 March 1922 and 4 April 1922; John Borgonovo, *The Battle for Cork: July-August 1922* (Cork: Mercier Press, 2011), p. 32.
23 Michael Hopkinson, *Green Against Green: The Irish Civil War* (Dublin: Gill and Macmillan, 1988), pp. 186-8; Dónal Ó Drisceoil, 'Irish Newspapers and the Treaty and Civil War,' in John Crowley, Dónal Ó Drisceoil, Mike Murphy, and John Borgonovo (eds), *Atlas of the Irish Revolution* (Cork: Cork University Press, 2017), pp. 661-4.
24 For a discussion of War of Independence funerals see: John Borgonovo, 'Political Percussions: Cork Brass Bands and the Irish Revolution, 1914-1922,' in Jack Santino (ed.), *Public Performances: Studies in the Carnivalesque and Ritualesque* (Logan: Utah State University Press, 2017), pp. 104-7; and unpublished paper John Borgonovo, 'The Politics of Mourning: Republican Funerals, Processions, and Burials, 1918-1921,' delivered at the Canadian Association of Irish Studies Annual Conference, 1 June 2019, Concordia University.
25 Ward, *In Their Own Voice*, p. 133; *Anglo-Celt*, 15 July 1922; *Irish Times*, 5 August 1922; *Freeman's Journal*, 14 April 1923.
26 *Nationalist and Leinster Times*, 9 September 1922; *Sligo Champion*, 23 September 1922; see also John Dorney, *The Civil War in Dublin: The Fight for the Irish Capital, 1922-1924* (Dublin: Irish Academic Press, 2017), p. 162.
27 Ryan, 'Splendidly Silent,' p. 29.
28 *Freeman's Journal*, 31 August, 13 October, 11 November 1922; *Kerry People*, 15 July 1922; *Kilkenny People*, 2 September 1922; *Irish Independent*, 4 October 1922; *Irish Times*, 4 December, 29 December 1922, 13 April, 14 April 1923; *Nenagh News*, 19 August 1922; *Sligo Champion*, 2 December 1922.
29 Three leading republican propagandists who became anti-Treaty, Bob Brennan, Frank Gallagher, and Erskine Childers, all held IRA military ranks and headed IRA publicity offices. Republican propaganda efforts remain relatively under-explored in historical literature, especially during the Civil War period.
30 See Tom Derrig's letter in Cormac O'Malley and Anne Dolan (eds), *No Surrender Here!: The Civil War Papers of Ernie O'Malley, 1922-1924* (Dublin: Lilliput Press, 2007), p. 298.
31 Brigid O'Mullane, MSP34REF1178.
32 For example - see 'Publicity and IRA GHQ Papers,' Lot 36, CD, MA.
33 OC Battalion 1 to OC Cumann na mBan, 6 January 1923, Material Found on Peg Flanagan, Blackrock, Lot 26, 2-3, Captured Documents, MA. See also: Eileen Barry, MSP34REF52674.
34 Mary O'Kelly, MSP34REF60441; *Irish Times*, 11 November 1922; Report of County Kilkenny Cumann na mBan Brigade, 8 November 1922, Papers Captured in Baby Club, Dublin, Lot 34, CD, MA.

35 Director of Publicity, Cumann na mBan, January 1923, Documents found on Eibhlín Coleman, Coole, Newport, Tipperary, Lot 92, Contemporary Documents, MA.
36 Brigid O'Mullane, MSP34REF1178.
37 For examples, see Christina Stafford Brooks, MSP34REF8968; Máire Comerford, MSP34REF60668; Gavin Foster, *The Irish Civil War and Society: Politics, Class and Conflict* (London: Palgrave Macmillan, 2015), p. 34. The infamous 'Red Cow' killing of three republican teenagers by Free State forces was one outcome. The three had been posting notices as a favour for a Cumann na mBan member who had been beaten up on such duty previously. See Yeates, *A City in Civil War*, pp. 140-5.
38 The slogans come from Borgonovo, *The Battle for Cork*, p. 48; O'Malley and Dolan, *No Surrender Here*, p. 219.
39 Brigid O'Mullane, MSP34REF1178; Sydney Gifford Czira, MSP34REF5713; Dorney, *The Civil War in Dublin*, pp. 149-50.
40 Máire Comerford, MSP34REF60668.
41 See the letter of Bob Brennan, Director of Publicity, Northern and Eastern Command, in O'Malley and Dolan, *No Surrender Here!*, p. 218; Eileen Barry, MSP34REF52674.
42 Lily O'Brennan, MSP34REF2229.
43 *Donegal News*, 12 August 1922; *Cork Examiner*, 14 September 1922; *Irish Independent*, 4 May 1923.
44 Lindie Naughton, *Markievicz, A Most Outrageous Rebel* (Dublin: Irish Academic Press, 2016), pp. 253-4.
45 For examples of such activity see the *Cork Examiner*, 18 August, 2 November, 23, 28 December 1922, 6 January, 28 February 1923; *Evening Herald*, 20 August 1922; *Donegal Democrat*, 5 January 1923; *Freeman's Journal*, 1 August, 23 October 1922, 5, 10 February, 3 March, 16 April 1923; *Irish Independent*, 22 July, 30 August, 9 December 1922 and 12 February 1923; *Nenagh News*, 6 January 1923; *Sligo Champion*, 16 December 1922. See also Eoin Swithin Walsh, *Kilkenny In Times of Revolution, 1900-1923* (Dublin: Merrion Press, 2018), pp. 158-9.
46 McCarthy, *Cumann na mBan*, pp. 190-1.
47 For example, see O'Malley and Dolan, *No Surrender Here*, p. 219; Borgonovo, *The Battle for Cork*, pp. 77-8; John Dorney, *The Civil War in Dublin*, p. 71.
48 Ward, *Unmanageable Revolutionaries*, p. 173.
49 While this chapter focuses on Cumann na mBan in the Irish Free State during the Civil War, Margaret Ward's chapter in this volume explores its activities in Northern Ireland during during the same period.
50 For example, see Liz Gillis, *The Fall of Dublin* (Cork: Mercier Press, 2011).
51 See Gillis, *The Fall of Dublin*; Yeates, *A City in Civil War*; Las Fallon, *Dublin Fire Brigade and the Irish Revolution* (Dublin: South Dublin Libraries, 2013).
52 Leslie Price, MSP34REF26980; Máire Carron, MSP34REF20238; Bríd Connolly, MSP34REF3977; Máire English, MSP34REF24424; Ina Connolly Heron, MSP34REF21565; Ward, *In Their Own Voice*, pp. 130-2; Dorney, *The Civil War in Dublin*, p. 77.
53 Gillis, *The Fall of Dublin*, pp. 60, 68, 78, 90; Ward, *In Their Own Voice*; Máire Carron, MSP34REF20238; Áine Ceant, MSP34REF3977; Ellen Lambert Stynes, MSP34REF56696.
54 Gillis, *The Fall of Dublin*, pp. 57-9; McCoole, *No Ordinary Women*, p. 91.
55 Mary O'Kelly, MSP34REF60441; Bridget Tomkins, MSP34REF548; Bridget Carrick, MSP34REF14221; Borgonovo, *The Battle for Cork*, p. 114; Áine Fitzgerald,

Endnotes

MSP34REF39275; Pádraig Óg Ó Ruairc, *The Battle for Limerick City* (Cork: Mercier Press, 2010), pp. 136-7.
56   Máire Fitzpatrick, MSP34REF53111.
57   Maura Kidney, MSP34REF6743; Brigid Mary O'Sullivan, MSP34REF51513; John Borgonovo, 'The Exile and Repatriation of Father Dominic O'Connor (OFM Capuchin), 1922-58', *Éire-Ireland*, 52, 3 and 4 (Fall/Winter 2017), p. 131; *Nationalist and Leinster Times*, 22 July 1922; John O'Callaghan, *The Battle for Kilmallock* (Cork: Mercier Press, 2011), p. 129; Borgonovo, *The Battle for Cork*, p. 109; Máire Fitzpatrick, MSP34REF53111; Ó Ruairc, *The Battle for Limerick City*.
58   Papers captured on Peg Flanagan, Lot 26/34, CD, MA.
59   Hopkinson, *Green Against Green*, pp. 172-8.
60   For a brief introduction to the system, see a series of circulars from the 1st Northern Division Intelligence Branch, 25-26 July 1922, Documents found on Miss Coyle, Lot 79, CD, MA. While women couriers were relatively common in the War of Independence, I am arguing that they became even more essential for dispatch work in the Civil War, owing to the faltering of rank-and-file IRA membership.
61   Brigid O'Mullane, MSP34REF1178; Leslie Price, MSP34REF26980.
62   For examples of dispatch couriers, see Catherine McGrath, MSP34REF6222; Elizabeth Egan, MSP34REF6329; Mary Russell, MSP34REF59935; Minnie Kennedy, MSP34REF34962; for 'call house' managers, see Hannah Blaney, MSP34REF51766; Nano Hourigan, MSP34REF6355; Mary O'Kelly, MSP34REF60441; Margaret O'Riordan, MSP34REF60615; Jane Shanahan, MSP34REF10154. See also the query, 'Are Cumann na mBan and Fianna being utilised as dispatch couriers in your area?' IRA GHQ Communications Department Form, 5 March 1923, Documents found on P.J. McDonnell, OC 4th Western Division, Leenane, Connemara, Captured Docs, Lot 19 (1/6), MA.
63   For examples, see Hannah Hanley, MSP34REF27316; Rose Sweeny, MSP34REF60037. See also O'Malley and Dolan, *No Surrender Here*, p. 258.
64   List of Addresses found in a notebook possessed by Ernie O'Malley, Lot 36, CD, MA.
65   Kathleen Connolly Barrett, MSP34REF2198.
66   Bríd Connolly, MSP34REF3977.
67   Maureen Ryan, MSP34REF52148.
68   Minnie Kennedy Harkin, MSP34REF34962; Nora Sullivan, MSP34REF21522; Rose Geoghegan, MSP34REF60007; Máire Comerford, MSP34REF60668; Annie Parkinson, MSP34REF56225; Agnes Boyd, MSP34REF57529; Rose Sweeney, MSP34REF60037.
69   Leslie Price, MSP34REF26980.
70   Dorney, *The Civil War in Dublin*, pp. 161-2. Quartermasters was a position at the IRA's company, battalion, brigade, division, and General Headquarters levels.
71   For examples see Rose Geoghegan, MSP34REF60007; Brigid Brawn, MSP34REF35546; Bridget Dunleavy, MSP34REF36642; Mary O'Kelly, MSP34REF60441; Minnie Kennedy Harkin, MSP34REF34962; Catherine Geoghegan, MSP34REF60079; Bridget Gill, MSP34REF1571; Margaret McCarthy, MSP34REF29945.
72   Cumann na mBan Proficiency Exams, Cumann na mBan Papers, Captured 7 February 1923, Lot 34, CD, MA.
73   *Cork Examiner*, 7 March 1923.
74   See Margaret Skinnider, MSP34REF1991. Thanks to Dr Mary McAuliffe for this reference. See also Skinnider's letter in Bríd Connolly, MSP34REF3977. Owing to the confused nature of the IRA Executive following the capture of the Four Courts and

the setting up of a new command structure in Munster by Liam Lynch, it is possible Skinnider was performing the quartermaster general function for the IRA's Eastern Command, which was headquartered in Dublin. See the testimony of Joe O'Connor, MSP34REF1878, and his explanation for his assumption to the Quartermaster General position after the capture of the Four Courts.

75 Máire Fitzpatrick, MSP34REF53111; Máire Comerford, MSP34REF60668.
76 Máire Fitzpatrick, MSP34REF53111.
77 Margaret Mary Fahy MacSherry, MSP34REF54707. See also *Irish Independent*, 16 May 1923; *Freeman's Journal*, 15 May 1923.
78 Máire Comerford, MSP34REF60668; Kathleen Kenny Blackburn, MSP34REF1967.
79 Mary Josephine Commins, MSP34REF4873.
80 McCarthy, *Cumann na mBan*, p. 199; Myrtle Hill, *Women in Ireland: A Century of Change* (Belfast: Blackstaff Press, 2003), p. 94. See also *Freeman's Journal*, 29 July 1922.
81 Máire Comerford, MSP34REF60668; Máire Fitzpatrick, MSP34REF53111.
82 *Irish Independent*, 5–6 July 1922; *Freeman's Journal*, 14 July 1922.
83 *Irish Independent*, 15 August 1922. See also *Kerry People*, 12 August 1922.
84 Kathleen Kennedy Cleary, MSP34REF3257; Margaret Mary Fahy MacSherry, MSP34REF54707; Rosanne Boland, MSP34REF34153; Siobhán Creedon Lankford, SP34REF29397.
85 Nora O'Sullivan, MSP34REF35989. Her brothers were the noted Cork No. 1 Brigade guerrilla leaders Pat and Micheál O'Sullivan.
86 *Irish Independent*, 13 February 1923.
87 Julia Ryan-O'Leary, MSP34REF60329.
88 McCarthy, *Cumann na mBan*, p. 199.
89 Ryan, 'Splendidly Silent,' pp. 23–43.
90 Pádraig Óg Ó Ruairc, '"The Women Who Died for Ireland" – Cumann na mBan fatalities in the War of Independence and Civil War,' *History Ireland*, 26, 5 (2018), pp. 36–8. Thanks to Pádraig Óg Ó Ruairc for sharing this article before it appeared in print.
91 O'Callaghan, *The Battle for Kilmallock*, p. 129.
92 Ó Ruairc, 'The Women who died for Ireland'; Nora Sullivan, MSP34REF21522.
93 Ibid.
94 *Cork Examiner*, 13 November 1922. Another Cork woman, Mary Egan of Charleville, died in disputed circumstances while on a trap with an IRA Volunteer fleeing a Free State raid. See *Cork Examiner*, 21 November 1922.
95 Elizabeth King McCarthy, MSP34REF60490.
96 McCoole, *No Ordinary Women*, p. 104.
97 Dorney, *The Civil War in Dublin*, p. 98.
98 *Irish Times*, 2, 11 November 1922, 8 March 1923; *Irish Independent*, 30 October 1922; *Nenagh Guardian*, 11 November 1922; *Cork Examiner*, 15 February 1923; *Connacht Tribune*, 14 April 1922; Dorney, *The Civil War in Dublin*, pp. 149–50; Military Service Pensions Collection, Pension Board interview with Margaret Kennedy, 17 September 1936; Bríd Connolly, MSP34REF3977; Brigid O'Mullane, MSP34REF1178.
99 For more detail, see McCoole, *No Ordinary Women*, pp. 88–137; McCarthy, *Cumann na mBan*, pp. 206–16; and Ward, *Unmanageable Revolutionaries*, pp. 190–8.
100 For an example see Nano/Annie McCrann, MSP34REF23419; Christina Stafford Brooks, MSP34REF8968.
101 Ward, *Unmanageable Revolutionaries*, p. 195.

102 For further discussion, see Linda Connolly, *The Irish Women's Movement: From Revolution to Devolution* (London: Palgrave and Macmillan, 2003).
103 Marie Coleman, 'Military Service Pensions for Veterans of the Irish Revolution, 1916–1923,' *War in History*, 20, 2 (2013), pp. 201–221; Marie Coleman, 'Compensating Irish Female Revolutionaries, 1916–1923,' *Women's History Review*, 26, 6 (2017), pp. 915–34.
104 Marie Coleman 'Compensating Irish Female Revolutionaries, 1916–23' *War in History*, 20, 2 (2013), pp. 915–34.
105 For example, see Siobhán Creedon Lankford, SP34REF29397; Margaret Clancy, MSP34REF1666; and Máire Comerford, MSP34REF60668.
106 For example, see Josephine O'Donoghue, MSP34REF55794, of Cork City, who was an intelligence agent working in the British Army's 6th Division. See also Sheila Wallace, 43D1846, and Nora Wallace, 34D2124, also of Cork City. Both of the sisters were leaders of the small Irish Citizen Army organisation in Cork, and were never members of Cumann na mBan. For Sheila Wallace's designated rank of Brigade OC of Communications, see the Cork No. 1 Brigade Headquarters Nominal Roll, MSPC-RO-27.
107 Máire Comerford, MSP34REF60668.
108 Supporting letter of Oscar Traynor, 29 September 1945, Máire Comerford, MSP34REF60668.
109 Dorney, *The Civil War in Dublin*, p. 77.
110 Maryann Gialanella Valiulis, 'The Politics of Gender in the Irish Free State, 1922–1937,' *Women's History Review*, 20, 4 (2011), pp. 569–78.
111 Aidan Beatty, *Masculinity and Power in Irish Nationalism, 1884–1938* (London: Palgrave Macmillan, 2017). For a discussion of unionist masculinity in Ulster during this period, see Jane McGaughey, *Ulster's Men: Protestant Unionist Masculinities and Militarization in the North of Ireland, 1912–1923* (Montreal: McGill-Queen's University Press, 2012).
112 John Borgonovo, *The Dynamics of War and Revolution: Cork City, 1916–1918* (Cork: Cork University Press, 2013), pp. 31, 89; John Borgonovo, 'Army without Banners, The Irish Republican Army, 1920–21,' in John Crowley, Donal Ó Drisceoil, Mike Murphy, and John Borgonovo (eds), *Atlas of the Irish Revolution* (Cork: Cork University Press, 2017), pp. 390–9.
113 Gavin Foster, *The Irish Civil War and Society*, pp. 41–6.
114 Sikata Banerjee, *Muscular Nationalism: Gender, Violence, and Empire in India and Ireland, 1914–2004* (New York: NYU Press, 2012), pp. 85–6.
115 Connolly, *The Irish Women's Movement*, pp. 65–71.

CHAPTER 5

1 A TD or Teachta Dála is a member of Dáil Éireann, the lower house of the Oireachtas (the Irish Parliament). It is equivalent to an MP or Member of Parliament.
2 For another recent re-appraisal of the first generation of women TDs, see Sinéad McCoole, 'Debating not negotiating: The female TDs of the Second Dáil', in Liam Weeks and Mícheál Ó Fathartaigh (eds), *The Treaty: Debating and Establishing the Irish State* (Dublin: Irish Academic Press, 2018), p. 138.
3 Caitríona Beaumont, 'After the Vote: Women, Citizenship and the Campaign for Gender Equality in the Irish Free State 1922–1943', in Louise Ryan and Margaret Ward (eds), *Irish Women and the Vote: Becoming Citizens* (Dublin: Irish Academic Press, 2018), p. 231.

4. Pat Thane, 'Women and Political Participation in England, 1918–1970,' in Esther Breitenbach and Pat Thane (eds), *Women and Citizenship in Britain and Ireland in the Twentieth Century* (London: Continuum UK, 2010), pp. 12–13.
5. Margaret Ward, *In Their Own Voice: Women and Irish Nationalism* (Cork: Attic, 1995), p. 86.
6. Margaret Ward, *Unmanageable Revolutionaries: Women and Irish Nationalism* (London: Pluto Press, 1983), p. 125.
7. Kathleen Clarke, *Revolutionary Woman 1978–1972: An Autobiography* (Dublin: The O'Brien Press, 1991), p. 164.
8. Louise Ryan, 'Why did only two women stand for election in 1918?', *Irish Times*, 10 December 2018: https://www.irishtimes.com/culture/heritage/why-did-only-two-women-stand-for-election-in-1918-1.3697445 (accessed 19 July 2019).
9. Ibid.
10. Ibid.
11. Ward, *Unmanageable Revolutionaries*, p. 135.
12. Ward, *In Their Own Voice*, p. 92.
13. Ward, *Unmanageable Revolutionaries*, p. 135.
14. Ward, *In Their Own Voice*, p. 93.
15. However, Markievicz's eligibility to take her seat in 1918 has recently come under question. The fact that she was married (but separated) to a Polish national would likely have disqualified her from the House of Commons as an alien, as would the that fact that she had been found guilty of treason (this would also have been the case for numerous male Sinn Féin MPs). See Mari Takayanagi, 'The Eligibility of Constance Markievicz,' *The History of Parliament*, 14 December 2015: https://thehistoryofparliament.wordpress.com/2015/12/14/the-eligibility-of-constance-markievicz (accessed 27 July 2019).
16. Clarke, *Revolutionary Woman*, p. 170.
17. Meg Connery, 'Letter to the editor,' *Cork Examiner*, 21 April 1921.
18. Mary Daly, 'The "Women Element" in Politics: Irish Women and the Vote, 1918–2008,' in Esther Breitenbach and Pat Thane (eds), *Women and Citizenship in Britain and Ireland in the Twentieth Century* (London: Bloomsbury, 2011), p. 81.
19. McCoole, 'Debating Not Negotiating, p. 138.
20. Margaret MacCurtain, 'Women, the Vote and the Revolution,' in Margaret MacCurtain and Donnchadh Ó Corráin (eds), *Women in Irish Society: The Historical Dimension* (Dublin: Praeger, 1979), pp. 46–57.
21. Catherine Lee and Anne Logan, 'Women's Agency, Activism and Organisation', *Women's History Review*, 28, 6 (2019), pp. 831–834.
22. However, see McCoole, 'Debating Not Negotiating', pp. 147–52.
23. Ibid., p. 147.
24. Debates on the 'Treaty between Great Britain and Ireland, Signed in London on 6th December 1921: Sessions 14 December 1921 to 10 January 1922: https://celt.ucc.ie//published/E900003-001/ (accessed 9 September 2020).
25. Sinéad McCoole, *No Ordinary Women: Irish Female Activists in the Revolutionary Years 1900–1923* (Dublin: The O'Brien Press, 2015), p. 164.
26. Maedhbh McNamara and Paschal Mooney, *Women in Parliament. Ireland: 1918–2000* (Dublin: Wolfhound Press, 2000), p. 75.
27. McNamara and Mooney, *Women in Parliament*, p. 80.

28 Charlotte Fallon, *Soul of Fire: A Biography of Mary MacSwiney* (Cork: The Mercier Press, 1986), p. 17.
29 McCoole, *No Ordinary Women*, p. 201.
30 McNamara and Mooney, *Women in Parliament*, p. 82.
31 McCoole, *No Ordinary Women*, p. 209.
32 Anne Dolan and William Murphy, 'Pearse (Brady), Margaret', in *Dictionary of Irish Biography* online: https://dib.cambridge.org/home.do (accessed 15 August 2020).
33 McNamara and Mooney, *Women in Parliament*, p. 82.
34 Dolan and Murphy, 'Pearse (Brady), Margaret'.
35 May Fox 'To the editor', *Irish Independent*, 25 February 1922.
36 McNamara and Mooney, *Women in Parliament*, p. 72.
37 McCoole, *No Ordinary Women*, p. 203.
38 McNamara and Mooney, *Women in Parliament*, p. 79.
39 Ibid.
40 Louise Ryan, 'Drunken Tans: Representations of Sex and Violence in the Anglo-Irish War (1919–21),' *Feminist Review*, 66 (Autumn 2000), pp. 73–93.
41 McCoole, *No Ordinary Women*, p. 85.
42 Ibid.
43 'Debate on the Treaty: https://www.oireachtas.ie/en/debates/debate/dail/1921-12-19/2/ (accessed 22 August 2020).
44 Fallon, *Soul of Fire*, pp. 79–80.
45 Ibid. p. 80.
46 'Debate on the Treaty: https://www.oireachtas.ie/en/debates/debate/dail/1921-12-19/2/ (accessed 22 August 2020).
47 Ibid.
48 Ibid.
49 Ibid.
50 Ibid.
51 Jason Knirck, *Women of the Dáil: Gender, Republicanism and the Anglo-Irish Treaty* (Dublin: Irish Academic Press, 2006), p. 78.
52 'Debate on the Treaty': https://www.oireachtas.ie/en/debates/debate/dail/1921-12-19/2/ (accessed 22 August 2020)
53 Ibid.
54 Ward, *Unmanageable Revolutionaries*, p. 174.
55 Ibid., p. 172.
56 Hanna Sheehy Skeffington, 'The Irish electorate', *The Freeman*, 10 May 1922, Margaret Ward (ed.), *Hanna Sheehy Skeffington: Suffragette and Sinn Féiner, Her Memoirs and Political Writings* (Dublin: UCD Press, 2017), p. 192.
57 Dáil Éireann debate on 'Irish Women and the Franchise,' 2 March 1922.
58 Ibid.
59 Ward, *Unmanageable Revolutionaries*, pp. 176–7.
60 McNamara and Mooney, *Women in Parliament*, p. 83.
61 Beaumont, 'After the Vote', p. 232.
62 Ibid., pp. 233–47.
63 Beaumont, 'After the Vote,' p. 233.
64 Maryann Gialanella Valiulis, 'The Politics of Gender in the Irish Free State, 1922–1937,' *Women's History Review*, 20, 2 (2011), p. 1.

65   Daly, 'The 'Women Element in Politics', pp. 81–3.
66   Geo. A Lyons, 'Women and the Franchise', *Irish Independent*, 11 November 1922.
67   P.S. O'Hegarty, *The Victory of Sinn Féin: How it Won it, and How it Used it* (Dublin: The Talbot Press, 1924), p. 103.
68   O'Hegarty, *The Victory of Sinn Féin*, p. 104.
69   Fallon, *Soul of Fire*, p. 102.
70   Frances Gardiner, 'Political Interest and Participation of Irish Women 1922–1922: The Unfinished Revolution', *Canadian Journal of Irish Studies*, 18, 1 (1992), p. 19.
71   Nationalist divisions moulded party politics in independent Ireland, which has historically been dominated by three parties: Fianna Fáil, Fine Gael and the Labour Party. The two largest parties, Fianna Fáil and Fine Gael, find their origins in a series of splits in Sinn Féin over the terms of the Anglo-Irish Treaty. Pro-Treatyites founded Cumann na nGaedheal, a predecessor of the centre-right Fine Gael, and the party formed the Free State government from 1923 to 1932. Fianna Fáil, historically the larger of the two parties and more centrist in its ideological platform than Fine Gael, was founded by Éamon de Valera in 1926. He and a number of other members left Sinn Féin following an unsuccessful motion to allow republicans to take their Dáil seats if and when the oath of allegiance was removed. Fianna Fáil entered government in 1932, with de Valera remaining as leader until 1959. It has formed the vast majority of governments in Irish political history, and only in 1989 did it require a coalition partner to govern. Meanwhile, following the loss of so many members, Sinn Féin would struggle financially and electorally until a revival in the 1970s. The decision by Labour, the political vehicle of the trade unions and organised labour, not to contest the 1918 general election to prevent a split in the nationalist vote has been linked to the weakness of the left in Irish twentieth-century politics, and it was the 'third party' in electoral terms until the 2011 general election. Some minor parties, such as the republican Clann na Poblachta (many of its members were alienated from Fianna Fáil), came and went during the first fifty years of independence.
72   Mary Clancy, 'Shaping the Nation: Women in the Free State Parliament, 1923–1937', in Yvonne Galligan, Eilís Ward and Rick Wilford (eds), *Contesting Politics: Women in Ireland, North and South* (Oxford: Westview Press, 1999), pp. 209–16.
73   Claire McGing, 'Women, Nationalism and Politics after the Easter Rising.' Paper presented at *RTE – Reflecting the Rising*, Dublin, 28 March 2016, pp. 15–18.
74   Interestingly, most female senators over the 1920s and 1930s held outwardly feminist views. Perhaps because there were more women in the Seanad than the Dáil, they regularly spoke out against gender-based discrimination. See Clancy, 'Shaping the Nation,' pp. 207–9.
75   Dáil Éireann debate on 'Civil Service Regulation (Amendment Bill)', 18 November 1925.
76   Clancy, 'Shaping the Nation, p. 206.
77   McGing, 'Women, Nationalism and Politics,' p. 17.
78   Ibid., p. 14.
79   Diane D. Kincaid, 'Over His Dead Body: A Positive Perspective on Widows in the U.S. Congress', *Political Research Quarterly*, 31, 1 (1978), pp. 96–104.
80   Gail McElroy, 'The Impact of Gender Quotas on Voting Behaviour in 2016,' in David Farrell, Michael Marsh and Theresa Reidy (eds), *The Irish Voter 2016* (Manchester: Manchester University Press, 2018), p. 166.
81   Manning, 'Women and the Elections,' p. 158.

82 Maurice Manning, 'Women in Irish National and Local Politics, 1922–1977,' in Margaret MacCurtain and Donnachadh O'Corrain (eds), *Women in Irish Society: The Historical Dimension* (Dublin: Arlen House, 1978), p. 96.
83 McNamara and Mooney, *Women in Parliament*, p. 17.
84 Daly, 'The "Women Element" in Politics,' p. 84.
85 McGing, 'Women, Nationalism and Politics,' p. 14.
86 McNamara and Mooney, *Women in Parliament*, p. 17.

CHAPTER 6

1 Peter Burke, *History and Social Theory* (Oxford: Polity, 2005), p. 11.
2 Louise Ryan, 'Drunken Tans: Representations of Sex and Violence in the Anglo-Irish War, 1919–21,' *Feminist Review*, 66 (2000), pp. 73–92.
3 For example, see various contributions in Laura Sjoberg and Sandra Via (eds), *Gender, War, and Militarism* (Santa Barbara: Praeger, 2010) and Jeffrey Burds, 'Sexual Violence in Europe in World War II, 1939–1945,' *Politics and Society*, 37, 1 (2009), pp. 35–73.
4 Ann Matthews, *Renegades: Irish Republican Women 1900–1922* (Cork: Mercier Press, 2010), p. 266.
5 Charles Townshend, *The Republic: The Fight for Irish Independence* (London: Allen Lane, 2013), p. 170.
6 Examples of such research include Lindsey Earner-Byrne, 'The Rape of Mary M.: A Microhistory of Sexual Violence and Moral Redemption in 1920s Ireland,' *Journal of the History of Sexuality*, 24, 1, (2015), pp. 75–98; Marie Coleman, 'Violence against Women During the Irish War of Independence, 1919–21' in Diarmaid Ferriter and Susannah Riordan (eds), *Years of Turbulence; The Irish Revolution and its Aftermath* (Dublin, UCD Press), pp. 137–56; Gemma Clark, *Everyday Violence in the Irish Civil War* (Cambridge: Cambridge University Press, 2014); Justin Dolan Stover, 'Families, Vulnerability and Sexual Violence During the Irish Revolution,' in Jennifer Evans and Ciara Meehan (eds), *Perceptions of Pregnancy from the Seventeenth to the Twentieth Century* (London: Palgrave Macmillan, 2017), p. 59; Julia Eichenberg, 'The Dark Side of Independence: Paramilitary Violence in Ireland and Poland after the First World War,' *Contemporary European History*, 19, 3 (2010), pp. 231–48; Thomas Earls Fitzgerald, '... and that created terror'. *The Dynamics of Civilian-Combatant Interactions in County Kerry, 1918–1923* (Unpublished PhD Thesis, Trinity College Dublin, School of Histories and Humanities, 2018); Brian Hughes, *Defying the IRA? Intimidation, Coercion, and Communities during the Irish Revolution* (Liverpool: Liverpool University Press, 2016).
7 For a discussion of these issues see: Sarah Benton, 'Women Disarmed: the Militarisation of Politics in Ireland 1913–1923,' *Feminist Review*, 50 (1995), pp. 148–72; Clark, *Everyday Violence*, p. 186; T.K. Wilson, *Frontiers of Violence: Conflict and Identity in Ulster and Upper Silesia 1918–1922* (Oxford: Oxford University Press, 2010); Coleman, 'Violence against Women During the Irish War of Independence,' pp. 137–56.
8 Clark, *Everyday Violence*, p. 195 concluded 'rape never became a weapon of war in Ireland.'
9 Charles Townshend, 'The Campaign of Fire: Everyday Violence in the Irish Civil War, by Gemma Clark,' *Irish Times*, 6 September 2014. The compensation claims documents were submitted to the Irish and British governments for damage and dislocation at the hands of groups 'engaged in armed resistance to the Provisional or Free State governments,'

or acting on behalf of 'any unlawful or seditious organisation'. The Irish government's files relating to personal injuries are largely missing, which has implications for studying attacks on women, but those for damage to property survive, along with the British records of more than 2,000 claims made by people 'who ended up in Britain after fleeing Ireland during the conflict'.

10 For an analysis see Linda Connolly, 'Sexual Violence in the Irish Civil War: A Forgotten War Crime?,' *Women's History Review*, published online 6 March 2020: https://doi.org/1 0.1080/09612025.2020.1735613

11 For a longer discussion see Connolly, 'Sexual Violence in the Irish Civil War.'

12 Jack A. Goldstone, *Revolutions: A Very Short Introduction* (Oxford: Oxford University Press, 2014), p. 8.

13 Margaret Keogh, BMH WS 273, referred to how British soldiers could only walk on one side of O'Connell Street, Dublin due to efforts to save Irish girls from them: 'A decent girl could not walk down the Post Office side without being molested. Then such girls got the name of a "soldier's totty".'

14 Shani D'Cruze, 'Approaching the History of Rape and Sexual Violence: Notes Towards Research,' *Women's History Review*, 1, 3 (1992), p. 379.

15 D'Cruze, 'Approaching the History of Rape and Sexual Violence', pp. 377–97.

16 Julia Eichenberg, 'The Dark Side of Independence: Paramilitary Violence in Ireland and Poland after the First World War'; Matthews, *Renegades*; Niall Whelehan, 'The Irish Revolution, 1912–23,' in Alvin Jackson (ed.), *The Oxford Handbook of Modern Irish History* (Oxford: Oxford University Press, 2014), pp. 621–39.

17 For a discussion see Coleman, 'Violence against Women During the Irish War of Independence,' pp. 137–56.

18 Conor Heffernan, 'Head Shaving during Ireland's War of Independence,' *Doing History in Public*, 3 December 2015: https://doinghistoryinpublic.org/2015/12/03/head-shaving-during-irelands-war-of-independence/(accessed 20 July 2020).

19 Mary Alleway, MSP34REF37069.

20 Madge Daly, BMH WS 0855. Mrs Geraldine Dillon, BMS WS 424. Seán Broderick, BMS WS 1677.

21 Deborah Pergament, 'It's Not Just Hair: Historical and Cultural Considerations for an Emerging Technology,' *Chicago-Kent Law Review*, 75, 1 (1999), p. 44.

22 Pergament, 'It's Not Just Hair,' pp. 42–59.

23 Ibid.

24 Ann Mah, 'This Picture Tells a Tragic Story of What Happened to Women After D-Day,' *Time*, 6 June 2018.

25 Anthony Beevor, 'An Ugly Carnival,' *Guardian*, Friday, 5 June 2009: 'As we mark the 65th anniversary of the D-day landings, Antony Beevor describes a dark side to the liberation parties: the brutal head-shaving and beating of women accused of collaboration.'

26 Claire Duchen, *Women's Rights and Women's Lives in France 1944–1968* (London: Routledge, 1994), p. 4.

27 Kristine Stiles, 'Shaved Heads and Marked Bodies: Representations from Cultures of Trauma,' *Strategie II: Peuples Mediterannaneens* (1993), p. 99: https://web.duke.edu/art/stiles/shaved_heads.html (accessed 10 May 2020).

28 See Paul Preston, 'Violence against Women in the Spanish Civil War,' *The Volunteer*, 23 August 2018.

29 Eichenberg, 'The Dark Side of Independence,' p. 240.

30 Heffernan, 'Head Shaving during Ireland's War of Independence.'

Endnotes

31 Eoin Swithin Walsh, *Kilkenny: In Times of Revolution 1900-1923* (Kildare: Merrion Press, 2018), pp. 274-5.
32 Leo Buckley, BMH WS 174.
33 Michael Higgins, BMH WS 1247.
34 Elizabeth Bloxham, BMH WS 632.
35 Margaret M. (Peg) Broderick-Nicholson, BMS WS 168.
36 'Summaries of Police Daily Reports,' CO 904/146.
37 In the case of Greece see: Katherine Stafatos, 'The Psyche and the Body: Political Persecution and Gender Violence against Women in the Greek Civil War,' *Journal of Modern Greek Studies*, 29, 2 (2011), pp. 251-77.
38 Hart, *The IRA and its Enemies*; Fitzpatrick, *Terror in Ireland*.
39 See Clark, *Everyday Violence*, pp. 186-8 for a discussion.
40 Townshend, *The Republic*, p. 170. See also Margaret MacCurtain, 'Women, the Vote and Revolution,' in Margaret MacCurtain and Donnchadh Ó Corrain (eds), *Women in Irish Society* (Dublin: Praeger, 1978), pp. 34-6. Cumann na mBan, *1918 Convention: Report* (Dublin: 1918), q. Aideen Sheehan, 'Cumann na mBan: Politics and Activities', in David Fitzpatrick (ed.), *Revolution? Ireland 1917-1923* (Dublin, 1990), p. 88.
41 D'Cruze, 'Approaching the History of Rape and Sexual Violence,' p. 389.
42 Julia Eichenberg, 'Review of Frontiers of Violence: Conflict and Identity in Ulster and Upper Silesia, 1918-1922,' *Irish Historical Studies*, 37, 147 (May 2011), pp. 499-500.
43 Liam A. Brady, BMH 676.
44 'Death of Kate Maher, 22 December 1920, Dundrum, County Tipperary,' National Archives, Kew: WO 35/155B/4. Dr Marie Coleman kindly sent an electronic copy of this file.
45 'Policy Reports: Summaries of Reports from Counties – Criminal Offences and Breaches of the Truce: Tyrone, Waterford, Westmeath, Wexford, Wicklow, 1921,' TNA, CO 904/156A. Sincere thanks to Aaron Ó Maonaigh for providing this source to me as NAUK, CO 904/156A.
46 Joanna Bourke, *Rape: A History from 1860 to the Present* (UK: Hachette, 2015), p. 15.
47 Ibid., p. 16.
48 For a discussion see: Coleman, 'Violence Against Women During the Irish War of Independence,' p. 141.
49 Earnest Blythe Papers, UCDA, P24/323(4).
50 James Maloney, BMH WS 152.
51 Margaret Ward, *Hanna Sheehy Skeffington: Suffragette and Sinn Féiner, Her Memoirs and Political Writings* (Dublin: UCD Press, 2017), pp. 182-6. The 'Statement of Atrocities on Women in Ireland signed' by Hanna Sheehy Skeffington, highlighted the atrocities committed by the Black and Tans against women and children.
52 Brian Hanley, 'Moderates and Peacemakers: Irish Historians and the Revolutionary Centenary,' *Irish Economic and Social History*, 43, 1 (2016), pp. 122-3. For a detailed discussion see also: Connolly, 'Sexual Violence in the Irish Civil War.'
53 Earner-Byrne, 'The Rape of Mary M.,' p. 75.
54 Séamus Fitzgerald, BMH WS 1737.
55 Earner-Byrne, 'The Rape of Mary M.,' p. 76.
56 'Death of Kate Maher, 22 December 1920, Dundrum, County Tipperary,' National Archives, Kew, WO 35/155B/4.
57 Ibid.
58 See John Borgonovo, *Spies, Informers and the 'Anti-Sinn Féin Society': The Intelligence War in Cork City, 1920-1921* (Dublin: Irish Academic Press, 2007), p. 108.

59   Tameside Central Library, Local Studies and Archive Centre MR 1/2/4. Diary of activities of Manchester Regiment (based in Ballincollig, County Cork) entry for 29 November 1920. Thanks to Andy Bielenberg for locating a copy of the original entry.
60   See Andy Bielenberg and James S. Donnelly, *Cork's War of Independence Fatality Register*: http://theirishrevolution.ie/1921-123/#.XDE6c2V8Pdk: 'At one point, after she had returned from a hospital visit, her hair was "bobbed" or shorn, as a punishment ordered by the local IRA battalion. Subsequently her house was searched (after a military raid) by order of the captain of the Ardgroom Volunteer Company, and in this search part of a letter from the RIC head constable in Castletownbere was found, along with five half-torn letters from other RIC members and two photographs of RIC men.'
61   Katherine Collins, MSP34REF34414.
62   Margaret Doherty, DP2100. For a full discussion of this case, see: See Linda Connolly, 'Sexual Violence and the Irish Revolution: an Inconvenient Truth?' *History Ireland*, 27, 6 (2019), pp. 34–9; Linda Connolly, 'Sexual Violence in the Irish Civil War: A Forgotten War Crime?', *Women's History Review*, published online 6 March 2020: https://doi.org/10.1080/09612025.2020.1735613.
63   'Discipline – Charge against Lieuts. Waters, Benson and Mulholland, Ballina', Military Archives, Dublin, A/11837. My thanks to the family of Margaret (Maggie) Doherty for allowing access to a copy of this file which is the subject of a forthcoming publication.
64   Margaret Doherty, DP2100.
65   For further discussion of this case see, Linda Connolly, 'Sexual Violence and the Irish Revolution.'
66   See John Horne and Alan Kramer, *German Atrocities, 1914: A History of Denial* (New Haven: Yale University Press, 2001), p. 200.
67   Bourke, *Rape*, p. 131; 'Discipline – Charge against Lieuts Waters, Benson and Mulholland, Ballina', Military Archives, Dublin, A/11837.
68   'Trim Criminal Quarter Sessions,' 24 March 1923, *Leinster Leader*, p. 11, states the case included the charge of rape.
69   Early publications that first detailed this case include: Seamus Hogan, *The Black and Tans in North Tipperary: Policing, Revolution and War 1913–1922* (Dublin: Untold Stories Publishers, 2013), pp. 420–2; Eamonn Gaynor, *Memoirs of a Tipperary Family – the Gaynors of Tyone 1887–2000* (Dublin: Geography publications, 2003), p. 206. See also John Dorney, *The Civil War in Dublin: The Fight for the Irish Capital, 1922–1924* (Dublin: Four Courts, 2017); Pádraig Yeates, *A City in Civil War – Dublin 1921–1924* (Dublin: Gill and Macmillan, 2015), p. 179; Clark, *Everyday Violence*, pp. 186–7; Linda Connolly, 'Sexual Violence and the Irish Revolution: an Inconvenient Truth?' *History Ireland*, 27, 6 (2019), pp. 34–9.
70   Mrs. E.M.W. Biggs, Irish Grants Committee, National Archives [London], CO 762/4/8.
71   Yeates, *A City in Civil War*; National Archives [London], CO 762/4/8.
72   Mo Moulton, *Ireland and the Irish in Interwar England* (Cambridge: Cambridge University Press, 2014), p. 212 draws attention to the following cases: Thomas John Day Atkinson and Mrs Cicely Helen Burrington Atkinson (assault, possibly sexual), CO 762/32/26; Mrs Norah Slattery (assault), CO 762/154/20; Mrs Margaret Fox (sexual assault), CO 762/17/22. Marie Coleman also discusses these sources in Chapter 7.
73   Mrs Bridget Doherty, BMH WS 1193, indicated women were also implicated in searching: 'They arrived at 5 o'clock in the evening. I was put into a room in my house where I was undressed by two female searchers.'

74 Joe Joyce, '24 July 1924: From the Archives: Three masked Free State army officers beat two young women with their Sam Browne belts and rubbed grease ...' *Irish Times*, 24 July 2012.
75 'Interview with Bill Bailey,' in Ernie O'Malley, *The Men Will Talk to Me: Kerry Interviews*, Tim Horgan and Cormac O'Malley (eds) (Cork: Mercier, 2012), p. 103.
76 See Pádraig Yeates, *A City in Civil War – Dublin 1921–1924: The Irish Civil War* (Dublin: Gill and Macmillan, 2015); Tom Doyle, *The Civil War in Kerry* (Cork: Mercier Press, 2008), p. 309.
77 Dominic Price, *We Bled Together: Michael Collins, the Squad and the Dublin Brigade* (Cork: the Collins Press, 2017), p. 210.
78 Ernest Blythe, BMS WS 939, p. 182. See also statements of: Cahir Davitt, BMH WS 1715, pp. 94–5; Kevin O'Sheil, BMH WS 1770.
79 Mary Walsh, BMH WS 556.
80 Mollie O'Shea, BMH WS 733.
81 This case was highlighted by Niall Murray, 'Role of Women Detailed in Pension Files,' *Irish Examiner*, 11 May 2018.
82 Delia Begley, MSP34REF32794.
83 Michael O'Regan, 'Stories of the Revolution: Ballyseedy and the Civil War's worst atrocity,' 11 December 2015, *Irish Times*: 'On 7 March, nine anti-Treaty prisoners, one of them with a broken arm, another with a broken wrist, and one, John Daly, unable to walk from spinal injuries, were taken by lorry to Ballyseedy Cross about two miles from Tralee. The hands of each prisoner were tied behind him. Each was tied by the arms and legs to the man beside him … A rope was passed completely round the nine men so that they stood in a ring facing outwards. In the centre of the ring was a landmine … The soldiers who tied them took cover and exploded the mine. The remains of the prisoners killed were flung far and wide, bits of bodies hung from trees in the wood that bordered the roadside.'
84 See: Élise Féron, 'Wartime Sexual Violence Against Men: The Hidden Face of Warfare,' (Tempere: Rowman and Littlefield), 28 November 2018: https://www.rowmaninternational.com/blog/wartime-sexual-violence-against-men-the-hidden-face-of-warfare (accessed 20 July 2020).
85 Brett Shadl, 'The Politics and Histories of Sexual and Gender Based Violence,' *Journal of Women's History*, 26, 1 (2014), pp. 185–94.
86 Connolly, *The Irish Women's Movement*.

CHAPTER 7

1 The Military Service Pensions Collection, the release of which is ongoing since January 2014, is available at http://www.militaryarchives.ie/collections/online-collections/military-service-pensions-collection/search-the-collection. A small proportion of the files, such as applications for service medals, are only available at present in the Military Archives building in Dublin.
2 Eve Morrison, 'The Bureau of Military History and Female Republican Activism,' in Maryann Gialanella Valiulis (ed.), *Gender and Power in Irish history* (Dublin: Irish Academic Press, 2009), p. 59.
3 Marie Coleman, 'Cumann na mBan and the War of Independence,' in John Crowley, Dónal Ó Drisceoil, Mike Murphy, and John Borgonovo (eds), *Atlas of the Irish Revolution* (Cork: Cork University Press, 2017), pp. 400–8.

4   Ruby Buchanan, 'A Study of the Treatment of the Republican Female Prisoners during the Irish Civil War (1922–23),' unpublished BA dissertation, Queen's University Belfast (2017).
5   The Cumann na mBan Series can be accessed in the 'Organisation and membership' section of the Military Service Pensions Collection website: http://www.militaryarchives.ie/collections/online-collections/military-service-pensions-collection-1916-1923.
6   For further elaboration of these points, see Marie Coleman, 'Military Service Pensions for Veterans of the Irish Revolution (1916–1923),' *War in History*, 20, 2 (April 2013), pp. 1–21; 'Compensating Irish Female Revolutionaries, 1916–1923,' *Women's History Review*, 27, 6 (2017), pp. 915–34; and 'Military Service Pensions and the Recognition and Reintegration of Guerrilla Fighters after the Irish Revolution,' *Historical Research*, 91, 253 (2018), pp. 554–72.
7   *Seanad Éireann debates*, vol. 19 (30 August 1934), cols 561–2.
8   John McCoy, 'Cumann na mBan Service: Memo on General Principles Interpreting Qualifying Service and Active Service under the 1934 Act "During Tan War Period",' 21 June 1939, Military Service Pensions Collection, CNM/163.
9   Memorandum by Gearóid O'Sullivan, 16 October 1924, MA, Military Service Pensions Collection, SPG/6/13.
10 Coleman, 'Compensating Irish Female Revolutionaries, 1916–1923.'
11 Tom Clonan, 'Granny was a freedom fighter but she never spoke about it,' in *Irish Times*, Health and Family Supplement, 29 March 2016, p. 3.
12 Kate Greaney, MSPDP15993.
13 Margaret Clancy, MSP34REF1666.
14 Kate Greaney, MSPDP15993.
15 Elaine Showalter, *The Female Malady: Women, Madness and English Culture, 1830–1980* (London: Panatheon Books, 1987).
16 See for example Tracey Loughran, *Shell Shock and Medical Culture in First World War Britain* (Cambridge: Cambridge University Press, 2017); Fiona Reid, *Broken Men: Shell Shock, Treatment and Recovery in Britain, 1914–1930* (London: Continuum, 2010); and Paul Lerner, *Hysterical Men: War, Psychiatry and the Politics of Trauma in Germany, 1890–1930* (Cornell: Cornell University Press, 2003).
17 Military Service Pensions Collection, M/124/25.
18 Army Pensions Act (1923), third schedule, paragraph 2.
19 Patrick Perry, MSP2D133.
20 Sinéad McCoole, *Easter Widows* (Dublin: Transworld, 2015).
21 MA, Military Service Pensions Collection, 1D475: Roger Casement; 1D43: George Geoghegan.
22 See for example MA, Military Service Pensions Collection, CON RAN 13: William John Coote.
23 http://centenaries.nationalarchives.ie/centenaries/plic/index.jsp (accessed 27 March 2018).
24 NAI, PLIC/1/4739.
25 See for example NAI, PLIC/1/1758: Edith Tyson and PLIC/1/2838: Mary Irwin.
26 Kathryn Milligan, 'The cultural cost of 1916: The Property Losses (Ireland) Committee and the Royal Hibernian Academy': http://inspiring-ireland.ie/cultural-cost-of-1916-property-losses-ireland-committee-and-royal-hibernian-academy (accessed 27 March 2018); NAI, PLIC/1/0588, Sarah Henrietta Purser: PLIC/1/0639: Estella Solomons.

27 Hanna Sheehy Skeffington, NAI, PLIC/1/3210.
28 NAI, Dept. Finance, FIN/COMP/2/14/105, 106 and 107; TNA, CO762/32/7, Annie (Neill) Collins.
29 See Niamh Mary Brennan, 'Compensating Southern Irish Loyalists after the Anglo-Irish Treaty, 1922–32', unpublished PhD thesis, University College Dublin (1994), Chapter 10.
30 Fergal Peter Mangan, 'Compensation in the Irish Free State, 1922–23,' unpublished MA dissertation, University College Dublin (1994), p. 3.
31 Andy Bielenberg, 'Southern Irish Protestant Experiences of the Irish Revolution,' in John Crowley, Dónal Ó Drisceoil, Mike Murphy, and John Borgonovo (eds), *Atlas of the Irish Revolution* (Cork: Cork University Press, 2017), p. 776; Niamh Brennan, 'A Political Minefield: Southern Loyalists, the Irish Grants Committee and the British Government, 1922–31,' in *Irish Historical Studies*, 119 (May 1997), p. 415.
32 Brennan, 'A Political Minefield,' p. 147; Bielenberg, 'Southern Irish Protestant Experiences,' p. 777.
33 Brian Hughes, 'Loyalists and Loyalism in a Southern Irish Community, 1921–1922,' in *Historical Journal*, 59, 4 (December 2016), pp. 1075–105; Paul Taylor, *Heroes or Traitors? Experiences of Southern Irish Soldiers Returning from the Great War, 1919–1939* (Liverpool: Liverpool University Press, 2015), pp. 44–7.
34 Gemma Clark, *Everyday Violence in the Irish Civil War* (Cambridge: Cambridge University Press, 2014), pp. 186–95. See also Pádraig Yeates, *A City in Turmoil – Dublin 1919-1921: The War of Independence* (Dublin: Gill and Macmillan, 2012) and Seán Hogan, *The Black and Tans in North Tipperary: Policing, Revolution and War 1913–1922* (Dublin, 2013).
35 A number of authors refer to her as Mrs Harriet Biggs, though her Irish Grants Committee file gives her name as Eileen M.W. Biggs. Civil registers of births and marriages indicate that she was born Eileen Mary Warburton Robinson, daughter of Robert Henry Robinson, an army surgeon, and his wife, Elizabeth, in Dublin in 1879 (which would have made her 43 at the time of the attack, although her age is given as 37 in other sources). In the 1911 census she was residing in the home of her sister, Mrs Grace Biggs, in Kilbarron, County Tipperary, where, in 1918 she married another member of the Biggs family, Samuel Dickson Biggs, www.irishgeneaology.ie and www.census.nationalarchives.ie (Bellvue, Kilbarron, County Tipperary). See also Linda Connolly, 'Sexual Violence in the Irish Civil War: A Forgotten War Crime?' *Women's History Review*, published online 6 March 2020: https://doi.org/10.1080/09612025.2020.1735613 and Linda Connolly, 'Sexual Violence and the Irish Revolution: an Inconvenient Truth?' *History Ireland*, 27, 6 (2019), pp. 34–9.
36 TNA, CO762/4/8: Mrs E. Biggs, Tipperary; Clark, *Everyday Violence*, pp. 186–7.
37 NAI, Dept. Justice, H5/386, Secretary, Dept. of Home Affairs to Chief of Police, 17 June 1922.
38 NAI, Dept. Justice, S. O'R to Secretary, Dept. of Home Affairs, 17 June 1922.
39 NAI, Dept. Justice, Thomas Sterling Berry to Minister for Home Affairs, 10 June 1922.
40 Ibid.
41 1911 census Ireland, Hogan family Dromineer, Monsea, Tipperary, http://www.census.nationalarchives.ie/pages/1911/Tipperary/Monsea/Dromineer/820022/ (accessed 19 June 2019).
42 *Nenagh Guardian*, 5 August 1922.

43 Military Service Pensions Collection, RO 192.
44 *Nenagh Guardian*, 5 August 1922.
45 Ibid.
46 TNA, CO762/4/8.
47 Ibid.
48 Deaths registered in the South Dublin Union District, death of Mary [sic] Peacock, 26 October 1924, www.irishgeneaology.ie; death notice of Margaret Peacock, *Irish Times*, 28 October 1924; obituary of Dr Pryce Peacock, *Irish Times*, 7 April 1927.
49 Deaths registered in the District of Dun Laoghaire, Rathdown, death of Samuel D. Biggs, 12 February 1937: www.irishgenealogy.ie (accessed 19 June 2019); death notice of Eileen Biggs, *Irish Times*, 9 October 1950; NAI, CS/HC/PO/4/104/400, Biggs, Eileen M.W., administration papers..
50 *Nenagh Guardian*, 5 August, 1922.
51 NAI, D/JUS H5/386: Dept. of Home Affairs note, 20 July 1923.
52 Military Service Pensions Collection, DP4458, Martin Hogan.
53 Clark, *Everyday Violence*, pp. 187–8.
54 TNA, CO762/17/22, Margaret Fox. I am grateful to Dr Mo Moulton for drawing my attention to this case.
55 TNA, CO762/40/0, Elizabeth McCormack [Gorman].
56 TNA, CO762/49/10, Delia Reidy.
57 TNA, CO762/40/6, Margaret McCormack.
58 TNA, CO762/62/19, Percy Hawkes Taylor.
59 TNA, CO762/32/26, Thomas and Cicely Atkinson.
60 TNA, CO762/51/8, Elizabeth Doyle.
61 TNA, CO762/66/8, Margaret O'Dowd.
62 TNA, CO763/131/8, Margaret Moore.
63 *Report of the Labour Commission to Ireland* (London, 1921), Appendix 3, pp. 80–1.
64 TNA, CO762/107/9, Bessie Churchill.
65 TNA, CO762/18/1, Ellen Wilkinson.
66 TNA, CO762/64/3, S.J. Heuston; CO762/118/16, Kathleen Fitzgerald; CO762/110/14, Kate Hayden.
67 TNA, CO762/191/9, Annie O'Shea.
68 TNA, CO762/62/8, Nora O'Mahony.
69 TNA, CO762/64/3, Margaret Colohan.
70 TNA, CO762/85/6, Bridget Ryan.
71 TNA, CO762/117/8, Agnes O'Halloran.
72 TNA, CO762/84/20, Mary O'Brien.
73 TNA, CO762/191/11, Anne Jones; 107/14: Alice Bevan; 51/9: Mary Sheridan; 110/7: Elizabeth Walpole; 51/13: Jesse Hunter; 191/2: Rachel Honner.
74 TNA, CO762/55/17, Emma Sophia McManus.
75 TNA, CO762/74/10, Mrs Waller-Sawyer.
76 Cal McCarthy, *Cumann na mBan and the Irish Revolution* (Cork: Collins Press, Revised edition, 2014), pp. 168–9.

CHAPTER 8

1 Andy Bielenberg, 'Fatalities in the Irish Revolution,' in John Crowley, Dónal Ó Drisceoil, Mike Murphy, and John Borgonovo (eds), *Atlas of the Irish Revolution* (Cork: Cork University Press, 2017), p. 753.

Endnotes

2 *Cork Examiner,* 16 February 1920.
3 *Cork Examiner,* 28-29 June 1921; TNA, Military inquests, WO 35/157a/57.
4 TNA, Military inquests, WO 35/159a/6; TNA CO. 904/148-50; Weekly summary of outrages against the RIC.
5 *Cork Examiner,* 13 July 1920; John Borgonovo, *Spies, Informers, and the 'Anti-Sinn Féin' Society: The Intelligence War in Cork City, 1920-1921* (Dublin: Irish Academic Press, 2007), pp. 31, 52, 93, 168-70.
6 TNA, Military inquests, WO 35/155a/31; TNA, CO. 762/161/4/2727 Application of David Medalie to Irish Grants Committee, *Cork Weekly News,* 18 December 1920.
7 TNA, Military inquests, WO 35/155a; *Cork Weekly News,* 18 December 1920.
8 TNA, Military Inquests, WO 35/147a/38; *Cork Weekly News,* 2 April 1921; William Regan, BMH WS 1069; William Buckley, BMH WS 1009.
9 A. Coyle, *The American Commission on Conditions in Ireland* (Washington DC, 1921), pp. 917-18; *Cork Examiner,* 30 September 1920.
10 M. Gyves, 'The Death of Mrs King,' *Mallow Field Club Journal* no. 28 (2010), pp. 33-52; Jeremiah Daly, BMH WS 1015; TNA, Military inquests, WO 35/153a/7.
11 NLI, O'Donoghue Papers, MS 31,301 (3 and 5), Ambush at Upton Railway Station.
12 *Cork Examiner,* 9 April 1921.
13 UCDA, Mulcahy Papers, P7/A/45, IRA order no 13, (9 November 1920) Woman spies.
14 Military Archives, Collins papers, Alexander Noble to de Valera, 8 September 1921.
15 UCDA, Mulcahy Papers, P7/A/26.
16 Military Archives, Collins papers A/0649; From Commandant Fifth Battalion to Cork No. 5 Brigade Headquarters, 21 October 1921.
17 Military Archives, Collins papers A/0649; From Commandant Cork No. 5 Brigade to adjutant, First Southern Division, 21 October 1921.
18 Military Archives, Collins papers A/0649; Travers Wolfe, solicitor to Minister for Defence, 16 March 1922.
19 *Skibbereen Eagle,* 28 January 1922.
20 Eve Morrison, 'Hauntings of the Irish Revolution: Veterans and Memory of the Independence Struggle and Civil War,' in Marguerite Corporaal, Christopher Cusack and Ruud van den Beuken (eds), *Irish Studies and the Dynamics of Memory* (Bern: Peter Laing, 2017). The taped interview was played at the West Cork History Festival (2017) at a paper presented by Dr Morrison. There are some other variations in local memory on the circumstances and location of Mrs Noble's death. I base this conclusion on exchanges with Fachtna O'Donovan, who has gathered information on the Noble case.
21 Terence de Vere White, 'The Shooting of Mrs Lindsay,' *Irish Times,* 17 October 1978. See for example, Imperial War Museum; Strickland Papers, pocket diary entry 20 June 1920 when Strickland came to lunch with his family. Her case has been given ample coverage in two publications, Seán O'Callaghan, *Execution* (London: Frederick Muller, 1974), which draws extensively upon the memory of some IRA members, notably Frank Busteed; Tim Sheehan, *Lady Hostage; Mrs Lindsay* (Cork: Lee Press, 1990).
22 Nevil Macready, *Annals of an Active Life* (London: Hutchinson and Co. 1924), p. 543. The military assumption that she would not be found out was implicit in the statement of the Solicitor-General for Ireland (Mr T.W. Brown) to the House of Commons, 4 August 1921, Hansard, fifth series, vol. 145, [1606]. Piaras Beaslaí, *Michael Collins and the Making of a New Ireland* (Dublin: Edmund Burke publisher, 1926), p. 191.
23 Imperial War Museum, Strickland Papers, pocket diary entry, 2 February 1921.

24 John Manning, BMH WS 1720; *Freeman's Journal*, 18 February 1921; *Irish Independent*, 18 February 1921. NLI, Seán O'Mahony Papers, MS 44,045/2. Letter from Jeremiah Murphy to J.J. Walsh, 19 February 1924. See pension claim of Mary Herlihy, who claims she attended Mrs Lindsay frequently and 'was given the particular duty of seeing that she was supplied with books' (MSP34REF62035).

25 UCDA, Mulcahy Papers, P7/A/21, 'The case of Mrs. Lindsay, Leemount, Coachford, County Cork' (written by Ethel Benson). On 1 April 1921 the motor car and 'one electric lighting set' taken from Mrs. Lindsay's was recovered by a Crown force searching party, when they located some IRA dugouts. The Tameside Central Library; MR1/2/4, Diary of activities of Manchester Regiment (Ballincollig) entry dated 28 January 1922.

26 *Irish Times*, 15, 19 March 1921; *Belfast Newsletter*, 19 March 1921.

27 Imperial War Museum; Strickland Papers, pocket diary entry 28 February 1921. For details of arrest and executions see TNA, WO 35/155B/1.

28 NLI, Seán O'Mahony Papers, MS 44,045, Benson to de Valera, 6 July 1921.

29 NLI, Seán O'Mahony Papers, MS 44,045 Minister for Defence to Mrs. Benson, 29 July 1921. This letter was read into the records of the House of Commons. UK Parliamentary Papers; Commons Sitting, 4 August 1921.

30 O'Callaghan, *Execution*, pp. 179–80. Sheehan, *Lady Hostage*, p. 158.

31 *Morning Post*, 23 March 1921.

32 NLI, Seán O'Mahony Papers, MS 44,045/1, Report on Mrs Lindsay signed OC Cork No. 1 Brigade, 19 July 1921.

33 Hansard, House of Lords Debate, 4 August 1921, vol. 43, cc.320-2; Nurse Cavell had become something of a British martyr, having been shot by the Germans as a spy during the First World War; TNA WO 35/146a Military Inquest of James Barrett.

34 NLI, Seán O'Mahony Papers; MS 44,045/1/C Minister for Defence to Mrs Ethel Benson 11 August 1921. The Lindsay case came up in the House of Commons Sitting, 4 August 1921.

35 F.P. Crozier, *Ireland for Ever* (London: Jonathan Cape, 1971), pp. 219–20.

36 Bridie Reilly, BMH WS 454.

37 NLI, Seán O'Mahony Papers, MS 44,045/1, report on Mrs Lindsay signed OC Cork No. 1 Brigade, 19 July 1921; Sheehan, *Lady Hostage*, p. 173. That Collins at least had been notified is corroborated in Piaras Beaslaí, *Michael Collins and the Making of a New Ireland* (Dublin, 1926), p. 191. But it appears that Beaslaí might also have been more misled on the details than he later implies in his book. See NLI, Piaras Beaslaí, MS 33914 (2), Editor, An t-Oglach to Chief of Staff, 12 July 1921.

38 Military Archives, IE/MA/CP/4/01, Brigade adjutant Cork No. 1 to Director of Information, 15 March 1921. This file was identified through the research of Cecile Gordan, 'The Case of Mrs. Lindsay,' *History Ireland*, 23 (September–October 2015).

39 NLI, Seán O'Mahony Papers, MS 44,045/1, report on Mrs Lindsay signed OC Cork No. 1 Brigade, 19 July 1921; O'Callaghan, *Execution*, p. 179; Michael Murphy, BMH WS 1547 even implies these executions were carried out by order from the Brigade OC (Seán O'Hegarty).

40 NLI, MS 33914 (1), Piaras Beaslaí Papers, letter from Director of Publicity to Minister of Defence, 7 July 1921; Ormonde Winter, *Winter's Tale: An Autobiography* (London: Richards Press, 1955), p. 302. UCDA, Mulcahy papers, P7/A/21 Letter from Editor An t-Oglach, 12 July 1921.

41 UCDA, Mulcahy papers, P7/A/21. Chief of Staff, IRA to the Divisional Commandant of the First Southern Division, 12 July 1921.
42 *Morning Post*, 23 March 1921, 30 July 1921, 2 August 1921, 10 August 1921.
43 Dennis Kennedy, *The Widening Gulf; Northern Attitudes to the Independent Irish State 1919–1949* (Belfast: Blackstaff Press, 1988), pp. 50–2. See for example *Belfast Newsletter*, 30 July 1921; Mrs Lindsay's late husband, Mr J.W. Lindsay had been a senior partner of Messrs. Crawford and Lindsay, Solicitors, Banbridge. *Irish Independent*, 5 March 1921; *Belfast Newsletter*, 4 August 1921.
44 NLI, Seán O'Mahony Papers, MS 44,045; The Director of Intelligence to the secretary to the Ministry of Defence, 21 February 1924. Also in this file see 'Memorandum: Mrs Lindsay's body,' which indicates that early in 1924 her un-coffined remains wrapped in canvas had been dug up yet again. A Rylane-based witness of this unceremonious removal, stated that 'the body was disinterred, placed in a horse and cart down to the "big road" thence transferred to a motor car,' which then drove east. Also see Sheehan, *Lady Hostage*, pp. 188–9, which argues that both bodies were handled in this way.
45 The full address given by the C/O at the Garrison Church, Ballincollig can be found in The Tameside Central Library, MR1/2/4, diary of activities of Manchester Regiment (Ballincollig) entry dated 28 January 1922.
46 *Irish Independent*, 30 January 1922; *Cork Examiner*, 30 January 1922. It is notable that this more public service did not take place in Cork city.
47 NLI, Seán O'Mahony Papers, MS 44,045, Crime Branch to the Private Secretary, Minister for Home Affairs 9 May 1924. This provides some corroboration for oral testimony gathered in a project on the 'History and Folklore of Knockraha' published in 1977, which refers to executions at 'Reinaslough', or 'Reanasallagh', while members of the Carrigtwohill company recalled the execution of a woman in that district, *Knockraha compiled edited and published by Knockraha Macra na Feirme* (Cork, 1977), pp. 34–6, 67. The rumour that she was buried in the area where Cork Airport was subsequently built is referenced in Olga Payne Clarke, *She Came of Decent People* (London: 1986).
48 O'Callaghan, *Execution*, p. 151.
49 UK Parliamentary Papers; Commons Sitting, 4 August 1921.
50 Marie Coleman, 'Violence Against Women during the Irish War of Independence, 1919–21,' in Diarmaid Ferriter and Susannah Riordan (eds), *Years of Turbulence: The Irish Revolution and its Aftermath* (Dublin: UCD Press, 2015), p. 141.

CHAPTER 9

1 *Irish Bulletin*, 9 July 1921. Publication of the *Irish Bulletin* began in November 1919 under the general editorship of Desmond Fitzgerald, and for some months in 1921, under Erskine Childers. Its main targets were opinion makers and so it was sent 'to pressmen, politicians, influential public figures, and heads of churches in Britain, Ireland and other countries' (Inoue, in Augusteijn, 2002, p. 88). Among the issues covered, along with the activities of Dáil Eireann and its ministries, the republican courts and police and other consecutive elements of republican propaganda, were the increasing 'acts of aggression' against the civilian population by the crown forces, and in particular, the attacks on the more vulnerable members of that civilian population, women and children.

2   Keiko Inoue, 'Propaganda II: Advanced Nationalist propaganda and the Moralistic Revolution, 1914–1918,' in Joost Augusteijn (ed.), *The Irish Revolution, 1913–1923* (London: Palgrave Macmillan, 2002), p. 91.
3   *The Irish Bulletin*, 9 July 1921.
4   Louise Ryan, 'Drunken Tans: Representations of Sex and Violence in the Anglo-Irish War (1919–21),' *Feminist Review*, 66 (2000), p. 78.
5   One of the first, and still essential, books was Margaret Ward's, *Unmanageable Revolutionaries* (Dublin: Attic Press, 1983), followed by, among others, Sinéad McCoole, *No Ordinary Women: Irish Female Activists in the Revolutionary Years* (Dublin: O'Brien Press, 2003); Louise Ryan and Margaret Ward (eds) *Irish Women and Nationalism: Soldiers, New Women and Wicked Hags* (Dublin: Irish Academic Press, 2004); Cal McCarthy, *Cumann na mBan and the Irish Revolution* (2007); Ann Matthews *Renegades: Irish Republican Women, 1900–1922* (Cork: Mercier Press, 2010); Senia Pašeta, *Women and Irish Nationalism 1900–1918* (Cambridge: Cambridge University Press, 2013); and Mary McAuliffe and Liz Gillis, *We Were There: 77 Women of the Easter Rising* (Dublin: Dublin City Council, 2016).
6   Peter Hart, *The IRA and its Enemies: Violence and Community in Cork 1916–1923* (Oxford: Oxford University Press, 1999); Anne Dolan, *Commemorating the Irish Civil War: History and Memory, 1923–2000* (Cambridge: Cambridge University Press, 2003); Joost Augusteijn, 'Accounting for the Emergence of Violent Activism Among Irish Revolutionaries, 1916–1921,' *Irish Historical Studies*, XXXV, 139 (2016), pp. 327–44; David Fitzpatrick, *The Two Irelands: 1912–1939* (Oxford: Oxford University Press, 1998).
7   This research includes Louise Ryan, 'Drunken Tans'; Lindsey Earner-Byrne, 'The Rape of Mary M.: A Microhistory of Sexual Violence and Moral Redemption in 1920s Ireland,' *Journal of the History of Sexuality*, 24, 1 (2015), pp. 75–98; Marie Coleman, 'Violence against Women During the Irish War of Independence, 1919–21' in Diarmaid Ferriter and Susannah Riordan (eds), *Years of Turbulence: The Irish Revolution and its Aftermath*, (Dublin, UCD Press), pp. 137–56. Other historians and researchers have looked at violence against women in this period including: Justin Dolan Stover, 'Families, Vulnerability and Sexual Violence During the Irish Revolution,' in Jennifer Evans and Ciara Meehan (eds), *Perceptions of Pregnancy from the Seventeenth to the Twentieth Century* (London: Palgrave, 2017), pp. 57–75; Ann Matthews, *Renegades: Irish Republican Women 1900–1922* (Cork: Mercier Press, 2010); Laura McAtackney, 'Gender, Incarceration and Power Relations During the Irish Civil War (1922–1923),' in Victoria Sanford, Katerina Stefatos and Cecilia M. Salvi (eds), *Gender Violence in Peace and War: States of Complicity* (New Brunswick, New Jersey/London: Rutgers University Press, 2016), pp. 47–63; Gemma Clark, *Everyday Violence in the Irish Civil War* (Cambridge: Cambridge University Press, 2014); Linda Connolly, 'Sexual Violence and the Irish Revolution: an Inconvenient Truth?' *History Ireland*, 27, 6 (2019), pp. 34–39; Linda Connolly, 'Sexual Violence a Dark Secret of War of Independence and Civil War,' *Irish Times*, 10 January 2019; Linda Connolly, 'Sexual Violence in the Irish Civil War: A Forgotten War Crime?' *Women's History Review*, published online 6 March 2020: https://doi.org/10.1080/09612025.2020.1735613.
8   Lil Conlon, *Cumann na mBan and the Women of Ireland, 1913–25* (Kilkenny: Kilkenny People Limited, 1969), p. 145.
9   Conlon, *Cumann na mBan*, p. 224.
10 *British Labour Commission Report*, 1921, p. 27.

Endnotes 251

11 Joanna Bourke, *Dismembering the Male: Men's Bodies, Britain and the Great War* (Chicago: The University of Chicago Press, 1996), pp. 12–13.
12 Lisa M. Todd, 'The Hun and The Home, Gender, Sexuality and Propaganda in First World War Europe,' in Troy R.E. Paddock (ed.), *World War I and Propaganda* (Leiden, Boston: Brill, 2014), p. 138.
13 D.M. Leeson, *The Black and Tans: British Police and Auxiliaries in the Irish War of Independence* (Oxford: Oxford University Press, 2010), p. 2.
14 Louise Ryan, 'Splendidly Silent: Representing Irish Republican Women, 1919-23,' in Anne Marie Gallagher, Cathy Lubelsk and Louise Ryan (eds), *Re-presenting the Past: Women and History* (London: Longman Publishers, 2001), p. 28.
15 Julie Peteet, 'Icons and Militants: Mothering in the Danger Zone,' in *Signs*, 23, 1 (1997), p. 108.
16 Ibid.
17 Anne Dolan, 'Spies and Informers Beware,' in Diarmaid Ferriter and Susannah Riordan (eds), *Years of Turbulence: The Irish Revolution and its Aftermath* (Dublin: UCD Press, 2015), p. 164.
18 Louise Ryan, 'Furies and "Die Hards": Women and Irish Republicanism in the Early Twentieth Century,' *Gender and History*, 11, 2 (1999), p. 263.
19 Justin Dolan Stover, 'Families, Vulnerability and Sexual Violence During the Irish Revolution,' in Jennifer Evans and Ciara Meehan (eds), *Perceptions of Pregnancy from the Seventeenth to the Twentieth Century* (London: Palgrave Macmillan, 2017), p. 59.
20 Michael Hynes, BMH WS 1173, p. 14.
21 *American Commission on Conditions in Ireland Interim Report*, May 1921, Appendix E, Robert McNamara, p. 132.
22 Stover, 'Families, Vulnerability and Sexual Violence,' p. 63.
23 Gemma Clark, *Everyday Violence*, p. 190.
24 Conlon, *Cumann na mBan*, p. 224.
25 Stover, 'Families, Vulnerability and Sexual Violence,' p. 62.
26 *American Commission on Conditions in Ireland Interim Report*, May 1921, p. 54.
27 Julia Duffy, MSP34REF11617.
28 Ibid.
29 Bridget O'Donnell, MSP34REF59841.
30 Ibid.
31 Edward Lynch, BMH WS 1,333.
32 Mary O'Neill, MSP34REF59221.
33 Ibid.
34 Katherine Collins, MSP34REF34414.
35 Christian Ahern, MSP34REF30738.
36 Margaret Brennan, MSP34REF1078.
37 *Irish Examiner*, 1 March 1920.
38 Annie Murphy, MSP34REF24721.
39 Ryan, 'Drunken Tans,' p. 83.
40 Helen Litton (ed.), *Kathleen Clarke: Revolutionary Women* (Dublin: The O'Brien Press, 2008), pp. 244–5.
41 *Irish Bulletin*, 9 July, 1921.
42 See, Linda Connolly, 'Towards an Understanding of the Violence Experienced by Women in the Irish Revolution,' *Maynooth University Social Sciences Institute Working Paper Series*, 9 (January 2019), pp. 7–16.

43 *Leitrim Observer*, 29 May 1920, p. 3.
44 Ibid.
45 *Weekly Irish Times*, 15 May 1920, p. 4.
46 *Irish Times*, 27 July 1920, p. 5.
47 Ibid.
48 James Maloney, BMH WS 1525, p. 27.
49 Ibid.
50 *Weekly Irish Times*, 24 July 1920, p. 4.
51 Coleman, 'Violence against Women,' p. 141.
52 *Skibbereen Eagle*, 6 November 1920.
53 *Belfast Newsletter*, 19 April 1921.
54 *Irish Times*, 13 June 1921, p. 5.
55 *Skibbereen Eagle*, September 1920, p. 7.
56 *Belfast Newsletter*, 21 October 1920, p. 6.
57 Amelia Wilmot, MSP34REF32473.
58 *Donegal News*, 15 January 1921, p. 3.
59 Erskine Childers, *Military Rule in Ireland* (Dublin: Talbot Press, 1920), p. 6.
60 Childers, *Military Rule*, pp. 11–12.
61 Ibid.
62 Robert Brennan, BMH WS 779 (Section 3), p. 593.
63 Julia Eichenberg, 'The Dark Side of Independence: Paramilitary Violence in Ireland and Poland after the First World War,' in *Contemporary European History*, 19 (2010), p. 240.
64 Eichenberg, 'The Dark Side of Independence,' p. 248.

CHAPTER 10

1 Nelly Furman, 'The Politics of Language: Beyond the Gender Principle?' in Gayle Greene and Coppelia Kahn (eds), *Making a Difference: Feminist Literary Criticism* (London: Routledge, 1985), pp. 59–79.
2 Valuable work has been done by Louise Ryan on representations of republican women in a range of primary sources, concentrating on 'how women who engaged in military conflict and transgressed gender roles have been depicted in a variety of primary sources'. See Louise Ryan, 'Splendidly Silent: Representing Irish Republican Women, 1919–23,' in Lubelska Gallagher and Louise Ryan (eds), *Re-presenting the Past: Women and History* (London: Longman, 2001), pp. 23–43. In terms of the literature written in the period, the fiction of Elizabeth Bowen, Frank O'Connor, Liam O'Flaherty and, more recently, Dorothy MacArdle has been subject to critical analysis, as has the broader genre of 'Big House' fiction, but the specific representation of women within these and other works has not received any sustained critical attention.
3 Cathy Caruth, *Unclaimed Experience: Trauma, Narrative, and History* (Baltimore: Johns Hopkins University Press, 1996), p. 11.
4 Rita Ann Higgins, quoted by Emily Berry in 'Spectacularly Endless: An Interview with Emily Berry,' *L.A. Times*, 7 March 2017.
5 Rita Ann Higgins, *Witch in the Bushes – Poems* (Galway: Salmon Publishing, 1988).
6 'Cultural criticism finds itself faced with the final stage of the dialectic of culture and barbarism. To write poetry after Auschwitz is barbaric.' Theodor Adorno, translated by Samuel and Shierry Weber, *Prisms* (Massachusetts: MIT Press, 1981 [1969]), p. 34; Susan Sontag, *Regarding the Pain of Others* (New York: Farrar, Strauss and Giroux, 2003).

Endnotes

7   Gerd Bayer, 'Trauma and the Literature of War,' in J. Roger Kurtz (ed.), *Trauma and Literature* (Cambridge: Cambridge University Press, 2018), pp. 213-25.
8   Bayer, *Trauma*, p. 213.
9   Seán O'Casey, *Juno and the Paycock* (London: Macmillan, 1923); Act II, 38.
10 Louise Ryan, '"In the Line of Fire": Representations of Women and War (1919-1923) through the Writings of Republican Men,' in Louise Ryan and Margaret Ward (eds), *Irish Women and Nationalism: Soldiers, New Women and Wicked Hags* (Dublin: Irish Academic Press, 2004), pp. 45-61.
11 Frank O'Connor, *Guests of the Nation* (London: Penguin, 2008 [1932]).
12 Ibid.
13 Peadar O'Donnell, *Adrigoole* (London: Jonathan Cape, 1929), p. 267. For more on O'Donnell's politics and literary practice, see Dónal Ó Drisceoil, 'My pen is just a weapon: Politics, History and the Fiction of Peadar O'Donnell,' *Irish Review*, 30 (2003), pp. 62-70.
14 Andreas Huyssen, *Twilight Memories: Marking Time in a Culture of Amnesia* (London: Routledge, 1994), p. 246.
15 See for example Chapter 2, 'What it means to Women' in Erskine Childers's pamphlet *Military Rule in Ireland* (Dublin: The Talbot Press, 1920) in which he details how 'raids upon private houses, for instance, which are minor features in the regime, number over 20,000 in the last two years alone' (pp. 8-9). Other archival material includes an article in *the Limerick Leader* on 30 June 1920 which quotes the opinion of 'a leading medical practitioner in Limerick' that 'if the present tension due to outrages like those being committed in our midst for some time past continues for any length of time a large number of people in the city, especially women, would become nervous wrecks. He added that he has treated more patients for nervous complaints or diseases within the past three months than during the whole of his previous career.'
16 In addition to the chapters in this volume, see also Ryan, 'Splendidly Silent,' pp. 23-43; Justin Dolan Stover, 'Violence, Trauma and Memory in Ireland: The Psychological Impact of War and Revolution on a Liminal Society, 1916-1923,' in Jason Crouthamel and Peter Leese (eds), *Psychological Trauma and the Legacies of the First World War* (London: Palgrave Macmillan, 2017), pp. 117-40; Gemma Clark, *Everyday Violence in the Irish Civil War* (Cambridge: Cambridge University Press, 2014); Linda Connolly, 'Sexual Violence and the Irish Revolution: an Inconvenient Truth?' *History Ireland*, 27, 6 (2019), pp. 34-9; Linda Connolly, 'Sexual Violence a Dark Secret of War of Independence and Civil War,' *Irish Times*, 10 January 2019.
17 Oona Frawley (ed.), *Memory Ireland Vols. 1-4* (New York: Syracuse University Press, 2011-2014); Guy Beiner, 'Probing the Boundaries of Irish Memory: From Postmemory to Prememory and Back,' *Irish Historical Studies*, 39 (2014), pp. 296-307; Emilie Pine, *The Politics of Irish Memory: Performing Remembrance in Contemporary Irish Culture* (New York: Springer, 2010).
18 Marianne Hirsch, *The Generation of Postmemory: Writing and Visual Culture after the Holocaust* (Columbia: Columbia University Press, 2012), p. 2.
19 Trevor's *Fools of Fortune* (London: Penguin UK, 2015 [1983]) is an exquisite exploration of the repercussions of violence which continue long after the traumatic event.
20 Jonathan Druker, 'The Path and the Pit: History and Traumatic Memory in Primo Levi's *If Not Now, When?*,' *Shofar: An Interdisciplinary Journal of Jewish Studies*, 33, 3 (Spring 2015), pp. 46-62, 49.

21. Caitríona Clutterbuck, 'The Irish History Wars and Irish Women's Poetry: Éiléan Ní Chuilleanáin and Eavan Boland,' in Jane Dowson (ed.), *The Cambridge Companion to Twentieth-Century British and Irish Women's Poetry* (Cambridge: Cambridge University Press, 2011), pp. 97–118, 114.
22. Cathy Caruth, 'Trauma and Experience,' in Cathy Caruth (ed.), *Trauma: Explorations in Memory* (Baltimore: John Hopkins Press, 1995), p. viii.
23. Caruth, *Unclaimed Experience*, p. 3.
24. Elaine Showalter, *Literature of Their Own: British Women Novelists from Bronte to Lessing* (Princeton: Princeton University Press, 1977), p. 52.
25. Paula Meehan, *Painting Rain* (Manchester: Carcanet, 2009).
26. Pilar Villar Argáiz, 'Telling the Truth About Time: The Importance of Local Rootedness in Paula Meehan's Poetry,' *Études irlandaises*, 35, 1 (2010), pp. 103–15.
27. Ní Chuilleanáin, Éiléan. *The Sun-fish* (Oldcastle. County Meath: The Gallery Press, 2009).
28. Éilís Ní Dhuibhne, 'The Old Woman as Hare: Structure and Meaning in an Irish Legend,' *Folklore*, 104, 1/2 (1993), pp. 77–85.
29. Ní Dhuibhne, 'The Old Woman as Hare,' p. 78.
30. Clutterbuck, 'The Irish History Wars,' p. 114.
31. Dori Laub, 'Bearing Witness or the Vicissitudes of Listening,' in Shoshana Felman and Dori Laub (eds), *Testimony: Crises of Witnessing in Literature, Psychoanalysis, and History* (New York and London: Routledge, 1992), pp. 54–74.
32. See Cynthia Cockburn, *The Space Between Us: Negotiating Gender and National Identities in Conflict* (London and New York: Zed Books, 1998); and Cynthia Cockburn, *From Where We Stand: War, Women's Activism and Feminist Analysis* (London: Zed Books, 2007); Miriam Cooke and Angela Woollcott (eds), *Gendering War Talk* (New Jersey: Princeton University Press, 1993); Wenona Giles and Jennifer Hyndman (eds), *Sites of Violence: Gender and Conflict Zones* (Berkeley, CA: University of California Press, 2004); Cynthia Enloe, *Bananas, Beaches and Bases: Making Feminist Sense of International Politics* (California: University of California Press, 2014).
33. Ryan, 'Splendidly Silent.'
34. Martina Evans, *Facing the Public* (London: Anvil Press, 2009).
35. Ryan, 'Splendidly Silent.'
36. Ernie O'Malley, *On Another Man's Wound* (Lanham: Taylor Trade Publishing, 2002 [1936]).
37. Ibid., p. 204.
38. Although the number of deaths was minimal in the burning of Mallow, the impact on the community was undoubtedly profound. *Cork's War of Independence Fatalities Register* registers two civilian deaths: one of Marion Quirke after the burning of Mallow, described as follows: 'A refugee in a Mallow graveyard like many other civilians on the night of the sacking of Mallow, Quirke became seriously ill and mentally deranged; she died about a month later'; the other of Hannah O'Connell: 'During the sacking of Mallow by British forces (in retaliation for a successful IRA arms raid on the military barracks there), a young woman identified by the surname Connolly spent the night cowering with other terrified inhabitants in the "Mallow Graveyard", and holding her three-day-old infant Rosanna, as much of the town burned. This young mother reportedly caught pneumonia and died shortly afterwards.' See: http://theirishrevolution.ie/.
39. Caruth, *Unclaimed Experience*, p. 9.

CHAPTER 11

1. Sister Hortense was known as Mother Hortense in the later part of her career, but the 'Sister' designation will be used throughout this article.
2. *Tuam Herald*, 16 April 1932. Some of the detail from the *Connacht Tribune* of the same date.
3. For a discussion of memory and commemoration see Guy Beiner, *Forgetful Remembrance Social Forgetting and Vernacular Historiography of a Rebellion in Ulster* (Oxford: Oxford University Press, 2019); Oona Frawley, *Irish Cultural Memory Volumes 1: History and Modernity* (Syracuse University Press, 2010); Linda Connolly, 'Honest Commemoration Reconciling Women's "Troubled" and "Troubling" History in Centennial Ireland,' in Oona Frawley (ed.), *Women and the Decade of Commemorations* (Indiana: Indiana University Press, 2021).
4. See for example Anne Dolan, 'Divisions and Divisions and Divisions: Who to Commemorate?' in John Horne and Edward Madigan (eds), *Towards Commemoration: Ireland in War and Revolution 1912–1923* (Dublin: Royal Irish Academy, 2013), pp. 145–53.
5. See for example Emilie Pine, 'Introduction: Moving Memory,' *Irish University Review*, 47, 1 (2017), pp. 1–6.
6. Maria Luddy, '"Angels of Mercy": Nuns as Workhouse Nurses, 1861–98', in Greta Jones and Elizabeth Malcolm (eds), *Medicine, Disease and the State in Ireland 1650–1940* (Cork: Cork University Press, 1999), pp. 102–20. The sisters had a former association with the workhouse, as unofficial teachers of girl inmates. They withdrew from the institution in 1860, however, on the appointment of a schoolmistress by the board of guardians ('Local Reports', *Tuam Herald*, 14 January 1860).
7. *Tuam Herald*, 30 August 1890, 14 January 1891.
8. *Tuam Herald*, 12 October 1918. The letter was originally published in 1904.
9. Donnacha Seán Lucey, 'These Schemes Will Win for Themselves the Confidence of the People: Irish Independence, Poor Law Reform and Hospital Provision,' *Medical History*, 58, 1 (2014), pp. 46–66 and pp. 48–50. Only the Castlecomer Union had availed of the facility in the legislation to separate hospital care from the poor law.
10. James P. Murray, *Galway: A Medico-Social History* (Galway: Kenny's Bookshop and Gallery, 1994), p. 80.
11. Quoted by Diarmaid Ferriter, *The Transformation of Ireland, 1900–2000* (London: Profile Books, 2004), p. 186.
12. Gabriel O'Connor, *A History of Galway County Council* (Galway County Council, 1999), pp. 127–8; Murray, *Galway: a Medico-Social History*, p. 80.
13. *Western People*, 18 June 1904.
14. Martin Ryan, WS 1417, pp. 19–20.
15. *Connacht Tribune*, 16 July 1921.
16. Bishop James Fergus, 'The Bon Secours Sisters and St Mary's Children's Home,' n.d. Copy in Glenamaddy Parochial House.
17. See Brian Heffernan, *Freedom and the Fifth Commandment: Catholic Priests and Revolutionary Violence in Ireland* (Manchester: Manchester University Press, 2014), pp. 97–121.
18. 'Boy prisoner dead,' *Irish Independent*, 26 October 1920; 'Dublin Executions,' *Connaught Telegraph*, 19 March 1921.
19. Born in 1889, Sister Hortense was christened Helena McNamara (shortened to Lena in her family) and was raised in a thatched farmhouse at Fossa Beg, Scariff, County Clare.

At 19, she entered the Cork novitiate of the Bon Secours, a French order, and she made her first profession of vows in Paris in January 1911.

20   Breen Timothy Murphy, 'The Government's execution policy during the Irish Civil War, 1922–3,' unpublished PhD thesis, NUI Maynooth, 2010, pp. 202–43; Nollaig Ó Gadhra, *Civil War in Connacht*, Cork: Mercier Press, 1999, pp. 86–92.
21   'Galway Defends the All-Ireland Republic, July 1922–May 1923,' *Eleven Galway Martyrs*, commemorative booklet (Tuam: 1985).
22   Ó Gadhra, *Civil War in Connacht*, pp. 82–3.
23   'Six executions in Tuam,' *Tuam Herald*, 14 April 1923.
24   'Reaction of Local Councils,' *Eleven Galway Martyrs*.
25   Ruairí Ó Brádaigh, *Dílseacht: the Story of Commandant General Tom Maguire and the Second (all-Ireland) Dáil* (Dublin: Irish Freedom Press, 1997); 'Tom Maguire: Commandant General, IRA (Second Division),' in Uinseann MacEoin, *Survivors: The Story of Ireland as Told Through Some of Her Outstanding Living People* (Dublin: Argenta, 1980), pp. 277–303.
26   'Tuam District Council,' *Tuam Herald*, 28 April 1923.
27   'Bodies Disinterred,' *Connacht Tribune*, 16 August 1924.
28   Murphy, 'The Government's execution policy,' pp. 244–77.
29   *Connaught Telegraph*, 1 November 1924.
30   'Laid to rest,' *Connacht Tribune*, 8 November 1924.
31   *Connacht Tribune*, 27 March 1926.
32   Ibid., 20 April 1940.
33   *Tuam Herald*, 23 August 1952.
34   Ibid., 17 November 1934.
35   Communication from Bríd Cottrell (Bon Secours Sisters) to John Cunningham, 29 August 2018.
36   *Tuam Herald*, 11 November 1961.
37   *Connacht Tribune*, 19 November 1921.
38   GC5/2, Galway County Council, 1922.
39   *Connacht Tribune*, 18 November 1922.
40   Ibid.
41   *Connacht Tribune*, 21 June 1924. See also ibid., 17 February 1923.
42   Ibid.
43   GC5/3, Galway County Council, 1924.
44   Special Correspondent, 'Children of Misfortune: Scandal of Glenamaddy Home,' *Connacht Tribune*, 21 June 1924.
45   *Connacht Tribune*, 9 May, 3 October 1925.
46   GC5/3, Galway County Council, 1924.
47   Ibid.
48   Letter dated 21 September 1925, GC5/3, Galway County Council.
49   GC5/3, Galway County Council, 1925.
50   Mother and Baby Homes Commission of Investigation, *Fifth Interim Report*, 15 March 2019, p. 59.
51   Catherine Corless, 'The Home,' *Journal of the Old Tuam Society*, 9 (2012), pp. 3–19. For an overview as to how the story emerged see Dan Barry, 'The Lost Children of Tuam,' *New York Times*, 28 October 2017: https://www.nytimes.com/interactive/2017/10/28/world/europe/tuam-ireland-babies-children.html (accessed 27 September 2018). For

work emanating from the Tuam Oral History Project see http://www.nuigalway.ie/tuam-oral-history/

52 See http://www.mbhcoi.ie/mbh.nsf/page/index-en. For a resource examining similar commissions internationally see http://www.lib.latrobe.edu.au/research/ageofinquiry/index.html. For discussion of institutional abuse and recent reactions see https://www.rte.ie/eile/brainstorm/2018/0903/991253-how-ireland-should-deal-with-the-issue-of-historic-abuse-cases/

53 For a discussion of the homes and the development of child welfare see Lindsey Earner-Byrne, *Mother and Child: Maternity and Child Welfare in Dublin, 1922–60* (Manchester: Manchester University Press, 2013); Sarah-Anne Buckley, *The Cruelty Man: Child Welfare, the NSPCC and the State in Ireland, 1889–1956* (Manchester: Manchester University Press, 2017); Conall Ó Fátharta, selected works in the *Irish Examiner*; Maria Luddy, 'Unmarried Mothers in Ireland, 1880–1973', *Women's History Review*, 20, 1, (2011), pp. 109–26; Donnacha Seán Lucey, *The End of the Irish Poor Law?: Welfare and Healthcare Reform in Revolutionary and Independent Ireland* (Manchester: Manchester University Press, 2015). For a discussion of changing attitudes to childhood see Sarah-Anne Buckley and Susannah Riordan, 'Childhood since 1740', in Eugenio Biaggini and Mary Daly (eds), *The Cambridge Social History of Ireland* (Cambridge: Cambridge University Press, 2017), pp. 327-343.

54 Elaine Edwards, 'Tuam babies: "Significant" quantities of human remains found at former home', *Irish Times*, 3 March 2017.

55 Mother and Baby Homes Commission, *Fifth Interim Report*, p. 64.

56 For access to all death certificates see www.IrishGenealogy.ie.

57 GC5/3, Galway County Council, 1924.

58 Virginia Crossman, 'Cribbed, Contained and Confined? The Care of Children under the Irish Poor Law,' *Éire-Ireland*, 44, 1 and 2 (Spring/Summer 2009), pp. 37–61.

59 Ibid.

60 GC5/3, Galway County Council, 1924.

61 John Cunningham, *Connacht Tribune*, 'What of the mothers?', 24 April 1998.

62 David Burke, 'A Voice from the Tuam Home,' *Tuam Herald*, 30 December 2015.

63 Burke, 'A Voice from the Tuam Home.'

64 Ibid.

65 Ibid.

66 Pádraig Stevens, 'We Stood Aside in Silence,' in Sarah-Anne Buckley and John Cunningham (eds), *Growing up in Galway: Histories and Memories* (Cork: Eva Books, 2017), p. 1.

67 Stevens, 'We Stood in Silence.'

68 June Goulding, *The Light in the Window* (London: Ebury Press, 2005), passim. Patricia Burke Brogan's *Eclipsed* was premiered in Galway in 1992.

69 See for example *Tuam Herald*, 31 August 1946, 24 September 1949, 23 September 1950.

70 'Archbishop Opens New Hospital,' *Tuam Herald*, 17 August 1946.

71 GC5/6, Galway County Council, 1928.

72 Alice Litster, *Report on Unmarried Mothers in Ireland*, Department of Local Government and Public Health, 1939.

73 GC5/6, Galway County Council, 1928.

74 GC5/4, Galway County Council, 1926.

75 GC5/6, Galway County Council, 1928.

76 GC5/4, Galway County Council, 1926.

77 *Tuam Herald,* 13 September 1919, 24 July 1920.
78 Ibid., 20 December 1947.
79 Ibid., 20 April 1985.
80 Mother Hortense McNamara, *Eleven Galway Martyrs.*

INDEX

Abbot, Fanny 135
abuse: court cases, *Irish Citizen*'s coverage of 28; domestic violence 28–9; in institutions 128, 214; servant girls, seduction of 28; under-reporting of 27, 28; in the workplace 29; *see also* hair cutting; rape; sexual violence; violence against women
academic publications, citation practices 5
Adorno, Theodor 184
Ahern, Christina 173
Aiken, Frank 131
Alleway, Mary (Mollie) 109
American Commission on Conditions in Ireland 90, 150, 166, 169–70, 171
Anderson, Benedict 10, 34, 46
Anglo-Irish Ascendancy 39, 45, 46
Anglo-Irish Treaty 7; anti-Treaty sentiment 71, 72, 94; Cumann na mBan and 71–2; Dáil debates 11, 64, 72, 92–4; negotiations 92; pro-Treaty propaganda 72; ratification 95; split 71–2; women TDs, opposition to 85, 89, 92–4, 96, 99
Army Pensions Act (1923) 122, 132, 133–4
arson 47, 60, 165, 171, 172–3, 175, 179; Black and Tans and 109, 172, 173; Cumann na mBan members and 80; IRA and 56, 155, 156, 201
Ashe, Thomas 51
Asquith, Herbert H. 23
Atkinson, Cicely Helen Burrington 124, 141
Atkinson, Thomas John Day 124, 141
Augusteijn, Joost 165
Auxiliaries 56, 141, 158, 166, 179

B-Specials 106, 120
Babington, Seamus 115
Ballyseedy atrocity 124, 126, 127
Banerjee, Sikata 84
Barker, Eileen 112

Barrett, James 157
Barry, Helena 81
Bayer, Gerd, 'Trauma and the Literature of War' 184
Beaslaí, Piaras 159
Beatty, Aidan 83
Begley, Delia 126
Belfast: fatalities 58; IRA arson attacks 56; sectarian tensions 58
Belfast Boycott 63, 64, 80
Belfast Cumann na mBan x, 10, 47, 48; Central branch 52, 64; Easter Rising (1916) and 50; fundraising 55; IRA and 52, 57–63; Irish language and 52; Lamh Dearg branch 52, 53, 58, 64; membership 64; military service pension applications 48–9, 59–63; post-1916 reorganisation 49–53; prisoners, support for 53–4; War of Independence and 48; West Belfast branch (Craobh Larthar) 52, 53, 64; *see also* Cumann na mBan
Belfast Newsletter 110, 159, 177
Belfast Prison 35, 36–7
Bennett, Lily 81
Bennett, Louie 23, 86–7
Benson, Ethel 156–7, 158
Berry, Thomas Sterling, Bishop of Killaloe and Clonfert 138
Bielenberg, Andy 12, 148–63
Biggs, Eileen Mary Warburton 117, 123–4, 137, 138–9
Biggs, Samuel 124, 137, 138, 139
Black, Rose 48, 61, 65, 66
Black and Tans 56, 105, 166; arson 109, 172, 173; attacks by 141, 166, 169–70; house invasions 168, 171; Mallow, sacking of 195; violence against women 109, 120, 126, 171, 176, 179
Bloxham, Elizabeth 114

259

Blythe, Ernest 53, 124–5, 134
Boland, Roseanne 80
Bon Secours Sisters 13, 198, 199; burial places 215; commemoration of executed republicans 204; Glenamaddy workhouse 201–2; perception of 211; private hospital established by 211; records, restrictions on 207, 215; republican prisoners and 201–2; *see also* Glenamaddy Children's Home; Tuam Mother and Baby Home
Borgonovo, John 6, 10, 68–84
Bourke, Joanna 119, 123, 167
boycotts 63, 64, 80, 141–5
Brady, Frances 48, 63, 66
Brady, Kathleen 63, 64
Brady, Liam A. 118
Brennan, Margaret 173
Brennan, Robert 35, 36, 178
Brennan, Miss S. 51, 52
Brennan, Una 178
British armed forces: female fatalities 149, 163; hair cutting and 109, 110, 114, 176–7; house raids 125, 176–8; IRA members, executions 156, 160, 162; IRA reprisals 150, 162, 163; Manchester Regiment 122, 159, 160; recruitment propaganda 178; reign of terror 166; sexual violence 92, 114, 121–2; War of Independence, behaviour in 168; *see also* Auxiliaries; Black and Tans
British Labour Party Commission 166
Broderick, Miss M. 76
Broderick, Seán 109
Broderick-Nicholson, Peg 109, 114
Browning, Ethelred 29
Brugha, Caitlín 97
Brugha, Cathal 73, 97, 156–7, 158
Buckley, Leo 113
Buckley, Sarah-Anne 13, 198–215
Bureau of Military History (BMH) 6; anti-Treaty activists' views on 48; Belfast, witness statements 48; Gonne's witness statement 10, 38; men's witness statements 67; northern IRA witness statements 48; perceived as 'Free State project' 48; sexual violence 115, 118; women's testimonies 13, 66–7, 130, 171, 187–8
Burke, Miss B. 114
Burke, Peter 103

Burke-Brogan, Patricia, *Eclipsed* 210–11
Busteed, Frank 158
Byrne, Catherine 63

Capa, Robert (photographer) 111
Carey, Nellie 150, 163
Carney, Winifred: arrest 65, 66; Cumann na mBan and 10, 51; Easter Rising (1916) and 10, 51; General Election (1918) 55, 86, 87; imprisonment 49; IRA and 54, 55, 57, 62–3; military service pension 48, 62; Northern Ireland Labour Party 87; Republican Prisoners' Dependant's Fund 55; Sinn Féin and 55, 86, 87; trade unionism 29; Transport Union and 51; White Cross work 55
Carter, Julia (later Devaney) 209–10
Caruth, Cathy 184, 188, 197
Casement, Roger 134
Cashel, Alice 52, 55, 203
Catholic Church: abuse 128; growing dominance of 96; women, attitude towards 1, 30, 96
Catholic clergy: republican funeral and 80; republican movement and 72, 155
Catholic hierarchy 30, 118; famine centenary and 213
Catholic institutions: abuse in 128; religious orders and 200; republicanism and 199; *see also* Glenamaddy Children's Home; Tuam Mother and Baby Home
censorship legislation 98
Childers, Erskine 74, 159, 164, 177–8
children: Black and Tans' attack 169–70; experiences of violence, effects of 187, 188; guerrilla war, house raids and 164, 165, 169, 171, 173, 178; illegitimate, Army Pensions Board and 134; illegitimate births in County Galway 212; illegitimate, putative fathers of 213; mortality rates 211–12; protection in wartime 167; survival rates in foster homes 211–12; *see also* Glenamaddy Children's Home; Tuam Mother and Baby Home
Churchill, Bessie 142–3
citizenship: feminists and 69; gender-based definition of (1922) 95
Civil Service Regulation Bill (1925) 97–8
Clancy, Margaret 132

Clark, Gemma 105, 165, 171, 187; *Everyday Violence in the Irish Civil War* 137
Clarke, James 155, 158, 159, 162
Clarke, Kathleen 134; Alderman for Dublin Corporation 90; Anglo-Irish Treaty debates 93; 'buffer state' metaphor 33–4, 39, 43; Cumann na mBan and 37, 51, 90; exercise time in prison 42; family background 90; Fianna Fáil and 97; General Elections 86, 89, 97; Gonne, perception of 40, 42; health in prison 43; 'hospital diet' in prison 41–2; house raid 173–4; imprisonment 10, 33–4, 37, 39–45, 90; IRB and 90; Irishness and 45; letters to her sister 38, 42–3, 46; Markievicz and 38, 39–40, 42–4, 45–6, 88; prison space, control of 43–4; republican courts and 90; *Revolutionary Woman* 44; Sheehy Skeffington, perception of 38; Sinn Féin Executive 90; social status and 39
Clarke, Thomas (Tom) 89, 93
Clutterbuck, Caitríona 188, 192
Coleman, Marie 166; compensation claims 11–12, 129–47; female fatalities 162; female military service 82; hair cutting 176; psychological violence, women and 108, 187
'collective amnesia' 103, 104
Collins, Katherine 122, 173
Collins, Michael 49, 54, 63; Craig, meeting with 64; death 65; funeral 74; IRA executions, information about 158; Treaty negotiations 92
Collins-O'Driscoll, Margaret 97–8
Colohan, Margaret 144
colonialism 19; alien culture of 17, 25; anti-colonialism 17, 18, 21, 26, 32; imperial culture, alien influence of 17, 20; nationalism and 24–5; pre-colonial past 32
Comerford, Máire 74, 79, 80, 83
commemoration: Civil War 7; Decade of Centenaries 5–6, 7, 8, 129, 165, 199; Donaghpatrick 203; Easter Rising 5, 18; female suffrage 5, 8; Great Famine, centenary of 213, 215; historiography and 4–9; of republicans at Tuam 13, 198, 199, 202, 204, 213–14, 215; women and 5–6, 8, 18

Commission on the Relief of the Sick and Destitute Poor 206
compensation claims 11, 105, 124, 135–6; *see also* Irish Grants Committee (IGC)
Compensation (Ireland) Commission 140
Conlon, Lil ix, xi, 26–7, 171; *Cumann na mBan and the Women of Ireland 1913–25* ix, 166
Connacht Tribune 201, 205
Connery, Margaret (Meg) 29–30, 88–9
Connolly Barrett, Kathleen 78
Connolly, James 26, 62
Connolly, Linda 1–14, 103–28, 137, 166, 174, 187
Connolly, Mrs 150, 163
Connolly, Nora and Ina 48, 49, 50
conscription, opposition to x, 33, 53, 90
Constitution of the Irish Free State (1922) 86, 95
Contagious Diseases Acts 27
Cork Assizes 176
Cork County: Bandon Valley, violence in 12; Dripsey ambush 155, 157, 163; fatalities 81, 149; female fatalities in the War of Independence 12, 148–63; IRA funeral 80; Mallow Army Barracks, IRA raid 150; Upton train ambush 151, 163
Cork Examiner 89
Corless, Catherine: 'Home, The' 206; infant deaths in Tuam 206, 211; research 13, 206, 211, 214
Corr, Elizabeth: Cumann na mBan and 10, 48, 50, 51, 57–8; Cumann na mBan Conventions 64, 65; funeral procession for Thomas Ashe 51; General Election (1918) and 54; Longford by-election campaign and 51; military service pension 62
Cosgrave, W.T. 79, 96, 124, 200–1
Costello, Thomas Bodkin 211
County Boards of Health (Assistance) Order 208
Coyle, Eithne 80
Craig, James 64
Crossman, Virginia 208
Crummey, Cissie 49
Crummey, Frank 49, 61
Crummey, Sarah 49
Cullen Owens, Rosemary, *Smashing Times* 22
cultural nationalism 21–2, 24–5, 91

Cumann na mBan ix, x, 10, 37, 68–71, 90; active service units 74, 79; activities 70–1, 130, 131–2, 168; annual conventions 51–2, 64, 65, 70, 86; anti-conscription campaign x; anti-Treaty majority 71, 72, 94, 96; Ardgroom branch 154; armed activity 80–1; arrests 80, 81, 82, 91; attacks on members 109, 122–3, 169, 171–4, 175, 178–9; Civil War and 6, 10–11, 71, 72–4, 75–82; conventional fighting, activities during 75–6; couriers for IRA 57, 61, 70, 76, 78; criticism of 26; dispatch work 70–1, 77–8; Easter Rising (1916) and 10; fatalities 81; fundraising 55; funerals, ceremonial responsibilities 72–3, 80; gendered mourning roles, repurposing of 72–3; General Election (1918) campaign 87; as guerrilla war combatants 77–82; *Heads Up* (newsletter) 74; home invasions 171; incarceration by Free State forces 81–2; Inghinidhe na hÉireann Branch x; intelligence work 70–1, 78, 130; internal structures 69–70; IRA and 56–7, 69–70, 73–4, 75–6, 131, 168, 172–3; IRA attacks 169; IRA newspaper special editions produced by 74; Irish language and 52, 65, 70; Irish Volunteers and 26, 27; Irish-Ireland ethos 68; male republicans' shaping of participation 84; membership 64, 71, 146; military role 68, 69–71, 79–81, 84; National Army, attacks by 74, 81; policy 86; pro-Treaty members 71, 74; proscription 57; publicity department 73–4; republican propaganda and 73, 74; scout and sentry activities 78, 172; sovereign independence, endorsed by 68; transformation of 26–7, 69–70; Treaty split 11, 71–2; Ulster branches 65; War of Independence and 10, 69; weapons, transport/distribution 79–80, 172; women's rights and 27; women's suffrage and 26, 68; *see also* Belfast Cumann na mBan

Cumann na nGaedheal 95, 97, 132

Cumann na Saoirse 74–5

Cunnane, Frank 202, 207

Cunningham, John 13, 198–215

Curran, John 112–13

Curran, Mary 112–13

Cusack, Sean 52, 54, 56, 60, 62, 63

Dáil Éireann: Anglo-Irish Treaty debates 11, 64–5, 72; Belfast Boycott 64; Cumann na mBan and 69; Democratic Programme 200; Department of Propaganda 164; First Dáil 88, 200; franchise debate (1922) 94–5; Oath of Allegiance and 92, 93; Provisional Government 71; Second Dáil 89–90; women TDs 11, 69, 72, 85, 89–91, 97; women's representation 95–9

Daly, Jeremiah 151

Daly, Madge 10, 34, 38, 42–3, 46, 109

Damage to Property (Compensation) Act (1923) 135, 136

D'Arcy, Tony 203

D'Cruze, Shani 107, 117

de Valera, Éamon 40, 52, 78; General Election (1918) and 54–5; IRA banned by 203; Markievicz's appointment 88; requests, missing women and 152, 156; Sinn Féin and 55; Treaty negotiations and 92

Decade of Centenaries 5–6, 7, 8, 129, 165, 199

Defence of the Realm Act (DORA) 33

Delaney, Elizabeth 48, 52, 53, 60, 64

Delargy, Mona 54

Derrig, Thomas 83

Devine, Anne 174

Devlin, Joseph (Joe) 50, 54, 55

Dillon, Geraldine 109

Doherty, Catherine 122

Doherty, Margaret (Maggie) 117, 122–3, 126, 127

Dolan, Anne 165, 168

domestic spaces: in conflict literature 192–3; transgression of 168–9, 170–1, 173, 179, 185–6, 187, 191; wartime propaganda and 167; *see also* home front

domestic violence 28–9

Donaghpatrick commemorations 203–4

Donnelly, James S. 148

Dorney, John 79

Doyle, Elizabeth 141–2

Doyle, Mary 117, 123

Dublin Metropolitan Police (DMP) 143

Duchen, Claire 111

Duffy, Julia 171–2

Duggan, Margaret 81

Duggan, Marion 31

Earner-Byrne, Lindsey 120, 121, 166

Index

Easter Rising (1916): aftermath 26–7, 91; centenary commemorations 18, 68; commemoration, women and 5; countermanding orders 10, 38, 50; Cumann na mBan and 10, 50; GPO and 10, 63; Property Losses (Ireland) Committee 135; 'Six Sycamores' sequence (Meehan) 189–91; women and x, 18, 48, 146
Eichenberg, Julia 111–12, 179
Emergency (1939–45) 203
English, Ada 69, 89, 91, 94
Euphemia, Sister (Bon Secours) 206
Evans, Martina 185, 189, 193–7; cultural memory 193, 194, 196; *Facing the Public* 193–4, 196; 'Knock' 196; 'Mallow Burns, 28 September 1920' 194, 195; mythical image 196; O'Malley's memoirs 194–7; *Petrol* 194; 'The Boy from Durras' 193, 194; 'Wooden Horse' 194, 195, 196

Feeney family 114
feminism 7; Gaelic civilization and 25–6; international women's movement 22; Janus-quality of 32; nationalism and 9, 17–21
Feminist Review 104
Fianna Fáil 82, 95, 97, 131, 203
Fine Gael 97
First World War 167–8
Fitzgerald, Kathleen 143
Fitzgerald, Seamus 120
Fitzpatrick, David 115, 165; *Terror in Ireland 1916–1923* 2
Fitzpatrick, Margaret 48, 59, 66
Flynn, Thomas 57, 58, 59, 61
Foster, Gavin M. 84
Fox, Margaret 124
Fox, Thomas 57
Furman, Nelly, *Politics of Language, The: Beyond the Gender Principle* 183

Gaelic civilization 24–6, 32; feminism and 25–6; gender equality and 25, 26, 32; Irish suffragists and 24–6; powerful female characters 25–6, 32
Gaelic League 25, 53, 57, 91
Gallagher, Mary 176
Galway Board of Health 204, 206, 207, 208
Galway County Council 200, 201

Galway Homes and Home Assistance Committee 204, 207, 211, 212
Gavan Duffy, Louise 74
Gaynor, Liam 59
gender: as category of historical analysis 3; models of gender relations 2; revolution and 3
gender equality: in Gaelic civilization 25, 26, 32; Proclamation of the Irish Republic (1916) 86
gender hierarchy, reassertion of 67
gender norms 193; conforming with 75, 83; transgression of 67, 80–1, 118
General Election (1918): Cumann na mBan and 54, 87; Irish Parliamentary Party and 54; Labour Party 86; Sinn Féin and 54, 55, 86; women candidates 86, 87, 89
General Election (1921) 85, 88–91
General Election (1922) 74, 80, 95
General Election (1923) 97
General Election (1927) 97
Geoghegan, George 134–5
Geoghegan, Margaret 134–5
Geoghegan-Quinn, Máire 88
'German Plot' 33, 34, 35, 53
Gifford, Sidney (John Brennan) 25, 32
Gillis, Liz and McAuliffe, Mary, *'We Were There': 77 Women of the Easter Rising* x
Gilmartin, Thomas Patrick, Archbishop of Tuam 13, 205
Glenamaddy Children's Home 204–6, 210, 213; conditions in 204–5, 210; mortality rate 204, 206, 211; 'ramshackle habitat' 205; *see also* Bon Secours Sisters; Tuam Mother and Baby Home
Glenamaddy Union 201–2, 208
Goldstone, Jack A. 1, 106
Gonne MacBride, Maud 10, 41; 'auto-suggestioning' and 41, 43; Clarke's perception of 39, 42; death of sister 38; imprisonment 33, 37, 90; Inghinidhe na hÉireann and 37; location in prison, claims about 44–5; Markievicz, perception of 38; meals in prison 41, 42; release from prison 39, 41; social status and 39; witness statement 10, 37–8, 41, 44
Gore-Booth, Eva 38, 40, 41
Gorman, Angela and Elizabeth 140
Goulding, June, *Light in the Window* 210–11

Government of Ireland Act (1920) 88
Greaney, Kate 132, 133
Great Famine, centenary of 213, 215
Greek Civil War (1946–49) 6, 111
Griffith, Arthur 36, 51, 92, 95
guerrilla warfare: British portrayal of 84; home front and 167–8; Irish Civil War 75, 76–82, 130; sexual violence in 106; War of Independence 69, 165, 179

Hackett, Mary 48, 54, 60
hair cutting 11, 104, 105, 106, 107, 108–16, 171; in Belgium 111; by British troops 109, 110, 114, 176; by the IRA 110, 112, 113–14, 122, 152, 153; in civil wars 111, 115; of collaborators/informers 111, 113–14; court cases and convictions 109–10, 112–13; during 'the Troubles' 109; films, depictions in 108; in France 110–11, 113; fraternising with soldiers/police 107, 109, 113, 170, 174–6; newspaper reports 109–10, 112, 120; perceived as 'lenient' punishment 115; photographic documentation of 111; in Poland 111–12; post-Second World War and 110–11, 113; RIC reports 114; symbolism of 108, 110, 174, 175; as violation of victims' feminity 112, 174; as a warning 122, 152, 153, 174
Hall, Mary 151, 163
Hall, Richard and Mary 151
Hanley, Brian 120
Haque, M.R. 19
Hart, Peter 47, 115, 165
Hartney, Mary 81
Harvey, Mary 51, 56
Hayden, Kate 143–4
Healy, Norah 121
Heffernan, Conor 108, 112
Heuston, Sarah Jane 143
Hibernian Rifles 130
Higgins, Michael D. 5–6
Higgins, Rita Ann 184, 189
Hirsch, Marianne 188
Hogan, Annie (Nan) 81
Hogan, Catherine 139–40
Holloway Prison 10, 33–4, 37–44, 90; comradeship 34, 38, 46; control of space 43–4; exercise time in 42; food, issues relating to 41; hierarchy, prisoners and 39, 41, 42; 'hospital diet' in 41–2;

hospital wing 45; hunger strikes 37, 41; sisterhood 38
home front: battlefront and 6, 193; children, house raids and 164, 165, 169, 171, 173, 178; churchgoers, attack on 169–70; First World War and 167–8; guerrilla warfare and 167–8; protection, gendered propaganda and 167; War of Independence and 167, 168–9; war in Palestine, violations 168; *see also* domestic spaces
Home Rule 23–4
Horne, John 123
Hortense, Sister (Bon Secours) 198, 204, 211, 212, 213, 214
Houston, Denis 54
Hughes, Brian 105, 137
hunger strikes 33, 37, 41, 63, 81, 89

India 9, 18, 19, 32
Inghinidhe na hÉireann x, 37, 55
internment 65
Irish Bulletin 74, 104, 164–5, 174, 177–8
Irish Citizen 25, 26; Connery's articles 29–30; court cases, rape/child abuse 28; Cumann na mBan, criticism of 26; hair cutting outrages 120; linen industry, working conditions 29; man-run system of society 27–8; 'Ruin of Young Girls in Ireland, The' 28; single mothers 31
Irish Citizen Army (ICA) 37, 76, 91; military service pensions 135; women and x 76, 91, 130
Irish Civil War (1922–23) 1; aftermath 82–4; anti-Treaty side 66; atrocities, desire to forget 103; Ballyseedy atrocity 124, 126, 127; Battle of Dublin 75–6, 83; ceasefire 77, 82; centennial commemoration 7; conventional phase 75; Cumann na mBan and 6, 10–11, 71, 72–4, 75–82; domestic space, transgression of 197; executions 13, 126, 198; female fatalities 81, 161; funerals 72–3; guerrilla phase 75, 76–82, 130; house raids 168; male combatants, killing of 12; patrilineal metaphor 6, 11; pensions awarded 130; violence, women and 8, 106; women and x–xi, 8, 68; *see also* Cumann na mBan; Irish Republican Army (IRA); National Army

Index

Irish Daily Mail 206
Irish Free State 9; anti-Treaty campaign, depiction of 84; Constitution 86; exhumations at Tuam workhouse 203; opposition to, women and 82; status of women 1–2; women, politics and 85
Irish Freeman 94
Irish Grants Committee (IGC) 11, 129, 136; economic lives of women 144–5; payments to female landholders 146; personal injury claims 142–4; rape case 138–9; southern loyalists and 137, 146; women and 137–46
Irish Independent 91
Irish Parliamentary Party (IPP) 23, 26, 50, 51, 54
Irish prison memoirs: gendered distinction in 34–5; men's narratives 34–7; women's narratives 33–4
Irish Republican Army (IRA) 48; 2nd Western Division 202, 203; 3rd Battalion (Tipperary No. 1 Brigade) 138; 3rd Northern Division 49, 56–7, 61, 65; 4th Battalion (Mid-Clare Brigade) 172; 5th Battalion (Castletownbere) 152–3; 6th Battalion (Cork No. 1 Brigade) 61, 155–6, 157, 158, 160, 163; Active Service Unit, Belfast 56, 58–9; active service units 79, 168, 172; Antrim Brigade 52, 56; Army Council 203; arson 56, 155, 172; attacks on Protestants 137–8; ban, de Valera and 203; Belfast Brigade 56, 57; Belfast Cumann na mBan and 52, 55, 57–63; bodyguard, Sinn Féin speakers 54; British portrayal of guerrilla campaign 84; C Company 54, 62; campaign in the north 56–9; Cavan Brigade 57; Cumann na mBan and 56–7, 69–70, 73–4, 75–6, 131, 168, 172–3; D Company 58; deaths in prison 203; Eastern Command 78; execution of women, GHQ directives 152–4, 158, 161; executions by British Army 156, 160, 162; female disappearances carried out by 151–60; female spy 177; flying columns 56, 78–9, 151, 155, 158, 165, 169; house raids 169, 170, 171, 173; internal structures 69; Mallow Army Barracks, raid on 150, 195; military rank, women and 82–3; National Army and 75, 77; newspaper, special editions of 74; Northern Divisions 61; northern offensive (1922) 65; rape 123–4, 137, 138–9; reprisals 105, 150, 162, 163, 169; RIC, attacks on 56, 149, 151, 169; secret IRA courts 118–19; support network of women 47, 48, 49, 59; violence against women 105, 122–3, 137, 169, 175, 179–80; women, hair cutting 110, 112, 113–14, 122, 152, 153, 175–6; women killed by 122, 149, 150–1; women, military rank and 82–3; *see also* Irish Civil War; Irregulars
Irish Republican Brotherhood (IRB) 50, 90
Irish Research Council 5
Irish self-determination 18, 32; feminists and 20, 21; suffragists and 19, 24, 32
Irish suffragists 9, 19, 21–2; British suffragists and 22; Cat and Mouse Act 38; constitutional groups 24; cultural nationalism and 21–2; cultural revival movement and 24–5; feminist analysis of society 18; Gaelic civilization and 24–6, 32; Home Rule, response to 23–4; international movement and 22; Irish MPs and 22–3; Irish Parliamentary Party and 23; man-run system of society and 27–8; militant groups 24; nationalism and 32; political divisions 24; self-determination and 19, 24, 32; 'ventilation of evils' 29–31; *see also* women's suffrage
Irish Times 96, 109
Irish Volunteers 52, 57, 132; assaults on women 105, 115; Cumann na mBan and 26, 27, 50, 52
Irish Volunteers' Dependents' Fund 91
Irish Women's Franchise League (IWFL) 24, 30, 86, 87, 89
Irish Women's Reform League 24, 29, 31; Watching the Courts Committee 28
Irish Women's Suffrage Federation (IWSF) 22, 23, 24
Irish Women's Suffrage Society (IWSS) 24
Irregulars (anti-Treaty IRA) 65, 116, 123, 202; executions 13, 198, 202–3

Johnson, Henry, Archdeacon 142
Johnson, Marie 55
Jordan, Sarah 118–19
Joshi, Rama 19
Journal of the Old Tuam Society 206

Katrak, Ketu H. 21
Keaven, Myles 200
Keegan, Bridget 109, 174
Kennedy Cleary, Kathleen 80
Kenny, Kathleen 79–80
Kettle, Mary 38
Kieran, Sister (Bon Secours) 214
King, Alice 150–1, 163
King, Anna 81
King McCarthy, Elizabeth 81
King, William (RIC inspector) 151
Kissane, Bill 2–3, 115–16
Knirck, Jason 93
Kramer, Alan 123

Lá na mBan (June 1918) x
Labour Party 87, 88
Lankford, Siobhán 80
Laub, Dori, 'Bearing Witness Or the Vicissitudes of Listening' 192
Leeson, D.M. 168
Lehane family 172–3
Leitrim Observer 170
Liddle, Joanna 19
Lindsay, Mary 154–61, 163; abduction by IRA 155–6; Dripsey ambush and 155, 158, 160; execution by IRA 156–7, 158; letters to General Strickland 156, 157; memorial services 159–60; newspaper coverage of case 157, 159, 161–2; request for her release 156; residence burned down by IRA 155–6
literature 183–97; autobiographies/memoirs 194; conflict, retrospective representations 185; cultural memory 193, 194, 196; domestic space in conflict literature 192–3; domestic space, transgression of 185–6, 187, 191, 197; Evans, Martina 185, 189, 193–7; hare, symbolism of 191; hidden legacies of women's experiences 189; inherited narratives 188, 189, 191, 192, 196–7; literary 'remembering' 184; Meehan, Paula 185, 189–91, 197; mid-century literary reflections 188; nationalist images of women 185–6; Ní Chuilleanáin, Éiléan 185, 189, 191–3, 197; Ní Ghríofa, Doireann 14, 216–17; poets' representations 185, 188–91; silences, recording 192; trauma 186, 187, 188, 189, 192; traumatic memory
190; women, limited narrative space 186, 187
Litster, Alice 211
Lloyd George, David 92, 162, 164
Local Government Act (1898) 200
Logue, Michael, Cardinal 30
Lynch, Finian 93
Lynch, Liam 73, 80, 81
Lynch, Robert 58
Lynn, Kathleen 86, 97, 173, 203
Lyons, Brigid 132

McAuliffe, Mary x, 12, 164–80
McCarry, Kate 97
McCarthy, Cal 55, 64, 68, 75, 80–1
McCarthy, Flossie and Jessie 124
McCarthy, Randal 124
McClean, Mary 48, 64, 66
McClintock, Anne 20, 32
MacConaill, Michael 58
McCoole, Sinéad 68, 90
McCorley, Roger 56, 57, 58, 60, 62, 65
McCormack, Margaret 140, 141
McCoy, John 131
McCullough, Agnes 55, 64
McCullough, Denis 50, 60, 64
McCullough, Una 51
MacCurtain, Margaret ix–x, 98
MacCurtain, Thomas 61
McDaid, Ailbhe 12–13, 183–97
McDermott, Jim 49, 57
McDevitt, Teresa 48, 53–4, 57, 59–60
McDiarmid, Lucy 10, 33–46
McDonnell, Kathleen 173
McEntee, Sean 35
McGillicuddy, Ellen 173
McGing, Claire 11, 85–100
McGowan, Martin 54
McGrane, Eileen 55
McGuill, Mrs 120
McKeever, Alice and Annie 48, 66
McKenna, Mrs 140
McKillen, Beth 26
McManus, Emma 145–6
McNally, Thomas 49, 56–7, 61
McNamara, Sister Hortense see Hortense, Sister
MacSherry, Margaret Mary 79, 80
MacSwiney, Mary 26, 69, 74, 90; American Commission and 90; Anglo-Irish Treaty debates 92, 93–4; General Elections

89, 95, 97; Irish language and 90; republicanism 90; Sinn Féin and 97
MacSwiney, Terence 53, 89, 90
Madden, Miss 176–7
Maeve, Queen 25, 26, 32
Maguire, Seán 198, 202, 203
Maguire, Tom 198, 202, 203, 213
Mahaffy, Elsie 40
Maher, Kate 121, 123
Mallow Army Barracks 150, 195
Maloney, James 120, 175–6
Manning, Maurice 98
Markievicz, Constance, Countess: Anglo-Irish Treaty debates 92, 93, 94; Clarke, conflict with 39–40, 42–4, 45–6; Clarke's perception of 38, 45; court-martial/death sentence 91; Cumann na mBan and 27, 87; Dáil Éireann and 88; death 97; Easter Rising (1916) and 37, 91; *Eire: The Irish Nation* 74; election to Westminster 32, 87; franchise debate 94; General Elections 86, 87, 89, 91, 97; Gonne's perception of 38; imprisonment 33, 37, 88, 90; Inghinidhe na hÉireann and 37; Irish Citizen Army and 76, 91; letters to her sister 38, 40, 43; meals in prison 41, 42; Minister for Labour 88; prison letters 10; social status and 39
masculine identity, nationalism and 83–4
Matthews, Ann 68, 71, 104–5
Meaney, Gerardine 24
Medalie, Sarah 149, 163
Meehan, Paula 185, 189–91, 197; *Painting Rain* 189; 'Six Sycamores' sequence 189–91; 'Them Ducks Died for Ireland' 189, 191
Mellone, Dora 32; 'Women in Ancient Ireland' 25
memory: 'collective amnesia' 103, 104; cultural memory 13, 193, 194, 196; 'postmemory' 188; traumatic memory 12, 13, 190
Military Archives x, 104, 119, 120, 122–3
Military Court of Inquiry 121, 124
Military Service Pensions Acts 82, 130, 131, 132
military service pensions applications 104; Belfast Cumann na mBan 59–63, 67; Cumann na mBan members 82–3, 122, 171–3; institutionalisation/nervous breakdowns 125–6; legislation 82;

Pensions Advisory Committee 48, 61, 62; Pensions Board 60, 61; referees 53–4, 57, 59–60, 61, 62–3
Military Service Pensions Collection (MSPC) x, 12, 129–35; active service, criteria 130, 131, 132; Belfast Cumann na mBan applications 48; Connaught Rangers 135; Cumann na mBan and 70, 130–1; Cumann na mBan membership returns 71–2, 130; dependency claims 134–5; disability pensions 132–3; IRA membership returns 71–2; neurasthenia, diagnoses of 132–3; Post-Traumatic Stress Disorder (PTSD) 132, 133; unmarried wives, dependency claims 133–4; violence towards women 122; women's testimonies 13, 187–8
Milligan, Alice 55
Moghadam, Valentine M. 2, 3
Moloney, Helena 26
Montgomery, Sean 59
morality: Catholic clergy and 30; double moral standards 9, 18, 29, 30, 31; social construction of female morality 29–30; social morality 30, 31
Morning Post 157, 159, 160
Morrison, Eve 66–7, 154
Mosse, George L. 20, 32
mother and baby homes: mortality rates 211–12; *see also* Glenamaddy Children's Home; Tuam Mother and Baby Home
Mother and Baby Homes Commission of Investigation 13, 206–7, 211
Moulton, Mo 124
Mulcahy, Richard 65, 124, 158
Munster Women's Franchise League 24, 90
Murphy, Amy 48, 57, 64, 66
Murphy, Annie 173
Murphy, Cliona 22
Murphy, Denis 157
Murphy, Kathleen 48, 50
Mydan, Carl (photographer) 11

Nairn, Tom 20, 32
National Archives of Ireland (NAI) 135–6, 147
National Archives (UK) 136
National Army: Ballyseedy atrocity 124, 126; Cumann na Saoirse and 75; female fatalities 81; Four Courts siege 83; IRA and 75, 77; Kenmare incident

116, 124–5; rape charges 122–3; sexual violence 106, 116, 120, 124, 128; unmarried wives, dependency claims 133; women incarcerated by 81–2; *see also* Irish Civil War
national identity: 'alien' influences and 17, 20; feminists and 18; traditions and 20, 21
National University of Ireland (NUI) 5
nationalism: colonialism and 24–5; feminism and 9, 17–21; gendering of 20; insider/outsider dichotomy 20, 21, 25; Janus quality of 20, 32; masculine identity and 83–4; men and 19, 20; muscular nationalism 84; rise in Europe 18; suffragists' demands and 32
Neill family 136
Newman, Agnes (*née* Casement) 134
Ní Chuilleanáin, Éiléan 185, 189, 191–3, 197; 'Ballinascarthy' 192; domestic space 192–3; hare, symbolism of 191; 'On Lacking the Killer Instinct' 191–2; silences, recording of 192; *Sun-fish, The* 191, 192
Ní Criac, L. 64
Ní Dhuibhne, Éilís 191
Ní Ghríofa, Doireann, *Brightening* 14, 216–17
Noble, Alexander 152, 153, 154
Noble, Bridget 122, 152–4, 161, 163
Northern Ireland: internment 65; nationalist minority 48; republicans in 47–8; sectarian tensions 58; unionist majority 47; violence (1918–22) 48
Northern Ireland Parliament 64, 88

Oath of Allegiance: teachers and 50; Teachtaí Dála (TDs) and 92, 93
O'Boyle, Nellie 48, 53, 57, 60–1
O'Boyle, Nora 64
Ó Brádaigh, Ruairí 213–14
O'Brennan, Lily 74
O'Brien, Art 78
O'Brien, Mary 145
O'Callaghan, Kathleen (Kate) 69, 89, 91, 93, 94–5
O'Casey, Seán, *Juno and the Paycock* 185
O'Connor, Frank 197; 'Guests of the Nation' 185–6
O'Connor, Rory 83
O'Daly, Major General Paddy 116, 124

O'Donnell, Bridget 172
O'Donnell, Peadar, *Adrigoole* 186–7, 197
O'Donoghue, Florence 158
O'Dowd, Margaret 142
Ó Duibhir, Eamon 35, 36
Office of Public Works (OPW) 136
O'Halloran, Agnes 145
O'Hegarty, P.S. 96
Old Age Pensions 200
Old Tuam Society 213
O'Mahony, Nora 144
O'Malley, Ernie 74, 124, 194–7; *On Another Man's Wound* 194, 196
O'Meara, Harriet 149, 163
O'Mullane, Brigid 73, 74
O'Neill, Mary 172–3
O'Neill, Sean 49, 57, 58, 61, 62–3
Ó Ruairc, Pádraig Óg 81
O'Shea, Annie 144
O'Shea, Mollie 126–7
O'Sullivan, Mary 142–3
O'Sullivan, Nora 80

Parliament (Qualification of Women) Act (1918) 86, 87
Parnell, Mary 149, 163
partition 64, 92
Paseta, Senia 69
patriarchal order 19, 31
Peacock, Margaret (Daisy) 139
Pearse, Margaret 51, 89, 90, 91, 93
Pearse, Pádraig 50, 89, 93
Pearse, William 89
Pergament, Deborah 110
Perry, Patrick 133–4
Perry, Rose 133–4
Peteet, Julie 168
Plunkett, George Noble, Count 51
Plunkett, Grace 51
Plunkett, Josephine, Countess 51, 55
Poblacht na hÉireann 74
Poor Law Amendment Act (1862) 208
Poor Law Guardians 200
Poor Law system 200–1
Price Barry, Leslie 65, 78–9
Priestley-McCracken, Elizabeth 28
prisoners: comradeship in 34, 35–6; Cumann na mBan's support for 53–4, 69; execution of republican prisoners 13, 126; 'imagined community' 34; republican women prisoners 81–2, 130;

see also Belfast Prison; Holloway Prison; Irish prison memoirs; Usk Prison
Proclamation of the Irish Republic (1916) 86
professions: male domination of 27; women and 27, 28, 29
propaganda: British Army recruitment 178; Department of Propaganda 164; pro-Treaty 72; republican 73, 74; Sinn Féin 53; wartime 167
Property Losses (Ireland) Committee 135
Protestants: attacks on 137-8, 141-2; depopulation 136, 146
Provisional Government 71, 95
Public Assistance Act (1939) 208
Purser, Sarah 135

Quinn, Nora 48, 53, 54, 62
Quirk, Mrs 150, 163

Radhakrishnan, Rajagopalan 20-1, 32
rape 104, 105, 106; British soldiers and 121-2; comparative study (Ulster/Upper Silesia) 117; court case 139; court cases, all-male juries and 28; female culpability, suspicion of 119; gang rapes 122-4, 137; a hidden crime 117; IGC compensation claims 137-40; institutionalisation/nervous breakdowns 124, 125-6, 127; IRA and 123-4, 137, 138-9; IRA/Sinn Féin court 118-19; newspaper coverage 28, 109-10; of pregnant women 120, 121, 140; psychological effects of 117, 122, 123-4, 127, 137, 139; reported to the Gardaí (1923) 119; reports in military archives 120; 'seduction' 28, 119; shame, victims and 139, 140; under-reporting by women 116-17; victims, burden of proof and 119; wartime rape 123; as a weapon of war 106, 118; *see also* sexual violence; violence against women
Redmond, John 23, 26
Redmond, William (Willie) 23
Reidy, Delia 140
Reilly, J.K. 35
Report into the Commission on the Relief of the Sick and the Destitute Poor, Including the Insane Poor 199, 204
Report on Unmarried Mothers in Ireland (1939) 211-12

Representation of the People Act (1918) 32, 85-6
republican courts xi, 13, 90, 139, 213
republican prisoners: Bon Secours Sisters and 201-2; execution of 13, 126
Republican Prisoners' Dependant's Fund 55, 90, 91
republican women 6, 72, 85; perception of 96; *see also* Belfast Cumann na mBan; Cumann na mBan
republicanism, Catholic institutions and 199
Rineen Ambush 172
Roman Catholic Church *see* Catholic Church
Royal Hibernian Academy (RHA) 135
Royal Irish Constabulary (RIC) 166; Belfast Volunteers, membership estimates 52; boycott 142-3, 144-5; compensation claims 142-3; Cumann na mBan, membership estimates 52-3; disbandment 142-3; IRA attacks 56, 149, 151, 169; violence against women, data on 105, 114-15
Royal Ulster Constabulary (RUC) 143
Russell, Mary 48, 54, 57, 58, 60, 66
Ryan, Agnes 49-50
Ryan, Bridget 144-5
Ryan, Louise 9, 17-32, 66, 67, 68, 187; Anglo-Irish Treaty debates 72; funerals, Cumann na mBan and 73; gendered violence in wartime 166; guerrilla warfare, women and 165, 168; home front, violation of 168-9; Sinn Féin, women candidates and 87; women in armed combat 81; women, nationalist images of 185; women, violence experienced by 104, 105
Ryan, Maureen 78
Ryan-O'Leary, Julia 80
Ryan's Daughter (film) 108

Scannell, Josephine 149, 163
Schmoll, Brett 6-7
Scott, Joan 3
Second World War, collaborators 111-12
sectarian tensions 58
sexual violence 5, 6, 11, 104, 105, 116-28; abuse in Church/State-run institutions 128; against men and boys 127-8; B-Specials 106, 120; British armed forces and 92, 114, 121-2; in the Civil

War period 106; in guerrilla warfare 106; IRA and 115, 123–4, 138–9; 'Irish exceptionalism' view 116; Irish Volunteers and 105, 115; Military Archives 104, 119, 120, 122–3; National Army 106, 116, 120, 124, 128; reported to the Gardaí (1923) 119; RIC reports 105; Sinn Féin court and 118–19; under-reporting by women 107, 116–17; in the War of Independence 104; witness statements 115, 118, 120; women's narratives of 120, 121; *see also* rape
Shadl, Brett 128
Sheehy Skeffington, Francis 26
Sheehy Skeffington, Hanna 10; Clarke's perception of 38; enfranchisement of women 94; General Election (1918) 86; hunger strike in prison 37, 41; imprisonment 33, 34, 37; nationalism and 24; property compensation claim 135; statement on atrocities against women 120
Showalter, Elaine 189
Sinn Féin 10, 25, 26, 97; abstentionist policy 87; anti-conscription pledge 53; Belfast propaganda committee 53; conscription, opposition to 53; Cumann na mBan and 51, 52, 73; General Election (1918) 54, 55, 86; General Election (1921) 88; General Election (1922) 95; Longford by-election (1917) 51; membership in Antrim 52; proscription 57; Ulster candidates elected (1918) 55; women election candidates 86, 87, 89; women members 53, 82, 86; women in politics, attitude towards 88; women's suffrage and 86
Sinn Féin clubs 52
Sinn Féin Court 119
Sinn Féin Executive 86, 90
Sisters of Mercy 200
Skibbereen Eagle 176
Skinnider, Margaret 79, 132
Slattery, Miss G. 114, 115
slum dwellings 30, 31
social status: Anglo-Irish and 39, 45, 46; height and 40–1
Solomons, Estella 135
Sontag, Susan, *Regarding the Pain of Others* 184
Spanish Civil War (1936–39) 6, 7, 111

Stack, Austin 36, 54, 78
Stevens, Pádraig (songwriter) 210
Stiles, Kristine 111
Stover, Justin Dolan 12, 169, 170, 187
Strickland, General 154–5, 156, 157
suffrage: legislation 85–6; *see also* Irish suffragists; women's suffrage
Sullivan, Eva 154
Sullivan, Nora 153
Swanzy, Chief Inspector 56, 61
Swithin Walsh, Eoin 112

Taylor, Essie 141
Taylor, Paul 137
Thane, Pat 86
Thébaud, Françoise 4
Tobin, Julia 112–13
Todd, Lisa 167
Tourmakeady ambush 202
Townshend, Caroline 117
Townshend, Charles 105, 116–17
Traynor, Oscar 83
Trevor, William 188
Truce (1921) 64, 70, 88, 92, 137, 161
Tuam Children's Home *see* Tuam Mother and Baby Home
Tuam Herald 209
Tuam Mother and Baby Home 13, 198, 206; admission to 209–10; 'adoptions' 208; applications to enter 207–8; assisted departures 208; boarding-out system 208, 210; catchment area 207; children, language used by 210; commemoration of infants and children 214; costs per head 212; death certificates for 796 children 206, 207, 211; deaths, causes of 211; executed IRA men, commemoration of 198, 199, 202, 204, 213–14; famine centenary, commemoration 213, 215; infants' mass grave 13, 199, 207, 215; mortality rate 206, 211, 212; 'otherness' of the children 210–11; vigil held at site 214; *see also* Bon Secours Sisters; Glenamaddy Children's Home
Tuam workhouse 13; Bon Secours Sisters and 201, 205–6; conditions 206; execution of anti-Treatyite prisoners 13, 198, 202–3; exhumations 203; Sisters of Mercy and 200; 'Tuam martyrs', commemoration of 199, 215

Index

Ulster Volunteer Force, women and 69
United Irish League 50, 52
unmarried mothers 13, 31; Glenamaddy Children's Home 204; incarceration of 'fallen' women 127; institutionalisation of 199; *Report into the Commission on the Relief of the Sick and the Destitute Poor, Including the Insane Poor* (1927) 199, 204; *Report on Unmarried Mothers in Ireland* (1939) 211–12; stigma, cultural and social 13, 212; *see also* Tuam Mother and Baby Home
Upton train ambush 151, 163
Urquhart, Diane 69
Usk Prison, Wales 34–6

Valentine, Emily 48, 54, 60, 66
Valiulis, Maryann 83
Vellacott, Jo 22
violence against women 5–6, 8, 11–12, 103–8; Black and Tans 109, 120, 126, 171, 179; British armed forces and 125, 166; 'collective amnesia' 103, 104, 116; documentation and 104, 106; domestic violence 28–9; gender-based 6, 106–7, 128, 175–6, 179–80; gender-specific punishment 11, 105; home invasions 12, 109, 125, 126, 169, 170, 172–5; house raids, effects of 177–8; IRA and 105, 122–3, 137, 169, 179–80; Kenmare incident 116, 124–5; loyalist women 11–12; paint, use of 116; patterns of 168; psychological effects of 187; RIC reports 105, 114–15; surviving evidences of 107; traumatic effects of 140, 179, 187; *see also* hair cutting; rape; sexual violence

Waller-Sawyer, Mrs 146
Walsh, Joseph, Archbishop of Tuam 213
Walsh, Mary 125
Walsh, Roisin 50, 55
War of Independence (1919–21) 1; atrocities, desire to forget 103; British crown forces, behaviour of 168; civilian population 165, 166; commemoration of ending 5; Cumann na mBan and 10, 48, 69, 73–4; deaths in Northern Ireland 58; female fatalities in County Cork 12, 148–63; funerals, IRA and 72; guerrilla warfare 69, 165, 179; hair, enforced cutting 110, 112; home front and battlefront 167, 168, 193; male combatants, killing of 12; Martial Law 164; O'Malley's memoirs 194; propaganda, Cumann na mBan and 73; Truce (1921) 64, 70, 88, 92, 137, 161; Upton ambush 151; violence experienced by women 8, 104–5, 109, 110, 114–15; women's role in x–xi, 47
war photographers 111
Ward, Annie 49, 64
Ward, Margaret ix–x, 4, 6, 8, 10, 47–67, 68; Cumann na mBan, transformation of 26–7; Cumann na Saoirse, views on 75; guerrilla warfare (1920–21) 69; *Unmanageable Revolutionaries* 4
Ward, Mary 149, 163
warfare: conventional 106; *see also* guerrilla warfare
Watching the Courts Committee 28
Westmeath Examiner 109
Wheeler, Anna 19
White Cross 55, 65
Wilkinson, Ellen 143
Wilmot, Amelia 177
Wilson, T.K. 117–18
Wind that Shakes the Barley, The (film) 108
Wisely, May 51, 64
women: Catholic Church and 1, 30, 96; conflict, traumatic memory of 12–13, 187–8; Constitution of the Irish Free State (1922) 95; enfranchisement 85–6; Irish womanhood, traditional images of 9, 18; as keepers of moral and social order 17; as keepers of national traditions 20, 30; legislative changes, restrictions and 95–6; literary representations of experience 183–97; martial responsibilities 69; modesty cult and 30; nationalist images of 185–6; portrayal as symbols of nation 20, 30; primary role of 96; republican women, perception of 96; rights of 29; roles ascribed to 17, 20, 21; violence, act of bearing witness 12–13; wages 31; women-in-the-family-model 2; working conditions 29, 30; *see also* unmarried mothers
women Teachtaí Dála (TDs) 11, 69, 85, 89–91, 95–100; Anglo-Irish Treaty, opposition to 85, 89, 92, 94, 96, 99;

Cumman na nGaedhael 97; franchise debate 94–5; perceived as 'honorary men' 98; political traditions inherited by 98; post-revolutionary 95–9; Sinn Féin 89–91, 97; 'sympathy vote' and 98

Women's Social and Political Union (WSPU) 24

women's suffrage 8, 9; British suffragists 22; centennial commemoration 5, 8, 9; Cumann na mBan and 26; franchise debate (1922) 94–5; Irish Parliamentary Party and 23; partial enfranchisement 32, 85–6; Sinn Féin and 86

Wood, Ella 149, 163

Woods, Seamus 57, 61, 62, 65

workhouse system 13, 200, 208–9

Wyse Power, Jennie 50, 65, 74, 86

Wyse Power, Nancy 50–1